D1506838

PRINCIPLES OF GENERAL MANAGEMENT

PRINCIPLES OF
GENERAL MANAGEMENT

The Art and Science of Getting Results Across Organizational Boundaries

John L. Colley, Jr.
Jacqueline L. Doyle
Robert D. Hardie
George W. Logan
Wallace Stettinius

Foreword by Robert F. Bruner

Published in Association with
The Darden Graduate School
of Business Administration

UNIVERSITY *of* VIRGINIA

DARDEN SCHOOL OF BUSINESS

YALE UNIVERSITY PRESS
NEW HAVEN AND LONDON

Set in Galliard type by Westchester Book Group.

Printed in the United States of America.

Library of Congress Cataloging-in-Publication Data

Principles of general management : the art and science of getting results across organizational boundaries / John L. Colley, Jr. . . . [et al.].
      p. cm.
      "Published in association with The Darden Graduate School of Business
         Administration."
      Includes bibliographical references and index.
      ISBN 978-0-300-11709-7 (cloth : alk. paper)
  1. Industrial management.   2. Strategic planning.   3. Corporate governance.   I. Colley, John L.
      HD31.P737 2007
      658—dc22   2006038986

A catalogue record for this book is available from the British Library.

The paper in this book meets the guidelines for permanence and durability of the Committee on Production Guidelines for Book Longevity of the Council on Library Resources.

10 9 8 7 6 5 4 3 2 1

We gratefully dedicate this book to our students,
who have enriched our lives and changed the world.

CONTENTS

FOREWORD

The commander-in-chief is always in the midst of a series of shifting events, and so he can never at any moment consider the whole import of an event that is occurring. Moment by moment the event is imperceptibly shaping itself, and at every moment of this continuous, uninterrupted shaping of events, the commander-in-chief is in the midst of the most complex play of intrigues, worries, contingencies, authorities, projects, counsels, threats, and deceptions, and is continually obliged to reply to innumerable questions addressed to him which constantly conflict with one another.

An order to retreat must be given to the adjutant, at once, that instant. And the order to retreat carries us past the turn to the Kaluga road. And after the adjutant comes, the commissary-general asks where the stores are to be taken and the chief of the hospitals asks where the wounded are to go, and a courier from Petersburg brings a letter from the sovereign which does not admit of the possibility of abandoning Moscow, and the commander-in-chief 's rival, the man who is undermining him (and there are always not merely one, but several such) presents a new project diametrically opposed to that of turning to the Kaluga road.

—Leo Tolstoy, *War and Peace*

The general manager has a predicament unlike any other. This person is subject to immense pressure from others, must have a bias for action, and yet must analyze carefully and comprehensively, often under conditions of incomplete information. General managers do not solve problems; they manage messes. Russell Ackoff, professor at the Wharton School, wrote, "Managers are not confronted with problems that are independent of each other, but with dynamic situations that consist of complex systems of changing problems that interact with each other. I call such situations *messes* . . . Managers do not solve problems: they manage messes." General management requires extraordinary preparation, mastery of a wide range of tools, skills, and concepts, and above all, qualities of leadership.

Unfortunately, we know less than we might like about the general manager's predicament, qualities, and training. Many of the popular books by or about general managers seem incomplete or offer bromides in place of wisdom. General managers themselves seem reticent to cast their insights in a form useful for teaching others.

The voice of the general manager has dwindled in the general consciousness. Some executives are reluctant to identify themselves as "general managers." The title fell into disfavor during the widespread corporate restructurings of the late 1980s and early 1990s that eliminated more than a million general management positions as companies sought to flatten their organizations. Not to be personally responsible for a customer relationship, the efficiency of a manufacturing line, or the design of a new product put you at risk for downsizing.

Universities, following the developments in the world of practice, shifted their research gaze from the general manager to specific skills and tasks, such as strategic analysis, organizational design, and performance evaluation. This lent scientific rigor to the research at the cost of inductive insight: The whole of general management is more than the sum of the parts. The individual pieces describe poorly the messes that general managers manage.

It is time for a fresh perspective on the predicament of the general manager. The more forward-thinking companies are returning to models of professional development that prepare general managers. Chief learning officers openly acknowledge that the major constraint on corporate growth is not capital, technology, or productive capacity—rather, it is the limited pool of *leadership*. Business schools are starting to return their resources toward leadership development in the cause of preparing general managers. We need a body of teaching and expository material that supports these trends.

I am especially pleased to introduce this book as a response to the needs of practitioners, educators, and researchers. It offers, in one volume, a valuable synthesis of the parts into the larger, vastly more interesting whole.

It yields compelling and practical ideas that can help to transform the functional specialist into a *general* manager. And it sounds the call for thoughtful practitioners, educators, and researchers to return their attention to general management.

To some extent, this book is a product of the tradition and values of the Darden School. Over the years, Darden's identity has been fashioned around the general manager. Our students typically graduate to work in functional assignments and then evolve into generalist leaders. Today, a careful survey would show that the vast bulk of our alumni are general managers. It is fitting that here, in 2006, just after the fiftieth anniversary of the founding of the Darden School, this book emerges to reaffirm and renew the legacy of Darden.

But to a larger extent, this book is the product of an extraordinarily talented team of professionals: John Colley, Jacqueline Doyle, Robert Hardie, George Logan, and Wallace Stettinius. They bring together years of work experience in general management and in graduate management education. They have been both a research team and a teaching team. This book not only summarizes their thinking from years of observation, but also presents ideas in a readily accessible fashion. As the senior member of this team, John Colley deserves special recognition: His vision and determination helped to preserve a focus on the general manager and to shape the team that produced this book. My colleagues and I commend John for his perseverance and sense of mission. And we thank the entire team for its contribution to the world of practice.

Acquire this book. Read it. Grow in your capacity to assume the perspective of the general manager. Thus, be ready to anticipate the impact of what Tolstoy described as the "series of shifting events . . . [and] most complex play of intrigues, worries, contingencies, authorities, projects, counsels, threats, and deceptions."

Robert F. Bruner
Dean and Charles C. Abbott Professor of
    Business Administration
Darden Graduate School of Business Administration
University of Virginia
Charlottesville, Virginia

The discipline of general management, also frequently referred to as business policy, comprises a broad range of topics that define the roles and tasks of the general manager. In general, the topics encompass the processes by which leaders plan, direct, coordinate, and reward the activities of employees to achieve the purpose of the organization. A description of this expansive process by Peter Drucker decades ago (*The Practice of Management*, New York: Harper and Row, 1954) is now a cornerstone of management theory. His process consists of five steps: planning, organizing, staffing, leading, and controlling. Drucker's early work still offers such a sound approach for considering the tasks of the general manager, that we have employed his steps as the starting point for the structure of this book. In addition to the original five steps, we have expanded some themes and added others to profile what we see as the roles and tasks of the general manager today. It is our hope that as events unfold, this framework might give general managers in any context—large or small business, functional department or profit center, for-profit or nonprofit organization—a way of thinking systematically about assessing and improving the effectiveness of their organizations.

Among the important challenges general managers face are key strategic and tactical questions relating to the total enterprise, including:

- In what businesses should the organization compete?
- How should we set goals for the businesses we choose?

- What are the most advantageous actions to take to achieve our goals?
- How should we organize, staff, and fund ourselves?
- How should we coordinate and control activities across a variety of functions and multiple locations?
- How should we assess our progress and performance and then hold people accountable?
- How should we inform, influence, and interact with various constituencies of the organization?
- How should we bring about meaningful change when it is required?

These questions must be answered as part of the vital decision-making process that goes on without pause for the life of a business, and answering them requires a very different mind-set from that of subordinate functional managers. Effective general managers have a perspective of the total enterprise in the context of both the present and likely future environments. They recognize that they must meet current goals by outmaneuvering rivals in today's competitive environment while simultaneously preparing to shape the kind of future they want for the business. This recognition often sets in motion the implementation of changes that will lead the organization in new and different directions. Accordingly, managing change effectively is a critical skill of general managers.

Maintaining an ability to relate to the functional or operational perspective, as well as the strategic, provides important insights for the general manager. In fact, strong general managers can recognize when and how to move between the two complementary perspectives, all with an eye toward finding the best possible path for the organization as a whole. Seeking an optimal position, however, with the goal of continually improving, involves many judgments based on often-competing goals and values. Thus, in nearly all organizations, general management involves dealing with complexity and ambiguity.

Recognizing the complexity faced by general managers has led some in the field to note that business is as much an art as a science. Indeed, there is a rational, analytical side as well as an intuitive, creative one. Both of these are of great consequence to the general manager. The variety of approaches to combine the art with the science gives rise to different individuals responding in different ways under similar circumstances. As a result, we observe changes in strategy and even culture when chief executive jobs turn over, even in highly successful organizations.

Implicit in these changes is perhaps one of the most important imperatives for the general manager: the requirement to take action. Only actions taken in the present can change the future. In effect, general managers must ask if they are doing today what is required to secure the future they desire for the organization and its stakeholders. This notion was well captured by Peter Drucker, who said, "The purpose of the work of making the future is not to decide what must be done tomorrow, but what should be done today to have a tomorrow" (*Managing for Results,* New York: Perennial Library, Harper & Row, 1986, p. 173). The ultimate strategy question is: Are we doing the things we need to be doing to have the kind of future we desire? After in-depth analysis and creative generation of responses, general managers should establish plans for their operations. They must then manage the workforce to implement the plans while keeping watch for the need to alter course.

Thus, the roles and responsibilities that define the job of the general manager are numerous and diverse, and this book is designed to explain the many related details. It covers the process of management and its related decision-making imperatives from the perspective of the general manager of an enterprise with profit-and-loss responsibility. Because well-trained, reasonable individuals in this role will choose different courses of action under the same set of circumstances, we do not propose that the approaches presented here will lead to "the right answer" for a given situation. It is our hope, however, that they will lead to better answers as a result of the considerations they entail.

The enterprises to which we refer may be a total company, a division of a decentralized corporation, or a profit center within either type of organization that includes all of the business functions. Our primary intent is to address the issues of the for-profit concern, although much of the material we present is applicable to those who manage in nonprofit or public enterprises.

During recent years there has been an emphasis on corporate strategy that has not been misplaced. Strategy is particularly important, whether deliberately pursued or not, but typically is not sufficient by itself to guarantee sustained success of an organization. As a result of this lengthy period of emphasis on strategy, the broader topic of general management has been left relatively uncovered in recent management literature for both the practitioner and the student. We should not overlook these other steps and components of management, which are also equally essential to prolonged survival as well as accomplishment. It is our hope that the following chapters will aid in reinforcing these significant concepts.

It is also our belief that, in an age of specialization, too many managers are becoming functional technocrats, intensively trained in their respective disciplines but not necessarily able to manage for the betterment of the entire organization. Functional managers need to understand the elements and nuances of general management if they are to relate and respond effectively to the general managers for whom they work and, ultimately, if they are to advance within the hierarchy of their organizations.

General management as a topic is a staple, in some form, of current business school curricula and the stated emphasis of a handful of schools. Certainly, if business schools are to prepare students to be leaders in the field of business, not to mention leaders of businesses themselves, their faculties must develop courses and programs to address this element of business education. Students also need to be aware of the importance of the topic. As they aim to meet the demands of recruiters seeking to fill jobs within the functional areas, students may not appreciate the import of the topic until after their course work has ended, and thus they may lose the opportunity to properly prepare themselves for their careers.

Consequently, we have written this book with the intention of highlighting the importance of the topic of general management for both students and practitioners, drawing on the combined experience of the five authors as a unique base of expertise. Our team of authors is drawn to this topic by many years of teaching in MBA (master of business administration) and executive education programs, particularly at the University of Virginia's Darden Graduate School of Business Administration, which has consistently maintained a dedication to general management and the training of general managers. Members of the group have had extensive practical experience in general management. Our collective service encompasses the roles of directors on and, for some, chairmen of more than seventy boards of directors; of chief executives and senior management positions; and of general management consultants for numerous corporations with varied attributes—large and small, headquartered in the United States and internationally owned, focused and diversified, public and private, for-profit and nonprofit.

We have attempted to combine our understanding of theory with our practical experience to produce a readable book that provides students and managers at all levels with an understanding of the general management perspective and with identification of the tools required to be effective general managers. In short, we have aimed to provide a realistic and instructive view of the topic. It is our hope that this book heightens our readers' interest in general management and aids those continuing in or entering into the role of general manager. The general manager's position is ever more essential as the corporation has become the primary organizational instrument by which our economic systems of capitalism, free enterprise, and competition operate for the greater good of our economy and society.

The Structure of the Book

This text consists of twenty-five chapters organized into five major parts, as follows:

- Part I (Chapters 1–3) begins with a broad introduction to general management, exploring its origins and establishment in the modern corporation and the economic and organizational contexts within which the general manager functions.
- Part II (Chapters 4–9) covers the various steps in the planning process, including the need for and the development of a strategy and its transformation into a strategic plan (including a set of strategic goals and objectives), a business plan (a financial plan covering a suitable planning horizon), and the annual plan, or budget.
- Part III (Chapters 10–16) presents seven analytical concepts that are essential to the successful execution of both the planning phase (Part II) and the taking-action phase (Part IV) of general management.

- Part IV (Chapters 17–21) covers the crucial actions that must be successfully led by the general manager, including staffing, organizing and aligning, integrating, and executing.
- Part V (Chapters 22–25) summarizes the various activities required to make it all work, including controlling and reporting, learning and innovation, public relations and advocacy, and our final reflections on general management.

ACKNOWLEDGMENTS

It is a great pleasure for us to acknowledge the support and assistance of a number of administrators, faculty colleagues, and students. Dean Robert F. Bruner of the Darden School has been a steady supporter of this project, along with the school's Research Committee. We also gratefully acknowledge the encouragement and support of Kathie Amato, former director of Darden Business Publishing. We especially acknowledge the Darden School's permission to include materials in the book that were previously copyrighted by the school.

We are very grateful for the steady, cheerful support of Barbara Richards, who is at her best when things are hectic.

We especially want to thank Mike O'Malley of Yale University Press for his support of this project.

Thanks also to the following present and former students who assisted with various parts of the effort:

Carla Andrews	Laura Jacobs
Jay Bliley	Scott LeTourneau
Neil Carter	Ben Sanders
Bill Donaldson	Robert Schoenvogel
Amber Gray	Julia Wilson

We are grateful to all of our students, both graduate students at the Darden School and participants in executive programs, who encouraged us to pursue the topics in this book over many years.

Finally, we thank our families, who have shared our quest to understand the complexities of business.

I

INTRODUCTION TO
GENERAL MANAGEMENT

Part I of this book introduces the reader to the roles and tasks of the general manager (GM) and the contexts within which these activities take place. These contexts (settings) include the broader economic system that determines the "rules of the game," the overall setting within which the business is governed and organized, and the general manager's personal orientation and management style.

A business operates within a system of economic, political, and social forces over which the general manager has very little, if any, control. These forces must be understood, along with the impact they are having and will continue to have on the business. To be properly understood, these governmental laws (federal, state, and local) and the rules stipulated by numerous regulatory agencies need to be seen in a broad historical context, as well as that of the current environment, and the trends that provide some clues about the future environment.

Chapter 1 discusses the impact of these outside forces on the general manager. The general manager usually has more influence and control on how the business is organized and governed, but even here, there are many other involved decision makers, who often make bringing about meaningful change time consuming and difficult. It makes a great deal of difference, for instance, whether the company is privately or publicly owned (different sets of laws, rules, and regulations) and whether it is focused on a single business, diversified within an industry, or diversified across industries. The organizational context determines whether the general manager is a chief executive officer (CEO) reporting to a board of directors, the manager of a group of profit centers, or the manager of a single profit center.

Chapter 2 discusses these organizational nuances, pointing out that all CEOs are general managers, but all general managers are not CEOs. The personal orientation and management style of the individual general manager interacts with and must conform to these macrocontextual scenarios. No one excels at everything, and general managers are no exception. They gravitate toward what they are comfortable with and what they find interesting. Other responsibilities are either delegated or ignored, often at great cost. The final piece of the puzzle through which they reach their personal "comfort zone" lies with the choosing of their staff or team. They are, of course, free to choose team members (subordinates) who complement them, providing coverage for areas in which their skills and experience may be lacking. Authoritarian general managers, however, may find themselves with a staff of "yes-men" and "yes-women." The general manager's management style tends, over time, to attract and retain subordinates who adapt and adjust to his or her predilections.

Chapter 3 describes the roles and tasks of the general manager. The roles include leader, advocate, visionary, disciplinarian, and coach, among others. The tasks include:

- Being responsible to the shareholders for earning an adequate return on their investment
- Being responsible for the relationships with other stakeholders
- Being responsible for the profit or loss from operations of the firm
- Managing the interfaces (integration) of the line functional departments—marketing, engineering, and operations

Part I thus introduces the reader to the pivotal responsibility in our economic system of capitalism, free enterprise, and competition—that of the general manager.

1

GENERAL MANAGEMENT IN ECONOMIC CONTEXT

General Management and General Managers

The terms *general management* and *general manager* have been in use since the early twentieth century, along with an extensive litany of substitutes, to refer to a field of study or practice and the associated practitioner in the realm of the modern corporation. As with most broad subjects, numerous interpretations of the terms exist, along with variations and inconsistencies in their form and application.

General management addresses sources of income or revenue (sales) as well as expenses, with the difference between these two measures determining a level of profit or loss. General managers therefore have what is commonly referred to as profit-and-loss (P&L) responsibility. In contrast, managers of the functional departments of a business, such as marketing, finance, operations, and engineering or research and development (R&D), are responsible for individual pieces of the P&L puzzle. General managers are presumed to take responsibility for a total firm or economic entity, so general managers are frequently described as having *an enterprise perspective.*

General managers may assume one of a variety of roles depending on the structure of the organization in which they operate. Common titles and roles for general managers in corporate organizations include chief executive officer (CEO), president, general manager, owner, business unit manager, division manager, group vice president, managing partner, and managing member, among others. The preeminent general manager is the CEO of a major corporation, to whom many of the other general management positions cited above eventually report. As a result, multiple levels of general managers are often employed within an organization.

CEOs of corporations are typically appointed by and report to a board of directors. In these situations, the CEO and board work together to operate the business effectively on behalf of its shareholders and stakeholders. The board governs and the CEO manages the corporation. Within the corporation, general managers other than the CEO are normally appointed by and report to the CEO. As noted, general managers have P&L responsibility, and some have the authority to manage a decentralized business or collection of businesses. In some corporations, the bylaws require the board to appoint certain lower-level general managers as corporate officers, but these managers clearly serve at the pleasure of the corporate general manager, the CEO.

General managers have numerous additional responsibilities within the corporation. As part of their duties, they must integrate the functions of the business to maintain viability and meet their organization's goals and objectives. The topic of goals and objectives is addressed in some detail later in this book; typically, this topic encompasses an overall pattern of results for meeting the firm's strategic goals and specified targets or targeted ranges for important financial measures, such as profit, return on investment, cash flow, and growth.

Coordinating and integrating the activities of the functional departments of the business are key tasks of the general manager and often are referred to collectively as "managing the functional interfaces." In the course of business, conflicts naturally arise among and between the functional managers. For example, marketing managers frequently would prefer to have numerous product variations and large inventories of finished goods to meet customer demands rapidly, but product proliferation and large inventories create added costs and complexity for manufacturing and warehousing and lead to increased capital investment. Manufacturing managers often would prefer stable demand forecasts and longer production runs in order to decrease volatility and lower costs, but long runs lengthen delivery times and slow responsiveness to ever-changing demand. Engineering managers would naturally prefer to overdesign products in the interest of durability and quality, but overdesign increases product costs without perceived benefit to the customer. The list of these potential conflicts and competing interests within a business could go on, and the general manager must effectively manage all such conflicts in the best long-term interests of the firm.

The general manager regularly must face difficult decisions involving forces outside the firm as well as those within. In some fashion, nearly all of these forces have an economic impact on the organization. Primary among the elements or parties exerting substantial force are:

- Owners (shareholders or equity holders) who invest in the corporation, whether public or private
- Employees of the organization
- Customers of the organization, including consumers and purchasers acting on behalf of other business organizations
- Suppliers of the organization from whom goods and services are purchased
- Communities in which the organization operates and competes
- Lenders who finance the debt of the firm
- The board of directors, whose primary tasks include governing the firm on behalf of all shareholders and hiring the general manager or CEO
- Laws and lawmakers as well as regulations and regulatory agencies that define the rules under which the firm competes
- Competitors who challenge any of the firm's products

Addressing and managing these stakeholders, elements, and forces are the heart of the general manager's role. This job is the crucial management task in today's organization, and the corporation is a vital instrument by which our current systems of capitalism, free enterprise, and competition operate for the greater good of our economy. The remainder of this book is intended to identify and explain the primary elements of general management and tasks of the general manager in the competitive environment of a free-enterprise marketplace. Before forging ahead, though, we would like to examine briefly some important elements of the historical context in which general management has evolved to its current state.

Evolution of General Management

Economic history began thousands of years ago and evolved as communities developed and grew. Over time, tools improved, craft skills advanced, and the efficiency of specialization was recognized. Bartering began first within and then among communities, and rudimentary economic systems burgeoned.

In an agrarian economy, the ownership of land was the source of wealth and often freedom. Landowning classes emerged that lived off the efforts of peasants and serfs. In order to protect their property and lands, the leaders developed military organizations that, over time, became larger and larger, necessitating the development of such management standards as chains of command and discipline in the ranks.

Sun Tzu wrote *The Art of War* some 2,500 years ago, yet many of this work's principles have applicability to modern management. Another early description of management appears in the Book of Exodus in the Bible, where Jethro, the father-in-law of Moses, speaks to him about managing the exodus of the Israelite males and their households out of Egypt. Jethro advises Moses to delegate—a skill that is essential to managing large operations as well as organizations. A plethora of other epic works has addressed principles of work, discipline, and human nature and still remains relevant to contemporary general management. Notably, Machiavelli provided an impressive summary of management advice to his patron, Lorenzo de' Medici, in his treatise to *The Prince* in 1521. While Machiavelli focused on principles for ruling, the work was written during a period of revitalization in Europe during which early forms of modern economic systems emerged. Nonetheless, Machiavelli's treatise remains one of the most forceful explanations of our inherent human nature, and the elegant writings of Sun Tzu and Machiavelli remind us of the enduring fascination with principles of management.

Free Enterprise, Capitalism, and Competition

A fundamental chapter in the evolution of current management thought was the emergence of democracy as a viable form of government. Democracy and its freedoms created an environment in which the free-market economic system of capitalism could take hold and flourish. There is a clear and logical connection between the concept of individual political freedom and the freedom of individuals to pursue their economic self-interests.

A paradox resulting from the development of a free-market system is that the collective pursuit of individual self-interest has created a prosperity that benefits the whole—that is, most of society. Free enterprise brings to the economies of developed countries the sustained energy of competition, in which the creative minds of countless individuals are unleashed to pursue their individual best interests, within the rules provided by laws and regulation. Adam Smith first wrote in 1776 that "an invisible hand of self-interest" moved to create a total environment in the best interests of "the many" when each of us acts to maximize our own individual interests.[1] While counter-intuitive in some respects, this remains an astonishing and liberating idea.

The concept of the invisible hand has led logically to the notion that as individuals pursue their separate interests, the intersections of their interests and objectives result in a natural state of competition. In the realm of business, competition among firms arises for raw materials, labor, customers, intellectual capital, and investment capital. This competitive environment typically leads to a "survival of the fittest" regimen that, over time, weeds out the weakest competitors and promotes survival of the most successful. While some people may fear this relentless ferreting out of the less effective, it is perhaps the most energizing aspect of systems of free enterprise and competition.

An additional key to the development of modern capitalism has been the mechanism by which the capital of many investors can be united to provide the large amounts of investment needed to fund extensive projects and massive enterprises. It is axiomatic that the greater the freedom of business enterprises to compete in search of expansive returns, the greater is the inclination of individual and institutional investors to provide the required capital. This capital is normally deployed in the funding of corporations, whose form we take as a given today. The corporation, however, is a relatively new form of business organization.

The Corporation

Early organizations engaging in trade or commerce were established as proprietorships or partnerships, where owners managed their own affairs and typically participated in the creation and delivery of goods and services. As business evolved, these simple forms of ownership were augmented with others that were generated to accommodate larger and more extensive organizations. The massive enterprises of today's economy have roots in the early companies of colonial-era Europe. The Muscovy Company (in 1555), the Spanish Company (in 1577), and the East India Company (in 1601) received history's first recorded business charters of incorporation during the reign of England's Queen Elizabeth I. The London Company, soon to be called the Virginia Company of London, followed in 1606.[2]

The U.S. Supreme Court, under Chief Justice John Marshall, made corporations possible legally in the early nineteenth century. Marshall himself defined a corporation in a Supreme Court opinion for *Dartmouth College v. Woodward* in the following terms: "A corporation is an artificial being, invisible, intangible and existing only in the contemplation of the law. Being the mere creature of law, it possesses only three qualities which the charter of its creation confers upon it, either expressly or as incidental to its very existence . . . [The most] important are immortality and, if the expression may be allowed, individuality; properties by which a perpetual succession of many persons are considered as the same, and may act as a single individual."[3]

In summary, the corporation is a creation of the law and has legal standing independent of its owners. Three features have made the corporation attractive:

- its unlimited life
- the limited liability of the owners
- the divisibility of ownership that permits transfer of ownership interests without disrupting the structure of the organization

Expansion of the use of the corporate form was fueled by the Industrial Revolution, which began in England around the mid-nineteenth century and launched the Western world's evolution from agrarian to industrial economies. Changes began in Britain with the introduction of steam power and powered machinery. Over time, energy to power machines was harnessed through water-driven mills, steam engines, and then the internal combustion engine and electricity, and the phenomenon of mass production emerged. Initially, commerce was essentially local, with local production and trade of products within the community. The revolution roared to life as farmers sought work in factories, towns were born, and prices of mass-produced goods became affordable to the new class of workers.

After its legal establishment, the corporation quickly became the preferred form of organization for larger enterprises. By 1919, corporations, while representing only 31.5 percent of the total number of businesses, employed 86 percent of the U.S. workforce and produced 87.7 percent of the total business output by value.[4]

The Industrial Revolution, driven by a wave of technological advances, created ever-larger organizations made possible by the corporate form. Within what was known as the second Industrial Revolution, the role of the general manager evolved. Larger organizations employed large numbers of workers, tasks and labor were divided, and a coordinating function became a necessity. The job of the general manager emerged, and hierarchical corporate structures became commonplace. These organizations were predecessors of the huge multinational and global businesses we see today, and their development was made possible by transportation and communication advances of the railroads, steamships, and telegraph. These advances allowed goods and information to travel rapidly across markets and concurrently expanded the feasible span of control within an organization.

Similar and related progress has been found in the rapid advances of the technological revolution driven by the computer, which has created and continues to create a very different type of global economy in what many call the Information Age. Syndicated columnist Thomas L. Friedman summarizes many of the attendant consequences as a "flattening" of the world, resulting in a leveling of the playing fields of competition.[5]

In the contemporary global economy, new business models are evolving as political boundaries are rendered economically obsolete in spite of protectionist laws. Economic theory tells us that these changes are not necessarily all bad. David Ricardo (1772–1823), an English economist, developed the free-trade theory of competitive costs, now called comparative advantage, in which he theorized that the global economy is not a zero-sum game. Rather, if a nation were to specialize in the production of goods in which it had a comparative cost advantage and then trade with another nation for goods in which it had a cost advantage, both nations would be better off than had they not traded. Extrapolation suggests there would be an overall gain in trade as well as income in all such trading countries. Many of these related advantages are evolving in the twenty-first century, but not all of the changes come without cost.

Adjusting to global competition has created structural shifts in certain economies, where short-run consequences have proven painful for those associated with industries whose work has faced stiff competition from or moved to other regions of the globe. Public policy makers often take this situation into account and lawmakers attempt to soften the impact, but no country can be successful in ultimately stemming the competitive tide using protectionist policies without great economic cost. Every country must learn to produce and compete, and managers must lead their companies to do the same, or perish.

In summary, the world is headed toward an increasingly global economy in which ever-larger corporations will continue to experience rapid, large-scale change. The challenges of a global economy place new emphasis on the role of the general manager. Past success is no longer an indicator of sustainable future achievement. In fact, mind-sets frozen by previous successful accomplishments may hinder the kind of thinking necessary to adapt to the future, much less create a new future. In the future, as in the past, the success of businesses will depend largely on how well they are led and managed by their general managers.

Ethical Considerations

Ethical considerations for managers encompass meaningful issues involving values. Hence, in some fashion, nearly every consequential decision a manager makes has an ethical component. The concept of stakeholder management, with a more recent variation of stakeholder capitalism, captures the essence of ethical decision making for contemporary managers and represents a growing trend that has increased the complexity of management for many senior executives schooled in previous traditions.

The traditional form of capitalism promoted by companies in the United States has been *shareholder capitalism,* whose goal is to create shareholder wealth. In the United States as well as in certain other countries, including the United Kingdom, Canada, and Australia, many of the legal standards governing boards of directors of companies address related responsibilities of board members to represent and act in the interests of the shareholders.

Another form of capitalism has mutated out of shareholder capitalism, as described by William Pfaff: "A new system has developed—manager's capitalism—in which the corporation came to be run to profit its managers, in complicity if not conspiracy with accountants and the managers of other corporations . . . because the markets had so disused corporate ownership that no responsible owner exists. This is morally unacceptable, but also a corruption of capitalism itself."[6]

Why did this happen? The issue is: Who are the owners, as opposed to shareholders, of a business? They are certainly not the overnight traders, or even the institutional shareholders, who prefer liquidity to control and long-term commitment. They, in effect, "rent" their shares as opposed to buying them for the long haul. The governance vacuum was filled by the boards and managers, who then were motivated by their own self-interests, with no controls to keep them within reasonable bounds.

Stakeholder management, on the other hand, is based on the premise that financial returns are not the sole consideration of a business. Rather, the best long-term results come about from higher-order efforts to attend to the interests of all stakeholders of the organization. In the United States, laws and regulations addressing consideration of stakeholder interests (other than those of shareholders) almost exclusively address protection of rights via prohibition of activities, situations, or environments that are currently or potentially deleterious, rather than an expressed duty to represent their interests.

As noted, stakeholder management embraces the view that businesses must manage relationships with all of their stakeholders, which often involves balancing conflicting interests. A review of the practices of many successful companies will reveal that they have a history of serving the interests of the stakeholders well. Constituencies commonly considered major stakeholders of a business include:

- customers
- employees
- suppliers

- communities in which the business operates
- shareholders or equity holders

One can readily see that an approach to decision making within a business that considers the interests of all stakeholders would require new ways of thinking for general managers who previously focused primarily on seeking financial returns. Many successful managers, however, already employ forms of stakeholder management, having embraced the notion that this enlightened approach to decision making serves the interests of the shareholders over the long term.

A related consideration for managers is the increasing expectation of the public for businesses to provide more transparency or disclosure, particularly in their approaches to dealing with controversial issues related to the law and fair dealings. These heightened expectations have come in the wake of numerous high-profile corporate scandals closely following the period of extremely high equity valuations between 1998 and 2001, which provided some managers extremely strong incentives to act unscrupulously.

Laws have evolved and regulations have been enacted to address business disclosures to the public, as well as their dealings with customers, employees, investors, and the environment. While some of these laws may have been written in favor of a special interest group in the name of the consumer or worker, most address past abuses that were outside the bounds of acceptable moral behavior. In spite of laws, however, some very successful managers have succumbed and will continue to succumb to temptations to engage in immoral and unlawful behavior. General managers should note that the standards related to their behavior on and off the job appear to be rising ever higher. Some of these standards address individual conduct, and others have been captured in the laws and regulations addressing the governance of corporations.

Corporate Governance

Corporate governance was thrust into the public spotlight at the beginning of the new millennium as a result of numerous scandals and the collapse or near collapse of several major American corporations. While the phrase is commonplace, corporate governance remains a vague concept for many citizens. Briefly, corporate governance refers to the act or process of governing corporate organizations. Corporate governance has evolved with the corporation itself, with many cornerstone U.S. laws and regulations enacted to counter the unrestrained greed and unscrupulous behavior of the robber barons who amassed great wealth during the days of the Industrial Revolution. As an eventual result, the governing of public corporations today has taken the form of representative government.

In U.S. public corporations, corporate governance creates a system for owners (shareholders) to elect individuals to represent their interests in managing the affairs of the firms. These individuals, or directors, collectively form the board of directors of the corporation. The board of directors delegates the responsibility for actual operations and day-to-day management to the chief executive officer (CEO), whom they hire. The CEO is accountable to the board of directors, which, collectively and individually, is responsible to the shareholders. In sum, this system of authoritative direction is known as *corporate governance*. We explore the responsibilities and duties of directors and the CEO in the context of the organizational structure further in Chapter 2.

Summary

As business and the corporation have evolved over the last century, so has the role of the general manager. In particular, the role of the CEO, the ultimate general manager in public corporations, has become progressively more important to the success of a business as businesses have grown in size and complexity. Rapid technological change in an increasingly complex and competitive global economy is bringing more and varied challenges to senior executives, heightening the significance of strong general management as a determinant of corporate success. As we point out repeatedly in this text, strength in general management comes about through insightful and sometimes lucky decision making, as well as disciplined and watchful implementation.

At the level of the general manager, decision science plays an important but notably limited role. Today's general manager faces a world that is complex, frequently unpredictable, and occasionally changeable. Creating models to capture its complexity and uncertainty can be challenging and even impossible. Plans, which must be made, may imply precision, but their implementation is difficult and much less precise work. Human behavior, while broadly and generally predictable, continues to surprise in individual circumstances. Therefore, the contents of this text—including the techniques, practices, and processes described within—should be considered tools of general guidance. Managers should be mindful that while the decisions required of them may be built upon seemingly precise analyses, the analyses themselves typically employ imprecise inputs and projections, and implementation of the decisions relies upon the performance and actions of workers.

We remind the reader that this work is not intended to provide in-depth reviews of the topic of strategic planning or any of the functional areas. Instead, it addresses broad principles of strategic planning and management of the functional interfaces, leaving the study of the more detailed topics to those specializing in the respective functional fields.

DISCUSSION QUESTIONS

1. What is the definition of a general manager?
2. How has the role of the general manager evolved?
3. Who are the major stakeholders of a corporation? Are general managers required to consider the interests of all major stakeholders in their decision making?
4. What is the difference between shareholder capitalism and stakeholder capitalism?
5. What is corporate governance?
6. What is the distinctive role of the general manager within our system of free enterprise, capitalism, and competition?

2

GENERAL MANAGEMENT IN ORGANIZATIONAL CONTEXT

We begin our examination of the position of chief executive officer (CEO) in an organizational context with a discussion of how the nature of the business ownership affects the structure. Then we shift our discussion to the level of the board of directors, for it is the board that ultimately represents the interests of the owners (shareholders) of the business and hires the CEO. We then discuss how the board interfaces with management and evaluates its performance. Finally we discuss how the CEO shapes the organization's structure.

The Nature of Business Ownership

The nature of a company's ownership—whether it is publicly or privately owned—has a significant effect on the organizational context in which the CEO functions. The ultimate authority for governing a publicly traded business resides with the board of directors, whose members are chosen by the shareholders to govern the company in their best interests and who appoint the CEO to manage the ongoing activities of the business. Thus, the board of directors governs the company and the CEO manages its day-to-day activities in accordance with goals and strategies mutually agreed upon by the board and management.

With private ownership, smaller businesses tend to be owner-managed, and the owners involved in the business represent themselves and their interests.

Within these two categories, further delineations need to be made to describe more accurately the ownership of the entity. For example, a publicly owned business may have a controlling shareholder or bloc of shareholders who exercise total control over the company, or it may have a widely fragmented ownership structure with no controlling individual or group. A privately owned business, on the other hand, may be owned and managed by a single individual or a group of investors (often a family) who exercise control.

Our discussion in this chapter is dedicated primarily to examining the publicly owned corporation, although much of the material is equally applicable to private businesses as well.

The Role of the Board of Directors

As the owners' representatives, the directors have a number of legal duties that define their fiduciary responsibilities. The most important duties of directors are those of loyalty, fair dealing, and care. In the United States, the individual states define these duties, with directors responsible for complying with the legal standards of the state in which the business is legally incorporated. Corporate laws vary from state to state.

As a broad summary, the primary duties of directors require them to be loyal to the company and place the interests of the corporation and shareholders above their own. In general, this implies that if there is a conflict of interest, directors must treat the corporation fairly in any dealings with it. Finally, directors must take the time and make the effort to fulfill their responsibilities thoroughly, which includes being reasonably well informed and, when they sense the need, making necessary inquiries to become informed. The duties of directors have evolved and broadened over the years, with the degree of accountability and the liability for failure to perform continually increasing in recent years.

The organizational tasks of the board of directors include hiring the CEO, which involves managing the CEO succession process, defining the CEO's responsibilities, evaluating the performance of the CEO, and determining top management compensation.

Hiring the CEO

Among the most important responsibilities of a board of directors is hiring the CEO. A poor choice may lead to the creation of problems and even result in failure, since an organization's leadership is a key determinant of its destiny. As such, the decision made by a board of directors in selecting and hiring the CEO is a fundamental determinant of the future of the enterprise.

Finding the right CEO is a matter of ensuring a situational fit between the skills and experience of the candidate and the current and projected needs of the organization. A rapidly growing technology business would require a different kind of leader than a mature retailer or manufacturer.

Succession Planning and Timing

Given the importance of the CEO, the succession planning process is a critical one for a board of directors. CEO selection is always in the context of choosing a successor to a current or recently departed CEO except for the situation of a start-up company. In circumstances of ordinary transition, the normal succession process may begin as early as two years in advance of a CEO's planned retirement. The appropriate committee of the board of directors, typically the governance committee, normally begins its process working with the outgoing CEO to review and revise the job description and develop an articulation of the personal characteristics desired in a new CEO.

The outgoing CEO will normally be involved in the process of choosing his or her successor unless there is some discord between the CEO and the board. Some CEOs do not want a role in choosing their successors, preferring to leave the task to the board. In most cases, though, the CEO will have developed a succession plan and will have groomed a successor or a pool of candidates within the company, with the board having been apprised of and involved in this process. If the board is pleased with the company's performance, competitive position, and long-term prospects, the board will be more predisposed to respect the CEO's succession plan or list of candidates, and a smooth transition will be the expectation.

Of course, not all transitions are orderly and planned. The circumstances under which the board must make its decision vary widely, with major variables including the following:

- Reasons for the change in leadership, spanning normal retirement, death or disability, resignation, and termination
- The time interval during which the board has notice of the change, varying from lengthy (years of long-term anticipation) to none at all (immediate and unexpected departure)
- The current condition of the business, as well as the trend or trajectory of its results. The current condition may be categorized broadly as strong, stable, weak, or in crisis mode; the trajectory or trend of results similarly may be characterized as positive/improving, stable/constant, or negative/declining.

When Immediate Action Is Required

There are instances in CEO transition when time is of the essence, for example, if the CEO leaves abruptly for another job, dies, or is incapacitated due to an accident or a health crisis. There may arise some scandal involving the company. There are many such events that require the board to move with what the U.S. Navy terms "all deliberate speed." All decision processes are expedited, and the board faces the task of finding and appointing a new CEO as rapidly as possible.

Because every company faces the risk of the CEO's unexpected departure, it behooves the board of directors to maintain a discreet contingency plan. Many boards require the CEO to provide annually the name of the person or persons who could assume the position of CEO, or this plan may be developed by the chair of the board and/or the chair of the board's nominating committee.

Each of the situations that result in a sudden need for a new CEO creates a unique dynamic for the board of directors. Emergency situations such as death or disability leave some members grieving for a respected friend; the event itself, though, usually creates no long-term fallout for the firm. Voluntary resignations cause employees and the public to ask why, wondering if the incumbent is aspiring to something different or evading something yet unannounced. In the case of a CEO resignation, the board must act quickly to ascertain the answers to these questions (if they are known) and determine an appropriate plan of action. An involuntary termination is more complicated. The board must deal with the consequences of the firing quickly, forcefully, and appropriately to contain damage to the firm, and then must turn immediately to the issue of finding a successor.

Regardless of the timing, boards with a need for a CEO should articulate their desires regarding the characteristics they seek in candidates. Such an exercise creates a structure for finding the best person for the position, whether the candidate is from within or from outside the organization. Boards should simultaneously examine and summarize the current needs, situation, and established norms of the organization, particularly those related to the position of CEO, as any candidate performing a diligent job search will want to evaluate these considerations.

The Desired Profile

A CEO requires a portfolio of attributes to be successful in the position. Because of the breadth of the requirements and the wide range of institutional needs, highlighted here are those traits common to the preponderance of public-company situations. These characteristics may be summarized broadly as demonstrated strength in:

- character
- technical competence
- administrative skills
- interpersonal and communication skills
- sharing of the core values of the organization

Boards seeking a CEO will naturally find additional important requirements upon careful examination of the particular circumstances of the firms they serve.

In addition to these characteristics, a CEO candidate must have the requisite experience, which translates into a certain level of maturity, along with relevant functional and general management experience.

Few candidates rise to the level of CEO of a major public company before the age of forty. On the other hand, few executives are appointed to CEO positions after the age of fifty-five because many companies now want their CEOs to serve a number of years before retiring between the ages of sixty-two and sixty-five. Attaining a position as CEO is thus somewhat dependent on luck or timing, as an opening must occur during the time frame in which an aspirant is considered eligible and qualified. The resulting selection of an individual who would be expected to hold the position for a decade or even two closes the door on anyone "coming of age" during that time frame and certainly on those who are contemporaries of the appointee.

Other Preferred Attributes

If the situation does not demand a dramatic change in strategy, the board might seek a strong consensus builder who would work with the current management team to continue current successful strategies. If the board feels that fundamental changes must be made, it should seek an effective change agent who would move the company into new realms, including those of new products or services, increased international presence, or the sale of assets or businesses no longer considered to be strategic necessities. Regardless of the need for change, prospective candidates for CEO should possess certain critical attributes. Many details may be added to each of the characteristics listed above, some general and others specific to the situation of a given company. As this text explores the roles and tasks of the general manager, additional details will become apparent.

Inside versus Outside Candidates

A primary choice the board faces in selecting a CEO under any circumstances is whether to promote from inside the organization or to hire from the outside. The natural tendency among most firms is to look inside first. Nearly all great companies work at creating a talent pool, which includes training and developing general managers so that one or more qualified candidates is always available for an orderly management succession. This is a process in which the board should be involved, as succession planning is their responsibility. In cases where no satisfactory inside candidate is available when an opening occurs, the board must conduct a search outside the firm to identify and recruit a qualified candidate.

If an organization is on a sound course and prospering, promoting a known and experienced candidate from within to continue the program is generally a sensible solution. If the organization is foundering, however, the board may be motivated to find outside talent to challenge the status quo and move the business to a better course. The board should also consider outside candidates in situations where directors feel the firm has not performed up to its potential given its industry, market positions, and other resources, such as intellectual capital.

Another factor that leads boards to seek new CEOs from the outside is the tendency of otherwise well-meaning directors to look at the management of competitors and peers with the view that somehow executives at other companies are just better than the insiders and that somewhere in the competitive world there has to be a better manager than the firm's internal candidates. When such a mood persists, it is almost impossible to placate the board, and the company will very likely bring in the most attractive outsider that can be lured to take the CEO position.

It is also quite prevalent that the board that hires an outsider to be CEO discovers his or her flaws only in due course after hiring rather than before, because it is very difficult to obtain straightforward negative feedback on potential candidates. Due to the current litigiousness of American society, few are willing to state for the record, or even off the record, their perceptions of anyone's negative attributes. A board thus will know the inherent weaknesses of internal candidates, who are then compared with an outside candidate or candidates whose problems are not apparent.

The Role of Headhunters

The tendency for a board to hire an outside manager as CEO is also enhanced by the steady growth in the use of executive search firms or "headhunters." These professional firms exist to identify, obtain references, and arrange interviews for candidates who are available to be considered for the CEO position and other management positions. The headhunters, of course, command handsome fees for their services, often equal to a year's total compensation for the executive position being filled.

When board members are inclined to check outside, perhaps just to be certain that they are not overlooking a strong candidate, they often and unwittingly set in motion a process that inevitably will lead to the appointment of an outsider. Consequently, boards should be careful in deciding whether to test the outside market unless they are reasonably sure that the insiders at hand are not adequate to fill the role.

The Position of CEO

General Responsibilities

The CEO has complete responsibility for achieving the immediate goals of the business and ensuring the effectiveness of all of its functions, as well as building an organization capable of long-term success. A critical skill of effective CEOs is the ability to surround themselves with highly talented teams, particularly with individuals whose skills, abilities, and personalities are complementary. Working with the team that he or she has brought together, the CEO develops the goals of the organization and the strategies for achieving those goals. The major goals and strategies are presented to the board for its advice and consent. After the board has approved the goals and key strategies, the CEO must lead the execution of the strategies and present timely and accurate reports of the progress and results to the board.

Title and Responsibility: The CEO and the Chairman of the Board

A major organizational issue for most large companies is whether to have a CEO who simultaneously serves as the chairman of the board of directors or to separate the two positions. Undoubtedly, two jobs exist: one to manage the affairs of the business, the other to organize and lead the work of the board in overseeing the affairs of the business as representatives of all shareholders. A majority of public corporations in the United States has combined the two positions, primarily reasoning that an organization needs a strong leader empowered to do his or her job. Combined positions remove the possibility of a rivalry developing between the CEO and chairman and eliminate any conflict between the agendas of the board and the organization. This practice of combining the positions, however, has recently been considered one of the sources of certain problems with corporate governance in the United States.

Concerns related to combining the positions of CEO and chairman of the board of directors primarily encompass the diversity of responsibilities and skills required for the two positions, as well as the apparent conflict of interest that arises when the CEO in effect chairs the body to which he or she is accountable. Given that the board (and especially the chairman) must evaluate the performance of the CEO, a person holding both positions is necessarily called on to evaluate him- or herself.

As a result, firms have begun to move toward the establishment of a non-employee chairman of the board, who works with the CEO to manage the board's work. A popular alternative in the wake of recent changes to federal and stock exchange regulations is the appointment of a lead director, who is prohibited from having direct ties to the organization through current or recent employment relationships. The lead director normally serves as the chair of the committee of outside directors, one of whose primary responsibilities is the evaluation of the CEO's performance.

A related issue is whether to have senior executives of the firm (in addition to the CEO) serve on the board of directors. As with most decisions, potential advantages and disadvantages accompany the options. When internal executives serve on the board as inside directors, the outside directors most often have a broader exposure to management, get to know the executives better, and learn more about the workings of the company. Board service may also be used as an important step in succession planning and the development of a potential future CEO candidate. An attendant risk, though, is that management directors will find it difficult to express disagreement with the CEO, potentially limiting the effectiveness of the board in considering multiple viewpoints.

The Board-Management Interface

The board of directors presides over the corporation by establishing appropriate policies that govern decision making in the organization. It also reserves the right to approve certain major decisions, including those involving capital investment, capital structure, the sale of assets, and mergers/acquisitions and divestitures. Boards are also responsible for the full, timely, and accurate disclosure of relevant events and performance to shareholders and for ensuring sound stewardship of shareholders' investments.

When operations are going well, a board generally has a straightforward job encompassing oversight of ongoing business affairs and response to proposals brought forward by the CEO. When crises arise, though, boards must respond promptly.

Each firm, through formal definition as well as practice and tradition, establishes a division of responsibilities between the board and the CEO. Both parties must be careful in this process, especially regarding the level of involvement of the board in the details of running the business. The majority of board members have, at most, a part-time interest in the company. Although they are obligated legally to represent the best interests of the shareholders, most have other full-time positions that limit the time they can devote to their oversight function. They must rely on the CEO (and top management) to keep them updated and apprised of important successes, opportunities, and problems.

A board that crosses the line by micromanaging the CEO and his or her decision making can undermine the effectiveness of the CEO and will find it difficult to hold the CEO accountable for poor results. On the other hand, a board that is too detached or passive may, in fact, be abdicating its role in the governance of the organization. Board members must strive to find the right balance between these two extremes, being proactive in carrying out their responsibilities as directors without interfering.

The Board's Role in Strategy Formulation

An important role of the board is to participate with the CEO in the development of the company's strategy and the plans for its successful implementation. As part of this process, the CEO normally prepares a list of the strategic options available to the company, explores the advantages and disadvantages of each option with the board, and recommends one or more to the board. (Details of this strategic planning process are presented in subsequent chapters.)

The CEO must consult the board on such matters because execution of the strategy often requires actions that must be approved by the board and/or the shareholders.

The Board's Oversight Responsibility

The board must maintain effective oversight of the CEO, the company, and its assets, and the CEO should willingly assist the board in carrying out these fundamental duties. A board must assert itself when necessary, challenge the CEO when trouble is apparent or suspected, and support the CEO in difficult situations when it believes that such support is warranted. The board also may be faced at times with the difficult decision of removing or replacing a CEO due to poor performance. In fulfilling its fiduciary role and in educating itself to evaluate senior management, the board must be informed regarding numerous relevant internal and external situations and trends.

Evaluating CEO Performance

The evaluation of the CEO's performance is such an important responsibility of the board that a separate board committee is nearly always dedicated to this task. In practice, evaluation of the performance of the CEO should be an ongoing process of observation and interaction as well as a comparison of actual results to projected progress toward agreed-upon goals and measures.

The board should also engage in a formal performance evaluation of the CEO periodically, and at least annually. This evaluation should be direct, candid, and in accordance with the charter of the compensation committee of the board. The discussions should address concerns, shortcomings, and positive achievements with frank dialogue involving all parties.

As one step in continually assessing the performance of the firm, the board and the CEO should regularly compare the firm's financial and operational results and status with those of available and relevant indexes and a select group of peer companies. In benchmarking a firm's performance, an analyst must first determine a set of attributes and measures on which to compare organizations. This set should depend on the nature of the firm, its industry, and its strategy. Core financial performance metrics should be included regardless, along with measures relevant to achieving competitive advantage in the industry of interest.

Compensation of the CEO

Compensation of the CEO and certain senior executives is generally administered by a compensation committee of the board of directors. New York Stock Exchange rules now require that this committee be composed entirely of independent directors within listed companies. Because of the visibility, magnitude, and special approach to CEO compensation, we treat it here with the examination of general management in organizational context. Compensation and rewards for other employees, as tasks of general management, are addressed in a later chapter.

Boards of directors aim to use executive compensation to pay for strong performance. The logic behind this goal is rather straightforward, but the reality of finding an effective implementation is complicated. A multitude of press exposés and lawsuits have reminded us in recent times of the potential pitfalls boards may face in addressing executive compensation. Numerous factors should influence CEO compensation, ranging from the size and industry of the company to the relative performance of the organization compared to that of peer firms.

Because the pool of potential, experienced CEOs is often limited, a board usually must match other firms, or meet the market, in terms of compensation to attract and retain a topflight CEO. Market forces also usually affect how much compensation is termed *guaranteed* (typically salary, benefits, and perquisites) and how much varies with the performance of the firm (short- and long-term incentives, often termed *at risk*). The at-risk compensation is intended to influence the executive to adopt the perspective of an owner, and as a result should be aligned with shareholder interests.

Because the intent is to influence the CEO to adopt an approach that benefits all shareholders, current and over the long term, some form of equity-based compensation is typically employed, often with vesting periods of numerous years.

The design of compensation plans must address both the levels and types of compensation to be awarded. In the wake of scandals in which senior executives banked millions while workers lost pensions and share values plummeted, shareholder activists have raised the question of how much compensation is enough or, more frequently, how much is too much income for the CEO. For the nonperforming CEO, anything over a reasonable base salary has been recognized as too much, and for the exceedingly poor performer, even that level of compensation has been deemed excessive, with many believing such executives should be terminated.

Regardless of the difficulties involved, boards must create compensation packages for their CEOs that generally consist of some combination of base salary, short-term incentives, long-term incentives, fringe benefits, and perquisites or perks. Boards must determine the appropriate level and mix of these components for their particular situations.

Employment Agreements (Contracts)

CEOs and senior executives are as a rule bound by contract with the firms for which they work. Such contracts usually include:

- severance agreements, which delineate how much and for how long an executive will be paid in the event of termination;
- noncompete clauses, which prohibit the executive from working in certain types of companies or in certain positions or industries for a specified period after leaving the firm; and
- change-of-control provisions, which offer the executive protection in the event of losing his or her job as a result of the sale of the company or any other event causing a change of control.

These latter provisions typically trigger a vesting of all stock options and restricted shares of company stock held by the executive. Severance agreements and change-of-control clauses are included in contracts with the good intentions of protecting the interests of loyal executives, but unfortunately, they have been instrumental on occasion in allowing nonperforming executives to walk away with large sums of money after only short or unsuccessful tenures in their positions.

Organizing for Success

With an understanding of the means by which the governance process puts the CEO in place, we now move on to discuss how the CEO goes about organizing the business to best meet its agreed-upon goals and objectives. The ideal organizational structure depends on a number of factors, including the size and type of business. In addition, a primary issue in establishing an effective organizational structure is the number of distinct businesses within the organization.

The organizing phase of general management consists of defining the authority, reporting, and support relationships through which the business will be conducted. Organizing also includes identifying where in the organization responsibility and authority to manage certain aspects of the business reside, whether it is with specific individuals or organizational positions. The authority delegated may allow a recipient to assume responsibility for a functional activity—such as marketing, manufacturing or operations, finance, engineering or research and development (R&D)—or for profit and loss (P&L) responsibility for a segment or segments of the business.

Organization is discussed briefly here and in more detail in Chapter 18, "Organizing and Aligning."

A Functional Organization

A primary approach to organizing a business is to employ a functional structure. A functional organization usually encompasses highly centralized control of the business. In such an organization, the marketing and sales of all of the firm's products are the responsibility of a marketing manager, whose department generates the company's revenues. Similarly, the manager of manufacturing or operations is responsible for the production of all of the products of the firm and thus manages most of the firm's assets, costs, and employees. The engineering (sometimes R&D) and finance functions are similarly conducted centrally.

In a centralized, functional organization, revenues and costs are not considered jointly except at the highest level—that of the CEO, president, or general manager. The responsibility for profits in such an organization clearly resides with its general manager, who must rely on a combination of sales efforts to produce revenues and expense budgets for cost control to provide a total result that generates a profit for the operation.

A Diversified, Decentralized Organization

The size and complexity of operations has led many companies to decentralize the management of the enterprise into a number of profit centers, which then tend to be functionally organized. In such an organization, the responsibility for conducting the firm's business in a segment of the company's markets is delegated to a profit center manager and his or her staff. The CEO or general manager determines the broad direction for the company, sets goals and objectives for the divisions, and makes changes in top-level executive personnel when necessary. The basic responsibility for profits resides with the divisions, and the overall company profitability is dependent on the performance of the divisions. This type of organization is usually referred to as a decentralized organization and the divisions are frequently referred to as profit centers.

A Project, Product-Line, or Matrix Organization

Companies or divisions that engage in long-running projects, or that have several different product lines within a profit center, may employ either a project, product-line, or matrix organization. In such organizations, specialized managers are designated to coordinate the activities of the functional managers for a given project or product line. These specialized managers report to the general manager and are expected to plan for and monitor functional operations and ensure the profitable operation of their product-line segments of the business.

Reacting to Needs for Organizational Change

Many companies find it necessary to change and adjust their organizations from time to time. A large number of alternatives are available to the manager attempting to accommodate various combinations of customer desires, available management talent, environmental factors, and significant internal situations. While the CEO or general manager operates within the context of how the business is governed and organized, he or she should not passively accept the organizational context, but instead participate in its shaping. Therefore, one of the key responsibilities of the general manager is to organize the business to achieve its purposes.

The Nature of the Business

The organizational structure of the business must take into account the nature of the business, which refers to the work or the activities that the business performs to fulfill its purpose. Manufacturers, retailers, service businesses, and professional service firms all perform very different activities. Within these broad groups, there is still wide variety in the activities carried out within specific types of businesses. Hospitals, airlines, and Internet service providers are all service companies, for instance, but each obviously encompasses diverse pursuits by its respective workforce.

Differences Within Functions

For example, one organizational choice within the marketing function addresses the sales force. Executives must decide whether to organize the sales force to specialize in particular products or markets, or whether to have one sales force that sells the full complement of product lines to all of the firm's customers. Similar decisions must be made regarding the organization of the engineering or R&D activities; the production or manufacturing facilities; and to a lesser degree, the finance and accounting staffs. Such internal functional decisions should be made in light of the firm's chosen strategy, which is addressed later in the text.

A Collection of Businesses

A fundamental factor in planning and developing strategy is whether a company is selling different products into different markets with different sets of competitors. Different businesses organized to function independently are often called subsidiary companies, divisions, strategic business units (SBUs), or simply profit centers. It has been apparent for decades (General Electric decentralized in the 1950s) that a functionally organized firm often has difficulty managing to the expectations of customers and competing effectively in multiple marketplaces. A natural step in the development of an organizational structure for multiproduct businesses is to reorganize the business into a hierarchy of profit centers, each of which has responsibility for most or all of the activities related to a particular product, product line, and/or market.

International Idiosyncrasies

Conducting business in multiple countries presents another set of organizational issues. One choice that firms eventually face is whether to have a global or a multinational organization. A multinational organization treats the operations of each country as a separate profit center or SBU. A global organization is similar to one large operating company with a functional organization. In a global organization, the sales organization reports to a manager of worldwide sales, and profits are only realized at the level of the CEO. Naturally, various permutations of these approaches exist in practice.

Organizing to serve markets and customers around the globe is a formidable challenge in most industries, particularly when customer desires vary across cultures. The complexity of managing global supply chains, international marketing efforts, currency issues, differing national laws and regulations, cultural factors, and taxes, among other weighty geopolitical issues, all in a dynamic global marketplace with ever-increasing competition, leaves many organizations constantly reassessing themselves for effectiveness and responsiveness.

Organizational Developments

In the past, when products and markets changed relatively slowly over time, and work was quite repetitious, workers were trained to perform their tasks with little need for judgment or innovation. The structures tended to be hierarchical and centralized, with an emphasis on the consistent execution of well-defined and straightforward activities. With the development and growth of the service economy as well as modern computing capabilities, the nature of work performed changed in many sectors of the economy, and requiring workers to use their knowledge and experience to assist in making decisions.

Organizational structures have changed over time as well, with current and emerging organizational structures tending to be flatter with fewer layers of hierarchy and more decentralized decision making. These changes in structure have brought about added importance of information systems, as they—rather than middle managers—keep management apprised of the goings-on in the firm. Selection and development of managers have also taken on added significance. With fewer checks and balances formerly provided by multiple layers of managerial review, senior executives and hence owners must rely on fewer managers to run operations, identify and solve problems, and report results accurately and honestly. Information and reporting systems play a critical role in these tasks, as does the recruiting of key personnel.

Management Is the Key

Regardless of the organizational structure implemented, the general manager at any level of the organization must supervise the heads of the functional departments he or she oversees and manage and coordinate the activities that require cross-functional cooperation. There is a tendency for functional units to become isolated and parochial silos as they focus on internal, departmental activities, goals, and measures. General managers must encourage and devise means for collaboration among the functional heads. Furthermore, general managers must work to develop a culture in which functional managers do not lose sight of finding the solutions and approaches that most benefit the organization as a whole rather than those that promote their own functions at a cost. Elements of this alignment of systems and structure are addressed throughout the text.

The management of these cross-functional activities in complex, often one-time undertakings is commonly referred to as project management. Such projects include new product introductions, capacity expansions, and unique efforts, such as major motion picture productions and construction projects. Successful companies develop the capability to manage these cross-functional project teams effectively, as well as everyday cross-functional efforts.

The Size of the Business

The size of a business affects a number of its attributes, and thus impacts the environment in which the general manager operates. Among the most prominent influences of the size of the business on the organization is the *span of control*. The term span of control typically refers to the number of subordinates that a superior can manage effectively. The appropriate number of subordinates varies naturally depending on the capability of the manager, the nature of the work performed by the subordinates, and the capability of the subordinates. When an operation grows beyond a manager's effective span of control, he or she must delegate, which may create a new layer of management and a different structure. The ability to delegate is an important attribute of an effective general manager, and one with which many successful individuals struggle as they are promoted to higher and higher levels within an organization.

Sales or revenue is a frequently used indicator of organization size, as is the number of employees. These indicators normally align and are useful in conveying the size of a firm and the breadth of its operations. There are exceptions, however, which occur when considering either one of the measures in isolation gives a false impression of the extent of an organization.

Some companies have few employees but large sales, which could result from large capital investments, a high degree of automation, and/or extensive outsourcing of production and support services. On the other hand, a highly vertically integrated firm will have a very large number of employees compared to others with similar revenues in its industry that purchase inputs from outside suppliers.

All of these situations influence the organizational structure of a firm, with larger size generally corresponding to more complex organizational structures. Of course, each situation must be examined for its context, as companies with a large number of employees in straightforward one-product businesses may face management issues more often associated with small companies.

Along with size, the organization of a business is also a function of the economies or diseconomies of scale related to its operations. Scale economies may be defined simply as advantages that arise as an organization increases in size. Most often, economies of scale refer to decreases in the average cost of production (typically, cost per unit) that correspond to increases in production output. To compete effectively, most businesses must be large enough to deliver competitive unit costs, and for larger firms, scale economies can contribute to competitive cost advantages.

In certain businesses, though, having operations beyond a particular size creates management challenges with no offsetting advantages. In such situations, average production costs actually increase with increases in size, and diseconomies of scale are recognized to have set in. For many years, check printing (optimal-sized plants) and mattress manufacturing (constrained by economic shipping distances) were conducted in strategically located plants. When demand at a plant grew beyond the optimum size or delivery zone, another plant was opened that was located closer to a growing segment of the market in order to avoid the diseconomies of scale that would have ensued. Economies of scale are discussed in more detail in Chapter 13.

Small Businesses

Very small businesses of ten to twenty employees are usually run by a general manager who is frequently the owner, perhaps with the assistance of a supervisor or two. As a business grows, the employees may be divided into teams, often based on the functions they perform. Such teams tend to be the building blocks of even the largest organizations.

As businesses grow larger—up to approximately one hundred employees—they are often led by a small team of three managers. One of the managers assumes the role of the general manager and usually also manages one of the three primary functions: sales, operations, or administration/finance. The other two managers head the remaining two functions. This situation describes the traditional beginnings of a functional management structure.

There are advantages to being small. Small businesses are simpler to manage, and communication is less encumbered, more efficient, and by and large informal. As a result, decision making can be much more rapid. A concomitant problem, though, is the inability of many small businesses to afford the management talent they need. The organization usually cannot afford a cadre of functional experts, and consequently, smaller businesses require more versatile managers.

Larger One-Business Organizations

Larger businesses are normally organized into functional departments, which can be subdivided into line and staff functions. Line functions are those that are directly involved in creating and matching demand for the firm's products with their supply. Variation in these designations may occur from organization to organization, but commonly the line functions include marketing and sales, which creates the demand volume; operations or production, which makes and delivers the product or provides the service; and R&D or engineering, which designs and improves the products and production processes.

The staff functions are intended to support the activities of the line functions. The principal staff functions are administration, human resources, and information systems. Each of these line and staff functions can be further subdivided in very large organizations. For instance, administration might include subfunctions such as finance, accounting, and legal services. Frequently, though, the finance department on its own is recognized as one of the primary functions of the organization. Similarly, human resources might be subdivided into personnel administration, training, and employee relations.

One of the dangers of size is the tendency to create excess layers of management within the functional departments and the firm. A general manager might be removed from the frontline workers by as many as ten layers of middle and senior managers, which is not an ideal situation for efficient management. Effective communication with employees and customers is much more challenging in these situations, and managers should diligently assess the logic of their structures periodically to ensure their effectiveness.

Types of Multibusiness Organizations

Multibusiness organizations take a number of forms, and the role of the general manager is somewhat different in each form. Common multibusiness organizations include mutual funds, investment companies, and diversified, decentralized organizations. Each is briefly described below.

THE MUTUAL FUND A mutual fund is a managed investment fund whose shares are sold to a number of investors. A mutual fund pools the capital of numerous individuals and sometimes corporate investors (frequently pension funds and endowments). The investments of a mutual fund may span a broad range of corporate and financial offerings, including stocks, bonds, and currencies, among others. A mutual fund normally holds a small percentage of the equity of each of its investments, but invests in a large number of companies and vehicles.

The major activities of the mutual fund firm revolve around investment analysis, buying and selling shares of stock or other securities, administration and record keeping, and managing relationships with the executives of investment companies. When the mutual company is publicly owned, additional activities deal with advertising and selling shares, stockholder communications, and regulatory compliance.

Because the mutual fund is not involved in the management of the companies in which it invests, it tends to be organized and operated as a single business.

THE INVESTMENT COMPANY An investment company buys large positions in a limited number of companies. The most well-known, publicly traded investment company is probably Berkshire-Hathaway, headed by Warren Buffett. Investment companies may also be private organizations that, similar to mutual funds, pool the capital of a number of investors.

The responsibilities of the general manager of an investment company are similar to those of the general manager of a mutual fund, except that investment companies rarely trade the shares they hold. Further, they are very involved as a rule in the management of the companies in which they invest, generally serving on their boards and consulting with management, especially with regard to strategic issues. The investment company has a highly decentralized management structure, meaning that the companies in which it invests operate independently from the corporate office and one another. Companies in the portfolio of an investment company function much like private, stand-alone businesses.

THE DIVERSIFIED, DECENTRALIZED COMPANY Diversified, decentralized companies are often referred to as holding companies, and they characteristically own all of, or a controlling interest in, a number of operating companies or businesses. Diversified, decentralized companies may be diversified within an industry (for example, in forest and paper products or packaged consumer goods) or across industries (with holdings in such diverse industries as aircraft engines, elevators, helicopters, fire extinguishers, and heating and air conditioning systems).

Idiosyncrasies of Multibusiness Organizations

The general managers of the operating companies, who are often referred to as (subsidiary) company presidents or division vice presidents, most often report directly to the CEO or chief operating officer (COO) of the parent holding company. Occasionally, an organization will have an additional layer of management (often called group heads) between the division general managers and the parent COO or CEO. This added level in the organization occurs most frequently in very large and diverse organizations.

In holding companies that do not have an industry focus, the businesses in the portfolio tend to be stand-alone entities with little or no interaction with the other businesses of the holding company. In holding companies with an industry focus, businesses within the portfolio are much more likely to interact. For example, one business might be a customer of another business, or two businesses with competing or complementary products might sell to the same customer or purchase from the same supplier.

Vertical integration, which creates the situation where businesses sell to and buy from one another internally, requires careful coordination among the separate businesses. Transfer pricing and delivery (commitment to internal order dates), in particular, present challenges for even well-run organizations. In many industries, management at each stage of the vertical integration in decentralized companies is assisted by free market forces that establish rational prices and can be used to mitigate internal conflicts over transfer prices.

The role of the general manager of a holding company depends on the degree to which decision making is decentralized. In a highly decentralized structure, the operating companies are run as self-contained units, and the parent holding company (or corporate office) provides very few support activities. In this scenario, decision making in the operating company generally involves advice and consent from the holding company CEO with regard to the strategies, plans, and capital spending of the operating company. The holding company CEO also has an ongoing oversight responsibility and can intervene if agreed-upon goals are not met, usually by replacing the operating company general manager.

If the activities of the operating companies are intertwined, the holding company CEO is responsible for their coordination. Some diversified, decentralized corporate offices provide services to the operating companies, which usually include specialized, administrative activities that can be performed better and less expensively at the corporate level, as well as management of infrequent but repeated major projects. These services often include financing activities, risk management (insurance), legal counsel, and the management of benefit plans and pensions. They may also include coordinated purchasing, credit management, and oversight of the construction of new facilities. In the holding company model, long-term debt is commonly held and equity issued only at the corporate level.

The all-important operating activities—selling and producing—are customarily left in the operating companies. There may be an effort to standardize some operating activities, based on best practices and/or the need to coordinate similar activities or inputs across subsidiaries. The holding company CEO is responsible for determining the degrees of integration and centralization and then for organizing the holding company staff to manage the activities that are taken on at the holding company level.

Summary

In a specialized and well-established process of representative governing, the owners of a business customarily elect the members of the board of directors to represent their interests. The board of directors, in turn, recruits and hires a CEO or general manager for the corporation, to whom the board gives the responsibility for the day-to-day running of the business. In the context of the organization, then, the typical CEO of a corporation reports to the board of directors, whose members are obliged to represent the interests of the shareholders in governing the corporation.

For the most part, the CEO has the responsibility and authority to organize the operations of the firm so that it will succeed in the short term as well as the long term. Numerous classical approaches to organization exist and are linked to various attributes of the firm. Primary attributes influencing organization structure are the scope of the organization, particularly the number of businesses in which it operates; the nature of the work; the size of the business; and the firm's geographic reach.

The role of the CEO, the preeminent general manager in the corporate organization, is critical to corporate success. A future of rapid technological change in an increasingly competitive global economy will continue to bring many new challenges and broaden the tasks of the contemporary CEO or general manager. We explore in Chapter 3 many important elements of the general manager's role and their obvious ties to the performance of the firm.

DISCUSSION QUESTIONS

1. What are the duties of the members of the board of directors?
2. How should the performance of a CEO be evaluated?

3. What are the dynamics of the board-management relationship?
4. Should an individual simultaneously hold the positions of CEO and chairman of the board? Why or why not?
5. What are the variables that should be considered in determining the most effective organizational structure for a business?

3

THE ROLES AND TASKS OF
THE GENERAL MANAGER

The responsibilities of the general manager of a business encompass a wide variety of roles and tasks. In some way, nearly every major role of the general manager involves making decisions. These decisions, ranging from straightforward to complex, may address simply whether to perpetuate the status quo in some facet of the organization (often viewed as no decision at all), or they may encompass considering a broad range of variables and options in the context of the global economy. The outcomes of this wide variety of decisions faced by a general manager, collectively and sometimes individually, will undoubtedly have a major impact on the fortunes of the business.

Managerial decision making involves consideration of various types of information, including fact and theory as well as opinion, conjecture, and, often, intuition. Managers might prefer clear-cut problems, where data and analysis align to lead to obvious rational conclusions, but decisions at high levels within the modern corporation are more often ambiguous. Decision making is frequently complicated by incomplete and/or inaccurate information, conflicts of interest and opinions, and strong uncertainty about potentially influential factors, as well as the possible outcomes. Finally, and all too frequently, the decisions must be made with a great deal of urgency. Considering the high stakes and complex decisions, one can reasonably describe the general management task as momentous.

The Essential Roles of the General Manager

Given the expansive range of roles a general manager must play and the lengthy time period he or she must consider, one can develop an extensive list of job responsibilities. Naturally, executives may delegate certain tasks to others in the organization, while they must perform certain tasks themselves. The role of the chief executive officer (CEO) as liaison to and member of the board of directors is explored in Chapter 2. A number of additional key roles that most general managers fulfill are listed and described below.

Manager of Profitability

One of the primary defining dimensions of general management is profit and loss (P&L) responsibility—that is, the responsibility for the "bottom line" of an organization's income statement. This encompasses not only managing the current profitability of the business but also providing a foundation to ensure future profitability. More than any other role, P&L responsibility separates the general manager from functional managers. At the level where revenues and expenses come together to determine profit or loss, the general manager must oversee the management of diverse yet interrelated structures, systems, entities, and constituencies.

These elements may include functional areas, operating divisions, and geographic markets; numerous revenue streams and a wide variety of expenses; capital investments that are the result of decisions to allocate resources, and cash resources that should be invested; debt instruments and their accompanying covenants, as well as equity vehicles; and finally, the broad range of stakeholders of the organization. General managers must manage the interactions of all of these elements to produce a smoothly functioning whole with the aim of earning a return on investment that is at once greater than the firm's cost of capital, superior to that of peer organizations, and sustainable.

Each business forms a segment of a value chain linking suppliers, distributors, and customers in a complex marketplace of competitors and consumers, all influenced by the economic and social trends of the day. A business must comply with the requirements and restrictions of regulatory guidelines and laws, under government oversight and media scrutiny.

These conditions are dynamic and set the context in which the general manager must function.

In addition to the environmental and economic contexts of the organization, the general manager must also understand the economic model of the business—that is, the important variables and relationships that determine profitability in a given business. Central to the economic model are the dynamic price-volume-cost relationships found in any business. Price affects volume, depending on the elasticity of the market, classically with lower prices resulting in increased demand and volume, and vice versa. Volume in turn affects unit costs and total costs, with a larger volume of output typically leading to scale economies and their accompanying lower costs. Furthermore, in some businesses, such as retailing or construction, there are relatively high transaction costs.

A high transaction cost means that a transaction, or sale, brings with it high incremental or variable costs. In such cases, volume changes have a large impact on expenses, and profits are not as sensitive to changes in volume. On the other hand, when transaction costs are relatively low, for example with airlines, volume changes do not impact expenses as much. Because there are high fixed costs in the airline industry, pricing and volume changes have an important impact on profitability due to their strong effect on revenues. Thus, the general manager must understand the drivers of profitability in the business, paying particular attention to determining which of those drivers he or she is able to affect. In summary, the resulting economic model of the business must be in concert with effective product, marketing, and pricing strategies that give the firm a strong chance for success, even in a highly competitive marketplace.

The Leader

As commander in chief of the organization, the general manager has the role of leading its members, "the troops," to achieve the firm's objectives. Numerous theories of leadership abound in all fields in today's world, and as a result, many differing notions exist of what the role of leader should encompass. We briefly describe a few of the primary elements of this role in the context of business below.

Leadership within an organization begins with motivating the workforce and with establishing, improving, or maintaining a performance-oriented, supportive culture. In carrying out these tasks, the general manager often acts as cheerleader, praising good efforts and rallying employees to perform, improve, and persevere. Leadership also includes setting goals and standards of performance and integrity that are reasonable and clearly understood throughout the organization. A large part of the leadership process is building and ensuring positive, trusting relationships with and among all layers of the organization, and even beyond the organization's boundaries to include customers and suppliers. Of course, leadership encompasses leading by example on all substantial fronts.

Leadership also requires being informed. The general manager, to be effective, must know what is actually happening within the organization as well as in its environment. Formal control systems for reporting and monitoring results should be in place to report on the important indicators or measures of the company's critical success factors as well as contributing influences and causes. Additional conversations with employees at all levels of the organization and with customers, particularly those accounting for the largest portions of revenues, provide essential information for the general manager and simultaneously demonstrate commitment to important constituents.

Further, a general manager may learn quite a bit about the organization and its functioning just by walking around and observing. In fact, casual involvement, if regular, might spur enhanced effort on the part of the observed. A leader should also cultivate relationships with a variety of trusted associates, both inside and outside the organization, as an added avenue of gaining information and perspective. In summary, a leader must be aware of the state of affairs within the organization and in its environment. In particular, when things are not going well and goals and standards are not being met, the leader must know how to determine the causes and when and how to intervene.

Additional elements of leadership may be found woven throughout the roles and tasks of the general manager. A few in particular deserve mention directly, especially those related to delegation and assumption of responsibility. A leader must be capable of delegating in order to be effective. If a leader has been successful in filling key positions with capable and trustworthy individuals, he or she will have at least these subordinates on whom to rely. Even with a competent and accomplished team on hand, not all general managers excel at delegating. In fact, for many self-reliant individuals, delegation is difficult.

Related to delegation is the requirement that leaders provide clear direction for their organizations. Without clarity, general managers cannot expect their teams to work together to achieve precisely what is desired, and only with clarity of direction can general managers legitimately hold subordinates accountable. Holding employees accountable is a prime responsibility of leadership in the role of general manager. Establishing accountability and consequences within an organization is crucial to smooth operations, yet this task proves difficult for many who are new to leadership roles.

Finally, a true leader is one who recognizes that the responsibility for the performance of the organization is ultimately his or hers alone. As President Harry S. Truman said, "The buck stops here."

Manager of Talent

The general manager has the responsibility to find appropriate people to fill key positions in the organization and place them in the right jobs. As a manager of talent (one metaphor is that of a casting director), a general manager also must ensure that the wrong people are removed from their jobs and, often, from the organization, because having the wrong people employed typically translates into lost productivity not only on the part of these individuals but also on the part of their superiors and subordinates. After employees are settled into proper positions, the general manager must ensure that they receive the training necessary to fulfill the requirements of their jobs and to fit in well with the firm's culture.

The general manager must also manage the pipeline of talent within the organization, anticipating future needs as well as meeting those of the day. Occasionally in this role, the general manager must orchestrate a reduction in employment. General managers today are spending more and more of their limited time in the role of manager of talent. They track and confer with employees who have been labeled high potential, and they work diligently to ensure that these employees are trained, engaged, and delivering on the commitments of their jobs. The competitive market for managerial talent in today's business environment creates an imperative for general managers to protect their investments in the human resources of their capable employees.

Visionary

In the role of visionary, the general manager must envision the future of the organization. This requires critically examining the business, its current performance and resources, and its evolving environment, in order to determine the need for change, for it is only through change that an organization may arrive at a different state. An organization rarely experiences lengthy periods when all is progressing smoothly and no changes are anticipated externally.

Frequent reasons for change in an organization include:

- A revised vision of where the business should be headed
- A crisis that requires immediate and ongoing response
- A desired culture shift
- Response to shifting environmental and/or competitive factors that have the potential to affect results
- A philosophy of continuous improvement

Acting as a visionary for an organization requires constant surveillance of the environment, monitoring of major forces of change, and anticipation of their impact on the business. The CEO or general manager should create a culture for change within the organization and be directly involved with all significant changes. The general manager and the team of senior staff together must model any desired changes themselves—that is, they must change if they want the organization to change.

Some of the desired changes will be immediate ones, while most will affect the future of the organization. In an ongoing cycle, the current period's performance results are fairly well determined in most businesses because today's results largely have been shaped by yesterday's decisions. Thus, the actions taken today set the pattern for tomorrow's performance, and when general managers consider or desire changes in the activities and results of the organization, they obviously are pondering the future. This consideration of the organization's future may be done in segments, as shown in Exhibit 3-1.

The first, immediate time frame for review has management focused on defending and extending the existing business in order to deliver continually improving results. This time period might be as short as six months in

EXHIBIT 3-1   Multiple Horizons in Managerial Decision Making

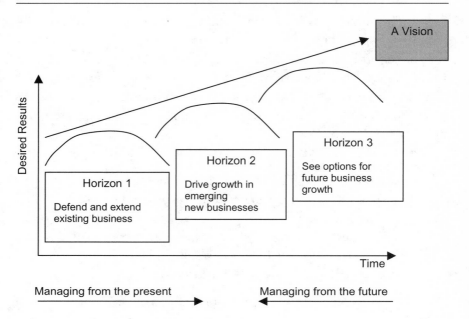

a field that is rapidly changing, but it generally lasts in the range of one to three years. Current momentum will carry certain organizations beyond the three-year horizon, but most businesses will need to be bringing new products and services to market within three years.

The subsequent, middle time horizon addresses an intermediate period, usually three to five years in length. In this phase, managers normally focus on identifying viable new businesses, or at least new products, processes, and services that will maintain an upward trend for the organization. Some of these new endeavors might already be in the organization's development pipeline. The second period, similar to the first, should be managed from the present, meaning that general managers and their teams should assess the current situations of their businesses and then determine what they should aim to change or maintain.

The final horizon in pondering the future deals with the longer term, perhaps as much as ten years into the future, or even more in some instances. The purpose of taking this long view is to assess the potential of the present momentum from the perspective of a clearly envisioned point in the future. Underlying this approach is the assumption that the momentum of the current business will carry the firm for a certain length of time before tapering off. The general manager should also consider the impact of initiatives that are already under way but have not yet come to full fruition. These initiatives might replenish the organization's momentum, but they too will have a limited life before their contributions wane.

New initiatives for the business almost certainly will be needed to meet the general manager's long-term financial goals. In transferring his or her perspective to the distant future, the general manager must reflect on the organization's stored potential, as well as the need for generation of future products and processes to carry the organization successfully into the future. Adopting a very long horizon forces a general manager to lay the groundwork for survival and success in the times ahead. Vignette 3-1 provides an example of the long-term effects of decisions within one major industry.

Every organization has a momentum that reflects its stage in its life cycle. This momentum has a direction and a force. The business is nearly always trending upward or downward, either slowly (gradually) or rapidly (precipitously), as illustrated in Exhibit 3-2.

Four broad strategic positions for the general manager regarding the momentum of a business are illustrated in Exhibit 3-2: growth, stability, retrenchment, and exit. The life cycle of a firm begins with the start-up phase and moves into a period of rapid growth if the business concept is valid. At some point, product life cycles, markets, and technology conspire to create maturity in the product concept. In considering the future of the organization, general managers are naturally influenced by the maturity of the industries in which they operate. As an organization approaches maturity, it is likely to find relative stability in its results and size.

VIGNETTE 3-1

When we consider the U.S. auto industry today, we realize that some of its managements' most serious problems have their roots in decisions made during the industry's successful times some twenty-five or thirty years ago. How might the industry's present be different if its managers at that time had thought more about the long-term results of their decisions?

EXHIBIT 3-2   The Strategic Continuum

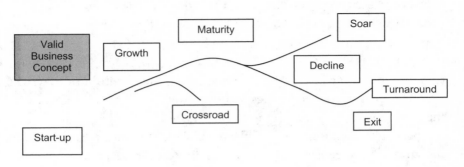

The challenge at this point is to reinvent the business—create a new or modified business concept that drives the company into a new era of growth. Many companies fail in this challenge and consequently enter into a decline. Unless a turnaround is engineered, the company will ultimately be forced to exit the scene through sale or liquidation.

The Architect of Organizational Purpose and Chief Planner

Planning may be divided into strategic planning (top level) and operations planning (lower level), and also into two distinct tasks: (1) setting goals and objectives for the organization, and (2) defining the strategies that will be employed to achieve those goals. The general manager personally should lead the firm's strategic planning efforts, beginning with an assessment of the organization's purpose, aspirations, and values, which are usually articulated in the mission, vision, and values statements of the organization. In some cases, an organization will not have these defining documents, but instead will rely on those of a parent organization. In many instances, organizations may not have taken the time and made the effort to put these significant ideas into words, or they may have statements that have not been used for years. The general manager should begin the strategic planning process by establishing or revisiting these critical, defining documents. The statements, which may need to be modified, should provide a directional platform for the organization, and the general manager should take a lead role in their development or refinement.

As a very brief overview, the starting point for strategy formulation is to gain clarity of purpose. Hospitals exist to treat patients, schools to educate, armies to defend, and businesses to satisfy customers. When leaders are unclear about the purpose of an organization, confusion proliferates.

Clarity about the purpose of the business begins with articulating the following attributes of the organization:

- Who are the core customers?
- What are their needs?
- Which of those needs does the firm intend to serve?
- What value does the firm intend to add in serving them?
- What skills and resources are required to meet those needs?

Other important questions include:

- What are the desires of leadership for the future of the organization?
- What are the values of the organization and its employees?

The purpose of a business is articulated in its mission statement. A company's mission statement is typically focused on its present business scope—"who we are and what we do." Mission statements broadly describe some combination of an organization's present capabilities, customer and/or business focus, and key activities. The vision, on the other hand, describes what the organization seeks to become or where it would like to go. The vision provides a lofty view of the future. Finally, the statement of values of an organization articulates the core values that all members of the organization should uphold and to which they should be held accountable.

The general manager typically calls upon a team of committed employees—often the executive team—to assist with the strategic planning process. If the team agrees that the defining statements of the mission, vision, and values are appropriate for the organization, they will affirm their commitment to the statements and use them as they move forward in the planning process. On the other hand, if the team determines the documents are no longer relevant for the organization, the general manager should launch a thorough and thoughtful process to revise them before proceeding.

In most years for most organizations, the mission, vision, and values remain unchanged from the previous planning period. Unfortunately, the status quo is often perpetuated as a result of a lack of attention rather than deliberate reaffirmation. When a general manager crafts or reaffirms the mission, vision, and values of the organization, he or she creates a foundation upon which to build a strategy and establish clarity of purpose within the organization. The contents of the documents may be used to establish standards to which a leader may hold subordinates accountable, and as such, become powerful tools for evaluating employees, projects, and strategies.

Primary steps in planning include setting appropriate financial and nonfinancial goals and objectives and then, with due consideration of likely future events, providing direction to the organization, and ultimately the board of directors, in terms of the businesses in which the firm will be engaged. The most common quantifiable corporate goals specify the general manager's expectations for profits, return on investment, cash flow, and growth. Stability (or predictability) of results is also desirable. As previously described, the stage of the industry life cycle in which the firm finds itself will have a strong impact on the results of the general manager's planning. Nonfinancial measures a general manager might monitor include indicators of critical success factors that affect or drive the financial performance, as well as measurements of progress on projects that address strategic issues or initiatives.

While the general manager oversees and coordinates operations planning, this work is done primarily by the functional managers, who are provided operational goals consistent with their function's role in achieving the company's goals. The functional managers then devise functional strategies for achieving their particular goals. Strategic management must be reinforced by a detailed operational planning and control system and an appropriate reward system that enhance the likelihood that the firm's operating units will effectively execute the strategies and achieve the desired results.

The approach to setting a direction for the organization is straightforward. Management must understand where the firm is currently positioned and determine where it wants the firm to go—that is, where it would like to see the firm positioned in the future. The general manager must then determine what needs to be done to realize that future. Exhibit 3-3 shows the flow of tasks that lead to strategies and are the means by which the desired future will be realized. The vision and the objectives describe the desired future, and the strategies describe how the firm will get there.

EXHIBIT 3-3   Tasks of Strategic Planning

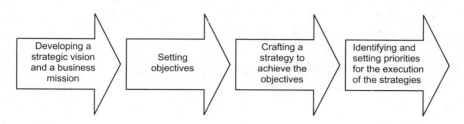

While this approach may be straightforward, the execution of strategic planning is not always clear-cut. As manager of this process, the general manager must coordinate numerous functions, activities, and even strategies to achieve the desired results.

Coordinator of Strategies

For the general manager, all decisions related to strategy should begin with a consideration of the customer. The acquisition of sales volume and revenue is a critical function, and the effort should begin with the selection of the market in which each business will compete and the identification of the customers the business desires to serve. General managers should then thoughtfully determine what those identified customers desire and ensure that the most effective products and/or services are offered to the chosen market segments. This process of pinpointing target customers and products/markets is discussed in more detail in Chapter 12.

A fundamental element of an organization's strategies is the pricing strategy. In most industries and for most companies, prices are set in the marketplace and not based on a consideration of the costs of the business. The combination of prices and the resulting volumes must produce revenues that exceed the total costs in order to produce a profit. This interaction of volume, costs, and revenues (termed the business model) must produce viable results in order for the organization to succeed. The planning process must continue until it arrives at a sustainable business model with which to move forward. The business model is discussed in more detail in Chapter 10.

Manager of the Functional Interfaces

Most businesses are organized into functional departments. The five basic functional departments and their general purposes are listed in Exhibit 3-4.

Two critical support functions are present within most businesses: administration and information systems. Administration, which generally comprises accounting and legal services, cannot be considered a money-making function, but ineptness in administration will bring major distress to a business. The information systems function has grown in importance in recent years and can be a distinctive competence that dramatically improves productivity and profitability in many businesses through the efficient and reliable collection and dissemination of information. This function can also constitute a major marketing tool.

Managing the interfaces between and among the functions is vital. The different functions should not be permitted to operate as separate, independent silos, but must be led to operate collaboratively across the organizational boundaries. Designing and managing these interfaces is another very important and distinctive responsibility of the general manager. For instance, new product development should be a responsibility of one of the functions, but both the marketing and the engineering departments

EXHIBIT 3-4   Function and Purpose of Departments

Function	Purpose
Marketing	Generates revenues for the organization by selling products and encouraging or stimulating purchases
Operations	Matches the supply of goods and services with the demand generated and promised by the marketing function
Engineering or Research & Development	Develops new and improves existing products, services, and production methods
Human Resources	Manages issues broadly related to recruiting, hiring, training, evaluating, and rewarding employees
Finance	Manages issues related to monetary resources and needs of the organization

play major roles in this critical task. The general manager should make such determinations in the best interest of likely success, and ensure that necessary collaboration is well managed by the functional managers involved. Moreover, the general manager should also ensure that appropriate systems or practices are in place to provide structure to this coordination. Cross-functional team meetings should occur regularly, in addition to the customary meetings of the executive team.

Monitoring the performance of the functional areas, both individually and collectively, and coordinating their ongoing activities should be undertakings of the top level of management led by the general manager. At the corporate or profit-center level, management must assess the relative performance of all of the functional departments, with special emphasis on the three basic departments: marketing, engineering or research and development (R&D), and operations or manufacturing. A business can likely be considered to be "under control" when the product, marketing, and pricing strategies of an organization are properly synchronized with its cost base. If trouble is known or suspected in an organization, analysis will be required to determine whether the essential functions are providing their respective contributions to success. Aspirations for each of the three departments include:

- Engineering will provide product leadership
- Marketing will provide sales leadership
- Operations/manufacturing will provide cost, quality, and delivery leadership

Excellence in operations processes, materials selection, quality control, and marketing expertise cannot offset the deleterious effects of a poorly designed product. Similarly, a well-engineered product that is manufactured effectively and at a competitive cost can be "given away" in the marketplace by an inept marketing function. Finally, superb engineering and marketing cannot offset poor quality or late delivery, both the responsibility of operations, where the majority of costs, assets, and people are employed. Thus, the general manager must consider the performance of each of the functional areas, particularly the basic functions, in the context of the organization's strategy. The general manager must also examine the consolidated results of the integrated whole.

Arbitrator and Counselor

A general manager acts as the head of the organization, and as a result, normally has the final voice in solving problems and disputes. Most conflicts will, or should, be resolved at lower levels of the organization, but occasionally some will rise to the attention of the general manager, especially those that have the potential to substantially impact the organization. Sometimes, though, they will encompass matters of less consequence that have been appealed to the highest court. In determining how to resolve specific conflicts or problems, the general manager as a rule will have to meet with the aggrieved or differing parties, and through such contact, will often be called upon to act as counselor as well as arbitrator. Effective leaders are seen as trustworthy and caring by their employees. Resolving conflicts and aiding employees provides a tremendous opportunity for the general manager to demonstrate that he or she cares about the employees involved and is deserving of their trust. Regardless of the level of confidentiality of the conflict, it is likely that word of the tenor of the talks will be reported to others within the organization. General managers should be aware that interactions in such circumstances might have greater consequences than those purely related to the issue at hand. This role requires skill in conflict resolution and counseling, fields that are more complicated than can be covered here.

Negotiator

One might expect that a general manager engaged in resolving conflict would benefit from a proficiency in negotiation. Such competence would certainly prove useful inside the organization, where the general manager might draw upon it to reach reasonable resolutions for opposing parties. Negotiation skills, though, can also have tremendous value in relationships that span the boundaries of the organization.

The business press frequently informs us of high-profile negotiations that take place between unions and managers regarding contracts for union members. Even more often, we hear reports of negotiations for the sale or purchase of a business. Similar situations occur regularly within organizations, but at lower levels and with less fanfare, such as negotiating deals with suppliers and customers regarding prices, quality, and delivery arrangements. Additionally, managers negotiate with one another within the organizational structure to set goals and establish budgets.

Typically, general managers will be involved in negotiations that will substantially impact their businesses. Having the capability to complete strategically important deals, therefore, is a valuable attribute for all general managers. At the highest level, some CEOs seem to have an inherent knack for completing deals, whereas others propose and posture, even get to the negotiating table, but for one reason or another just cannot close the deal. What enables some CEOs to complete dozens of deals over many years, while others are stymied? If a CEO has a need to emerge as the clear victor in all negotiations, he or she more than likely will be unwilling or unable to make the kinds of concessions necessary in the normal give-and-take of reaching a deal.

Advocate

As we examine external roles of the general manager, we recognize the role of advocate along with that of negotiator. The role of the CEO has evolved to encompass the major activities of serving as the company's public spokesperson, liaison to the investing community, representative at major industry events, public educator, influencer of domestic policy, and in some cases, player or diplomat in the global sociopolitical economy. These activities have grown to demand a hefty share of many CEOs' schedules, and the shift toward an external orientation has created a demand for the CEO to have additional skills. Chapter 24 explores this role in detail.

Vignette 3-2 describes the path of one general manager through the early years of his career. In the brief description provided, it is apparent that the general manager assumed many roles.

Complicating Factors

The general manager's job, as evidenced by the lengthy list of roles, is complex. We repeatedly emphasize this notion and present here a number of complicating variables that are based on material from the U.S. Marine Corps book, *Warfighting*,[1] which describes the nature of war. There are remarkable parallels between the nature of war and the nature

VIGNETTE 3-2

Carlyle Publications was a major publisher of a variety of daily and weekly trade publications for more than seventy-five years. It recently was acquired by a well-managed and highly successful broadcasting company, and as part of its plan to rejuvenate Carlyle, the new owner began to hire promising master of business administration (MBA) graduates and put them into positions with line-operating responsibility. One of these new hires, Robert Lake, specifically asked to be assigned to the weakest of Carlyle's many properties. He assumed that in this placement he would be able to make the greatest impact and achieve the most recognition. Lake was naturally aggressive, focused, unusually energetic, and talented.

Lake was granted his request and was assigned to a paper where he and the paper's publisher, Phil Bush, worked closely together for some months as Lake absorbed the dynamics of the business. Lake began to spend most of his time in the field getting to know the manufacturers who were collectively the advertising base of the paper. He first met the few who were active advertisers, but then became determined to meet all the players in the industry. He soon found that the vast majority of these prospects had an extremely negative opinion of both Phil Bush and the paper. Despite developing a real fondness for Lake, they would not consider any advertising expenditures except perhaps immediately before and/or during the four trade shows their industry held each year. The primary objection of these nonadvertising manufacturers was that the paper ignored the segments of the market they served, and as a result, it had little value for them. They felt that the paper's editorial focus was aimed only at a few high-end urban retailers, which was a customer and sales category that few of the manufacturers considered important. Middle America was their market, and their manufacturing approach was to make long production runs in search of the lowest cost.

The industry the paper served was located mostly in the southeastern and southwestern regions of the United States, but the trade paper had only one part-time journalist residing in this area. The journalist was a solid, competent business reporter who was well respected throughout the industry. The stories he filed with the paper's editor, though, were seldom published, without explanation. The mind-set at the paper, personified by Phil Bush, was that there was little noteworthy outside the large northeastern city where Carlyle was headquartered.

For almost two years, Robert Lake repeatedly advised Bush about why the nonadvertising manufacturers thought so poorly of the paper, but Bush seemed content with the status quo and made no meaningful changes. Finally, in disgust, Lake went to Carlyle's general manager (GM) to whom Bush reported directly. Lake described the situation and his personal frustration. He insisted that there was an available market that could provide exceptional returns if Bush would just position the paper properly and focus on its advertising base and its natural readership—retailers throughout the country. Lake told the GM that he wanted Bush's job, immediately, and that he would breathe new life into the paper, just as the new owner wanted.

The general manager pointedly rejected Lake's request and admonished him on the spot for making such demands. Lake promptly resigned, realizing that his effort to restore the paper's prestige would only be seen as a power play against Bush.

Lake decided that he would execute the opportunity himself and promptly went into action. He raised $75,000 among three friends, one of whom lived in the southeast and became the chair of Lake's board of directors. The southeastern-based reporter immediately responded to Lake's invitation and came on board, along with one salesperson and a secretary. Lake then bartered commercial space in one of the trade show market buildings for advertising space when he began publishing. His most important vendor relationship, however, was made with a contract printer whose high-speed offset presses could produce high-quality color documents that contrasted starkly with the newsprint and poor reproductions that his former publisher used. Lake's strategy was to bring a fashion dimension to his new paper through the use of color, and in the process, he would collect much greater ad revenues driven by the color premiums he believed the manufacturers would pay. The use of color would also make his editorial product distinctive and set it apart from any of the competition.

The manufacturing sector was the source of Lake's ad revenue, and the retail sector was his natural readership base. His editorial product, covering a broad array of retailers, would become the link between the two. His most challenging objective was to demonstrate the value of trade (business, as opposed to retail) advertising, and in the process, organically grow the entire market.

Because of his cultivation of associations with industry leaders throughout his travels, Lake possessed an enormous amount of industry data, including an assessment of the strengths and weaknesses of individual companies. He also was aware of the scarcity of communications across industry segments except during the trade show markets. Lake was convinced that he could shift the industry out of its historical emphasis on production and into a new era focused on marketing, following emerging fashions and changing styles and using his paper as the primary communication vehicle.

As his property grew rapidly over the years, Lake increased the frequency and size of his publications and relentlessly added high-performance salespeople and well-qualified business journalists. He ruthlessly held both groups to his own high standards of behavior and performance, and modeled and developed a culture of high performance. Lake's former publisher, Bush, did not take Lake seriously as a competitor for several years, and eventually was terminated by the parent's senior management.

(*continued*)

VIGNETTE 3-2 (*continued*)

After the tenth year in business, Lake had succeeded in organically growing the market by a factor of four, 80 percent of which he captured. Late in the twelfth year of the new paper, Lake and his investors sold the paper to an international business publisher for $40 million, with an additional $10 million earn-out designed to be distributed among Lake's 105 employees. The deeply embedded culture of high performance established by Lake remained, and the earn-out was accomplished.

of business. Complicating factors with which the general manager must deal include:

- *Friction:* Uncontrollable events go awry and make decisions and actions difficult. Examples include natural disasters and other unpredictable events, physical constraints, competitors' actions, operating problems, and difficult personalities.
- *Uncertainty:* The fact that there are unknowns about the future.
- *Disorder:* Disorder is a reality of the marketplace that is particularly evident when practice is compared to the implied neatness of various theories and principles.
- *Fluidity of Situations:* Each episode in a business is the temporary result of a unique combination of circumstances and requires, to some degree, an original solution. No episode, though, can be viewed in isolation—each merges with those coming before and after in a continuously evolving pattern of activity with abundant fleeting opportunities and unforeseen events.

Action: The Importance of Execution

Strategy and planning come to life in effective action. Carefully crafted strategic initiatives and plans are of little value until they are executed successfully, and successful general managers realize that effective execution requires the right people to do the right things consistently.

A strong multiyear history of solid performance consists of sequential individual years of successful results, and a successful year usually comprises strong quarterly performance. Similarly, failures develop gradually in most firms, rather than in one catastrophic moment. Discipline and dedication are required to ensure successful strategy implementation and sound performance. An organization's general manager, as well as the leadership team, must model these traits of discipline and dedication and, in doing so, establish standards for the employees and set the true tone for the culture. Further discussion of the deliberate and sustained effort that is required to ensure the best odds for an organization's success is presented in Part IV.

Summary

The general manager's role encompasses the responsibility for the organization achieving its purpose, for its profitability and financial performance, and for the effectiveness of all of its functions, both currently and in preparing for the future. The general manager does not have the luxury of choosing a functional focus, but instead must take interest in and responsibility for all parts of the business as well as the integrated whole.

A primary duty of the general manager is to get the best people possible for the key positions in the firm. General managers must surround themselves with cadres of executives who have complementary talents and personalities because no individual is capable of running an organization of substantial size independently. Working with this team, the general manager must confirm the purpose of the organization, develop its goals, and devise the strategies for achieving those goals. At the top level of a firm, the major goals and strategies are presented to the board for their advice and consent. After the board has given its approval to the goals and key strategies, a CEO must find ways to execute the strategies and present timely and accurate reports of the progress and results to the board.

Details of many of the activities described in this chapter are presented in later parts of the text. Part II begins this development with a discussion of planning as part of the general management process.

DISCUSSION QUESTIONS

1. What are the essential roles of a general manager?
2. Are certain roles more important than others? If so, which ones are most important? If not, why not?
3. How does the analogy of "architect" fit the general manager?
4. What factors complicate the tasks of the general manager?
5. How can an aspirant general manager best prepare for the responsibilities of the position?

II

THE GENERAL MANAGEMENT
PROCESS: PLANNING

At any point in time, every business organization is at a given position in its long-term journey. It has a degree of momentum from that point in some direction. The question is whether the momentum is moving the business in the direction desired by those who are responsible. It is reasonable to ask first whether management knows the preferred destination, or even where the business can feasibly hope to move. And, if the destination is known, does management know what actions should be taken to maximize the likelihood of getting there? The answers to these questions are the essence of strategic planning.

We want to stress that this is not a book about strategy, but one about general management. We acknowledge the critical role that strategy and its formulation play in general management, and we highlight process fundamentals in Part II. There are numerous books on strategy formulation and strategic planning, but we strive here to relate the processes in the next few chapters to their roles within the sphere of general management.

Some may interpret this discussion as implying that formal strategic planning is the only path to success. We all should know that this is not the case. There are many accounts of success based on luck or intuitive genius. There is no substitute for entrepreneurial thinking in the creation and execution of strategy. Sometimes, success is being in the right place at the right time, but even such good fortune must be recognized and exploited. There almost always needs to be a degree of intentionality, which, at a minimum, increases the chances of success and the attainment of superior performance.

Entrepreneurs create and execute strategies in a variety of styles. At one end of the continuum is the strength of the entrepreneur's personality and his or her intuitive judgment—he or she is the driving force. In the middle is an effort to create strategy in response to a given situation (problem or opportunity). At the other end of the continuum is a systematic management process that is imbedded in the way the business operates.

When is an entrepreneur-driven planning style sufficient, and when is a more systematic approach necessary? As long as the business possesses a sustainable competitive advantage—say, a patent or an unassailable cost advantage—the entrepreneur's drive and intuition may be sufficient. A systematic approach to strategic planning is more essential in larger, more complex, and more competitive businesses.

Creating and executing strategy should be viewed as a process. General managers often think there is a need to have a strategic plan, and they will have a retreat—an event—to generate one. They may produce a data-laden document and/or articulate some goals. Such an event and the resulting document seldom have any lasting impact on the future of the organization.

The process is paradoxical in that it requires both the intense, hands-on involvement necessary to get a "feel" for the situation and the detachment that provides an objective perspective. Detachment means removing ourselves emotionally from the situation—literally, standing back as if we are not involved and assessing what is going on. What would a newly arrived person with a fresh perspective do differently from current plans? It is very difficult for anyone to rationally evaluate his or her own plans or actions.

Chapters 4 through 9 describe the step-by-step development of a process for strategic planning:

- Chapter 4 describes the pressures that drive managers to need a systematic approach to strategic planning.
- Chapter 5 discusses the forces necessary to drive sustained superior performance.
- Chapter 6 introduces the essential element of competitive analysis and its role in the development of a viable strategy.

- Chapter 7 treats the role of strategic planning in the development of a firm's purpose, direction, and goals.
- Chapter 8 presents the level of detail required to produce a three-year business plan, with special attention to the scale of intended operations and the resources that will be required—people, skills, facilities, capacity, and capital.
- Chapter 9 describes the culmination of the strategic planning effort—the development of the annual plan or budget. All efforts in the organization will be focused on bringing about the results anticipated in the budget.

Part II thus describes in detail the steps required to produce a "plan of action" for a business. The degree of relevance and elegance with which the plan is developed will likely determine the business's future success.

4

THE EFFICACY OF STRATEGIC MANAGEMENT

Today's competitive business environment demands the evaluation of results. In the economic context of a free market built on the precepts of capitalism and competition, managers are constantly under pressure to perform and to explain their performance. This attribute of a competitive marketplace is logical; if investors are to make informed decisions about buying and selling shares of corporations, they should have access to all available accurate, current information. Performance has numerous dimensions.

Some managers have a disdain for strategy and strategic planning, assuming these methods are too theoretical for practical use. Every successful company, however, benefits from an effective strategy. The strategy might have been developed through formal analysis, trial and error, intuition, or just luck. Regardless of its origin, a strategy was indeed executed, whether managers were aware of it or not.

Most large and many small firms rely on a deliberately chosen strategy to direct their activities toward achieving desired results. After implementation of a strategy, competitors react, and the firm's strategy requires revision to respond to the new competitive environment and to meet new challenges. There is no stopping point, but instead a perpetual competitive cycle.

Businesses may take steps to prepare to enter the strategic management process, either initially or anew. This chapter addresses a number of considerations and steps in this procedure, beginning with a variety of evaluators of a firm's performance, whose measurements should be considered in devising performance goals. We move on to discuss some initial steps in the strategic management process, and finally, a checklist is presented to assist managers in gauging the readiness of an organization to commence the strategic management process.

Evaluators of Corporate Performance

Chief executive officers (CEOs) or general managers of public or private companies are under continuous, relentless pressure from their various constituencies to outperform their competitors and provide a sound return on investment. In particular, stockholders evaluate the performance of a company in terms of the profits earned, the dividends paid, the performance of the market price of the company's stock, and the public image of the company and its management. Performance counts.

Customers regularly appraise a business's performance in terms of the value it delivers, the quality and reliability of its products, and the ability of the organization to meet delivery dates. Vendors demand timely payment of obligations. Government agencies maintain surveillance over such operational factors as market share and pricing policies, antitrust regulations, pollution control, equal employment opportunities, and many other important attributes of the business.

Bankers evaluate companies in terms of their ability to make debt repayments, various financial ratios, cash position, and general overall financial strength. The bankers' assessment of the risk inherent in a firm's operations directly affects the firm's access to debt and the interest rate the firm must pay for borrowed funds.

Perhaps most importantly, the board of directors has performance expectations as well. In addition to analyzing financial performance and trends, the board monitors, among other things, the quality of strategic decisions, whether strategic goals are being achieved, and how well change is being managed. They may also look at how well the leadership role is being fulfilled. Members of the board have a fiduciary duty to monitor the performance of management and the organization on behalf of the shareholders whose interests they represent. Their duty extends beyond results to the activities, initiatives, and systems employed to produce the results of the current period and the investments and approaches made to generate the results of the future.

The Professional Evaluators

Financial institutions, which have a significant influence over the market for corporate stocks, employ analysts to guide their investments. The market price of a company's stock and the accompanying PE (share price to earnings) ratio are important indicators of the investment world's assessment and expectation of performance, and a major determinant of the firm's ability to raise capital by issuing public securities. Financial analysts thus exert considerable leverage over the availability of equity funding for a firm. What, then, are the principal attributes of performance that these professional evaluators prefer? Consider the most obvious measurable results (or expectations): profits; return on investment; cash flow; growth; and, finally, predictability of results.

Professional investors and analysts assess the adequacy of the operating results of a business through a complex evaluation of the interrelationships of these attributes. The preferences among the performance criteria have changed over time, with five- to ten-year periods in which growth, or return on investment, or then stability were preferred. The measures of financial results have gradually become more sophisticated, with transitions having occurred from "earnings" to "earnings per share" to "return on equity" to "free cash flow."

The first level of assessment considers the earnings, earnings growth, and return on investment sustained over time, together with their volatility, compared with other firms in the same industry and with general stock market performance. It is possible for a business to report consistently high levels of profitability, yet not be able to provide internally for its cash needs, especially in fast-growth situations. On the other hand, inherently cyclical businesses with large asset bases and correspondingly large cash flows from depreciation may have highly volatile earnings while cash flows remain impressive. Financial analysts and bankers therefore look beyond the levels of profitability reported, to the cash the business would need to sustain its operations over the long term. Along with these favorable performance attributes, financial analysts ultimately prefer "predictability of results."

Forecasts, Not History

Financial analysts guide investors in their choices of firms and in the timing of their investments. A need to forecast future profits is inherent in the process of capital formation in a competitive, free market system because investment decisions are based on the anticipation of future profits, not on past performance. Companies that do not have consistent earnings patterns fare better with private ownership because public companies are under continuous pressure to produce consistently favorable earnings and earnings growth, regardless of even expansive cash flows.

Analysts must depend on the CEO or general manager to explain the firm's strategies and for assistance in the process of attempting to forecast the level and volatility of the company's future profit performance. Corporate officers of public companies regularly provide public projections of anticipated future profits and possible strategic or operational problems that may emanate from a variety of international, economic, and demographic factors. These public pronouncements build a degree of credibility (either good or bad) for the CEO or general manager and the company with the investment community. The level of esteem in which the manager and his or her company is held is a major determinant of the company's stock price, its borrowing rates, and even its borrowing capacity from lending institutions. Vignette 4-1 describes the feelings of a CEO of

VIGNETTE 4-1

The CEO of a Fortune 100 company was asked about his attitude regarding the tendency of professional financial analysts to focus on the reported quarterly financial results of his company. He stated that he felt the short-term focus on performance provided a valuable discipline for his organization. He said he found that if he consistently met his quarterly earnings targets, the financial analysts would listen to his strategy. He also said that if he failed to meet his targets, the analysts would not even be interested in his strategy.

In response to the same question regarding the focus on quarterly results of public companies, a very senior, lifelong executive of a major financial institution explained that the focus simply resulted from the availability of the data. His thought was that since the data were available, the financial analysts would be derelict if the information was not taken into account.

a Fortune 100 company and a senior executive of a large financial institution about the focus of the professional investment community on the quarterly results of public companies.

It is reasonable that financial analysts should prefer a stable and improving earnings pattern, which suggests a high degree of market acumen and management control. Within any industry, some companies consistently react to all of the exigent factors influencing their competitive markets and sustain higher earnings than their competitors, with essentially similar facilities, labor arrangements (union or nonunion), and raw material costs.

Subjective Evaluations

Beyond the figures, the analysts and bankers form opinions regarding their level of confidence in a firm's board of directors and its CEO or general manager, its business concept and strategies, the growth potential available in its market segments, its degree of product line focus or diversification, and additional subjective attributes that cannot be quantified, such as the culture of the organization.

These realities of the spectrum of business performance evaluators and their relentless expectations add immeasurably to the complexity of the general manager's job. While few businesses achieve long-term superior performance, the general manager should view sustained superior performance as an ultimate goal. The goals set by the leaders of organizations can have a powerful effect on the achievements of their employees, and as a result should be appropriately high and communicated effectively.

The Need for Strategic Choices

Effective strategic planning greatly enhances the likelihood of outstanding corporate performance. Placing a great deal of emphasis on strategy, though, will neither guarantee success nor lead unerringly to the desired results for a general manager. Unexpected catastrophes as well as serendipitous windfalls have befallen well-managed and poorly managed firms alike. The weight of logic, however, supports the notion that an effective strategic management process would more than likely enhance a firm's ability to achieve favorable results.

Many companies have persevered in their efforts to implement a comprehensive strategic management system, in spite of organizational resistance to change and doubters of its effectiveness. In subsequent chapters of this book, we address numerous details of providing the strategic direction and management control required for successful ongoing operations. We summarize here some important choices that many general managers face in the strategic management process.

Industry Attractiveness

A wide range exists in the inherent attractiveness of different industries. Numerous factors contribute to the attractiveness of an industry or major industry segment, and the relative importance of each is subject to the individual preferences of the managers who compete in the industry. One important dimension, especially when considering results, is profitability. Profitability varies widely among industries, both in the short term and the long term, indicating that certain industries produce (on average) higher levels of profitability than others. A quick review of the industries of the Fortune 500 reveals that 2005 returns on revenues ranged from 28.9 percent for mining and crude oil production to negative 10.6 percent for airlines. Similarly, 2005 returns on shareholders' equity ranged from 41.5 percent for household and personal products to 4.2 percent for telecommunications (airlines were not listed).[1] As demonstrated, companies competing in certain industries actually lose money. In every industry, though, regardless of the median or average rate of profitability, some companies are a great deal more profitable than others.

Factors other than profitability contribute to an industry's attractiveness. Exhibit 4-1 presents a number of attributes commonly used to assess the attractiveness of an industry. It is well known that certain companies with strong management are able to achieve superior returns, even in difficult industries. It is much more difficult, though, to achieve sustained superior performance, particularly outstanding results compared to the broad market, when competing in an unattractive industry.

Sustained success is derived from the combination of effective strategies and excellent execution. As shown in the two-way table in Exhibit 4-2, successful organizations *do the right things* (have an effective strategy) and also *do things right* (achieve operational excellence). Even when organizations

EXHIBIT 4-1   Common Attributes of Industry Attractiveness

• Size (units and dollars)	• Capacity utilization
• Growth rates	• Technology requirements, life cycles, threats
• Cyclicality and seasonality	
• Number and types of competitors	• Regulation and taxation
• Competitive structure	• Labor availability and unionization
• Profitability and margins	• Energy and inflation impact
• Raw material supply	• Social and demographic trends
• Barriers to entry and exit	

have well-run operations, if they *do the wrong things*, success is unlikely. If the organization is very capable at making something for which there is no demand, the operational excellence counts for naught. The absence of both an effective strategy and operational excellence produces certain failure in virtually every instance. A strong strategy supported by elements outside operations—for instance, cost leadership based on a cost-effective location or differentiation based on sole access to a branded component or a desirable patent—can sustain weak execution until competitors catch up. It is very unlikely, however, for any degree of strong execution to lead to sustained success given an ineffective strategy, which would entail doing the wrong things well.

Innovation Is Essential

Numerous examples make the point that effective new strategies can undermine established strategic positions. Southwest Airlines, CNN

EXHIBIT 4-2   Strategy, Operations, and Organizational Success

		Strategy	
		Effective	*Ineffective*
Operations	*Excellent*	Sustained success	Success unlikely
	Poor	Possible short-term success	Certain failure

(Cable News Network), and Nucor Steel are well-known and touted examples demonstrating the effectiveness of new strategies. Each of these companies created strategies that recast the competitive rules of their industries and permitted them to establish sustainable leadership positions. These very successful companies not only innovated with processes and products but also created new business concepts and led with innovative strategies.

A business concept is the underlying logic—a strategy—for serving a market. A new business concept makes the old business concepts obsolete by introducing more effective, faster, or less-expensive ways to meet customer needs. The business strategy that takes shape with the implementation of a new business concept consists of doing different things, not doing the previous things better. It may result in advantages for the initiator that result from differentiation from competitors in perceived value, or from lower costs and price, or both. Details of some well-known new business concepts are described in Vignette 4-2.

Effective strategies, however, do not last forever. Circumstances change,

---

VIGNETTE 4-2

When airlines were deregulated in the 1970s, the major airlines developed the business concept of the hub-and-spoke (a system of routing air traffic in which a major airport serves as a central point for coordinating flights to and from other airports). This was very successful for most of them, but Southwest Airlines instead introduced a low-cost, point-to-point concept for its routes. Southwest chose not to compete directly with the major airlines, but to attack them where they were weakest. During the late 1990s and into the early 2000s, when other airlines were losing money, Southwest remained profitable.

The story of innovative business concepts goes on and on, in industry after industry. CNN created specialized news channels—a business concept very different from that of the traditional networks. Nucor Steel used the mini-mill concept (steel-mill technology that achieved cost advantages by melting scrap steel rather than refining iron ore) to gain substantial market share at the expense of "big steel." Dell rewrote the competitive rules within the computer industry by selling built-to-order computers direct to customers.

Innovation has been and continues to be limited only by the creativity of entrepreneurs.

and strategies lose their effectiveness. If the fifteen years prior to 2000 are divided into three five-year periods, we find that twenty-four companies were ousted from the S&P (Standard & Poor's) list of the one hundred largest companies in terms of market capitalization in the first period, twenty-six were replaced in the second period, and forty-one in the third period. Clearly, effective strategies (and their related business models) come and go, and only the most persistent continue on with superior performance.

All of this is not to say that operational execution is unimportant. Even the most ideal strategy for a firm's situation has no value unless implemented properly.

Beginning to Think Strategically

Exhibit 4-3 shows significant issues the general manager needs to understand and associated commitments implied in the launching of a strategic management effort. The first step in this process is for the general manager to determine whether the collective management of the company is ready for the effort.

In deciding to move forward with the strategic management process, the general manager should:

- Understand the current status of the company
- Define clearly the urgent need for positive change
- Identify outstanding issues that require immediate attention
- Determine the readiness of the organization to proceed
- Determine how the effort should unfold

Vignette 4-3 describes the reaction of the new CEO of a major corporation to a question about his strategic vision for the company.

A realistic assessment of the current situation is thus the first step in the strategic planning process for any business organization. It is a prerequisite to understanding whether a business needs to and is ready to implement a strategic management process. Many organizations are not ready for a variety of reasons, including the immediate need to address pressing issues within the business. A general manager must be open to this possibility or face the prospect of failure.

EXHIBIT 4-3   The Commitment to Strategic Planning

What General Managers Should Understand	Associated Commitments
• What they don't know	• To learn
• What strategic management entails	• To change the way they think about and manage their businesses
• Why they are doing strategic planning	• To agree that it is necessary to achieve their goals
• What the potential benefits of strategic planning are	• To agree that the potential benefits are real and worth the effort
• What the potential problems of strategic planning encompass	• To solve them
• How to engage in critical thinking and decision making	• To learn to think analytically and make decisions rationally, both individually and as a team
• How to engage in creative thinking and innovation	• To learn to be innovative and entrepreneurial
• Concepts of strategy	• To learn what they encompass and how to apply them to their situation
• A management model for their organization	• To agree on the way they will manage the business
• The process for creating strategies	• To design a process to implement strategic management in their organizations
• The importance of execution	• To learn how to execute the strategies effectively

VIGNETTE 4-3

When Louis T. Gerstner took over the management of IBM in April 1993, he rapidly assessed the existing situation. In late July, he announced at a press conference, "There has been a lot of speculation as to when I'm going to deliver a vision for IBM, and what I'd like to say to all of you is that the last thing IBM needs right now is a vision."[2] He had concluded from his assessment of the situation that IBM had experienced rapidly declining revenues, a plummeting share price, and a looming cash crisis, and that a rapid turnaround had to be engineered before he could think about the long-term future.

Calls for Action

Many managers run reasonably successful or very strong businesses without giving much, if any, thought to strategic management. This fortunate circumstance could result from a number of situations, including any one or a combination of the following:

- The ability of the general manager and management team to make intuitively effective strategic decisions
- A strong industry in which the firm is a very good operator, and therefore has had little perceived need for an emphasis on strategy
- A competitive advantage, which may or may not remain sustainable

Even in such fortuitous circumstances, the general manager may be led to become interested in the long-term strategy of the business by some event or situation that may indicate a need for action:

- For successful companies with strong current operating results, the perception of a need for action may emanate from a gnawing discomfort that key attributes of the business have begun to deteriorate
- Introspection might be precipitated by an aspiration to elevate the performance of the company to a new, higher level
- The general manager may be searching for a way to reenergize the growth and/or the profitability of the company
- For a small company with growth aspirations, it may mean trying to determine the best means by which to grow
- For a company that is experiencing operational problems, it might be a perceived need to search for effective solutions
- It could be the intellectual curiosity of the general manager as he or she searches for better ways to manage the business

An organization suffering trauma or serious decline may react to its current situation by beginning a strategic planning process:

- Management may be under pressure to improve the results or face the prospect of replacement
- Management incentive compensation may be "underwater" (of no value), and purchased shares may have lost significant value, with the outlook for a turnaround bleak

- Unexpected threats to the business or disruptive technology might have caught management off guard

The basics of strategic planning may be an appealing starting point for seeking remedies to such situations.

A principal strategic role of the general manager is to define the need for change. This duty obviously relates to understanding the need, but it also includes determining the degree and pace of change required. Will incremental, evolutionary change suffice, or must the organization undertake transformational change with a challenging deadline, as with a disruptive technology? When an organization is in crisis, the situation demands strong and decisive leadership and aggressive action. On the other hand, if the organization is currently performing well, there is often time for change to occur in a gradual, evolutionary mode.

How Does the General Manager Describe the Situation?

The CEO and the board must have a mutual understanding of the state of the business before progressing through the strategic management process. Numerous attributes of the organization's situation should be addressed. Their relative importance will naturally vary from organization to organization. An assessment of the business situation should include the following essential attributes:

The Number of Businesses

As noted previously, it is important to determine whether there is more than one business within the organization since competitive strategies are formulated at the business level. If there are a number of businesses, the general manager should define the relationships between them. If a holding company structure exists, the general manager should determine and describe the functions it performs. If the organization includes more than one business where some are clearly the major businesses and the others are not strategic material, the board and the CEO should concentrate at this stage on those that are important. The less-important businesses would command attention only if they presented a significant opportunity or problem.

Organization Structure, Leadership, and Management

An organization chart will provide a brief overview of the reporting structure and identify key managers. An assessment of the situation should consider leadership and management capabilities within successive organizational levels, addressing such questions as:

- Does the leadership think strategically, or is it primarily operationally oriented?
- What is the attitude of leadership toward the business's strategy?
- Is the talent of leadership and management good enough in quality and quantity to meet the challenges of running the business?
- How much change are members of leadership and management willing and ready to manage?
- Does management function as an effective team, or are there serious tensions between certain individuals?

Size and Complexity

The size and complexity of a business is a major determinant as to whether management should begin a formal strategic management process, and if so, at what level of effort. The larger and more complex a business, the more likely that strategic management will have benefits commensurate with the effort required.

The Goals of the Owners or Key Managers

The objectives of the owners and key managers are an overriding consideration, and provide the context within which the performance of the business will be judged. It is important to ascertain what these objectives entail and whether they present serious limitations to or encompass conflicting opinions about acceptable strategic choices.

Business Definition

Each business should be described in terms of its key markets and customers served, their needs and desires, and the perceived value provided to them by the organization's products. The general manager should understand any unique, sustainable competitive advantages of the organization. The needs and desires of the customers assist in identifying the skills that are required to meet and fulfill them (often referred to as the critical skills of the business), which become important considerations in the business concept, the competitive strategy, and the functional strategies.

The Life Cycle Stage and Health of the Business

The board and CEO should assess the general status of each business, both in terms of the stage of its industry life cycle and major products, and of its overall health and stability. Some questions they might seek to answer for each business include:

- Is the business in a start-up stage, a growth stage, or a mature stage of the life cycle?
- What is the market potential, both currently and expected over time?
- Has the business enjoyed a pattern of success? If so, is success expected to continue?
- Has the business experienced hard times, and does it therefore require a turnaround?
- If needed, is a turnaround practical? If not, can the troublesome business be sold on favorable terms?
- Is there any kind of crisis or serious problem in the business? If so, what is the associated level of urgency?

Financial Picture

The board should know the level of profitability of each business, its cash flow history and projections, and the associated levels of and trends in other key financial measures. This assessment should address the adequacy of the capital structure and whether it presents problems or opportunities.

Marketing Strategy

The board and management should understand the attributes of the marketplace and how each business sells its products. Useful questions in this line of inquiry include:

- Are the markets growing, mature, or declining? What are the expected rates of change?
- Is the firm a leader, a laggard, or somewhere in between? The details should include facts about the firm's competitors and its positioning in the market.
- How are orders won in the marketplace? Which of the customers' needs and desires drive most sales decisions?
- Does the firm have a competitive advantage? If so, what does it entail? If not, does the business suffer from a competitive disadvantage? How might it be described and quantified?

Operations

The operations of the business are critical to delivering its products and their perceived value to the customer. Management and board members may use the following questions to understand the key characteristics of operations:

- How satisfied are customers with the business's products and delivery?
- Is the firm efficient in its combination of cost and quality? Are major products considered a good value?
- How many different outlets or production locations are in use? Do they provide any special advantages as a result of their location? What is the current market value of these investments (assuming they are owned)?
- What is the available production capacity? How does usage compare to availability?
- What production processes are being used? Are these processes current, and how effectively are they equipped technologically to compete?
- What is the inventory policy of the business? How do inventory levels and turns compare to those of similar businesses? How often do stock outs occur?
- What are the skill levels and demographic characteristics of the workforce? How well do the employees meet the challenges

of producing the firm's products? How does their productivity compare with that of other organizations performing similar tasks?

- Does the firm possess any special skills that are important?
- Is innovation occurring regularly?
- Is there a commitment to continuous improvement?

Infrastructure

Infrastructure refers to the systems that make the business run effectively, and are often taken for granted. Management and board members might consider the following questions related to infrastructure:

- Are safety and security priorities of the business?
- Does the business have employees with the skills, tools, and necessary support to execute the business processes effectively? Is there an effective training program in place?
- Are the Management Information Systems in place to support effective internal controls and management reporting? Does the control system function effectively?
- Are compensation systems in place that attract the necessary talent and properly reward performance?
- How effective are the internal and external communications systems?

These somewhat lengthy lists illustrate the complexity of assessing the situation for any business. They include general topics which the board and the CEO should explore and about which they should reach a mutual understanding. These discussions could bring up additional topics that may or may not be relevant to describing and understanding the situation of the business. The board of directors and the CEO must mutually sense what is important and follow through by taking the next steps in the planning process. For some organizations, this should entail putting the planning process on hold while significant and urgent shortcomings are addressed. In general, the purpose of the exercise for management and directors is to get an accurate feel for the situation and decide together whether and how the firm should proceed.

Determining the Readiness of the Organization for Strategic Planning

After a careful assessment of the business's situation, the board and the general manager have to make a judgment call about whether the company and its management are ready to proceed with a formal strategic management process. An illustrative checklist is presented below that should aid in this decision.

A Readiness Checklist

A number of factors may be used to determine a firm's readiness to proceed with the strategic management process. Businesses with positive answers to the majority of the following questions are prepared to begin with a strong likelihood of success. Organizations with a preponderance of negative answers to the questions are not as ready as would be desired. Questions assessing readiness include:

- Does the general manager understand strategy, strategic planning, and their respective costs and benefits? Is he or she committed to the effort in a meaningful way?
- Are there any pressing business issues or crises?
- Are the politics in order? This means that there must be no hidden agendas, and the board and management must be willing to challenge the status quo. Openness and willingness to change should encompass:
  - Examining new ways of doing things
  - Asking hard questions
  - Facing difficult choices
  - Making tough decisions that are best for the organization
- Is it realistic to make the necessary commitment of resources to complete the effort? Immediate resources needed include management and board time and energy, and monetary funds.
- Is there a commitment and ability to gather the required information, internally and externally?
- Are there good working relationships and trust among the key members of the management team and between the board and management?

EXHIBIT 4-4   Readiness for Strategic Management for Various Business States

		Condition	
		Strong	*Weak*
Momentum	*Improving*	May be ready	Depends on the nature of the weakness. May be ready, but may have to go slowly until the condition improves sufficiently to support the effort.
	Stable	May be ready	Probably not ready until the weak conditions are remedied.
	Declining	Not ready. Decline must be stabilized, if not reversed.	Not ready. Potentially a crisis requiring an immediate turnaround.

- What is the condition and momentum of the business? The impact of these two attributes of the business on readiness for strategic planning is described in Exhibit 4-4.

Are the Key Success Factors in Place?

Exhibit 4-4 reinforces the principle that strategic management is most likely to succeed within companies that are reasonably strong and want to extend and defend their existing strategies, and/or develop new ones to ensure their long-term future. If the current situation is not a good base from which to grow the business, management must at least stabilize it enough to buy the time to reposition the company strategically, and the business must be in a strong enough condition to survive while the new strategy establishes itself.

Note that the term "May be ready" is used in Exhibit 4-4. The uncertainty of this phrase relates to the management's, and especially the CEO's, attitude toward strategy. If the CEO harbors a skepticism or cynicism about the utility of the process, he or she will almost certainly fail to make the commitment necessary for the effort to be successful. If the CEO views the undertaking as a loss of control or a threat to his or her authority, perhaps instigated by one or more key board members, he or she typically will oppose the effort or provide hesitant support. Entrepreneurs often do not have the patience and discipline to lead a successful formal strategic management effort. In other situations, the CEO may perceive the need and energetically lead the project, but some key operating managers may actively or passively resist rather than assist. In all of these situations, the board and the CEO have to keep in mind that if they want to succeed, they will have to "change the people, or change the people." Thus, the first attempt to initiate change should address motivating the reluctant individuals to willingly support the change efforts. If this effort to "change the people" fails, management may have to revert to removing the opposed individuals and replacing them with more willing counterparts.

As an overview, the value of implementing strategic management as a rule is determined by the circumstances. If things are going well, a strong condition exists with positive momentum, and there are no opportunities or threats that require a change in strategy, introducing a major strategic management effort may add little current value. It might, however, create a formal means of protection against arriving at a less-desirable state in the future.

If, however, things are going reasonably well and there is room for improvement in the current business, strategic management can provide an effective tool for identifying issues, sharpening management's focus, and coordinating decision making, all of which ideally would lead to improving momentum and strong future conditions.

Finally, strategic management adds the most value when there is a need for organization-wide strategic change because the existing strategies are beginning to weaken, or when opportunities and threats suggest the need for new strategies.

In many cases, the board and CEO of a business will or should conclude that they are not ready to begin to embark on the implementation of a formal strategic management process. The reasons will vary, but generally fall into one of the following two categories:

Current Issues Require Attention

One cluster of reasons for caution is the presence of too many pressing survival issues that must be addressed currently if the business is to have a future. This was the situation described previously in the example of Gerstner at IBM (Vignette 4-3). The most practical approach under these circumstances is to identify the issues and begin to deal with them. A thorough description of the business's situation will bring these matters to light; management and the board should already be well aware of most of the issues.

Culture

The second cluster of reasons for caution involves realistically identifying that the culture of the organization—along with the prevailing negative or inappropriate attitudes of key managers—needs attention. Strategic planning is about performance and change. Many corporate cultures are not performance oriented and are very resistant to change. It is remarkable how entrenched people can be in preserving the status quo in spite of evidence that the company's future is bleak. People will often cling to the clearly unsuccessful approaches of the past until it is too late, and make concessions to reality only after some calamity has befallen them or the situation.

Difficult cultural situations also commonly occur under circumstances related to top management. One classic example occurs when the company is led by a strong entrepreneur who has an exceedingly authoritarian style. The strategic planning process is not consistent with this managerial approach. A cultural mismatch also can be found when many of the managers have a narrow operating mentality and are not interested in strategic thinking about the future, do not understand it, and/or do not think it is applicable to their situation. If key members of the management team think this way, until they are convinced otherwise, it will be at best difficult and more likely impossible to make meaningful progress in implementing a strategic planning process, especially if the business is not in a dire situation. With opposition rather than leadership from key managers, the results will not be worth the effort. Again, the board and/or the CEO must "change the people or change the people" to progress successfully.

If there are important reasons to move forward with strategic management—a crisis, a vision, or the CEO's commitment to change as a philosophy—new managers may have to be hired into key positions to lead the effort. If the company's culture is a barrier, an organizational development effort should be initiated to change the culture. Progress for this initiative takes time, and often requires some painful decisions about the retention of long-term employees.

Forging Ahead

Finally, if the board and the CEO conclude that the organization should proceed with a formal strategic management effort, it may be prudent to select someone to lead the program—from either inside or outside the firm. Most firms will find an experienced executive or consultant helpful because of his or her strategic planning experience and objectivity. The importance of positive chemistry with the CEO and other key managers cannot be overstated. The role of the project leader should be as a coach in designing and executing the strategic planning process.

Summary

The three chapters in Part I introduce the economic context and the organizational context within which the general manager functions, along with descriptions of the roles and tasks associated with this critical position in our system of free enterprise, capitalism, and competition. This chapter has discussed the essential preliminaries that must be conducted to launch a successful strategic management effort. The remaining chapters in Part II describe the systematic steps necessary to develop a strategic plan and its associated business plan (three-year horizon) and annual plan or budget.

DISCUSSION QUESTIONS

1. Who are the important evaluators of performance for a business? What does each evaluator desire?
2. What is a business concept?
3. What should a general manager consider in assessing the situation of a business?
4. What should a general manager consider in determining whether an organization is ready to begin a process of strategic management?
5. What is the meaning of the phrase, "change the people, or change the people"?

5

THE STRATEGIC MANAGEMENT PROCESS

The strategic thinking phase of strategic management requires a review at the level of each business the organization operates, and if there is more than one, at the corporate or parent level as well. We begin this chapter by examining the corporate level, and then move to the business or divisional level. Many of the lessons for and concerns of the general manager at one level are shared by the general manager of the other.

Corporate strategy formulation consists of looking toward the future, providing direction to the firm beginning with the industries in which the firm chooses to compete when appropriate, and setting suitable goals and objectives for expected corporate financial performance. Strategic thinking must be followed by a detailed operational planning system that enhances the likelihood that the firm's operating units will achieve the desired results. With appropriate goals and objectives set and strategies for achieving them in place, the firm must decide how it should be organized to provide the best environment for achieving the desired results.

The Strategic Management Process

Businesses operate through a continuous process of setting goals, assessing performance, taking corrective action, and monitoring results to ensure improved performance. Members of management must detect problems and identify new opportunities through an effective control system and their personal knowledge of the business, as illustrated in Exhibit 5-1.

EXHIBIT 5-1   The Strategic Management Process

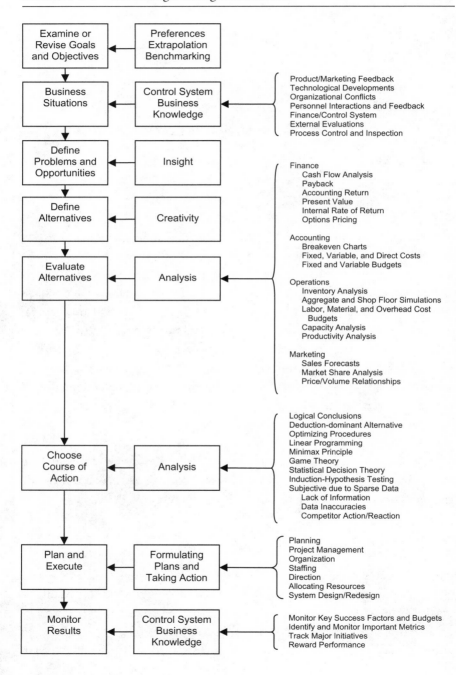

The general manager is the director of this process, and should ensure that such a system functions continuously in the organization.

Suggestions of continuity might indicate to some that the strategic management process is solely a reactive one, engaged only in response to the identification of problems and opportunities. This is hardly the case. The strategic management process should be employed not only as a reactive process but also as a formal process deliberately employed at regular intervals (commonly on an annual basis).

When a new business opportunity or symptom of a problem is detected, management must ensure its careful definition. Defining problems requires a detailed insight into the workings of the business and an understanding of new opportunities, along with a sound understanding of the market and competitive environment. The creative portion of the strategic planning process involves deriving feasible approaches and alternative strategies to capitalize on the opportunities or counteract the problems that have been identified. The more alternatives that can be put forth for investigation, the more effective the action taken is likely to be. Conversely, if the number of alternatives explored is limited, the best approach to the situation might not be brought forward.

Each of the reasonable alternative courses of action should be analyzed to determine its advantages and disadvantages and its economic cost and effectiveness. The additional revenues, likely costs, and necessary investment must be estimated, and the anticipated results determined or predicted. The manager involved in the decision making must choose a course of action with which to respond to the problem or opportunity. There are many ways to make this decision, including reacting to an overwhelming set of positive circumstances, conducting an in-depth analysis of relevant data, or literally playing a hunch.

Some decisions are fairly easy to make. A proposal for a new tool may provide a sufficient cost reduction to recover the investment in a year. In such cases, the manager has little difficulty choosing a course of action. In other cases, where the preferred course is not so evident, the analysis process is likely to be complex and to involve uncertainty. In many situations, the managers must speculate about the future actions of customers and competitors, anticipate costs and economic factors, and make assumptions about raw materials, suppliers, and regulation—among other factors.

Under these circumstances, the decision makers will never have enough data to formulate a definitive conclusion. In addition to making projections about external factors that they cannot control, managers may misjudge the ability of their organizations to execute.

Lower-level and relatively straightforward decisions are more apt to be accompanied by sufficient data to support the use of analytical tools and techniques. Conversely, higher-level, more strategic decisions are normally made in an environment of insufficient data and uncertain estimates about the actions and reactions of competitors, customers, suppliers, equity holders, and other stakeholders of the organization; trends in the market, economy, and society; and even the organization's ability to execute the strategy. These are frequently the defining strategic decisions for corporations. The ability to handle these situations is what identifies chief executive officers (CEOs) as effective or ineffective. CEOs that can consistently make successful strategic decisions in these situations are priceless.

After a course of action is chosen, the manager must ensure that the decision is properly executed. This involves planning for and taking action. Planning is a vital skill of successful organizations, as discussed further in this chapter. Execution, or taking action, is covered in detail in the five chapters of Part IV.

The final task in the process of strategic management is to ensure that actions happen as they have been planned. The manager must determine the key success factors for the organization and provide for the continuous monitoring of results through effective control systems. The manager must rely on the control system and his or her knowledge of the business to assess the myriad of complicating factors and ensure the achievement of the desired results. This brings us back to the means of detecting problems or opportunities, which begins anew the circular, endless process of strategic management.

Establishing Corporate Strategic Objectives

A strong driver of sustained superior performance in nearly all businesses is consistent, logical, and demanding goal setting. Setting goals starts at the top of the organization with the board of directors, whose members set goals and establish commensurate rewards for the CEO or general manager and senior management. Goal setting should cascade through the organization to the level of the hourly worker. Regular monitoring and reporting of progress toward targets and objectives is a sound step toward establishing a long record of superior performance.

Measures of Financial Performance

In order to establish achievable corporate goals and objectives, management must first consider the link between corporate expectations and the ultimate generic reason for the existence of most corporations. Public corporations exist primarily to provide investors an adequate return on their investment. With this in mind, we revisit the most obvious measurable results described earlier. They are:

- Profitability
- Return on investment
- Cash flow
- Growth (in revenues and profit)
- Stability (or predictability) of results

A sound capital structure of the business is also an underlying aim, and is often captured by the ratio of long-term debt to owners' equity.

While the emphasis on one or more of these measures may lessen or intensify over time, they collectively represent the most important financial measures of corporate performance for most businesses. Preferably, the general manager would want to jointly maximize this collection. We recognize and explore in Part III the interrelationships among some of the variables, realizing that improvement in one sometimes results in pressure on another.

It also is pointed out in Chapters 3 and 4 that the external agencies that appraise the performance of public companies gradually have become more demanding in the measures they prefer, with transitions from profits (earnings), to earnings per share, to return on equity, to free cash flow (cash flow after providing for capital needs).

A fundamental challenge for the general manager is to produce results that achieve the preferred level of each performance measure. Frequently, this feat is difficult, if not unrealistic, leaving the manager to seek the best possible results with some degree of balance among the measures. This challenge is heightened by numerous complicating factors, regardless of whether the company is focused on a given market, diversified within an industry, or diversified across industries.

Synergies between and among a group of diversified, decentralized profit centers are discussed briefly here and in more detail in Part IV of the book. If we assume that trying to achieve synergy among a group of divisions (or business units) is at least as troublesome as it is apt to be constructive, corporate results are tied directly to the sum of the results of the divisions that make up the organization (less the costs related to the corporate office). Consequently, each division should have an individual set of desirable and achievable goals with respect to profit, return on investment, cash flow, and growth.

If we assume capable division management and reasonable corporate goals, and the achievable composite results still fail to meet the expectations of corporate executives, board members, and independent appraisers, the only feasible remedy is to change the mix of divisions in the corporate portfolio through acquisitions and/or divestitures. When certain division managers are weak, however, the CEO should change the managers of underperforming profit centers to affect the composite results.

The Corporate Goal for Share Price

Professional financial analysts have an important role in determining the price at which a company's stock trades, based on their assessment of the company's long-term prospects. If the company wishes to increase the valuation of its shares, in most cases, it must improve its performance with regard to the key performance factors. In a diversified corporation, a rapid and substantial improvement in performance is most likely to come through restructuring the businesses in its portfolio. The CEO or general manager could trade away or sell one or more of the profit centers (divisions) that are performing poorly and/or acquire additional businesses whose performance would enhance the corporate results. For the focused business, rapid turnaround may be more elusive and require a longer horizon to effect.

An additional consideration encompasses the stock price multiple to be sought. Most investment managers seek to lessen the risk in their portfolios by holding shares in a variety of industries. The shares of the leading performer within each industry are thus likely to be in demand, and due to laws of supply and demand, stock price multiples for leading firms are likely to be greater than the averages within their industries. As a result, a primary strategic decision for the management of a firm is whether it will strive to be a leader or a follower within its industry. A straightforward comparison of the company's results to those of its competitors will reveal the inherent stock price likely to follow from its existing portfolio or operations.

While a small number of firms are rewarded with higher share prices as a result of their leadership positions within their industries, an even smaller number of companies transcend these stock price levels because their performances are truly outstanding compared to the many thousands of public companies. These companies generally enjoy multiples of share price-to-earnings greater than twenty-five, meaning investors pay more than twenty-five times the earnings per share of these companies to purchase a share. These stock price levels are rarely awarded to firms unless they consistently, over some period of years, earn returns on equity greater than 20 percent and grow earnings per share at a rate greater than 15 percent per year, compounded. Very few focused or diversified firms consistently exceed both of these criteria and achieve long-term stock price multiples greater than twenty-five.

The CEO or general manager must articulate the company's aspirations regarding its target stock price multiple and put in place strategies that provide a reasonable chance of success. Because the share price multiple derives from numerous other performance metrics and characteristics of the business, these attributes should be carefully considered in the planning process.

Setting Specific Corporate Goals and Objectives

Consider the corporate expectation for profits. If each division or operating unit is performing in an outstanding fashion compared to competitors or comparable companies, corporate edicts that attempt to increase profits are likely to be counterproductive for most firms. If the level of profits emanating from each unit is as strong as can reasonably be expected, then the total corporate profit level is likely as great as can be achieved (in the short term) with the given portfolio of businesses (divisions).

Consider a firm's return on investment. The current operating divisions compete in a set of industries and markets with characteristic degrees of asset intensity and requirements for working capital. If each division is performing at an outstanding level with regard to asset management, compared to competitors and comparable companies, then total corporate assets and the return on these assets are as effective as they are likely to become in the near future.

Corporate-level growth potential also needs to be considered, given that each operating division faces a competitive situation in which its industry has some prevailing growth rate. It may be a mature industry, in which growth is tied directly or indirectly to the rate of population growth, such as the soap industry or the textile industry. In such situations, it is usually the best strategy to hold steady a division's market share by growing at the market rate.

In fast-growing industries, such as the computer industry or the cellular telephone industry, the division may choose to grow at a rate less than, equal to, or greater than the market rate. If a division in a fast-growing industry chooses to grow at a rate less than the market rate for any set of reasons, it can be argued that the value of the division would diminish over time and a better strategy would be to sell the division immediately. If the division intends to grow at the market rate or faster (increasing its market share), the parent company in most situations will need to provide the cash needed to fund the rapid growth.

What total corporate performance can reasonably be expected? The resulting corporate performance on each measure will be the sum of the results from the divisions—a sort of weighted average of the division results on each measure—combined with the cost of the corporate office. An important concern for corporate management is how well this composite set of financial results will play with the external evaluators of the company's performance.

In summary about corporate-level goals and objectives, a company and its general manager must choose its fundamental goals with regard to aspirations for its share price. The management and board then must choose to compete in a set of businesses from which the desired level of performance can be reasonably expected. Finally, the general manager must ensure through the strategic planning process and control system that the divisions perform to their expected levels. Major, rapid adjustments to the company's performance potential can be achieved only by altering the makeup of the company (restructuring) or changing the leadership of the profit centers.

Setting Profit Center Goals and Objectives

Establishing long-term objectives, goals, and strategies is a fundamental step in the strategic planning effort of any focused company or division, regardless of the generic strategies in place (focus or niche, differentiation, or cost leadership).

- Strategies may be offensive or defensive. Offensively, strategies are directed at capturing market share from competitors, creating and opening new markets, and expanding existing ones. Alternatively, defensive strategies may be devised to protect the existing situation and defend against competition.
- Strategies must be formulated with recognition of existing outside influences, including those brought on by the overall economic situation of the business and its industry.
- Strategy formulation also must recognize an organization's inherent strengths and weaknesses.
- Strategies should reflect the personal interests and objectives of the company's owners and management.

Translating Strategic Objectives into Planning Goals

A company's strategic objectives are usually broad desires for the organization expressed in general terms and aimed at supporting or enhancing a business strategy. Before an operational plan can be developed, these strategic objectives must be refined into planning goals. Examples of this conversion are shown in Exhibit 5-2. Before launching the planning goals, managers should ensure the derived goals are realistic and attainable with a reasonable degree of risk. Consider the strategic planning goal in Exhibit 5-2 of improving return on assets from 12 percent to 20 percent. Management must identify and understand the means by which the return on assets would be improved. Appropriate questions might include those addressing which specific new products, advertising programs, inventory reduction programs, scheduling developments, or new facilities (perhaps with

EXHIBIT 5-2　Translating Strategic Objectives into Planning Goals

Strategic Objectives	Planning Goals
1. To improve return on assets	1. Increase return on assets (after taxes) from 12% to 20%
2. To increase overall profit	2. Increase overall profit margin from 4% to 6%
3. To increase sales by:	3. For each product:
a. Improving market penetration in existing markets	a. Product A: Increase market share from 15% to 20%
	Product B: Increase market share from 20% to 25%
b. Opening up new markets, diversification	b. Move product from development to production (planned market penetration, 5%)
	Purchase a company in the XYZ industry
4. To increase manufacturing productivity	4. Purchase new equipment
	Establish a methods-engineering department
5. To improve management-union relationships	5. Establish new industrial relations department and examine management's approach to labor problems

automation) would be developed to bring about the improved results. After sufficient examination to ensure that each goal is feasible, management adopts a set of planning goals for input into the next stage of the planning process. A more detailed review of return on investment is provided in the next section as an example of an examination of a particular planning goal.

Return on Investment

To devise more detailed operational goals, a manager may separate a return-on-asset goal into two factors, the return-on-sales ratio (profits to sales) and the sales-to-assets ratio, also called the asset turnover rate. Thus:

$$\frac{\text{Profit}}{\text{Assets}} = \frac{\text{Profit}}{\text{Sales}} \times \frac{\text{Sales}}{\text{Assets}}$$

EXHIBIT 5-3   Projected Return on Assets

Year	Return on Sales	Turnover Rate	Return on Assets
1	8.0%	1.5	12.0%
2	8.5%	1.7	14.5%
3	9.0%	1.8	16.2%
4	9.5%	1.9	18.0%
5	10.0%	2.0	20.0%

In a long-range plan, the improvement in return on assets projected in Exhibit 5-2 would be scheduled in detail, year by year, as shown in Exhibit 5-3.

Once detailed goals have been set, the components of the return-on-sales ratio and the asset turnover rate should be planned in greater detail. Profit as a percentage of sales is highly dependent on the extent of competition in the industry, the degree of labor intensity, characteristic wage and material costs, and overhead costs of the business. The turnover rate for a product line is largely a function of the output or production per dollar of capital invested that is achievable in a given industry. Thus, the more capital intensive the industry, the more difficult it is to achieve a high turnover rate. On the other hand, within a given industry, the relative turnover rate varies among the competing companies and is manageable through an organization's scheduling efficiency, inventory control, wage and work-rule systems, facility utilization, workforce levels, and management of accounts receivable. General managers should be aware of the elements that make up or contribute to the measures they use to evaluate the performance of their operations, and in particular, which of those component elements they may influence to achieve their desired results.

Cash Flow

A critical measure for nearly all general managers, particularly for those at the top of their respective enterprises, is cash flow. The availability of cash is vital for a business to remain a going concern, so that it may pay its creditors—including, among others: suppliers for goods purchased; lenders for the use of their funds; and probably most importantly, employees for their work. A profit center's operating results and the changes in its financial status may be combined and summarized to provide a measure of the organization's cash flow. The profit after tax that is retained in the business (not paid out in dividends) plus non-cash charges to income such as depreciation and amortization are typically considered sources of cash. Uses of cash, in addition to those accounted for in arriving at the profit-after-tax figure, classically include planned capital expenditures and additional working capital required for growth in sales. The sources must be greater than the uses if a firm is to have positive free cash flow. It is possible for a successful and profitable business to reach an untenable cash situation if the cash required to support its growth is continually greater than the cash being generated. Analytical relationships among cash flow, growth, and investments are developed in Chapter 11. These relationships aid in the establishment of feasible, self-reinforcing sets of operating goals.

Summary of the Comparison Process

How, then, can realistic goals be set for focused companies, diversified companies, or profit centers within diversified companies? For the most part, goals must be derived from comparisons with similar organizations. Internal comparisons may be made with other operating units of the organization when appropriate, or with an organization's own past performance. External comparisons may be made with similar businesses or a peer group of comparable organizations, as mentioned previously in the discussion of CEO compensation.

Because of its usefulness, discussions of the process of benchmarking are interspersed within this text. An additional treatment is provided in Chapter 13, where generic steps in benchmarking are examined, as well as the process's particular application to assessing productivity. The lessons, however, are transferable to nearly any measure of interest. Difficulties typically arise, as noted, in establishing an effective collection of peer organizations to which performance or activities may be compared, and in collecting the data to be used in the process.

Comparing operating results to goals provides an indication of the level of current performance. If results are below expectations, management must decide whether the business is being run poorly or whether the goals themselves are unrealistic. The comparison process must assess the strategic position of the business as well as the details of operating performance.

When an organization finds itself in the enviable position of leading the peer group on a number of measures, the general manager might desire to set his or her sights higher, perhaps on the moniker "best in class," or on the goal of being a top performer among public companies on important strategic measures. As an ultimate goal, general managers might seek to be known as "world class" or "premium" in their operations.

If an organization is at the top of its peer group with regard to numerous important performance measures, a highly disciplined general manager might create goals that stretch the organization beyond its current mode of operation. This approach has taken on several names in practice, including setting stretch objectives, establishing breakthrough objectives, and even creating a unifying "Big, Hairy, Audacious Goal."[1] Exhibit 3-1 in Chapter 3 shows a similar, long-term concept, driven by a vision for the future of the organization. The general topic of continuous improvement is developed further in Chapter 17.

Commitment to Action: Strategic Planning

When managers behave ethically, what they know seldom gets them into trouble. Problems more often arise because of what management does not know. If important facts are not known, the general manager may be unaware of the company's limitations. Embracing strategic planning means being willing to learn, having the intellectual curiosity to find out what is not known, and being aware that there will always be additional unknowns.

Similarly, in practice, the general manager never fully masters or perfects the processes of creating and executing strategies. Environments, competitors, and business practices shift continually, and effective general managers are constantly learning and changing throughout their careers, as illustrated in Vignette 5-1.

The Catalysts for Action

The catalysts for action (change) vary with each organization, and it is important to understand the circumstances in any specific situation. There are essentially three basic catalysts that incite strategic planning efforts:

- A crisis
- A vision
- A philosophy of continuous improvement

Crises have a way of breaking down resistance and building a consensus toward a need for change. It is better for the organization when the crisis is prospective—that is, anticipated to occur at some future point in time, and the opportunity still exists to avoid or minimize its consequences. Crises do not automatically lead to change, however. Denial of the problem is often so great that people become frozen in their thinking, even in the face of obvious threats to the survival of the organization. In these cases, the prospect of a crisis might not be sufficient to mobilize action until it is too late. If the general manager is preparing to face a potential crisis, he or she should clarify for the organization the nature of the crisis and the types of actions necessary to deal with it successfully.

A vision is a more positive catalyst for redirecting the likely future of the firm, one for which management will change because it wants to achieve some significant goal. A common vision can be a unifying and motivational force for all members of an organization. If a vision is to be effective as a catalyst for change, the general manager must ensure that it is clearly and widely communicated and its influence is noticeably modeled by management.

Another positive catalyst for strategic change is a philosophy of continuous improvement. An organization that truly seeks to improve continually embraces change as a way of life. Employees at all levels of the organization take action and experiment because they are constantly searching for opportunities to enhance all aspects of their work.

Whatever the catalyst, it is imperative that the general manager demonstrates his or her belief that changes in the organization are necessary. The general manager is the ultimate role model for change in an organization—both inside the organization and out.

Potential Benefits and Problems of Strategic Planning

An understanding of the potential benefits of strategic planning—both for the business and for its individual employees—can provide strong motivation for embracing the effort for the first time, or for the first time in earnest if other failed or weaker efforts have preceded it. The benefits of a strategic planning effort relate to the catalysts that precipitated it. By dealing with the crisis, achieving a visionary goal, or bringing about significant improvement, the assumption is that the business will at least survive and, hopefully, grow and prosper. Jobs are preserved or created, and opportunities arise for people to be promoted and to increase their earnings.

The defining benefit of adopting strategic planning is the deliberate creation of a successful business. This outcome will benefit the organization as a whole, and it is important that key managers are able to find a personal benefit in it as well. If, however, certain members of the management team have a vested interest in the status quo because they will otherwise in some way lose power, prestige, pay, or even their jobs, they will have difficulty seeing the benefit of the change for the organization.

Consequently, if some managers in key positions will be disadvantaged in the process of strategic planning (which happens frequently), the general manager must recognize and deal with the situation as early as possible. If such action is not taken, the organization is almost certainly going to be burdened by an impediment to meaningful change.

As detailed in Chapter 4, a general manager entering into the process of strategic management should first develop a detailed knowledge of the current situation. The need for specific and accurate industry and functional knowledge cannot be overstated. In a similar vein, a sound projection of the future environment and the forces that are driving change is also required for a quality strategic planning effort. Potential problems arise when a genuine effort is not made in any of these endeavors, as they provide crucial input for subsequent steps and form the foundation on which goals, strategies, and plans will be built.

Subsequent steps of the strategic planning process involve setting desired goals and objectives and determining the major changes necessary to reach them. From these starting points, business strategies should be crafted, drawing upon the information gathered about the situation and likely future. The final challenges are to develop and execute plans to achieve the objectives via execution of the agreed-upon strategies. These solutions involve a sound process of analysis and decision making, drawing on the best minds in the organization and expert advice.

Challenges and problems might derail the strategic planning process, though two basic problems involve the personnel of the organization: Some may not want to see the effort succeed, and others simply may not be capable of making the desired result happen. A lack of desire for the effort to succeed, or more actively, a desire for the effort to fail, may be defined as resistance to change and may arise from many motivations. If the general manager feels that resistance exists at the leadership level, he or she must deal with the problem firmly and promptly, or the entire effort is likely to be sabotaged. Resistance at lower levels can often be overcome by good communications, effective training, accountability for support of the effort, and clear and consistent action by management that demonstrates a commitment to moving the effort forward. One approach to implementing a new process is described in Vignette 5-2.

Those employees who are unable to perform within the demands of the

VIGNETTE 5-2

A company had undertaken a long-term project to upgrade the operational systems in a very large manufacturing facility (five thousand people, hundreds of projects, and tens of thousands of parts and subassemblies). The project—to develop the most modern and cost-effective systems for accounting, materials requirements planning, purchasing, inventory control, production control and scheduling, and shipping—had involved dozens of management information systems (MIS) specialists and large numbers of cooperative first-line and middle managers for a period of several years.

The systems for overhead (paper-related) activities had been implemented successfully, with significant savings associated with the release of some five hundred overhead workers. Employees who were replaced by these automated systems were able to be absorbed at higher wage rates in the rapidly growing factory workforce that had resulted from the lowest overhead rate in the company's industry. The large reduction in the overhead workforce had thus been accomplished with no involuntary separations. Some workers, however, had declined the direct factory jobs available and sought employment elsewhere.

The time arrived when the company was ready to install the final portion of the total system, the shop floor control piece. This work-in-process control system was intended to improve the plant's performance regarding inventory levels, schedule effectiveness, and worker efficiencies, and bring about further cost reductions through the replacement of numerous expediters and factory-floor schedulers. The general manager correctly anticipated the likelihood of serious resistance to the implementation of the new system.

The general manager preempted any resistance to the new system by meeting with all of the manufacturing department's first-line supervisors in the company cafeteria. He simply told them that the implementation of the system was essential to the survival of the division (a crisis, by his definition) and that every effort had been made to ensure that the system would support everyone to work at the best factory in the world. He closed the meeting by stating that the specialists had worked for two years or so to develop the new system, that he personally had checked out the results, and that the system would work to the benefit of everyone with their cooperation.

The general manager instructed the supervisors that any questions about the workings of the system should be directed to the head of the systems development effort. Finally, he told the group that because the successful implementation of the system was essential to the survival of the division, anyone who did not support the new system could not continue to work at the company. The system was subsequently implemented with great success. The general manager had ensured success by taking a strong stance that was clearly understood by all involved.

new system at its implementation may be subdivided into two groups—those who just do not have the aptitude to learn the necessary skills and tools, and those who do not possess the skills but can be trained. The solution is to reassign to more fitting positions or terminate those whom training will not help, and to train those who are both able and willing. Depending on the nature of the change involved, this approach might entail removing large numbers of workers from the organization and replacing them with new hires who possess the requisite skills to move forward with the new approach. This is often the case when a firm must develop a turnaround strategy that sends the organization off in a direction substantially different from that of its past.

Committing to Make the Process Work

Process is especially important in complex situations. A great deal of thought and effort therefore must go into designing a process for creating and implementing strategic planning. In fact, this book extensively addresses process. Most organizations that struggle with strategy do so because they have not designed processes that are effective for their respective situations.

Implementing strategic planning in an organization and truly making it a part of the management philosophy and processes of the business is difficult work. There are many formidable obstacles to success, and unless there is an abiding commitment, they will not be overcome and the effort will eventually die out.

Perhaps the most intimidating potential obstacles to successfully implementing strategic planning are the personalities of the members of the management team. Many people find the work of learning and deliberate and analytical thinking extremely challenging. They may prefer doing something tangible where they can see immediate, short-term results, or performing familiar tasks where there is little new ground and small risk of failure. Others, including managers, may demonstrate a resistance to change that has fairly deep psychological roots. Regardless of the reason, general managers must be able to recognize, if not anticipate, such resistance and be prepared to deal with it, much in the fashion that they would deal with those lacking the skills to participate in the process or its anticipated resulting organization.

Designing the Strategic Management Process

A management process should be custom designed for the business in which it is to be implemented. In designing a strategic management process to fit the circumstances of a business, the general manager might consider addressing the following topics:

- The desired outcomes of the process
- The logical starting point
- The level of the planning effort
- The organization of the process
- The participants and their training

Each of these topics is addressed below.

The Desired Outcomes of the Process

As with many artistic as well as scientific endeavors, designing a strategic management process might best begin with an envisioning of the outcome. Because no two situations are exactly the same, neither are any two sets of outcomes; thus, no two processes should be identical. A general approach, however, might provide guidance to any organization.

As mentioned previously, early steps in the process should involve developing descriptions of the current state of the organization as well as customer needs and desires, all of which require an objective assessment of the status quo. The process should also encompass developing an idea of where management wants to take the business and where it can realistically expect to take it, which sets the strategic goals for the organization and should identify key issues that will have to be addressed to move the organization in the preferred direction. Common outcomes are three planning documents: the strategic plan, the business plan, and the annual plan, which collectively provide direction for action. These plans are discussed in detail in Chapters 7, 8, and 9.

The Logical Starting Point

A general manager should seek to identify a logical starting point for instituting a strategic planning process in his or her organization. As described earlier, clarity of purpose is the foundation for the strategy of every organization. If ambiguity exists in the organization about its purpose, seeking clarification is a logical and sound place to begin. The general manager should begin elsewhere only if the mission and vision statements are viable and current and have recently been affirmed.

Many organizations are not as clear about purpose as they should be. Start-up businesses are frequently fueled by naive enthusiasm, with no clear understanding of the customer base. Successful businesses may see confusion in their purpose evolve as market or technology changes alter the competitive landscape. This latter case is particularly vexing when an "old guard" of management is trying to hold onto a past that is slipping away.

Still another starting point may be directional decisions. Recall that direction indicates the organization's orientation with regard to growth. Given the market situation and the company's position in it, the business may choose to:

- Attempt to grow, either internally or by acquisition
- Diversify
- Expand globally
- Maintain its current size
- Merge, retrench, or seek an exit

Determining a direction is an essential early step in forming strategic plans, one that is often taken for granted.

The current competitive strategy—how the business gains a competitive advantage—can also provide a starting point for strategic planning. The general manager may want to maintain a winning approach or abandon one that is obviously not working. In this context, the general manager should also evaluate the business concept. As previously described, a business concept deals with how the business operates. If the concept is the same as that of all of the competitors, the general manager will place added emphasis on execution. If, however, the concept is innovatively different, management will have to be vigilant to confirm its economic viability and to protect the organization's distinctive territory.

Underlying all of these elements of strategic planning is the business model of the organization (covered in Chapter 10, "The Business Model"), which describes the mechanisms used by the business to create and sustain financial viability. Examining the financial condition and/or the profitability of the business may function as a logical starting point for strategic planning, particularly when the firm is troubled financially, or, conversely, tremendously profitable.

The Level of Effort

The appropriate level of the effort for the strategic planning process depends on the size and complexity of the business, as well as how quickly management desires to bring about strategic change. Four variables may be used in determining the level of the strategic planning effort: time required; personnel demands; depth of analysis; and preferred outcomes, as shown in Exhibit 5-4. The level of effort has been categorized as abbreviated, moderate, or extensive, with corresponding time requirements of one month, three to six months, and a repeating twelve-month cycle, respectively. The outcomes should provide a straightforward consensus on the purpose of the organization, its direction, and the major strategic issues, regardless of the level of effort, and with more extensive endeavors, may also encompass a deeper understanding of the current situation, the likely future environment, and anticipated changes in how the business will be managed. For all levels, the initial effort should be followed by annual reviews and refinements.

The Organization of the Process

The general manager should organize and manage implementation of a strategic planning process as a unique project. Such an approach requires identification of defined tasks and the creation of a work plan with action steps, schedules, and assigned individual responsibilities. For a variety of reasons, the general manager may appoint a senior, well-respected member of the management team to be champion of the process. A champion should possess certain characteristics, including a passion for the strategic planning process, strong organizational skills, and the ability to provide effective project management for the effort, for it is the champion's responsibility to keep the effort on task and on schedule. The champion should also possess openness to new ideas and change, as well as a willingness to recognize shortcomings in current approaches, because all of these are necessary for a truly successful strategic planning effort.

The general manager may also appoint a steering task force, chaired by

EXHIBIT 5-4 Level of Planning Effort

	The Planning Effort Must be Consistent with the Complexity of the Situation		
Level	Abbreviated	Moderate	Extensive
Time Required	1 Month	3–6 Months	12–Month Planning Cycle
Personnel Involved	• In a smaller organization, entire staff and board • In a larger organization, key managers and board	• In a smaller organization, entire staff and board • In a larger organization, senior managers, key middle managers and board • Some external stakeholders provide input	• In a smaller organization, entire staff and board and extensive input from external stakeholders • In a larger organization, large numbers from all major internal and external stakeholders
Depth of Analysis; New Information to Be Gathered	• Little or none	• Some	• A lot. Bottom-up info from associates, customers, and suppliers and objective info about the environment
Primary Outcomes Sought from the Process	• Consensus on purpose (Mission), direction (Vision), competitive strategy, functional strategies, and key strategic issues • Guidance to staff on developing detailed annual operating plans • Action on critical issues	• Consensus on purpose (Mission), direction (Vision), competitive strategy, functional strategies • Greater understanding of operating environment (SWOTs) and related issues • Integration of program and management and operations goals and objectives into budgeting process • Action on major issues	• Consensus on purpose (Mission), direction (Vision), competitive strategy, functional strategies • Greater understanding of operating environment (SWOTs) and related issues • Integration of strategic management in basic management processes • Actions to address broad range of issues

the champion. The larger the organization, the more formal this structure will be. A steering task force normally consists of persons who represent a diversity of talent and viewpoints that are representative of the organization as a whole. This means the members of the group should represent the important functional areas and several layers of management. Other personal characteristics include:

- Rationality and open-mindedness
- Solid knowledge of the business
- Availability to participate fully

The steering task force functions best when it has an administrator who provides staff support for the project and manages the related communications, record keeping, and logistics. In a small business with an abbreviated effort, the general manager may be the champion, and the senior management group may serve as the steering task force.

Participants

The selection of the participants in the strategic planning process will reflect the level of effort that has been determined to be necessary. Individuals are typically invited to participate because of any of the following reasons:

- Their input will be of value
- Their support in implementation will be critical
- The general manager wants to provide them with the benefits of the experience as part of their personal management development

In order to participate fully in the process, the participants should have training in the following areas:

- The concepts of strategy
- The planning process
- The workings of an effective team

Members of management should also be trained in the areas cited above, regardless of their level of participation in the formal planning process. The approach to efficiently presenting the essential aspects of strategic planning to a management team, naturally, should depend on the experience and skill level of the individual members. If the team members are well trained in management theory and have extensive collective experience, they already will intuitively know most of the fundamentals. If, however, they are home-grown operating managers, much of this methodology will be new to them. The solution is to design a workshop or short course that covers the material with an emphasis on applying these principles to the company's situation. In addition to learning the concepts, there is also value in the team having a common, interactive, and mutually enriching learning experience.

Summary: The Competitive Arena

As noted previously, the careful definition of business segments is a cornerstone of the strategic management process. A company must develop, nurture, and implement basic strategies for each business in which it engages. For a holding company, however, strategies must also address the appropriateness of the various business units (and potential acquisition targets) for inclusion in the corporate portfolio.

In order to proceed with the strategic planning process, the general manager must have a realistic knowledge of the business as it is currently operating, which may be described in terms of both its condition (strong or weak) and its momentum or trend (improving, stable, or declining). A strong business condition implies that past strategies have worked well. A positive current momentum suggests that current strategies are effective. Regardless of the condition and momentum, the general manager should be committed to developing and formulating more effective new strategies after a careful review of the related characteristics of the organization and its environment, including its competitors.

Finally, the CEO or general manager should determine how the firm wins orders in the marketplace. The purpose of the assessment is to identify the value-adding activities the firm is able to perform better than its competitors. The sustainability of these advantages should be considered—that is, how difficult would it be for a competitor to reach the firm's prevailing level of performance? Naturally, for many general managers, a more compelling concern is how their organization will be able to reach the level of performance of their leading competitors. The groundwork for addressing such issues is covered in Chapter 6, "Fundamentals of Strategy Formulation."

DISCUSSION QUESTIONS

1. What are the differences between strategic goals and financial goals?
2. How might a general manager transfer goals into action?
3. What role does critical thinking play in strategic planning?
4. Why is process so important in strategic management?
5. How does a general manager determine the starting point for a company's strategic management process?

6

FUNDAMENTALS OF STRATEGY FORMULATION

In Chapter 5, we are introduced to the strategic management process and its components, and we explore the concept of setting goals for an organization. We are also introduced to the notion of a necessary beginning of the strategic planning process and accompanying groundwork to which a general manager must attend before launching this process in an inexperienced organization. For many businesses, though, particularly larger ones, the process is well under way, both as a reactive course of action and as a formal and regular practice.

The strategic management process, as laid out in Exhibit 5-1, addresses the ongoing scanning and analysis that should accompany deliberate management of an organization. As noted, a firm's approach to strategy formulation should have similar elements of scanning and analysis, decision making, implementation, and monitoring, all under the direction of goals and objectives set for the organization. The process for strategy formulation, once established in a ready organization, typically follows a regular calendar. As noted in Chapter 5, the level of effort accompanying the process may vary depending on a number of relevant factors.

In this chapter, we intend to provide guidance for a general manager establishing or undertaking a process of strategic planning with the aim of developing a strategy for his or her organization. We recognize that scores of volumes have been written on this subject, with entire texts devoted to individual elements of the process, and that legions of consultants offer guidance and expertise on the matter, with multitudes of specialties. Thus, it is not our intent to provide a comprehensive review of strategy analysis, a field of study in itself. Instead, we hope to present a general and robust approach to strategy formulation, a process with fundamental components that would guide a wide range of general managers through a basic effort of settling on a strategy for their respective organizations. Given this caveat, we must note that numerous conceptualizations of strategy formulation for businesses have been promoted over the past half century or so. As with the strategies they produce, the approaches themselves vary in content and effectiveness. Individual managers will have personal preferences for how they wish to go about strategy formulation, just as they will have preferences for how their organizations will compete. That is not to say that certain approaches are categorically better than others, but that managers must find those with which they are comfortable and which suit the situation of their organizations at the time they are employed. As we have noted, different managers in the same situation will devise different strategies requiring varying approaches to implementation.

We provide below a brief listing of the fundamental steps in strategy formulation that will be addressed in this chapter:

- Review values, ambitions, and goals of key constituents
- Revisit and confirm definition of businesses
- Revisit and affirm the defining documents of mission, vision, and values
- Assess what is happening in the environment
- Assess the current situation of the business
- Develop alternative strategies for the business
- Determine the strategy the business will pursue
- Confirm capabilities within the organization and develop a plan to fill gaps
- Set priorities for implementation

The process of strategy formulation, as well as its outcomes, should vary with the circumstances of the organization; and within the same organization, it should vary over time (the state of affairs will naturally change as an organization matures). Changes will emanate from responses to variations in the external environment as well as from internal factors. Like most facets of management, the strategy formulation process is very likely to be ever evolving. Most approaches to strategy formulation, though, will encompass in some way the basic steps cited above.

As noted, one primary outcome of the process should be a statement of strategy for an organization, to be applied until a newer strategy replaces it. In general, a statement of strategy describes how the organization plans to compete in its chosen competitive arena. A subsequent outcome of the strategic planning process is the strategic plan. Chapter 7 addresses the strategic plan and its components. The subsequent portion of this chapter will address the steps of strategy formulation.

A Review of Preliminary Efforts

Several activities that are central to the strategic planning process are discussed in previous chapters. We briefly review them here with highlights of their respective roles in our process of strategic planning. They include understanding the motivations and desires of influential constituents of the organization; identifying separate businesses under the umbrella of the organization; defining the organization through the mission, vision, and values; and understanding the economic model of the organization.

Understanding Internal Thresholds and Ambitions

A useful and worthy first step in entering into the strategic planning process is taking stock of the perspectives and desires of any influential constituents of the organization, including the board of directors, founders, and major shareholders or shareholder groups, as well as senior managers of a parent corporation if the organization is a subsidiary or division. Strong preferences among these stakeholders should not necessarily influence the process the strategic planning group follows, but they may present constraints on or guidance for the range of options open for the planners to pursue. Issues to consider include personal ambitions, values, attitudes toward risk, business philosophies, and ethical beliefs. In a proprietary business, there is no economic power independent of the proprietor, thus it is obvious that his or her goals and limitations shape the business strategy. These predilections are also apparent in corporate settings where economic power is separate from ownership.

Many smaller businesses and even some larger public ones are family controlled, if not family owned, which introduces its own set of dynamics and considerations. Relationships involving spouses, parents, children, siblings, and even more distant relations are more apt to complicate many business issues rather than simplify them, including strategy formulation. Conflicts may arise as a result of differing agendas and abilities, as well as conflicting emotions such as jealousy, resentment, and fear. As a family-controlled business matures and subsequent generations inherit portions of the businesses' equity, the ownership base fragments, complicating issues further. In these situations, critical issues in the businesses traditionally include employment roles and succession of heirs, along with the dividend policy. For some of the heirs, the regular payment of dividends provides a major source of personal income. Thus, it is not surprising that few family businesses survive as many as three generations with ownership intact.

Aside from the family situation, the personal factors that most affect strategy formulation and implementation in businesses of all sizes are the ambitions and capabilities of the primary shareholder. The primary shareholder's personal situation—including such factors as age, health, emotional ties to the business, and dependence on dividends for income—may serve as a major factor in strategic decisions. An older owner who is approaching retirement and seeking financial security by means of a liquidity event is going to view opportunities and risks differently than a younger person seeking to make his or her fortune. These influences apply equally well to individuals or blocs of important owners with minority interests.

All of the above-mentioned factors can create significant complications in the formulation of strategic decisions about the future directions in which the business should proceed. For example, the decision to discontinue or sell off the flagship brand of the organization simply might not be an option when the founding family maintains a controlling interest.

Formulating strategy may become particularly delicate for the strategic planning team when the requirements of the business no longer coincide with the abilities and/or needs of the controlling owners or board members, who may include members of senior management. This situation might arise when successful businesses become the victims of market changes or obsolescence of some kind. In some cases, owners may be forced to make difficult choices between meeting the needs of the business to ensure continued success and exiting the business so that their personal needs might be met. For example, an entrenched board with strong industry ties might be unwilling to venture into more diversified holdings or offerings, especially if the new ventures would thrust the organization into unrelated industries. Knowledge of all such proclivities should assist the planning team in developing its range of feasible alternatives for the organization, an appreciation for likely reluctance or resistance that might accompany certain recommendations, and the necessary support for favored recommendations.

Established goals and objectives should also be strongly considered throughout the strategic planning process, some of which might have been shaped by the influential stakeholders, as described. Evaluators of the outcomes of the process, whether they are managers in the parent organization or board members of a focused business, will likely find the results unacceptable if they fail to meet the communicated hurdles of performance. Exhibit 5-1 shows the examination and revision of goals and objectives of the business as the starting point of the strategic management process, as it is with deliberate strategic planning.

Defining Businesses

As noted previously, defining businesses in a multibusiness organization is an important step in the groundwork of the strategic management process. Strategies are crafted at the level of the individual business, where competition occurs among organizations for the business of customers. Simply put, a strategy describes how a business in a competitive environment will compete and establish or maintain an advantage over competitors. Because competition and survival must take into account profitability, strategy formulation clearly falls among the primary duties of the general manager.

The definition of the business is important because it shapes the way one thinks about strategic planning. Businesses can be defined in a variety of ways, including in terms of the following or combinations of the following:

- What they do (products or services)
- How they do it (processes)

- What they are capable of doing (resources and capabilities)
- Where they do it (geography)
- For whom they do it (customers)
- What the product or service does (product function)
- What needs and desires they fulfill (customer needs)

For example, if a company made kitchen stoves, how might it define itself? It might address the product or the customers for whom the product is made. An enlightening way of thinking about this question might be to consider what the product does—it cooks. What are the characteristics of a good cooking device from the customer's perspective? Convenience, safety, and reliably precise heating are some desirable attributes of the product, along with energy efficiency and attractiveness, among others. How quickly the product cooks, though, would make a marked difference in the type of technology employed. Certainly, the desires vary with customer groups, and the better management understands customers' needs and desires, the better it can answer the questions related to making an improved product and establishing sustainable advantage over competitors.

The Foundation: Mission, Vision, and Values

As mentioned in Chapter 5, the definition of the business might serve as a good starting point for the strategic planning process. Regardless of whether it is the first step, upon the initiation of a strategic planning effort, the members of the team should revisit the organization's mission, vision, and values statements. These defining documents truly lay the foundation for strategy formulation. They reveal, in general, what the organization aims to do in the present and near term, what it would like to become over the long term, and what it values in action, intent, and character. That which is *not* included in these statements is also of great consequence, especially the mission statement.

We recognize that numerous definitions for the mission, vision, and values have been promoted over the years. It is not our intent to add to these lists with innovative conceptualizations. Instead, we offer here, as in Chapter 3, general descriptions and guidance, recognizing that many organizations already employ suitable, carefully crafted statements. What is important to the general managers is that they find the documents, as well as the process to formulate them, useful in decision making.

The mission, vision, and values statements should be created or revised with care and diligence in order for them to be useful in providing guidance and clarity of purpose for an organization. They should form a foundation on which a strategy for the organization is built. If we return to the material of Chapter 3 where we describe the role of the general manager as being architect of organizational purpose, as well as chief planner, we may find broad definitions similar to the following:

MISSION The mission of an organization describes its purpose and often the different areas of business in which it competes, including products, markets, and/or geographic regions. The mission statement addresses the organization's intent for the present, even though it may be employed for lengthy periods of time.

VISION The vision of an organization is forward looking. It describes what the organization wishes to become or where it seeks to go. The vision statement should include aspirations, and often utilizes inspirational language addressing excellence and competitive leadership.

VALUES The statement of the values of an organization should encompass important attributes of employees and culture in which the organization takes pride and to which its members pledge allegiance. The values often describe how employees of the organization will conduct business, both with one another and with other constituents outside the firm.

An important principle of general management related to the mission, vision, and values is the necessity of clarity of purpose and norms of behavior for any organization. Clear purpose and guidelines for behavior create a context for the decision making and actions of management and employees alike, and relate to daily duties as well as critical, strategic moves. Purpose and values should be acted on consistently, and their pursuit should be recognized and rewarded. Nearly all organizations of notable size or maturity have statements of mission, vision, and values. Benefits accrue to those who use them and act upon them.

Understanding the Current Status and the Environment

Before a strategic planning team devises a strategy, it should first gain a reasonably thorough understanding of the important, relevant elements of the organization's current status and environment, as well as anticipate its likely future situation. The content produced from such endeavors will guide the strategy formulation effort. The process of assessment, however, should become continuous, as changes constantly occur. The sooner an organization learns of significant issues in its operations or environment, the more likely it is to implement a timely, successful response. We see this notion of continuous scanning in Exhibit 5-1, which describes the strategic management process, and we revisit it here in reduced form in Exhibit 6-1.

The results and outcomes of a continuous scanning mechanism typically include decisions and actions to address an organization's problems and/or opportunities. The benefits extend beyond the results, however, to more informed, day-to-day decision making and knowledge of the individuals involved. Thus, the organization benefits from the process itself. The discipline of the activities requires the employees involved to be well informed, which, in some cases, results from necessary participation in industry events (such as trade shows or conferences). Through their efforts, these employees become aware of where and how much information is available, as well as what is not available. This knowledge allows management and the strategic planners to estimate what their competitors are likely to know, and not know.

The process of gathering information and gaining understanding as an early step in formulating strategy may be divided into two main efforts: external and internal assessments. We begin with a review of useful external appraisals.

The Industry and Market Landscapes

Knowledge of an organization's industry and its more specific markets is particularly important in the formulation of strategy. The status of and trends in both undoubtedly will have an effect on an organization's business. Both are likely influenced by a number of forces and factors, as well, and all of import should be considered in the process of formulating strategy.

EXHIBIT 6-1   The Strategic Planning Process

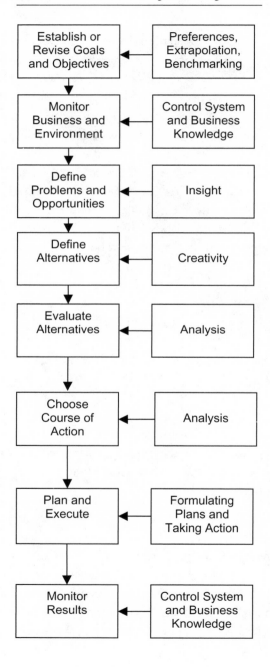

Given the breadth of this topic, managers and planners should develop a systematic methodology for assessing issues that are significant to the organization. We offer some general guidance below, but also submit that managers should tailor and enhance the approach for the specifics of their respective organizations. Planners should keep in mind that data they gather on activities other than their own is likely to contain some errors and imprecision. As a result, they should view the information they gather as a tool to provide broad insight rather than precise measurements and descriptions.

Defining Customers

A primary issue that planners should address early in their process is defining the business's customers. The valuable yet simple questions of "Who are our customers?" and "What do our customers need and desire?" may provide fundamental direction for the strategic planning process. The ultimate end of the strategy formulation process is for the organization to have clear accounts of which needs and desires of which customers the organization aims to meet, how it will meet those needs and desires, and how it will win orders to do so in a competitive marketplace.

An enlightening step in understanding customers is creating profiles of current customers as well as those the organization has lost over the previous planning cycle. These profiles naturally will vary greatly depending on the type of product produced or service delivered, and a range of relevant and potentially relevant attributes to examine should be identified.

As a subsequent move, the strategic planning team should critically assess the needs and desires of the customers and potential customers of the organization. Creative, insightful, and open employees should be assigned to this task, which should be given considerable attention. Determining what customers truly wanted and needed—not just what employees within the organization have always thought they want and need—is a valid and necessary cornerstone of strategy formulation. A survey of lost accounts or lost orders often provides valuable information for this investigation. Managers and planners assigned to this task might also want to consider defining in a relevant manner what customers do not want and need. At the end of the process, the answers to these basic questions identifying the organization's customers and their needs may in fact be different from those at the outset.

Examining the Industry

Definition of an organization's industry is also a useful early step for an external scan. In designating an industry, planners define a relevant arena to explore and analyze. The previous exploration of customers and products should add guidance to any hazy understanding of industry definition. In addressing the industry, planners might consider first the attractiveness of the industry, taking into account such factors as those listed in Exhibit 4-1. Public data sources, such as reports from government agencies as well as government and commercial databases (for example, EDGAR, Federal Reserve Economic Data, and Standard and Poor's Research Insight database) may prove very useful starting points.

Notable elements of industry attractiveness usually include the competitive dynamics of the industry. Michael Porter has classically defined five forces that drive industry competition, and has described a valuable approach to assessing the overall competitive dynamics of an industry.[1] This approach has come to be known as a five-forces analysis. Porter's five forces of competition include:

- Threat of new entrants
- Threat of substitute products or services
- Bargaining power of buyers
- Bargaining power of suppliers
- Intensity of rivalry among current competitors

Porter submits that the five forces jointly determine the intensity of competition and profitability in the industry, and that effective competitive strategy takes action to create a defendable position against the five forces or to determine where it can influence them in its favor. An in-depth review of each of the forces should provide planners with a broad base of information to use in devising strategies, whether or not they choose to follow Porter's approach.

Examining the Market

The market in which a business operates may have characteristics that are somewhat different from the industry in general. The market is usually defined by some combination of type of customer, product, and/or geography, and identifies a narrower segment than the entire industry. Important factors general managers and strategic planners will want to understand about the market include:

- *Market Size* — How large is the market or market niche for which the firm is competing (in units and dollars)? How does it compare to other segments? What are the expected growth rates for the relevant markets or segments?
- *Market Share* — What share of the market does the firm command?
- *Market Coverage* — How much of the available market is the firm covering to achieve its market share? Would additional coverage possibly yield a greater share?
- *Market Structure* — Is the market fragmented with a lot of relatively small competitors, or has it been consolidated around a few large competitors?
- *Market Position* — Is the firm a leader (Number 1), runner-up (Number 2), or one of a number of followers? The company's position is important in determining realistic strategic options available to the general manager.
- *Market Maturity* — How mature is the market? Is it growing, mature, or declining, and if so, at what rate is it changing?

Other market-related factors of interest to the manager and strategic planner might include:

- Market cyclicality and/or seasonality
- Market share distribution among competitors
- Market sensitivity to product offerings and price changes
- Costs of customers to change providers (switching costs)
- Pricing power among competitors

Depending on the stage of a business within the growth, stability/maturity, or retrenchment phases of market maturity, the general manager has available a number of feasible strategic alternatives for addressing identified problems or opportunities. Exhibit 6-2 identifies a sampling of these alternatives for each stage of market growth.

Financial characteristics are also an essential consideration when deciding

EXHIBIT 6-2   Strategic Alternatives for Varying Industry Growth Phases

Growth	Stability/Maturity	Retrenchment
• Start-up	• Maintain the status quo	• Harvesting
• Organic growth	• Internal improvements	• Downsizing
• Growth by acquisition	• Pause/proceed with caution	• Turnaround
• Diversification		• Divestiture
• Global expansion		• Selling out
		• Liquidation

to enter, remain in, or leave a market. These include profitability and margin structure, capital intensity, capacity utilization, and financial barriers to entry and exit.

Industry and Market Changes

It is possible that some of the desired information regarding the market was identified in the review of the industry. The differentiation is not material; strategic planners should focus on what is essential to the business and its environment, regardless of designation. Indeed, numerous economic, environmental, and sociological trends in the external environment should be of interest to the strategic planner. They exist in some stage of formation, prevalence, or decline and may have widespread or concentrated effect. The planner does not need to closely monitor all such trends, which could certainly prove overwhelming, but instead he or she should endeavor to capture relevant current and projected impact on the organization and its competitive environment. This effort might encompass factors and forces at the level of the economy, industry, market, and even a component market niche or specific locale.

While industries change within the context of the macroenvironment, they change independently of it as well. Industries move among phases of growth, maturity, and decline as the patterns of their sales evolve over time. The competitive structure in industries changes over time, as well, for a number of reasons. Cost structures may shift as a result of productivity improvements or technological advances, for example. Mergers may reshape competitive positions within an industry. Most importantly, new business concepts may rewrite the competitive rules. The retailing industry in the last twenty years provides a good example of these sources of transformation. The major discounters have dramatically reduced distribution costs, leading to ever-lower retail prices on most merchandise. On the other hand, specialty high-end merchandisers have prospered, while traditional department stores have suffered as a result of cultural shifts.

Not surprisingly, most industries are also experiencing global influences in some way. These may be related to any number of facets of their operations, most markedly those associated with serving global markets themselves or with serving those who serve and supply global markets. In fact, the movement of certain organizations into international markets may force such expansion on the bulk of its supply chain when the business expanding its operations is in a position to demand it of its distributors and suppliers. Other compelling effects involve dealing with global customers who now own domestic companies, or responding to the necessity of moving operations to lower-cost labor markets overseas to remain competitive. The general manager must anticipate possible or likely changes that will result from these global influences and seek the necessary support, often from outside the organization, to respond to them effectively.

In regulated industries in particular, modifications of legislation and regulations present unavoidable cause for change. The airline, trucking, financial services, health care, and all types of utility industries are impacted by frequent changes in government regulations. Even in unregulated businesses, numerous rules and regulations affect various attributes of the competitive landscape, including the environment, workplace safety, minimum wage rates, discrimination in employment, fair trade practices, antitrust provisions, and so forth. The impact of all such issues has led to the trend of chief executive officers (CEOs) spending increasing amounts of time advocating and lobbying on behalf of their organizations, industries, and even customers, both domestically and in the global marketplace. Advocacy is discussed in more detail in Chapter 24.

Similar to the impact of globalization, e-commerce may affect a business through customers, or through suppliers, or both. The phenomenon of e-commerce is changing the way many businesses sell their products or provide their services, whether they compete in business-to-business (B2B) or business-to-consumer (B2C) markets. Even when transactions are not electronic, much pre-transaction information is communicated electronically. There is also a rapidly growing use of the Internet to support administrative communications within a supply chain.

Industries tend to cluster into strategic groups or markets where the important competitive battles take place. These battles are characterized by a set of rivals competing for the business of a common set or overlapping sets of customers across a changing landscape. The CEO or general manager and strategic planners must grasp any material change in the market and the impact it will have on competition and competitive advantage. This might include how the structure of the market is changing as a result of mergers, new entrants, or firms leaving the market. The general manager must determine whether the firm's products or services, prices, or delivery methods should be changing in response, and he or she should decide how to proceed. A difficult situation typically accompanies threats from substitute products that are more effective and/or less expensive.

Competitors and the External Environment

As a further step in the process of monitoring the situation, the assessment of the market combined with the previously suggested review of customer wants and needs inevitably leads to a comparison of offerings among competitors. A transitional query, which may aid the strategic planning team in understanding customer desires and competitor offerings—and to which the team should return repeatedly—is how orders (or sales) are won in the marketplace. This questioning may be used as a beginning to understanding what competitors have done in the past, are currently doing, and are likely to do in the future.

Competitors

This approach may be carried out by seeking and articulating information about numerous aspects of the competition, including each major competitor's goals, leadership, resources, capabilities or competencies, and perceived strengths and weaknesses. An effort also should be made to determine each competitor's major customers, current strategy, sources of advantage, and potential means of attacking other organizations. Managers and planners should also revisit any benchmarking analyses completed to compare their organization's results to those of competitors, and supplement these analyses as they deem necessary to gain a sound understanding of relative competitive standings. Here, managers and planners must be careful to recognize organizations as having composite profiles of performance with strengths and weaknesses. If, instead, they compare their organization's results only to the best performance for each measure, an unrealistic picture of the competition will result, and they will overlook important insights about individual competitors' weaknesses.

It is equally important for managers and planners to examine the trends in performance among competitors, both current and those likely to develop in the future. They should determine whether any pending changes will strengthen or weaken individual competitors, and which competitors, if any, are undertaking new strategic initiatives. For potential future competitors, managers and planners must anticipate what their strategies and situations might be.

Analyzing competitors often encompasses difficulties in ascertaining all desired information. A variety of proactive methods of discovery exist, including the following:

- Establishing personal relationships with owners and managers of competing organizations, both at the principal level and at the employee level. People in an industry frequently come to know one another over time and often will exchange information.
- Maintaining careful sales records, especially those related to lost orders or customers. These may reveal on whom competitors are concentrating, as well as their pricing strategies. Informal conversations with common customers can be useful. These discussions may yield helpful information, particularly if it is the result of unobtrusive but focused questioning.
- Talking with common suppliers, particularly representatives who service competitors' plants or stores.
- "Mystery shopping," using a professional service or on one's own, when possible.

- Consulting public records, including SEC (Securities and Exchange Commission) reports, local and trade press, real estate transactions, credit reports, and the like.
- Retaining investigative services, such as consultants or private investigators.
- Purchasing privately generated reports about competitors. These documents are often developed and sold by independent firms and may be most useful in assessing a private business or division of a larger corporation whose individual results are not publicly available. Managers should be cautious, however, in using this information, as these reports frequently contain estimates and extrapolations. As a check, a manager might also purchase the document reporting on his or her own organization to determine overall veracity, as well as to see what competitors who purchase the same may learn.
- Hiring knowledgeable workers from competitors.

Driving Forces

The concept of driving forces is related to but different from industry or market competitive forces. Driving forces are important to the general manager because much substantial change often may be traced to a few driving forces. To anticipate their impact, the general manager should first identify the prevailing driving forces for the current and near future environment, and understand their trends and their potential impact on the industry, the business, and the business's customers. In the same way that managers should choose to focus on those industry elements likely to impact their businesses and competitive situations, so should they limit their attention to those driving forces they anticipate will do the same.

It is essential for every manager and strategic planning team to choose from among all of the extant factors, the three or four critical forces that are the prime drivers for their market or industry. Care must be taken to identify those that will have the most profound impact on the business. For some businesses, the key force will be technology developments. For others, such as health-care providers, a driving force might be a demographic trend such as the aging of the population. While economic forces eventually affect all businesses, some businesses are more affected by a given force than others.

Macro Trends

In addition to considering driving forces and their potential future effects, managers and planners should also examine how relevant elements of the organization's environment are changing and anticipate their likely future states. Broad macro forces to consider include political, economic, and social influences, including technology, globalization, demographics, energy, education, security and terrorism, governmental changes, and political transitions, both domestic and abroad. Many of these forces indicate the likelihood of a move toward a knowledge-based economy for more advanced markets and rising standards of living on a broad scale. The relative importance of the effects of these elements constantly evolves for businesses, and as a result, managers must track those that are or may be particularly relevant to their operations.

Stakeholder Changes

In addition to monitoring the relevant forces and trends in the environment at large, managers and planners should also focus on any substantial changes occurring with stakeholders outside the organization. As a reminder, major stakeholder groups outside the organization are typically recognized to include customers, suppliers, members of the communities in which the organization operates, and external equity holders. Managers and planners should also deliberately explore changes occurring with internal stakeholders. The following section discusses the assessment of the situation and trends within the organization, which includes an examination of internal stakeholders.

Assessing the Internal Situation

After establishing a reasonably sound understanding of the external environment and potential relevant changes, managers and planning teams should turn their attention toward their own organizations. The purpose of this self-assessment is to understand the organization's position in its competitive circle and to examine the likely sustainability of any advantages the firm may hold over its competitors. The order of the suggested assessments below should be varied to suit the logic of the strategic planning team.

Performance Assessments

As one facet of evaluating the internal situation, the general manager should assess the effectiveness of the current strategies, whether they are articulated or not. One approach involves focusing on the financial statements as a first step. Managers and planners should determine whether financial objectives are being met and assess the trends the statements reveal.

The earlier examination of competitors called for a review, supplementation, or generation of benchmarking results comparing the performance of the organization to that of its competitors. These results provide valuable insights into how the organization is positioned relative to its competitors on a variety of measures, regardless of how well it has achieved its own goals. Managers and planners should focus on those measures that describe financial health as well as those that are central to achieving a competitive advantage in the organization's marketplace. Performance of this comparison and analysis should lead to an overall assessment of the organization's financial strength, as well as that of its competitors. Because financial statements are historical, their review should be supplemented with an examination of projections and trends.

Many managers find useful a system that categorizes each firm's performance and trends for the primary measures examined. This system might be as simple as identifying whether a performance measure for a particular competitor is above or below the average for the competitive circle, and the same for its rate of improvement. For example, Company X might have a compound annual growth rate of net income measure among the top half of competitors, but with a below-average rate of improvement. Some analysts prefer more sophisticated approaches. Chapter 13 provides a discussion of additional methods of assessing relative performance.

Because financial strength, in general, dictates the breadth of options and power of responses available to individual competitors, the insights garnered from the comparison of results should prove valuable. For example, a business barely meeting its debt coverage will have far fewer strategic options available in the near term than one with an arsenal of a generous amount of excess cash. The examination of measures central to competitive advantage (covered in more detail later) may provide similarly useful information.

Financial statements provide a host of useful insights but do not necessarily reflect how well strategic objectives are being met (assuming an organization has articulated such objectives). In addition to the financial situation, managers should evaluate the progress toward the achievement of strategic objectives, such as market share, customer retention, quality, productivity, and product and process innovations.

Strong organizations regularly monitor progress toward financial and strategic goals. The strategic planning process gives all organizations the opportunity to pause and deliberately assess the organization's performance toward its internally developed goals, as well as determine how it compares to others in its competitive circle. The assessment may be integrated later with other inputs to develop a strategy and strategic initiatives for the organization.

Market-Facing Assessments

As noted above, an extremely useful concept for managers and planners is how orders are won in the marketplace, which usually is strongly related to customer wants and needs. The strategic planning team should revisit or articulate the order-winning criteria for the organization's market, in general, and then determine how the organization itself wins orders. An honest assessment is necessary, particularly so that consideration may be made of the sustainability of the organization's competitive advantage, should one be recognized. A business may win orders for any number of reasons, with the classic order-winning criteria encompassing cost, quality, and delivery. Innovation and service are frequently included as well, but in reality an accommodating or persuasive sales force may win sales. An analysis of customer feedback or a customer survey could provide insights into this issue. Feedback should be considered from external and internal customers, where appropriate.

Drawing on their considerations of what wins orders in the marketplace, planning team members may construct graphical representations to aid in their understanding of the competitive situation and how their organization compares to others in the competitive circle. These representations can be developed using any number of variables, but those that are typically most useful encompass the criteria identified as explaining how orders are won. Chapter 12 provides a detailed discussion of one approach to graphical analysis of competitive positioning.

Assessments of Competencies and Capabilities

It is useful for management to take stock periodically of the competitive tools of the organization—its resources, capabilities, and competencies—as well as its major obligations. The strategic planning process provides an opportunity for this review, which may also be extended to include resources that the organization could easily attain. While this review may be at the level of the firm, it is often most useful when extended to the functional level as well. The purpose is to provide the planning team with an assessment of what stores the organization has readily available to draw upon in executing a strategy—whether the current strategy or a revised approach—as well as what obligations may stand in the way. Once a strategy has been chosen, the team should revisit the notion of resources, capabilities, and competencies to determine how the collection should be reconfigured to support the organization going forward.

The notion of resources frequently refers to assets of the organization, but it may also encompass broader categories of elements that might be used to compete in the marketplace. Resources may be categorized to include such items as cash or other liquid assets; property, plant, and major equipment; patents and other intellectual property rights; contracts and long-term leases or arrangements; alliances and relationships; and employees and their skills and knowledge.

Managers and planners may also want to take stock of the organization's major obligations at this time. These obligations, which should include options, debt and other liabilities, and major taxing commitments, have the potential to affect the ability of the organization to implement certain strategies effectively, and so should be considered deliberately in the process of formulating strategy.

Understanding the capabilities of the organization is also important to the planning team, for capabilities typically leverage resources into actions that lead to implementing a strategy. Similar to resources and obligations, the planning team may take stock of the organization's capabilities. Numerous approaches to categorizing capabilities may be employed and the one selected should be related to the specifics of the organization. One systematic approach is to catalogue the primary capabilities of each of the functions of the firm, including those addressing management, labor, capital equipment (where appropriate), and technology.

Competencies are closely related to capabilities, and their assessment might provide additional insights to a strategic planning team. Certain distinctions among levels of competencies have been promoted over the years, with primary categorizations including competencies, core competencies, and distinctive competencies. General definitions follow:

- A *competency* is an internal activity that a firm performs better than most other internal activities.
- A *core competency* is a well-performed internal activity that is central (not peripheral) to a firm's strategy, competitiveness, and profitability.
- A *distinctive competency* is a competitively valuable activity that a firm performs better than its rivals.

When a planning team understands its customers and what they want, those factors that are critical to meeting the customers' identified needs and desires may be defined. These factors are sometimes referred to as critical success factors. Successful firms align their competencies with the market's critical success factors.

In order to maintain success over an extended period, an organization must establish a clear advantage over its competitors. Competitive advantage is an oft-used term in strategy analysis and formulation, yet its definition is somewhat elusive. Classic sources of competitive advantage include either offering similar products at lower prices or offering differentiated products at premium prices.

In the process of analysis leading to the formulation of a strategy, the strategic planning team should carefully determine which organizations in its competitive circle maintain a competitive advantage and the source of the advantage. The perceptual mappings related to product, market, and pricing strategies referenced in Chapter 12 may assist in visually demonstrating the various firms' approaches to competition. A review of the benchmarking data may also be useful in providing a record of profitability over time. Organizations that have maintained relatively high levels of profitability over the period examined are strong candidates for possessing a competitive advantage.

If the planning team determines that its own organization maintains a competitive advantage, the general manager and the team should carefully understand the sources of the advantage and begin a process of determining how to defend against competitors attempting to emulate it. Their approach to strategy formulation should become more defensive, because competitors will likely attempt to imitate the successful strategy the organization has developed. One method of defense is to limit competitors' access to the resources and/or capabilities that would allow them to emulate the winning strategy.

Assessments of Internal Change

Just as the general manager and planning team should review the external environment for significant changes, so should they assess patterns of internal change. Numerous approaches to categorizing such change exist; the planning team should find one that works well with their approach to the planning process. One method might include analyzing each function and the important functional interfaces, along with major internal stakeholder groups. Given the discussion of competitive advantage, reviewers should particularly examine skills necessary to maintain competencies and address critical success factors.

Identifying Opportunities and Threats

Most strategy implementation efforts are aimed at exploiting opportunities and/or countering threats. Managers have the advantage of being able to select the opportunities to pursue. Threats, on the other hand, are likely to be imposed upon the organization. Before opportunities may be pursued or threats countered, managers and planners must recognize them. Much of the groundwork for their identification will have been laid if the previous steps of the strategic planning process have been followed.

To identify opportunities for and threats to the organization and any potential strategy selected, managers and planners should perform a deliberate review of various elements of the environment, including:

- The industry (for substitute products or disruptive technologies);
- Competitors (to assess their strengths and weaknesses);

- The general environment (for economic, social, political, or technological events and trends); and
- The organization's specific environment (for shifts in market characteristics). In particular, managers should listen to their customers' feedback and questions, which may be unsolicited or solicited through customer feedback surveys.

Advantages often accrue to the organization that is the first to acknowledge and exploit applicable new developments. A head start normally provides the first-mover advantages of experience, scale, and recognition over later entrants. On the other hand, advantages sometimes accrue to followers, who learn through observation and typically invest far less than leaders.

The strategic planning team should carefully consider identified opportunities and threats and devise ways of exploiting them. One consideration should be the resources and competencies required, and whether they are available within the organization or easily acquired. If not, the team should consider how they might acquire them. Assessing the window for the opportunity in terms of time is also a useful endeavor, as is cataloguing the attendant risks and developing approaches to minimize them. Reasonable questions for the planning team are whether the risks are appropriate for the organization to assume, and equally important, if it is advisable for the organization to risk *not* acting.

In this process of creatively exploring the situations related to identified opportunities and threats, management might also consider creating additional opportunities through the use of stretch objectives or breakthrough strategies, by which they identify somewhat expansive goals or envisioned futures and then work to bring about the desired results. Management might consider, for example, what it would take to ensure that the organization would win all of its bids or capture all of the business of its largest customers. Members of the management team should explore how they might achieve the outcome, or at least move in that direction. The identification and exploitation of an opportunity is the essence of success. Widespread recognition should be given to employees who find ways to innovate. Bets should be placed on multiple new products and services, and some typically will pay off handsomely. Managers must be prepared to lose their total investment, though, on projects that fail.

Threats are external conditions in the firm's environment that carry potentially negative consequences. Examples of threats are changes in customers' needs or tastes, substitute products, inadequate supplies of skilled labor or raw materials, new government regulations, and potential litigation. Threats must be sought out and evaluated continually. Numerous questions might assist management in assessing identified threats to the organization, including how likely and how soon the threats are to materialize, what their potential impact might be if they do materialize, and how the organization might mitigate their effects. Ignoring threats could lead to failure. General managers must be attentive to identifying and monitoring potential threats; a failure to do so could end in devastating results.

A general manager periodically must be sure to think the unthinkable about his or her company and its products and services. This exercise will stretch the general manager's thinking and assist in uncovering valuable opportunities.

How to Compete: Setting Strategy

At this point in the process, the preparatory work is completed and we are ready to adopt a strategy and prepare the strategic plan, the subject of Chapter 7. The strategic alternatives inevitably include the three generic strategies described by Michael Porter and mentioned earlier. To quote Porter, "In coping with the five competitive forces, there are three potentially successful generic strategic approaches to outperforming other firms in an industry:

- Overall cost leadership
- Differentiation
- Focus

"Sometimes the firm can successfully pursue more than one approach as its primary target, though this is rarely possible as will be discussed further. Effectively implementing any of these generic strategies usually requires total commitment and supporting organizational arrangements that are diluted if there is more than one primary target."[2] Thus, even though the three generic strategies are not mutually exclusive, Porter warns that the successful implementation of each is a formidable task. By this point, the general manager should have considered the available alternatives and decided which strategy provides the greatest chance for success to the organization.

After a strategy is articulated, the head of each functional department should consider how his or her organization will support the business strategy. These thoughts should be developed into a set of functional strategies that describe how the functions will support the business strategy.

The next step in the process is to revisit the assessment of resources and capabilities/competencies to confirm that the capability is in place to pursue the chosen strategy effectively. This will include determining what activities the firm needs to keep, divest or dispose of, and acquire. The goal is to close the gap between the current state and the desired state that is required to implement the agreed-upon strategy. If resources are unattainable within the necessary time frame, revision is required for some combination of the size or scope of the goals or the time frame for achieving the goals. Gaps identified in this process might include needs in management, labor, finances, capital equipment, technology, research and development (R&D), customer relations, project management, and/or management information systems. The goals here are to leverage resources into capabilities and competencies, and to focus on the goals or priorities that are identified as having the greatest impact on customer-perceived value. These priorities for action must be embraced by the functional managers, who must integrate their activities to bring about the desired future. The successful implementation of the strategies will require extensive cross-functional collaboration. Contingency plans for coping with a range of possible roadblocks to success must be prepared after thinking through the likely contingencies.

Summary

Just as Sun Tzu titled the seminal work he produced *The Art of War,* we note with humility that there is indeed an art associated with business strategy and management. The "art" is in the translation of strategic planning to implementation. The general manager and all functional managers must introspectively ask themselves what they are going to do differently to achieve the new (or reconfirmed) strategy, the related functional strategies, and the concomitant goals and priorities. Success will come about only through changes in action.

DISCUSSION QUESTIONS

1. What are the "preliminaries" necessary for the successful formulation of strategies? Describe them.
2. What are the differences between the mission, the vision, and the values?
3. How does management ensure that it understands the industry, the market, and the ongoing changes to them?
4. What must the general manager understand about the competitors and the external environment?
5. How does the general manager's choice of the means to compete become imbedded in the organization?

7

THE STRATEGIC PLAN: PURPOSE, DIRECTION, AND GOALS

This chapter addresses the development of the planning documents that articulate and communicate the broad plans to implement the organization's strategy and achieve its goals. Carefully documenting the strategies and plans for achieving them is an important discipline that forces management to sharpen its thinking and bring issues into focus. The written documents are the fundamental bases for the all-important communications effort that is essential to executing the plans successfully.

The end product of the strategic planning effort consists of three documents:

1. The strategic plan
2. The business plan
3. The annual plan

This chapter addresses the first of these three documents, and Chapters 8 and 9 address the business plan and annual plan, respectively.

The Planning Cycle Calendar

The planning documents should be produced on a regular basis according to a planning calendar that integrates planning into the normal management processes of running the business. Many businesses use an annual planning calendar that is organized with the year divided into four quarters and each quarter divided into three planning months. The months of this calendar consist of four weeks in the first and second months and five weeks in the third month of each quarter. This calendar has the virtue for planning purposes of dividing the year into four thirteen-week quarters, within which each month's plan and results can be calculated by aggregating weekly results. This approach eliminates the month-end "closings" that require dealing with accounting accruals and deferrals.

An annual strategic planning calendar can be built on three-month quarters. A sample division of broad tasks among the quarters follows:

- *First Quarter (1Q):* Examine the internal situation and scan the environment; formulate the business strategy
- *Second Quarter (2Q):* Prepare the strategic plan
- *Third Quarter (3Q):* Determine resource allocation (including capital expenditures); finalize the planned capital expenditures in order to fix the investment and asset base for the following year; outline performance measures for management control; prepare the business plan
- *Fourth Quarter (4Q):* Prepare the annual plan (the budget)

Some organizations compress the planning calendar into as little as four to six months, or less, which can be effective in relatively simple situations. Some companies choose to examine an especially important subject each year. Because the process is an annual cycle that is repeated every year, the organization may take some time to become effective at its implementation. The first one or two times through the cycle may prove to be difficult learning experiences, and the results may not be as polished as desired. In these cases, management should be careful that perfection does not become the enemy of reasonableness. The plans should be prepared as completely as possible, with the notion that efforts to improve both the process and its outcomes will continue each succeeding year. Despite the amount of preparation performed, companies naturally learn to improve the process over time.

The strategic plan must be revisited annually and should be revised and brought up to date as necessary. Strategies themselves, however, should not change drastically very often, and then only when there are substantial changes in the company's situation. If strategies lack some extended continuity, the organization will almost certainly suffer from confusion that accompanies a lack of coherent direction.

The business plan, however, must be revised every year, dropping the current year and adding an out-year. This type of approach is known as a "rolling planning horizon," much like a rolling three-year employment contract that must be renewed annually. The annual plan also should be prepared anew every year. Properly constructed, it should be a more detailed version of the first year of the business plan.

Many companies have two rather disconnected planning tracks—strategic planning and annual planning, or budgeting—which lack established procedures for tying the budget back to the strategic plan. The sample method described in this chapter and section addresses this lack of continuity and promotes instead a sequenced and derivative approach to developing the planning documents. Here, the business plan flows from the strategic plan, and the annual plan flows from the business plan. The annual plan is thus linked to the strategic plan through the business plan.

The Level of Detail

A common concern of managers relates to the level of detail that should be included in the planning documents. An appropriate level may be found by considering the ultimate users of the planning documents, typically managers at all levels of the organization who must execute the chosen strategies. Primary objectives of the planning documents are the communication of strategies and their respective rationales, along with clear articulation of the specific results to be achieved by the organization. The planning documents provide the framework or context for lower-level, more detailed planning and decision making. Other audiences for these documents are members of the board of directors who must understand and approve the plans, and especially the company's lenders, who also will desire to understand the firm's plans for the future.

The three basic plans of an organization are prepared almost exclusively for inside audiences who generally have a good understanding of the business and business concepts. Additional planning documents for outside audiences such as shareholders, financial analysts, and customers have very different objectives and are often subject to legal restrictions. These additional documents may include forward projections of expected quarterly earnings, potential major acquisitions or divestitures, and other substantial and sometimes sensitive information. While they may be derived from the internal planning documents, the external communications typically must vary substantially in scope and presentation.

The internal planning documents should be simple and straightforward enough to convey important information and conclusions in a very understandable manner. Remember that the process that generated the documents began with strategic thinking—including an assessment of the firm's current situation and the operating environment—and a thoughtful projection of the future. Much of the information, analysis, and assumptions that led to the strategic decisions should be included in the strategic plan.

The Planning Horizons

The horizons of the three planning documents of interest vary in length: As proposed here, the annual plan or budget has the shortest horizon of the three—one year—and is a detailed development of the first year of the business plan. Because one purpose of the business plan is to project resource requirements, the business plan's horizon needs to encompass the lead times necessary to acquire the requisite resources. For businesses that have major capital assets that take years to bring online—a paper mill, for example—the planning horizon might be quite long. For most businesses, a three-year planning horizon is most suitable for the business plan.

The strategic plan, by definition, must have the longest time horizon. Most of the important issues addressed in the strategic plan extend up to approximately five years in the future.

Strategic Objectives

The key to moving from planning to action lies in establishing overall, long-term strategic objectives and appropriate strategies and methods for their attainment. Recall that strategic objectives are typically broad desires for the organization expressed in general terms and aimed at supporting the business strategy. Examples of strategic objectives might be to establish service in the western United States, to begin to offer the option of Internet sales, or to exit a segment of the existing business.

In order to develop the business plan (three years in length) and its more detailed annual plan (the first year of the business plan), members of management must refine and translate the company's strategic objectives into specific planning goals. The process of converting strategic objectives into planning goals is discussed in Chapter 5, with related, sample illustrations provided in Exhibits 5-2 and 5-3.

The strategic objectives may begin with addressing the desired positioning of the company in regard to such attributes as market share, markets served, relative quality, and production and service delivery costs, along with any other significant attributes that differentiate the company relative to its competitors. These broad strategic objectives result from and lead to the firm's aspirations for its share price as a multiple of its earnings. As described in Chapter 5, the chief executive officer's (CEO's) or general manager's desires regarding the sought-after share price multiple will point the way to a specific set of planning goals for expected (required) levels of profits, return on investment, cash flow, and growth of net income, along with a pattern of stability (or predictability) of results. These requisites hold whether the firm is focused to compete within a narrow market segment of a broader industry, or diversified to compete in a number of markets within an industry or across a number of industries.

The Comparison Process

A majority of CEOs and general managers are content with performance levels and the resultant share price multiples that, at best, place them in the pack of competitors rather than in leadership positions within their universe of direct competitors or within the select group of very successful firms whose long-run, sustained performance transcends specific industry comparisons. At the first competitive level, within a specific industry, a focused public company that consistently leads its direct competitors in financial performance normally will command the highest share price multiple within its set of competitor companies. The resulting share price multiple will vary, depending on a number of factors, including the attractiveness of the industry within which the business competes. The overall median share price multiple across the entire industrial spectrum will vary from time to time, but for the sake of discussion, we assert it to be in the range of sixteen to nineteen, for a universe of the largest one hundred, five hundred, or one thousand public U.S. companies. (This range of multiples, as a rule, varies with the general performance of the public markets over long cycles, as do the multiples typically earned by the best performers.) A profit center (division or subsidiary of a larger firm) will also benefit from utilizing a similar comparison process to evaluate its performance.

A second level of strategic aspiration characterizes a few of the most demanding and effective CEOs and general managers. This much smaller number of aspirants to outstanding share prices lead their organizations to levels of long-term, consistent financial performance that result in share price multiples significantly greater than those normally attributed to industry leaders. These general managers and their firms, for the most part, achieve share price to earnings per share multiples greater than twenty-five (significantly greater than the overall medians of sixteen to nineteen) by consistently earning profit levels sufficient to provide returns on shareholder equity greater than 20 percent. In general, they also attain sustained growth rates in net income greater than 15 percent per year over at least a five-year period and generate internal cash flows sufficient to fund the growth without any additional equity infusion and its resulting dilutive effect on existing shareholders.

The strategic assessment of the firm and of the external environment places every business at some current position with a prevailing degree of momentum as compared to its direct competitors. The wise CEO or general manager seeks first to enter the top echelon of the corporation's peer group, and second, to become the dominant firm within its set of competitors. When or if the firm becomes the dominant performer within its competitive universe, then the exceptional CEO or general manager sets his or her sights on the level of performance that will transcend that of other firms with which the organization does not compete, and subsequently, most other companies in its economic sector. This progression or hierarchy of performance objectives (and related results) exists for firms that are focused, diversified within an industry, or diversified across industries. Indeed, there are high-performing firms of each type. Without a motivated general manager, though, the likelihood of prevailing success is extremely small for any organization.

The Strategic Plan

A strategic plan's contents will vary from firm to firm, depending on the traditions and emphases of the management and the planning teams charged with their preparation. As with all of the components of the strategic management process, we propose here a sample approach to generating a strategic plan. In general, the goals of the strategic plan include:

- Articulation of the strategies required to achieve the objectives of the organization
- Articulation of and setting priorities for the issues related to the execution of the strategies
- Establishment of initiatives for each of the identified strategic issues, and action plans for each initiative
- Construction or maintenance of an accurate strategic performance measurement system

Most organizations also include reiteration of the strategic objectives. Some also insert statements of their mission, vision, and values or code of conduct as part of the strategic plan. The contents of these documents are indeed relevant to the strategic planning effort, and hence the strategic plan. The mission, vision, and values, however, typically are not updated with the regularity of the strategic plan.

The strategic plan is a high-level conceptual document that sets the direction of the organization. Along with the defining documents of the mission, vision, and values, it creates the context and boundaries within which all lower-level decisions should be made. It should not focus intently on operational or tactical details, but instead address strategic concerns. It should be grounded in the realities of the current situation, and establish aggressive yet realistic objectives. Its primary focus is describing how the business will achieve those objectives. Objectives are the broadest aspirations for the business, while goals are the stepping-stones necessary to reach those objectives. If there is more than one business within an organization, a set of plans should be designed for the corporate or holding-company level, as well as for each business.

The general approach to the structure of the strategic plan should be the same regardless of the level of the business it addresses. One notable difference arises in the content of the strategic plan in addressing the identified strategies for the organization. While the corporate-level strategic plan focuses predominantly on issues related to structuring the portfolio, the strategic plan for a business addresses operating issues, such as products, markets, costs, pricing, and delivery. Elements of a sample strategic plan are outlined below. The sample is applicable to both the corporate level and the business level, with differences highlighted, when relevant.

The Capital Structure and Related Financial Goals

As part of its goal-setting efforts, management should establish capital structure strategies for the firm. These capital structure strategies specify the amount of leverage (debt) the firm intends to employ and the expected sources of capital. In order to attract investors and/or secure financing from lenders at a desired cost (interest rate), the organization must present an appropriate history and projection of future financial performance. As a result, goals for financial performance must be set accordingly so that the firm can reasonably expect to attract the capital necessary to fund its operations and planned capital expenditures. These goals should also realistically reflect the risks as perceived by investors, which may be captured in the cost of funds lent or the expected rate of return for investments. Capital structure and financial goals should be established as guidelines or broad policies at the strategic planning stage of the planning process, while more detailed financial plans will be developed during the business planning exercise. As these financial plans are developed, new or revised insights may lead to further refinement of the strategic planning guidelines or policies. Capital structure and financial goals are relevant attributes of a strategic plan for both a multibusiness holding company as well as a firm with a single focused business.

Strategies to Achieve the Objectives

As noted previously, strategies are especially different, as a rule, when one compares holding companies to focused businesses. The strategic plan for any type of organization should include a summary of the identified strategy or strategies developed during the strategy formulation process.

HOLDING-COMPANY STRATEGIES Strategies for holding companies deal primarily with meeting portfolio objectives, which are for the most part financial in nature. Consequently, these corporate strategies focus mostly on the kinds of businesses in which the corporation wishes to compete in order to meet its objectives, and may address how the organization plans to acquire the missing pieces as well as approaches for identifying businesses that are intended to be divested. Corporate strategies do not include competitive business strategies, which are crafted by the management of the subsidiary businesses and which are essential to their success. Lastly, the corporate strategies include functional strategies only for those functions to be performed at the corporate level. These functions tend to be narrower than the traditional functions of a business and might include such activities as construction of new production facilities or shared purchasing.

OPERATING BUSINESS STRATEGIES Operating businesses are single businesses operating either independently or within a larger business. The strategies for operating businesses should be included as a centerpiece of their strategic plans and include directional, competitive, and functional strategies. As described in Chapter 6, directional strategies indicate broad growth intentions; competitive strategies articulate how the firm intends to compete; and, finally, functional strategies are developed for each of the major functions to indicate how it will support the directional and competitive strategies of the organization.

Priorities for the Issues Related to Executing the Strategies

Among the central inputs to the planning process at both the corporate and business levels are identified strategic issues, which broadly articulate the strategic actions that must be planned—the pursuits that must be accomplished—to implement the chosen strategy and achieve the related strategic objectives. The strategic planning team should generate a list of strategic issues during the late stages of the strategy formulation process and as they articulate the strategic objectives of the organization. These issues should be tied to strategic objectives, and the planning team should develop a priority ranking of the issues it identifies.

Priorities can be set for addressing the key issues based on the highest anticipated benefit or impact combined with the degree of difficulty or requirements for resources. Various combinations exist of the level of benefit expected and the degree of difficulty of implementation, as shown simply in the table in Exhibit 7-1. Consequently, different teams will often rank issues differently, depending on their perceptions of the attributes of the issues under consideration. Along with the priority ranking of issues, the team should develop a list of indicators of progress and success for each of the identified issues, as well as metrics to define the indicators. These indicators of success and relevant measurement metrics should be reasonably high level, with the details developed and addressed in the annual plan.

Recall the strategic objective of expanding service to the western region of the United States mentioned earlier in this chapter. Supporting issues for this objective might include those of market feasibility, location of production to meet demand from the new region, and reevaluation of the business model given potential changes in scale, costs, and complexity. As a further step toward implementation, each issue should be broken down into initiatives, for which action plans should be developed.

Initiatives Addressing Identified Issues

As a more detailed step toward planning and implementation, each of the strategic issues identified in the strategic plan should be broken

EXHIBIT 7-1   Setting Priorities for Addressing Strategic Issues

		Degree of Difficulty	
		Low	*High*
Benefit	*High*	Highest priority	Requires most planning
	Low	Do when convenient	Lowest priority

down or segmented into a set of initiatives. Initiatives are actions identified as necessary to address the issues and implement the strategies of the organization. Emphasis should be placed on the initiatives that are to be undertaken in the near future, while action planning for those issues that are being deferred can be at a very broad level. For example, for the issue of locating production with the objective of expanding to serve the western United States, initiatives might include, to name a few: identification of potential facilities in the West; site and community analyses for the potential facilities (especially addressing availability of resources, including skilled labor); cost analyses for establishing facilities (production and/or warehousing) versus servicing demand from the established base; and transportation studies. One can extrapolate further to envision action plans and timelines for each of these initiatives, with necessary sequencing imposed.

As a note, the nomenclature used in the sample strategic plan presented here, particularly strategic *objectives, issues,* and *initiatives,* is merely one approach to codifying a hierarchy of analysis that should be present in some form in an organization's strategic plans. Terms and definitions might vary, but all organizations should attempt to identify central objectives of their strategies whose achievement appears essential to successful implementation, along with ever-finer levels of activities that would lead to the achievement of those objectives.

Strategic Performance Measurement Systems

A common management adage tells us, "That which does not get measured does not get managed." Many managers and analysts have found truth in this saying and should recognize that it applies as much to strategy as to operations. Corporate financial performance can be measured quite effectively, but most companies have difficulty measuring the nonfinancial attributes of their performance. The problem lies first in identifying what should be measured, and then learning how to measure it. Logical starting points for developing approaches for measuring performance against nonfinancial strategic goals include revisiting strategic objectives and assessments of customer needs and desires. An illustrative example is provided in Exhibit 7-2, which reveals the goal-setting process for one particular strategic plan.

EXHIBIT 7-2 Building Goals in the Strategic Plan

Goal-Setting Steps		Examples
Step 1	Identify a (nonquantitative) critical success factor necessary to achieve a strategic objective, issue, or initiative	• Reliable delivery of products to customers
Step 2	Identify indicators for the success factor	• Meeting promise dates • Meeting request dates
Step 3	Identify a metric for each indicator	• Percentage of orders with on-time delivery (meeting promise date) • Average days late for late deliveries (past promise date) • Percentage of orders meeting request dates • Average days late for orders not meeting request dates • Percentage of orders later than a specified length of time (standard) past promise date • Average days late above a specified length of time (standard) past promise date
Step 4	Set a goal for each indicator	• 95 percent on-time deliveries • 90 percent request dates met • Two-day standard for delivery dates • Seven-day standard for request dates

Measuring and reporting strategic performance indicators is a valid early step toward addressing any related problems. Of course, problems must be identified and their severity understood before they can be solved. In order to truly resolve concerns, the organization must develop an understanding of the causes of inadequate performance, and may rely on the elements of the strategic plan to lay the groundwork for such tactical cause-and-effect analyses.

Communicating the Plan

After the strategic plans of a business are set, numerous constituents of the organization must be led to understand the strategic plan because their support is critical to its success. The board of directors, managers, and certain key employees constitute the initial, primary internal audience. The CEO or general manager will also want to communicate the company's plans to external audiences, including customers, investors, investment analysts, and funding sources, among others. Effective communications require a well-thought-out plan that delivers a compelling message consistently and repetitively to gain and then sustain the understanding and hopefully enthusiastic support of the external constituencies.

Numerous effective approaches to communicating chosen elements of the strategic plan are available to management. Selected examples of methods employed include the following:

- The CEO or general manager gives speeches at special events announcing or promoting the strategy
- The senior management team uses all-employee or all-shift meetings to rapidly and personally present the strategy to employees and to demonstrate their commitment
- Training sessions are employed as a means of developing understanding
- The organization develops and distributes newsletters, brochures, and posters, as well as direct mail to the homes of employees
- For external audiences, briefing sessions or one-on-one presentations are made by members of the senior management team

Communication materials should be carefully reviewed before their presentation. Management should be careful to keep proprietary and sensitive information confidential, for information is a formidable tool in competition.

Summary

Important tasks of the general manager include developing or overseeing the development of the organization's planning documents. These documents characteristically articulate and communicate the organization's strategy and goals, and the plans for achieving them. Putting into writing the firm's objectives and identified relevant strategies for achieving them is an important discipline for management, and requires managers to employ logic and analytical thinking. The written documents, properly used, are the basis for the all-important communications efforts necessary to inform constituents and prepare for the execution of the plans.

It is customary that the broad strategic plans of the organization be viewed and organized as three separate but related documents, as mentioned earlier:

1. The strategic plan
2. The business plan
3. The annual plan

The strategic plan creates the context for the more detailed planning that takes place in the business plan. The strategic plan builds on the purpose of the business to articulate the direction management wants to take and the strategies intended to bring about the desired future. The business plan, on the other hand, focuses on the scale at which the firm intends to operate, the resources required to operate at that scale, and the impact of addressing the previously identified strategic issues. The annual plan is focused on the detailed actions required to make the next year of the desired future a reality. Chapters 8 and 9 address the business plan and annual plan, respectively, in detail.

DISCUSSION QUESTIONS

1. What is the purpose of a strategic plan?
2. What is the difference between a holding-company plan and an operating-company plan?
3. How are strategic objectives translated into action?
4. To whom should a strategic plan be communicated and why is communication of the plan so important?
5. How are the strategic plan, the business plan, and the annual plan linked with one another?

8

THE BUSINESS PLAN: SCALE AND RESOURCES

The business plan and annual plan are intended to project the aggregate performance of the organization by capturing all potential sources of revenue and expenses, and, consequently, profit or loss. These two plans should include detailed product, marketing, and pricing plans for each business, whether focused or part of a diversified collection. For an organization to maintain long-term prosperity, the expected revenues and the costs to generate them for each business must demonstrate a viable economic model in terms of expected income levels, return on investment, and cash flow. Similarly, the asset base and the resultant capital structure must provide adequate levels of funding for the various operational and strategic initiatives. With these mechanisms in order, the focus of the multi-year forecasts in the business plan is ensuring that planned trends are expected to provide positive results, meet agreed-upon goals, and demonstrate continuous improvement. The general manager, with his or her responsibility for profit and loss, should use the plan to aid in directing the business to the desired future.

Scenario Planning

Recall that a company's business plan provides a multiyear look ahead for the business, with its first year forming the basis for the annual plan. The business plan that is finally adopted by the organization will be based on a single set of objectives and goals, but the managers using the plan recognize that any number of events could occur to substantially alter the projections. To consider the potential reasonable range of outcomes, managers frequently find the use of scenario planning very helpful in the process of arriving at the plan's final version. Scenario planning may be approached in either or both of two ways. One approach is to explore scenarios and potential outcomes tied to very specific events, such as obtaining a sizeable contract, adding a major piece of capital equipment, or receiving patent approval for a potentially lucrative product or technology. The other approach is to project a band of potential performance—a worst case, a probable case, and a best case—to provide a range of possible outcomes for the organization.

The use of scenarios provides a means to understand the sensitivity of the business plan to adjustments in a number of key variables and allows the general manager to be reasonably sure that there is sufficient flexibility in the firm's planning and resources to deal with reasonable risks and launch contingencies. The development of the business plan should begin with a baseline scenario (the final expectations for the current or base year) with projections for the future years (the planning horizon) that assume a continuation of current operations, augmented only by known or anticipated changes. Managers may then investigate a range of scenarios that reflect a variety of initiatives and circumstances that might lead to even further variations in the plans.

The primary types of scenarios that should be tested include those with combinations of the following:

- A variety of volume (revenue) levels, price levels, and variations in product mix
- A variety of expense and efficiency scenarios (cost-driven margin changes)
- A variety of capital investment scenarios, including debt and equity options

The Planning Horizon

The general manager must choose a time horizon for the business plan. As noted in previous chapters, the horizon should be long enough to cover the lead times necessary to obtain required resources and to provide evidence of the directional trends that the derived plans reflect, whether positive or negative. On the other hand, management should not attempt to reach so far in the future that projections lack substantive relevance. Most businesses find that three years constitute an effective planning horizon. This leads to a common practice in which companies use the current year as a baseline and then project the next three years in the business plan. Examples of the need for a longer horizon include situations where the business must plan further ahead to add major pieces of equipment, facilities, or locations, or where it is evaluating proposals for long-term financing. The years farthest into the future are usually developed in less detail, and would presumably be increasingly less accurate.

Rolling Plans

Most companies utilize a rolling planning horizon, updated annually. This approach encompasses maintaining a continuous three-year plan (or some other horizon) by adding a new year at the end of the horizon, dropping the base year, and updating the remaining years of the plan. Management thus prepares a business plan annually (to implement the strategic plan) that replaces the previous year's plan, reflects recent events, and includes the most current expectations for the future.

Organizational Layers

Because the business plan is an important tool for management, the general manager must determine how the operations of the organization will be represented in the plan. If the company produces a single product in a single location, only one business or organizational layer will be represented in the business plan. At the other end of the spectrum, a multibusiness enterprise will consist of multiple layers, the top layer of which is the corporate office. In the plan, the corporate office entry should include expenses attributable to the corporate office and also encompass a roll-up of the financial results of the organization's individual businesses. The final or bottom layer of such a multilevel plan is typically the business level, whose entities are often referred to as subsidiaries, divisions, profit centers, or strategic business units (SBUs).

The plans for a division or SBU may be disaggregated as well. The planning units for a division may be constructed to reflect any of a number of substructures or categorizations of the business, including product mix, market segments, or production centers/service locations. The purpose of dividing the results of the business is to identify logical units that reveal where the business is making or losing money. This endeavor requires devising planning units that are distinctive and reasonably self-contained in terms of the forces that shape profitability, hence the oft-used designation of profit centers.

The number of layers a business plan contains will be a function of the firm's size and organizational structure. The best business plans are those that are built upward from the profit-center level, through any divisional or group levels, to the total corporate level. Management must set goals for and measure performance at each level of the business plan, beginning first at the level of the profit center.

The Planning Baseline

The general manager traditionally begins the development of a business plan in the third quarter of a given fiscal year. As described earlier, the business plan and the annual plan can be developed more effectively after the firm's capital budget has been set, usually by the end of the second quarter. Details regarding the allocation of capital within the organization are provided in Chapter 15. The process of establishing the business plan begins with the current year's financial results. The baseline, or beginning point for the planning horizon, is calculated by taking year-to-date results and adding the best (most realistic) expectations for the ending results for the final quarter of the current year. This baseline then becomes the starting point of the model that produces the business plan. Assumptions must be made about additional possible future changes, which can either be intended (the organization plans to take action to make them happen) or emergent (anticipated to result from external sources of change).

The intended future changes within the organization include those driven by the initiatives that need to be undertaken to address the strategic issues identified in the strategic plan. Management may use the planning model, often a spreadsheet, to test the impact of planned initiatives and a variety of assumptions or scenarios. The goal of this phase of the planning effort is to understand as much as possible about the potential impact of future changes on the business. The general manager will ultimately select the operational path that appears the most promising and is considered most likely to lead to achieving the firm's strategic objectives and goals, both immediate and long term.

The exercise of scenario planning is immensely improved by a detailed, assumption-driven computer model similar to one utilized in the preparation of the financial exhibits presented in this chapter. The model must reflect assumptions about the drivers of revenues, expenses, assets, and liabilities. The spreadsheet-based model presented here contains three interlocking sections—the income statement, the balance sheet, and the cash flow statement—and is designed so that when any assumption is changed, the entire set of financial statements is recomputed. For example, one of the key inputs to be varied in the model at an early stage is the scale of the organization in terms of volume of revenues, which, in turn, drives the need for required resources and characteristically affects costs.

Sources of Changes in Revenues

In determining the revenues of the organization represented in the business plan, a manager (or planner) must make assumptions about unit prices and unit volumes. To do so, the manager should carefully consider each major source of change in these elements. Primary sources of change to consider include the following:

- The impact of planned strategic initiatives described in the strategic plan. These should be listed, and the amount and timing of the impact projected and added to the baseline forecasts.
- The impact of market trends. The maturity of the market, for example, normally has a marked impact on future revenues.

- Projected changes in market share. These changes should reflect the competitive position of the firm in the market and any plans for change.
- The impact of possible additional changes, both internal and external. This broad category, by definition, has the most risk of error in its forecasts.

Sources of Changes in Expenses

As with revenues, a manager or planner must make assumptions about expected changes in expenses. These assumptions should align with the projected changes in volume. Assumptions about expenses may be categorized as one of the following types of change:

- Changes in variable expenses that are driven by the projected volume changes.
- Changes that may result from volume projections that relate to the need for increased capacity, and hence affect overhead costs.
- Changes that result from the impact of planned strategic initiatives described in the strategic plan. These should be listed, and the amount and timing of the impact projected and added to the baseline.
- Anticipated changes in variable expenses that are due to shifts in the unit costs of purchased goods and services, including, for example, raw materials, labor, and energy.
- The impact of other possible internal or external changes, which may or may not be tied to volume changes. As noted, this type of forecast has the highest risk of error.

Theoretically, nearly all expenses eventually vary with volume in the event of large changes. In any planning period, however, expenses can be separated into fixed and variable categories within existing or planned capacity constraints.

Fixed costs or expenses, sometimes referred to as period expenses do not vary with volume, except when new capacity is added or existing capacity is eliminated.

Variable expenses change with unit volume, and so they are transaction driven. Among the obvious examples of these expenses are the costs of goods purchased for resale by the owners of retail establishments and the raw materials used in manufacturing businesses. Labor costs, too, should vary over time with the fluctuation of volume, but in any short period of time, labor costs may, in fact, constitute a committed and consequently fixed expense. We strongly recommend here that labor costs be considered variable expenses for purposes of developing the business plan. In making short-term, tactical decisions about prices, however, labor costs normally should be considered fixed.

There is a tendency to think of labor as the only variable personnel costs. In fact, a significant portion of selling, general, and administrative (SG&A) overhead expense varies with volume. For purposes of preparing the business plan, those SG&A expenses that are driven predominantly by volume should be viewed as variable—for example, sales expenses.

In general, variable expenses are characterized as a given percentage of sales revenues, so the estimating process for variable expenses may begin with establishing the current variable expenses as a percentage of current sales revenue. There are pitfalls to applying this logic, though, which occur if changes take place in price levels, productivity, costing rates (for instance, hourly labor rates or medical benefit costs), or the product mix. It is therefore imperative that explicit assumptions be made about these costs.

The general manager may use the contribution principle in examining the economics of the business plan. The contribution principle dictates that no profit is earned until total contribution (revenues minus out-of-pocket costs) covers total overhead expenses (both fixed and variable), after which all contribution is profit. The relationships captured in the principle allow management to compute break-even points between revenues and costs. One approach to addressing the financial strategic and operational goals is to manage the price/volume/cost/capacity relationships in order to maximize contribution.

Fixed expenses, which, as noted, typically vary only with substantial capacity adjustments, normally are broken down into manufacturing or operating overhead, administrative expenses, and marketing expenses. Because they are fixed, and thus do not vary with volume, they cannot appropriately be projected as a percent of revenue. Fixed costs, therefore, usually are expressed as absolute amounts. Again, managers should start with the current amounts, and make adjustments for known changes.

Fixed expenses may be classified as cash expenses (such as monthly lease payments) or non-cash expenses (such as depreciation and amortization). Non-cash expenses do not require cash outlays during the period but are represented as expenses on the income statement, and therefore reduce income taxes. In examining depreciation expenses, managers should note whether the asset being depreciated will eventually have to be replaced, perhaps to take advantage of new technological developments.

The Economic Model of the Business

A major intent of developing a business plan is to create a profitable economic model for the business that accurately reflects the relationships between volume, prices, costs, and capacity. In order to do this, managers must first understand the elasticity of the market's reaction to price. The general manager must then understand how volume drives (or affects) costs. This understanding can have an important strategic impact, for changes in price may provide a means of altering volume (revenues and/or units), and volume changes may impact the costs of the organization.

As mentioned above, conventional economic wisdom tells us that all costs are fixed in the short run and all costs are variable in the long run. Managers should keep this generality in mind, recognizing that, as expected, there are certain exceptions. Among the exceptions is the notion that certain costs are always variable, such as purchased raw materials and goods bought for resale. Companies with minimal vertical integration enjoy more flexibility than those embracing it because they purchase more of their inputs from outside the organization, and as a result most of their major costs are variable. Companies that outsource more of their components also have more strategic flexibility, but are also more vulnerable to supply chain disruptions.

The business plan provides a means to project the resources required to operate at the projected scale, including capital, workforce, and capacity. To implement a strategy successfully, a firm or business must have the required resources when needed, which necessitates advance acquisition, or no later than "just in time." To manage this process effectively, the general manager must have a process for constantly planning ahead to address the firm's needs, given the goals that resulted from the strategy formulation.

The Sustainable Growth Rate

The sustainable growth rate (sometimes referred to as the cash-balancing growth rate) is the maximum rate of revenue growth that an organization can maintain indefinitely using only internally generated cash flow and the required additional debt to maintain an established capital structure. General managers should understand this important and relevant concept, particularly when composing and reviewing the organization's business plan. A company may grow at a rate that exceeds its cash-balancing growth rate in the short term by employing incremental borrowing, but the company will eventually run out of cash or credit availability to support operations. This cash-balancing growth rate provides a benchmark for determining realistic limits on a firm's growth and is discussed in Chapter 11.

The Model for the Business Plan

As previously suggested, the model of the business plan should be developed to reflect the economic structure of the business. The following section describes a basic and generic spreadsheet format that should be adjusted to account for those specific attributes unique to any business. In this chapter, which addresses the business plan, and in Chapter 9, which addresses the annual plan, the process of developing models for these key plans is illustrated using JL Inc., a sample company with sales of two product lines (businesses). We want to emphasize that our purpose with JL Inc. is to illustrate the business planning process with a sample company. The input data shown in the exhibits and reflected in the forecast results represent the probable case for the future of the business. Subsequent sensitivity analyses show possible results for a best case (reflecting more optimistic assumptions) and a worst case (more pessimistic assumptions), which bracket the probable case (most likely assumptions). The JL Inc. model includes a base year and the forecasts for three subsequent years.

The detail required in the inputs for the spreadsheet reflects the essential, thorough information required to produce a valid business plan. The spreadsheet reminds the general manager that management of the larger picture of a business's overall results is rooted in managing the details.

The Input Data

The generic business plan requires numerous inputs. These inputs include corporate assumptions about overhead expenses, capital investments (expenses), and the capital structure, as well as forecasts for unit sales, prices, and costs. Each of these inputs is described below.

Corporate Assumptions

The spreadsheet should be initiated with a set of appropriate data and forecast assumptions about corporate expenses, the firm's capital plan, and its debt/equity structure. These data are input for the base year (the baseline) and for the prospective years. The corporate assumptions are applied to the product information (to be input) to produce the final corporate estimates.

Unit Sales Forecasts

The unit sales form the foundation of the product plans. Unit sales for the base year and for the years in the planning horizon for Product 1 and Product 2 are shown in Exhibit 8-1. This exhibit also shows the growth rate

EXHIBIT 8-1   JL Inc. Unit Sales Forecast

Probable Case (in thousands of units)			
	Base Year	*Year 1*	*Year 2*	*Year 3*
Product #1	36,500	41,975	48,271	55,512
Product #2	5,800	6,380	7,018	7,720
Total	42,300	48,355	55,289	63,232
Growth Rates				
Product #1		15.0%	15.0%	15.0%
Product #2		10.0%	10.0%	10.0%
Total		14.3%	14.3%	14.4%
Product Mix %				
Product #1		86.8%	87.3%	87.8%
Product #2		13.2%	12.7%	12.2%

EXHIBIT 8-2   JL Inc. Unit Pricing Forecast

	Probable Case			
	Base Year	Year 1	Year 2	Year 3
Unit Prices				
Product #1	$1.11	$1.18	$1.25	$1.32
Product #2	$3.47	$3.57	$3.68	$3.79
Annual % Increase/Decrease				
Product #1		7.0%	6.0%	5.0%
Product #2		3.0%	3.0%	3.0%

in unit sales for each product line for each forecast year and the product mix for each year. These essential data will be combined with other inputs to delineate the revenues and direct expenses for each product.

Unit Pricing Forecasts

The prevailing unit prices in the base year and those estimated for the future plan years are shown in Exhibit 8-2, along with anticipated price increases for each product line for each plan year.

Unit Cost Forecasts

Exhibit 8-3 provides various cost and resource estimates for each product line in the base year and the expected escalations or reductions for subsequent years. These basic cost elements are summed to produce a total cost per unit (total variable cost) for each product for each year.

Revenue, Cost, and Contribution

Exhibit 8-4 combines the planned price per unit and the variable cost per unit (previously input as shown in Exhibits 8-2 and 8-3) to provide values for the contribution per unit for each product each year. The unit sales and the price per unit (previously input as shown in Exhibits 8-1 and 8-2) are combined to produce the forecast revenues for each product line for each year. The variable cost per unit multiplied by the forecast unit sales provides estimates of costs for each product for each year. Subtracting variable product costs from product revenues provides estimates of total contribution to profit and overhead for each product and in total for each year.

EXHIBIT 8-3   JL Inc. Unit Cost Forecast

Probable Case-Product #1

	Base Year	Year 1	Year 2	Year 3
Material Cost ($/unit)	$0.28	$0.29	$0.30	$0.32
Labor Requirement (hours/unit)	0.005	0.005	0.005	0.005
Direct Labor Rate ($/hour)	$52.74	$55.38	$58.15	$61.06
Direct Labor Cost ($/unit)	$0.26	$0.28	$0.29	$0.31
Variable Overhead ($/unit)	$0.25	$0.26	$0.28	$0.29
Total Cost per Unit	$0.79	$0.83	$0.87	$0.92
Annual % Increase/Decrease				
Material Cost		5.0%	5.0%	5.0%
Labor Requirement		0.0%	0.0%	0.0%
Direct Labor Rate		5.0%	5.0%	5.0%
Variable Overhead		5.0%	5.0%	5.0%
Total Cost per Unit		5.0%	5.0%	5.0%

Probable Case-Product #2

	Base Year	Year 1	Year 2	Year 3
Material Cost ($/unit)	$1.58	$1.66	$1.74	$1.83
Labor Requirement (hours/unit)	0.016	0.013	0.010	0.009
Direct Labor Rate ($/hour)	$43.70	$45.89	$48.18	$50.59
Direct Labor Cost ($/unit)	$0.70	$0.59	$0.51	$0.45
Variable Overhead ($/unit)	$0.25	$0.26	$0.28	$0.29
Total Cost per Unit	$2.53	$2.51	$2.53	$2.57
Annual % Increase/Decrease				
Material Cost		5.0%	5.0%	5.0%
Labor Requirement		−20.0%	−18.0%	−15.0%
Direct Labor Rate		5.0%	5.0%	5.0%
Variable Overhead		5.0%	5.0%	5.0%
Total Cost per Unit		−0.8%	0.6%	1.8%

The Projected Income Statements

The projections for sales, variable product costs, SG&A expenses, and various overhead and asset projections provide the information needed to prepare an income statement for the business plan (the base year plus three forecast years). The income statement is shown in Exhibit 8-5.

EXHIBIT 8-4 JL Inc. Revenue, Cost, and Contribution

<table>
<tr><th></th><th colspan="4">Probable Case</th></tr>
<tr><th></th><th>Base Year</th><th>Year 1</th><th>Year 2</th><th>Year 3</th></tr>
<tr><td>Unit Sales:</td><td></td><td></td><td></td><td></td></tr>
<tr><td>Product #1</td><td>36,500</td><td>41,975</td><td>48,271</td><td>55,512</td></tr>
<tr><td>Product #2</td><td>5,800</td><td>6,380</td><td>7,018</td><td>7,720</td></tr>
<tr><td>Price per unit:</td><td></td><td></td><td></td><td></td></tr>
<tr><td>Product #1</td><td>$1.11</td><td>$1.18</td><td>$1.25</td><td>$1.32</td></tr>
<tr><td>Product #2</td><td>$3.47</td><td>$3.57</td><td>$3.68</td><td>$3.79</td></tr>
<tr><td>Cost per unit:</td><td></td><td></td><td></td><td></td></tr>
<tr><td>Product #1</td><td>$0.79</td><td>$0.83</td><td>$0.87</td><td>$0.92</td></tr>
<tr><td>Product #2</td><td>$2.53</td><td>$2.51</td><td>$2.53</td><td>$2.57</td></tr>
<tr><td>Contribution per unit:</td><td></td><td></td><td></td><td></td></tr>
<tr><td>Product #1</td><td>$0.31</td><td>$0.35</td><td>$0.38</td><td>$0.40</td></tr>
<tr><td>Product #2</td><td>$0.93</td><td>$1.06</td><td>$1.15</td><td>$1.21</td></tr>
<tr><td>Product Revenue ($ in millions):</td><td></td><td></td><td></td><td></td></tr>
<tr><td>Product #1</td><td>$40.34</td><td>$49.63</td><td>$60.50</td><td>$73.06</td></tr>
<tr><td>Product #2</td><td>$20.10</td><td>$22.78</td><td>$25.81</td><td>$29.24</td></tr>
<tr><td>Total</td><td>$60.44</td><td>$72.41</td><td>$86.31</td><td>$102.30</td></tr>
<tr><td>Variable Product Costs ($ in millions):</td><td></td><td></td><td></td><td></td></tr>
<tr><td>Product #1</td><td>$28.88</td><td>$34.87</td><td>$42.10</td><td>$50.84</td></tr>
<tr><td>Product #2</td><td>$14.69</td><td>$16.03</td><td>$17.74</td><td>$19.87</td></tr>
<tr><td>Total</td><td>$43.57</td><td>$50.90</td><td>$59.84</td><td>$70.71</td></tr>
<tr><td>Total Contribution ($ in millions):</td><td></td><td></td><td></td><td></td></tr>
<tr><td>Product #1</td><td>$11.46</td><td>$14.76</td><td>$18.40</td><td>$22.22</td></tr>
<tr><td>Product #2</td><td>$5.41</td><td>$6.75</td><td>$8.07</td><td>$9.37</td></tr>
<tr><td>Total</td><td>$16.87</td><td>$21.51</td><td>$26.47</td><td>$31.59</td></tr>
</table>

The Projected Balance Sheets

Exhibit 8-6 shows the forecast balance sheets for JL Inc. The existing base-year balance sheet entries are combined with forecast changes to product-related working capital and planned capital expenditures to produce the forecast balance sheets for the business plan. For strategic purposes, it is useful to plan for a target capital structure; in the case of JL Inc., the desired capital structure is represented by a ratio of debt to total capital

EXHIBIT 8-5 JL Inc. Projected Income Statement

Probable Case ($ in millions)

	Base Year	Year 1	Year 2	Year 3
Sales	$60.439	$72.410	$86.309	$102.296
Cost of Goods Sold				
Material	$19.261	$22.776	$26.946	$31.895
Labor	$13.681	$15.370	$17.584	$20.431
Variable Overhead	$10.624	$12.752	$15.310	$18.385
Fixed Overhead	$8.163	$8.408	$8.660	$8.920
Depreciation	$1.175	$1.859	$1.934	$1.808
Total Cost of Goods Sold	$52.905	$61.165	$70.433	$81.438
Gross Margin	$7.534	$11.245	$15.876	$20.858
Selling, General & Administrative				
Sales Expense	$0.604	$0.724	$0.863	$1.023
G&A Expense	$1.567	$1.646	$1.728	$1.814
Total SG&A	$2.172	$2.370	$2.591	$2.837
Operating Income	$5.363	$8.876	$13.285	$18.020
Corporate Overhead	$0.907	$1.086	$1.295	$1.534
Gain/Loss on Sale of Assets	$0.000	$0.502	$0.000	($1.005)
Interest Income	$0.199	$0.276	$0.596	$1.032
Interest Expense	$0.873	$1.074	$1.353	$1.804
Other Income	$2.512	$2.512	$3.014	$3.265
Profit Before Tax	$6.294	$10.005	$14.248	$17.974
Income Tax	($2.203)	($3.502)	($4.987)	($6.291)
Net Income	$4.091	$6.503	$9.261	$11.683
EBITDA[1]	$5.631	$9.648	$13.924	$18.294

[1]EBITDA = Operating Income + Depreciation − Corporate Overhead

of 35 percent. As mentioned earlier, this level of debt to total capital roughly corresponds to an AA bond rating by most rating agencies. As an illustrative step, the entry for cash shown on the balance sheet in Exhibit 8-6 is separated into two parts: the minimum cash balance, representing the amount needed on hand to maintain operations and the designated capital structure under the scenario shown; and excess cash, which represents the amount of cash on hand beyond the minimum level required to establish the desired capital structure.

EXHIBIT 8-6   JL Inc. Projected Balance Sheet

Probable Case ($ in millions)				
	Base Year	Year 1	Year 2	Year 3
Excess Cash	$0.000	$5.610	$16.679	$31.344
Minimum Cash Balance	$6.648	$7.965	$9.494	$11.253
Total Cash	$6.648	$13.575	$26.173	$42.596
Accounts Receivable	$1.784	$2.172	$2.625	$3.147
Inventory				
Raw Materials	$2.913	$3.419	$4.068	$4.842
Work-in-Progress	$2.286	$2.636	$3.051	$3.467
Finished Goods	$4.873	$5.271	$6.091	$7.062
Total Inventory	$10.072	$11.326	$13.210	$15.371
Total Current Assets	$18.504	$27.074	$42.008	$61.114
Gross Fixed Assets	$20.093	$20.595	$22.102	$22.102
Accumulated Depreciation	$7.535	$6.379	$8.313	$9.117
Net Fixed Assets	$12.558	$14.216	$13.789	$12.985
Other Assets	$2.512	$2.662	$2.822	$2.991
Total Assets	$33.573	$43.952	$58.619	$77.090
Accounts Payable	$2.392	$2.765	$3.184	$3.681
Net Assets	$31.182	$41.187	$55.435	$73.409
Debt	$10.914	$14.415	$19.402	$25.693
Equity	$20.268	$26.771	$36.032	$47.716
Debt/Total Capital	35.0%	35.0%	35.0%	35.0%

The Projected Cash Flow Statements

Exhibit 8-7 shows the summary of the cash flow resulting from the projected availability of net income for each year and the associated changes in various asset and liability accounts. The projected cash flow statements are organized into three sections: cash flow from operations (resulting from net income, depreciation, gain/loss on sale of assets, and working capital changes); cash flow after investing (as a result of changes in fixed and other assets); and cash flow after financing (reflecting the changes to maintain the target capital structure, including the impact of any dividend payouts).

EXHIBIT 8-7   JL Inc. Projected Cash Flow Statement

Probable Case ($ in millions)			
	Year 1	Year 2	Year 3
Net Income	$6.503	$9.261	$11.683
Depreciation	$1.859	$1.934	$1.808
Gain/Loss on Sale of Assets	($0.502)	$0.000	$1.005
Change in Receivables	($0.388)	($0.453)	($0.522)
Change in Inventory	($1.255)	($1.884)	($2.161)
Change in Payables & Accruals	$0.373	$0.419	$0.497
Cash Flow From Operations	$6.590	$9.278	$12.311
Additions to Gross Fixed Assets	($4.019)	($1.507)	($2.512)
Sale of Fixed Assets	$1.005	$0.000	$0.502
Change in Other Assets	($0.151)	($0.160)	($0.169)
Cash Flow after Investing	$3.425	$7.611	$10.133
Change in Debt	$3.502	$4.987	$6.291
Cash Flow after Financing	$6.927	$12.598	$16.423

Performance Indicators

Exhibit 8-8 shows various performance measures (values, ratios, and growth rates) that can be compared to JL Inc.'s goals and objectives. We mentioned earlier that a premium-company designation, from the viewpoint of investment professionals, would require achievement over a period of years of a compound average growth rate of net income greater than 15 percent, an average return on equity greater than 20 percent, and sufficient cash flow to support operations and debt service without the need for additional equity. Premium companies often are rewarded with share prices that reflect a stock price multiple of earnings per share of twenty-five or greater. An examination of Exhibit 8-8 reveals that the proposed business plan for JL Inc. forecasts a compound annual growth rate of net income greater than 40 percent, returns on equity greater than 24 percent, and increasing levels of free cash flow (which leads to increasing amounts of excess cash available) during the forecast three-year period.

Most measures of JL Inc.'s operating performance show a pattern of

EXHIBIT 8-8 JL Inc. Performance Indicators

	Probable Case			
	Base Year	*Year 1*	*Year 2*	*Year 3*
Asset Turnover	1.80x	1.65x	1.47x	1.33x
Operating Income Return on:				
Sales	8.9%	12.3%	15.4%	17.6%
Assets	16.0%	20.2%	22.7%	23.4%
Net Assets	17.2%	21.5%	24.0%	24.5%
Net Income Return on:				
Sales	6.8%	9.0%	10.7%	11.4%
Assets	12.2%	14.8%	15.8%	15.2%
Net Assets	13.1%	15.8%	16.7%	15.9%
Equity	20.2%	24.3%	25.7%	24.5%
Cash Flow from Operations After Capital Expenditures ($ MM)		$2.57	$7.77	$9.80
Compound Annual Growth Rates				
Sales		19.8%	19.5%	19.2%
Assets		30.9%	32.1%	31.9%
Operating Income		65.5%	57.4%	49.8%
Net Income		59.0%	50.5%	41.9%

continuous improvement over the planning horizon. A number of the return measures are negatively impacted in year three, though, by the very low return earned on excess cash. Because excess cash is typically invested in marketable securities and similar instruments, the returns it earns are normally well below those earned on capital invested in the operations of the business. As a result, a buildup of excess cash will depress the earnings and returns of a healthy business. On the other hand, excess cash can be a very effective strategic weapon.

Sensitivity Analyses

At this point in the process, the investigation of a variety of scenarios can be revealing to the general manager. Estimating the effects of a variety of assumptions should assist the general manager in determining a range of volume levels representing worst case to best case, from which he or she may estimate the most likely volume level. Many companies will use the most likely volume as their planning goal, while others will set somewhat higher goals.

Two scenarios were created using the business plan model for JL Inc. to bracket the probable case described above. Reasonable adjustments to the levels of unit sales, costs, and prices created plausible best and worst case scenarios by which the sensitivity of the business plan to various fluctuations could be studied. Exhibits 8-9 through 8-12 show the sensitivity of sales, net income, return on equity (ROE), and free cash flow, respectively, to the best and worst case scenarios. The models show that the results of this company are very sensitive to changes in volume. We note that the achievement of the probable case of assumptions would produce results that would represent a premium company (as described in this book), and any results on any key parameters that exceed the probable scenario will only enhance that strong performance. One may also note, however, that any results on key parameters represented in the

EXHIBIT 8-9   JL Inc. Sensitivity Analysis—Sales

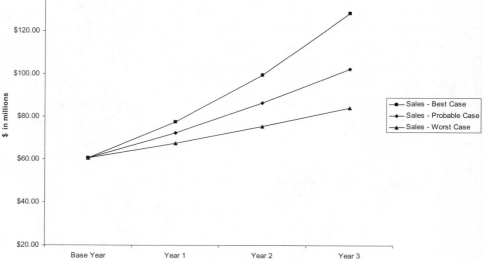

EXHIBIT 8-10   JL Inc. Sensitivity Analysis—Net Income

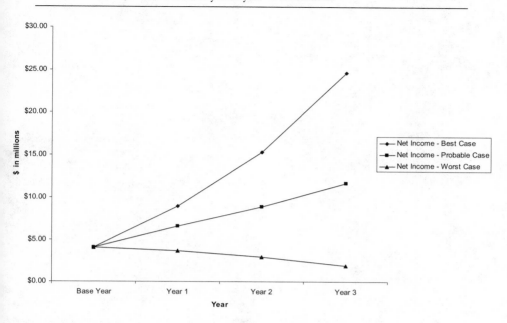

EXHIBIT 8-11   JL Inc. Sensitivity Analysis—Return on Equity

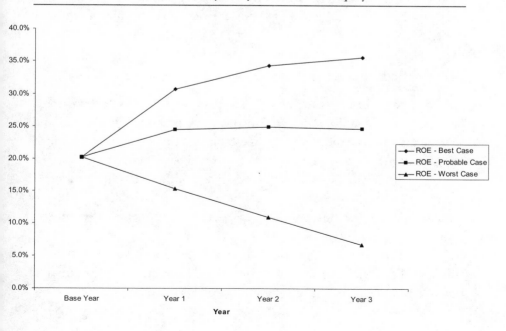

EXHIBIT 8-12   JL Inc. Sensitivity Analysis — Free Cash Flow

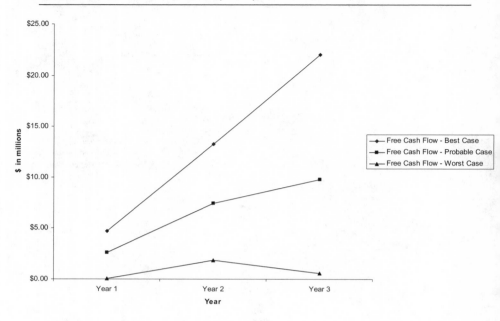

model that are less effective than those in the probable case will put JL Inc.'s meeting of the threshold requirements for a premium company at risk.

The Results

The effort to create the business plan results in a set of projected financial statements for each year in the strategic planning horizon and sets the direction of the firm over an established timeline using quantified financial terms. At its conclusion, the effort will have increased the general manager's understanding of the future drivers of the firm's financial prosperity and identified related uncertainties and risks. Contingency plans may accompany the business plan and address any identified potential, substantial risks.

The business plan developed must be supported by a set of obligatory subplans that are essential to the creation of the baseline assumptions and possible future changes. These subplans are addressed below.

Plans Supporting the Income Statements

The income statements should be supported by a number of more detailed plans. These supporting plans provide information useful in monitoring and managing the performance within the organization. Supporting plans for the income statements should include at least the following plans:

- *Marketing and Sales Plan:* This plan describes how the targeted revenues will be generated in terms of their sources and the efforts that need to be made to realize them.
- *Volume/Capacity Plan:* This plan compares the targeted volume to the available capacity, with emphasis on any seasonal demands or other peaks and valleys in expected demand. If the organization expects to have excess capacity over the planning horizon, managers should consider the possibility of reducing capacity, if possible, or rethinking the marketing plan to determine if there are ways to generate more volume.
- *Workforce/Staffing Plan:* The staffing plan is actually a subset of capacity planning. Management wants to ensure that the workforce has the skills and includes the number of people necessary to deliver the projected volumes. Where volumes are unpredictable, management may seek flexible staffing solutions. If the organization will be overstaffed in certain areas, management should explore the possibility of transferring workers to areas of growth, if possible. The general subject of staffing is discussed further in Chapter 18.
- *Expense Plan:* The expense plans will necessarily be developed after the expected volumes are known and the detailed staffing plan is designed.
- *Research and Development (R&D) Plan:* Development of the R&D plan is an exercise to identify which R&D projects management expects to undertake and to project their expected costs and impact on operations. The maturing of a project that will generate new revenue may require that the volume, capacity, and expense plans be revisited.

Plans Supporting the Balance Sheets

The projected balance sheets for the business plan should be supported by several detailed plans (similar to the supporting plans for the income statements) to aid the management in achieving its goals. Plans supporting the balance sheets should encompass three essential segments of the balance sheets, which include the following:

- *Trading Capital:* Accounts receivable and inventories are generally projected in terms of days (of sales) for accounts receivable and days of cost of goods sold (COGS) for inventory. Accounts payable and accrued expenses likewise relate to volume and should be detailed in this plan.
- *Capital Budget:* This exercise focuses on planned capital spending, which may encompass numerous purposes, including capacity expansion, replacing worn-out equipment, and enhancing quality and productivity. Details of capital allocation/reallocation are provided in Chapter 15.
- *Capital Structure:* This supporting plan addresses financing the firm's asset requirements and/or operating cash needs, which is especially relevant in a seasonal business. The capital structure plan is usually responsive to the cash flow projections described below.

Plans Supporting the Cash Flow Statements

The final element of the business plan relates to the projected cash flows for each year in the planning horizon. The purpose of the cash flow statement is to delineate the firm's cash requirements (or generation) over the time horizon of the business plan. The forecast cash flows are supported by the plans underlying the income statements and the balance sheets.

Summary

An organization's business plan is intended to allow managers to review the anticipated forecast of financial results related to the implementation of the strategic plan. The model of the business plan may be initiated as a spreadsheet, with a set of assumptions, including those about corporate expenses, the firm's capital plan, its debt/equity structure, and essential product sales and cost forecasts. To assist with planning, the model outputs should include an income statement, balance sheet, and cash flow statement. A general manager employing such a model should also have access to calculations of a variety of performance indicators that summarize the forecast results relative to a company's operational goals and objectives. With manipulation of the model inputs, a manager may conduct a set of sensitivity analyses in which the variability of forecast results relative to changes in input values can be estimated. Finally, the model should include a series of detailed supporting plans to aid the general manager in monitoring and managing performance.

Once generated, the detailed plans that support the business plan also should be tested against the previously adopted operating goals, including those addressing revenues, direct costs, and expenses, as well as the resulting expected levels of net income and its growth, return on equity, and cash flow.

At the aggregate level, managers may test the attractiveness of the business plan using a number of key ratios, as described above and in Exhibit 8-8. These measures of performance that may be used to evaluate the efficacy of the business plan also are used later to evaluate actual performance and are discussed in more detail in Chapter 22, "Controlling and Reporting." The general manager should aim to be as certain as possible that the business plan provides for meeting the firm's financial growth and profitability targets. Without such planning and subsequent monitoring, a general manager is unlikely to lead an organization to achieve and maintain the status of being a premium business.

This chapter and its companions, Chapters 9 and 10, reinforce the absolute necessity for converting the conceptual elements of the strategic plan into the myriad of details that must be managed to achieve the strategic objectives.

DISCUSSION QUESTIONS

1. What factors determine the appropriate length of the planning horizon?

2. Why is it necessary to provide the planning data in such detail?
3. What is the reason for separating the cash balance between "minimum cash" and "excess cash"?
4. What should the general manager learn from sensitivity analyses?
5. Which elements of JL Inc.'s business plan reflect a pattern of continuous improvement?

9

THE ANNUAL PLAN: ANTICIPATED ACTIONS

No strategy has value until it leads to action. Whereas the strategic plan is about direction and momentum, and the business plan is about the scale of future operations and the requisite resources, the annual plan is about action. It is about what will be done during the next year to create the kind of future the general manager desires, with an emphasis on meeting the current operating goals. It is important to keep in mind that a strong future consists of a series of strong individual years. A down year in profitability, whatever the reason, causes a pattern of results and forecasts often referred to as the "hockey stick syndrome," in which profits in a given year dip below the prior year's plan, but are then forecast to increase nicely thereafter. The reference derives from the similarities between the shape of the graph of profits over time and the profile of a hockey stick. Firms inflicted with the "hockey stick syndrome" never seem to have a strong year. Instead, their plans and performance continually move through time with results that are subpar, but with seemingly endless optimistic forecasts.

To avoid this pattern, managers should commit to pursue actions to improve upon current operations so that the firm achieves greater profitability and is in a better position to defend and extend its current successful strategies. At the same time, management must also be laying the groundwork for the envisioned future, pursuing moves such as entry into new markets, the launching of new products or services, the adoption of new production processes, and, on occasion, the development of new business concepts. The initial steps for new processes and continuing action for on-going endeavors are represented in the details of the annual plan.

It is vitally important that the organization implement a logical and disciplined approach to the development of the annual plan (also commonly referred to as the budget) that reflects the complexity of the current situation. (Here, we use the terms *annual plan* and *budget* interchangeably.) The process presented in this chapter is one that has been effective, with some variations, in a number of companies. Many companies undoubtedly employ equally effective yet different processes that reflect their distinct management philosophies and the nature of their businesses. While the presentation in this chapter provides a brief example, numerous and varied sources are available that describe budgeting and annual planning in more detail.

The Situation

The budgeting process invariably reflects the current business situation, which sets the context for and defines the issues that must be addressed in the annual plan or budget. If substantial changes are occurring for an organization, such as very rapid growth or retrenchment (significant downsizing, for instance), the annual plan or budgeting exercise may prove difficult. Because management must deal with the amount and pace of both growth and other changes, the chief executive officer (CEO) or general manager of an organization almost certainly is learning as he or she goes along and is therefore very likely to make mistakes. Major challenges in such situations relate to determining how best to respond to the most critical aspect of the change effort, such as expanding the workforce rapidly or determining how extensive the expense reductions have to be. The planning effort is most important when it is also the most challenging.

The planning effort is likely to be far less challenging, though, when the business is mature, the environment consistent, and the organization changing little. Management in such situations, as a rule, considers current performance and projects a repetition, perhaps with an emphasis on continuous improvement on a broad spectrum of measures. The annual planning process, then, requires scant analysis and virtually no innovation.

Overview of the Annual Plan or Budgeting Process

As noted in Chapter 8, the annual plan flows from the business plan. The business plan is typically developed in the third quarter of the fiscal year, and therefore begins with a baseline of the current year with the expected year-end results projected. As discussed earlier, the first year of the business plan is the foundation for the development of the annual plan or budget for the upcoming year. In this process, the development of the annual plan begins when management delivers the first year of the business plan to the operating managers for their comments and ultimate concurrence. The first year of the business plan is refined through a process of analysis and negotiation until it gains the commitment of the operating managers to its successful execution. This annual plan or budget then becomes the revised plan for the first year of the final business plan. All efforts throughout the organization will subsequently be focused on successfully executing the annual plan.

Using the first year of the business plan as the starting point, senior management usually sets the overall goals for the organization and the supporting, specific targets for each planning unit (marketing, manufacturing, and engineering) in a top-down, decision-making process. The operating managers then develop their plans and budgets to achieve these goals or targets in a bottom-up process. If the operating managers believe the targets to be unrealistic, they communicate this up the chain, and negotiate what they think are more realistic targets. The way this process actually works depends on the culture of the organization. The managements of some organizations are very firm and assume an attitude that if the operating manager will not agree to meet stipulated goals, he or she will be replaced by someone who will commit. Others take a more collegial approach of trying to determine what is most reasonable in the circumstances. In most cases, personal goals and objectives for the operating managers are tied to the agreed-upon annual plan and, consequently, so are their bonuses. As a result, management at multiple layers of the organization is motivated to achieve the goals of the annual plan.

It is axiomatic that if goals are unrealistically aggressive, management is setting itself up for failure. The general manager should be concerned if lower-level operating managers do not know how to meet the specified goals, or feel strongly that the goals cannot be met. The essential commitment in regard to the likelihood of meeting any goal is the commitment of the person who has the responsibility for achieving the goal. A failure to address these issues at the front end of the budgeting process will lead almost invariably to disappointment later.

When management proceeds with what is referred to as the baseline technique (described here), the tendency is to accept current expenses as reasonable and to concentrate on possible changes (increases or decreases) in those expenses. The zero-based approach, alternatively, requires that every expense be justified on its merits regardless of current expense levels. The zero-based approach is obviously more demanding because it sets a higher standard of accountability, and requires more in-depth analysis.

The goals set for the subsequent year and incorporated in the annual plan should address the completion of the relevant strategic initiatives and their components, as well as focus on the important specific drivers of prosperity in the organization's business model.

Developing the Budget

Using the first year of the business plan and the guidance of the agreed-upon goals, management may develop detailed budgets for every level, integrating the supporting (functional) plans described in Chapter 8. The reader is reminded that supporting detailed plans must be developed for any budget to be meaningful and effective. Many of the results of the functional plans are incorporated in the budget as assumptions regarding unit sales, prices, costs, working capital levels, and so forth.

Projecting the Costs of Planned Strategic Changes

When an organization's plans include substantial strategic change, managers should assess the probability of achieving the planned operating goals set for the organization. At the outset of strategic changes, management often should expect reduced earnings and cash flow from operations. In most cases, as the strategic initiatives are completed, however,

EXHIBIT 9-1   Separating Strategic Expenses

Sales	$10,000	$10,000
Expenses	$9,000	$8,500
Operating Profit	$1,000	$1,500
Strategic Expenses		$500
Pretax Profit	$1,000	$1,000

management should look for improved financial results. Management should ensure that the impact of planned strategic changes on operational results is incorporated into the annual plan or budget. The results of this incorporation may best be understood by means of a revised income statement format. Consider, for example, the two formats of the income statement shown in Exhibit 9-1. The configuration in the second column shows the strategic expenses separately, rather than combined with the normal operational expenses. The table reveals that current operational earnings are actually higher than shown initially by the amount of the strategic expenses. This format has the advantage of separating the spending on current, operational activities from the strategic expenses that are intended as investments for the future.

The Level of Detail

Senior management must determine how the budget for the organization will be structured. As with the business plan, the annual plan or budget for an organization may be disaggregated to address any number of substructures or groupings of operations within the organization. The annual plan should naturally contain a budget for each unit addressed by the business plan. This first approach to structuring the annual plan segregates the organization by planning units, which are organizational units within the business and should align with the units of the business plan.

In addition, the annual plan may also contain budgets for various segments of the organization not addressed by the business plan but for which management would like a budget for use as a managerial tool. These additional segments need not have responsibility for both profit and loss, as was the case with the business plan. Instead, budgets may be developed for cost centers as well as profit centers. For example, an internal distribution center or research laboratory would very likely have a budget of its own, but neither of these operations generates revenues for the organization. Even small businesses benefit from segmenting their operations for budgeting purposes.

An additional and complementary approach to segmenting the business for budgeting purposes is to employ a marketing perspective. Management may, for example, partition the business using the follow approaches:

- By location (geographic area)
- By type of customer
- By individual customer
- By marketing channel
- By product

The data organized in the budgets of these various market segments and the reports of actual sales can be analyzed to show any combinations of these variables that are of interest to management. Budgets are powerful managerial tools and for most organizations represent a primary mechanism for implementing strategy. General managers should use the budget process within the organization to address logically all aspects of the operations, disaggregating the budgets to do this in a meaningful way.

Budget Fundamentals

The annual plan or budget becomes the point of focus for most of the management and hourly employees for the coming year, and whether by design or not, the budget thus becomes a means of strategy implementation as all workers strive to follow its guidelines and achieve its goals. The annual plan, together with its supporting plans at various levels of the organization, will have been prepared during the third and fourth quarters of the preceding year. Ideally, all elements (estimates) and projections of the plan will have been agreed to by those who must bring about the results, regardless of their role in the plan's preparation. Thus, the sales forecasts will have been prepared by and/or agreed to by the sales and marketing organization. Similarly, scheduled productivity improvements will have been agreed to and endorsed by each affected unit or department manager, and so on. This describes what may be referred to as a "budgeting principle." The CEO or general manager will need to ensure that the budget he or she takes to the board of directors and the professional financial analysts is endorsed and supported by those who must "make the results happen."

A Spreadsheet for the Annual Plan or Budget

In the approach presented here, the budget for the coming year is subdivided into budgets for each quarter of the year. These "quarters" may be regular calendar quarters (January–March, and so on) or they may be "fiscal" quarters (as mentioned earlier), each consisting of thirteen calendar weeks, in the pattern of two four-week fiscal months followed by one five-week fiscal month.

A spreadsheet may be developed that subdivides the annual plan or budget into quarterly increments to facilitate control and corrective actions. There are numerous questions to be answered in this process of subdivision. Are seasonal or cyclical patterns of sales expected? At what point or points during the year will price changes be implemented? When, during the year, will planned capital expenses actually take place? Will working capital needs and related cash needs be smooth or erratic during the year?

The answers to these and other questions allow for the preparation of a quarterly worksheet for planning and control. The spreadsheet is similar to the business plan spreadsheet described in detail in Chapter 8, but the input data and the resulting financial statements show quarterly budgets along with the year-to-date totals.

Corporate Assumptions

The annual plan spreadsheet is initiated with the same set of corporate data and forecast assumptions about corporate expenses, the firm's capital plan, and its debt/equity structure as the business plan spreadsheet. These data are input for the year and subsequently subdivided to provide quarterly statements. The corporate data overlay the product information, that is, they are added to the sum of all the product data to produce the final, comprehensive corporate estimates for each quarter and for the year.

Quarterly Unit Sales Forecast

Exhibit 9-2 shows the forecast total unit sales for each product broken down into the expected sales for each quarter. As can be seen, the spreadsheet would allow for the insertion of any seasonal or cyclical pattern of unit sales. For illustrative purposes, the sample company, JL Inc., is assumed to have level quarterly sales.

Quarterly Unit Pricing Forecast

The expected price increases for the year are planned to take effect in the first quarter, as shown in Exhibit 9-3.

Quarterly Unit Cost Forecast

Similar to the pattern for price increases, all of the projected changes in costs and resource requirements are planned to take effect in the first quarter, as shown in Exhibit 9-4. (The spreadsheet should allow for the changes to take effect in any quarter.)

EXHIBIT 9-2   JL Inc. Quarterly Unit Sales Forecast

	Base Year	Year 1-1Q	Year 1-2Q	Year 1-3Q	Year 1-4Q	Year 1
Probable Case (in thousands of units)						
Product #1	36,500	10,494	10,494	10,494	10,494	41,975
Product #2	5,800	1,595	1,595	1,595	1,595	6,380
Total	42,300	12,089	12,089	12,089	12,089	48,355
Annual Growth Rates						
Product #1						15.0%
Product #2						10.0%
Total						14.3%
Quarterly Distribution (% of annual units sold)						
Product #1		25.0%	25.0%	25.0%	25.0%	
Product #2		25.0%	25.0%	25.0%	25.0%	
Product Mix %						
Product #1		86.8%	86.8%	86.8%	86.8%	86.8%
Product #2		13.2%	13.2%	13.2%	13.2%	13.2%

EXHIBIT 9-3   JL Inc. Quarterly Unit Pricing Forecast

		Probable Case				
	Base Year	Year 1-1Q	Year 1-2Q	Year 1-3Q	Year 1-4Q	Year 1
Unit Prices						
Product #1	$1.11	$1.18	$1.18	$1.18	$1.18	$1.18
Product #2	$3.47	$3.57	$3.57	$3.57	$3.57	$3.57
Annual % Increase/Decrease						
Product #1		7.0%	0.0%	0.0%	0.0%	7.0%
Product #2		3.0%	0.0%	0.0%	0.0%	3.0%

Projected Quarterly Financial Statements

Exhibits 9-5, 9-6, and 9-7 provide quarterly income statements, balance sheets, and cash flow statements for the annual plan or budget for Year 1. These statements provide the focus for all activities throughout all levels of the organization. As with a jigsaw puzzle, all of the relevant pieces of the business (sales, costs, assets, liabilities, and cash flows) must fit together to lead to a successful year.

Quarterly Performance Indicators

The indicators shown in Exhibit 9-8 allow management to detect any adverse trends in results early enough for timely corrective action to be taken. As described earlier in this chapter, numerous detailed plans and budgets for functional and market-based activities provide usable information related to successes and problems.

Suggested Actions Related to the Annual Plan or Budget

General managers should aim to start the new budget year with obvious, logical actions to get the year off to a good start. As part of this endeavor, the general manager, at the end of a year of strong performance, should take every possible ethical and legal action to defer sales into the next year and prepay expenses in order to begin the coming year with a solid head start on meeting the budgeted financial and strategic goals.

EXHIBIT 9-4   JL Inc. Quarterly Unit Cost Forecast

Probable Case—Product #1

	Base Year	Year 1-1Q	Year 1-2Q	Year 1-3Q	Year 1-4Q	Year 1
Material						
Cost ($/unit)	$0.28	$0.29	$0.29	$0.29	$0.29	$0.29
Labor Requirement						
(hours/unit)	0.005	0.005	0.005	0.005	0.005	0.005
Direct Labor						
Rate ($/hour)	$52.74	$55.38	$55.38	$55.38	$55.38	$55.38
Direct Labor						
Cost ($/unit)	$0.26	$0.28	$0.28	$0.28	$0.28	$0.28
Variable Overhead						
($/unit)	$0.25	$0.26	$0.26	$0.26	$0.26	$0.26
Total Cost						
per Unit	$0.79	$0.83	$0.83	$0.83	$0.83	$0.83
Annual % Increase/Decrease						
Material Cost		5.0%	0.0%	0.0%	0.0%	5.0%
Labor Requirement		0.0%	0.0%	0.0%	0.0%	0.0%
Direct Labor Rate		5.0%	0.0%	0.0%	0.0%	5.0%
Variable Overhead		5.0%	0.0%	0.0%	0.0%	5.0%
Total Cost per Unit						5.0%

Probable Case-Product #2

	Base Year	Year 1-1Q	Year 1-2Q	Year 1-3Q	Year 1-4Q	Year 1
Material Cost						
($/unit)	$1.58	$1.66	$1.66	$1.66	$1.66	$1.66
Labor Requirement						
(hours/unit)	0.016	0.013	0.013	0.013	0.013	0.013
Direct Labor Rate						
($/hour)	$43.70	$45.89	$45.89	$45.89	$45.89	$45.89
Direct Labor Cost						
($/unit)	$0.70	$0.59	$0.59	$0.59	$0.59	$0.59
Variable Overhead						
($/unit)	$0.25	$0.26	$0.26	$0.26	$0.26	$0.26
Total Cost per Unit	$2.53	$2.51	$2.51	$2.51	$2.51	$2.51
Contribution						
Margin per Unit	26.9%	29.6%	29.6%	29.6%	29.6%	29.6%
Annual % Increase/Decrease						
Material Cost		5.0%	0.0%	0.0%	0.0%	5.0%
Labor Requirement		−20.0%	0.0%	0.0%	0.0%	−20.0%
Direct Labor Rate		5.0%	0.0%	0.0%	0.0%	5.0%
Variable Overhead		5.0%	0.0%	0.0%	0.0%	5.0%
Total Cost per Unit						−0.8%

EXHIBIT 9-5 JL Inc. Projected Quarterly Income Statement

			Probable Case ($ in millions)			
	Base year	Year 1-1Q	Year 1-2Q	Year 1-3Q	Year 1-4Q	Year 1
Sales	$60.439	$18.103	$18.103	$18.103	$18.103	$72.410
Cost of Goods Sold						
Material	$19.261	$5.694	$5.694	$5.694	$5.694	$22.776
Labor	$13.681	$3.843	$3.843	$3.843	$3.843	$15.370
Variable						
Overhead	$10.624	$3.188	$3.188	$3.188	$3.188	$12.752
Fixed						
Overhead	$8.163	$2.102	$2.102	$2.102	$2.102	$8.408
Depreciation	$1.175	$0.465	$0.465	$0.465	$0.465	$1.859
Total Cost						
of Goods Sold	$52.905	$15.291	$15.291	$15.291	$15.291	$61.165
Gross Margin	$7.534	$2.811	$2.811	$2.811	$2.811	$11.245
Selling, General & Administrative						
Sales Expense	$0.604	$0.181	$0.181	$0.181	$0.181	$0.724
G&A Expense	$1.567	$0.411	$0.411	$0.411	$0.411	$1.646
Total SG&A	$2.172	$0.592	$0.592	$0.592	$0.592	$2.370
Operating Income	$5.363	$2.219	$2.219	$2.219	$2.219	$8.876
Corporate						
Overhead	$0.907	$0.272	$0.272	$0.272	$0.272	$1.086
Gain/Loss on						
Sale of Assets	$0.000	$0.502	$0.000	$0.000	$0.000	$0.502
Interest Income	$0.199	$0.055	$0.060	$0.070	$0.091	$0.276
Interest Expense	$0.873	$0.256	$0.275	$0.263	$0.280	$1.074
Other Income	$2.512	$0.628	$0.628	$0.628	$0.628	$2.512
Profit Before Tax	$6.294	$2.876	$2.360	$2.382	$2.387	$10.005
Income Tax	($2.203)	($1.007)	($0.826)	($0.834)	($0.835)	($3.502)
Net Income	$4.091	$1.869	$1.534	$1.548	$1.551	$6.503
EBITDA[1]	$5.631	$2.412	$2.412	$2.412	$2.412	$9.648

[1]EBITDA = Operating Income + Depreciation − Corporate Overhead

Not all years get off to a good start, however. As a general rule, many successful general managers conclude that if revenues are more than 10 percent below forecast levels by the end of February (or the second month of a fiscal year) it is very unlikely that the shortfall will be recovered to meet the original annual plan, unless they are aware of some specific industry

EXHIBIT 9-6   JL Inc. Projected Quarterly Balance Sheet

Probable Case ($ in millions)

	Base Year	Year 1-1Q	Year 1-2Q	Year 1-3Q	Year 1
Excess Cash	$0.000	$0.000	$0.000	$2.798	$5.610
Operating Cash	$6.648	$7.965	$7.965	$7.965	$7.965
Total Cash	$6.648	$7.965	$7.965	$10.763	$13.575
Accounts Receivable	$1.784	$2.172	$2.172	$2.172	$2.172
Inventory					
Raw Materials	$2.913	$3.419	$3.419	$3.419	$3.419
Work-In-Progress	$2.286	$2.636	$2.636	$2.636	$2.636
Finished Goods	$4.873	$5.271	$5.271	$5.271	$5.271
Total Inventory	$10.072	$11.326	$11.326	$11.326	$11.326
Total Current Assets	$18.504	$21.464	$21.464	$24.261	$27.074
Gross Fixed Assets	$20.093	$20.595	$20.595	$20.595	$20.595
Accum. Depreciation	$7.535	$4.986	$5.450	$5.915	$6.379
Net Fixed Assets	$12.558	$15.610	$15.145	$14.680	$14.216
Other Assets	$2.512	$2.548	$2.586	$2.624	$2.662
Total Assets	$33.573	$39.622	$39.194	$41.565	$43.952
Accounts Payable	$2.392	$2.765	$2.765	$2.765	$2.765
Net Assets	$31.182	$36.857	$36.429	$38.800	$41.187
Debt	$10.914	$14.719	$12.758	$13.580	$14.415
Equity	$20.268	$22.138	$23.672	$25.220	$26.771
Debt/Total Capital	35.0%	39.9%	35.0%	35.0%	35.0%

conditions that might rescue the firm from the situation. Action should be taken in these circumstances to immediately alert senior management to the threat to achieving previously committed/budgeted results, so that corrective action can be taken to salvage the committed results to the extent possible, and to prepare a new plan that reflects the best-achievable results.

It is thus better to start over with a new budget that takes into consideration the new circumstances. If the general manager were to wait several months to take action, the organization would not have enough time left in the year for any feasible cost reductions to have the desired effect. A delay in taking appropriate action therefore compounds the deleterious effect of the drop in revenues and requires more extreme cost-reduction measures.

EXHIBIT 9-7   JL Inc. Projected Cash Flow Statement

	Probable Case ($ in millions)				
	Year 1-1Q	Year 1-2Q	Year 1-3Q	Year 1-4Q	Year 1
Net Income	$1.869	$1.534	$1.548	$1.551	$6.503
Depreciation	$0.465	$0.465	$0.465	$0.465	$1.859
Gain/Loss on Sale of Assets	($0.502)	$0.000	$0.000	$0.000	($0.502)
Change in Receivables	($0.388)	$0.000	$0.000	$0.000	($0.388)
Change in Inventory	($1.255)	$0.000	$0.000	$0.000	($1.255)
Change in Payables & Accruals	($0.373)	$0.000	$0.000	$0.000	($0.373)
Cash Flow From Operations	$0.562	$1.999	$2.013	$2.016	$6.590
Additions to Gross Fixed Assets	($4.019)	$0.000	$0.000	$0.000	($4.019)
Sale of Fixed Assets	$1.005	$0.000	$0.000	$0.000	($1.005)
Change in Other Assets	($0.037)	($0.037)	($0.038)	($0.039)	($0.151)
Cash Flow after Investing	($2.489)	$1.961	$1.975	$1.977	$3.425
Change in Debt	$3.805	($1.961)	$0.822	$0.835	$3.502
Cash Flow after Financing	$1.317	($0.000)	$2.798	$2.813	$6.927

Flexible or Variable Budgets

Many companies routinely employ an accounting technique known as flexible or variable budgeting. Flexible budgets are prepared based on the most likely or expected set of revenues and reasonable estimates of variable costs and fixed expenses, but are subsequently adjusted for actual changes in sales volume. The budgeted amounts for variable expenses then reflect the volume changes and allow actual expenses to be compared effectively to the adjusted budgeted amounts, revealing relative performance of the operating units. A major principle of flexible budgets is that these automatic adjustments are normally recommended only for changes in volume of less than 10 percent. The conventional wisdom is

EXHIBIT 9-8   JL Inc. Quarterly Performance Indicators

			Probable Case			
	Base Year	Year 1-1Q	Year 1-2Q	Year 1-3Q	Year 1-4Q	Year 1
Asset Turnover	1.80x	1.83x	1.85x	1.74x	1.65x	1.65x
Operating Income Return on:						
Sales	8.9%	12.3%	12.3%	12.3%	12.3%	12.3%
Assets	16.0%	22.4%	22.6%	21.4%	20.2%	20.2%
Net Assets	17.2%	24.1%	24.4%	22.9%	21.5%	21.5%
Net Income Return on:						
Sales	6.8%	10.3%	8.5%	8.6%	8.6%	9.0%
Assets	12.2%	18.9%	15.7%	14.9%	14.1%	14.8%
Net Assets	13.1%	20.3%	16.8%	16.0%	15.1%	15.8%
Equity	20.2%	33.8%	25.9%	24.6%	23.2%	24.3%
Cash Flow from Operations After Capital Expenditures ($ MM)						$2.57
Annual Growth Rates						
Sales						19.8%
Assets						30.9%
Operating Income						65.5%
Net Income						59.0%

that when changes to the budgeted volume exceed 10 percent, the budget should be rebuilt completely. This approach would allow for adjustments in semi-fixed costs to accommodate the more substantial changes in scale.

Projecting the Future

As described above, the budget is subdivided into three-month periods referred to as quarters. It has become common practice for the CEOs and general managers of publicly traded companies to publicly announce—usually before an audience of professional financial analysts— the expected financial results for future periods, typically the next quarter. The estimates provided usually include revenues and net income, often expressed as earnings per share. A great deal of emphasis is placed on these projections by the investment professionals and the CEO. As discussed earlier, the accuracy of these projections either reinforces or diminishes the credibility of the CEO. If the company subsequently meets the projections, the investment community will likely attribute the accuracy of the forecasts to a strong, fundamental understanding of the company's capabilities on the part of the CEO and a high degree of management control over the numerous factors that influence corporate performance.

The Focus on Quarterly Results

As described in Vignette 4-1 (Chapter 4), the focus on quarterly results as key measures of corporate performance emanates from the requirement that these data be submitted to the Securities and Exchange Commission (SEC) by all public companies. The professional financial analysts are thus obliged to take the available data into consideration in assessing the CEO's grasp of the business's issues and the apparent degree of effective management control. The focus on quarterly financial results of public companies has its roots in controls put in place by the SEC to ensure that the investing public remains informed about a company's performance.

Summary

These vignettes and anecdotes illustrate the close scrutiny under which CEOs and general managers must function. Over time, executives create a reputation for both the knowledge of their businesses and the degree of control they have in place, which serves as a formidable asset in maintaining value in and loyalty to the organization's public shares. Knowledge and control are derived from the disciplined work of managers within the organization to create and execute plans, especially the annual plan. The process described in this part of the book delineates details required to produce first a strategic plan, then a business plan (with more specific details for, say, three years), and finally an annual plan or budget that provides for effective short-term action steps that lead ultimately to the achievement of the strategic goals.

General managers achieve high performance over the long term through the careful crafting and successful execution of a series of annual plans.

DISCUSSION QUESTIONS

1. How does the annual plan or budget relate to the first year of the business plan?
2. What is the utility of providing quarterly forecasts of all key input data and the resulting financial statements?
3. How does management determine when the existing annual plan or budget should be revised?
4. Which of the quarterly results should the general manager closely monitor?
5. How should the general manager divide his or her time between monitoring current-year results and planning for the future?

III

ANALYTICAL CONCEPTS FOR
THE GENERAL MANAGER

Part I of this book describes the roles and tasks of general managers and the economic and organizational context within which these activities take place. Part II covers the strategic planning process from the initial impetus for clarity propounded by the investment community (the sources of capital) to the preparation of the annual plan or budget, which provides a detailed plan of action for the organization in the immediate future. Part IV covers the detailed topics related to the numerous ways in which general managers take action.

"Analytical Concepts for the General Manager," is inserted between Parts II and IV to describe the methodologies that would be useful to the general manager in both planning and taking action. Part III includes the following:

- Chapter 10: The Business Model
  Three primary structural variables constitute the business model: the profit structure of the business, the capital intensity of the business, and the prevailing economies of scale.

- Chapter 11: The Relationship between Cash Flow and Growth
  This chapter presents analytical relationships between a firm's growth and cash flow. These relationships provide tools that assist in the process of developing feasible, self-reinforcing sets of operating goals, and in making efficient trade-offs among conflicting objectives.

- Chapter 12: Product, Marketing, and Pricing Strategies
  Management at the corporate or profit-center level must assess the relative performance of the three basic business functions: marketing, engineering, and manufacturing or operations. This chapter discusses the product, marketing, and pricing strategies that must be properly synchronized with the cost base if a business is to be "properly controlled" from a top-level standpoint.

- Chapter 13: Relating Productivity and Firm Growth
  The conceptual underpinnings of a strategic emphasis on employee productivity are addressed in this chapter. All-important behavioral aspects of managing the workforce are also discussed, including relevant, potential influencers of the inclination of employees either to resist attempts to improve productivity or to assist willingly and energetically in achieving productivity gains.

- Chapter 14: Residual Income, EVA, and Corporate Capital Charges
  The performance of a profit center can be evaluated using return-on-investment measures, a ratio of profit to investment, or through various forms of residual income measures. Chapter 14 discusses both approaches to evaluating financial performance, with the specific aim of relating the earnings of a division to the investment required to generate those earnings.

- Chapter 15: The Allocation (Redeployment) of Capital (Cash)
  The allocation of available and anticipated levels of cash to strategic and operational initiatives constitutes one of the most important duties of the general manager. A firm begins competing with a prescribed capital structure consisting of a combination of debt and equity. This chapter stresses the great strategic value attributable to a strong balance sheet.

- Chapter 16: Share Repurchases
  Share repurchases have become a widely used strategic tool for U.S. corporations. Many highly regarded companies regularly buy back their shares as a matter of policy. This chapter explores the reasons why corporations repurchase shares, how share repurchase plans are implemented, and the implications of those plans. Analytical methodologies are presented that allow for

the calculation of the likely effect of share repurchases on share prices.

The tools and techniques described in the chapters in Part III will be of use to general managers in strategic planning, taking action, and control activities.

10

THE BUSINESS MODEL

The general manager has the responsibility to operate a business to maximize long-term shareholder value for the investors. Profit is the reward for successfully creating or attracting customers; the potential for profit attracts investors; and the realization of profit (or expected realization of profit) ultimately increases shareholder value. The general manager must therefore translate the intent to satisfy customers into a viable financial framework, given the business model of the firm.

The organization sets goals and objectives based on measurable results to guide management and the organization to create value. Goals typically encompass aims for profits, return on investment, cash flow, growth (in revenues and profit), and stability (or predictability) of results. A sound capital structure of the business is also an underlying aim, and is often captured by the ratio of long-term debt to owners' equity. The achievement of these objectives, individually and collectively, is the primary task of the general manager. Their realization, though, often requires that trade-offs be made among the several objectives. For instance, trade-offs normally must be made between cash flow and growth, which is demonstrated in Chapter 11. Similarly, the pursuit of growth may require the acquisition of expanded facilities that require capital investments and will usually have a deleterious effect on the goal of return on investment, at least in the near term. This chapter discusses a number of financial and accounting concepts, collectively called the business model, which relate to the various elements of the financial workings of the firm. Here, we use the exhibits presented in Chapter 8 in the business plan to illustrate the business model for the hypothetical company JL Inc.

Financial Prerequisites for Success

In order for a business to be viable over the long term, it must satisfy two critical financial requirements. First, the business must be adequately capitalized (funded); that is, it must have the capital resources to support its operations, given the strategies and the nature of the business (cyclical, rapid growth, and the like). Second, the business must be profitable. This means that the business must be capable of producing a level of profitability consistent with the goals of its investors and lenders (the suppliers of equity and debt), and with the risk inherent in its chosen product/market segments.

The business model, mentioned briefly in earlier chapters, is a complex system of interrelated parts that must function in harmony with one another for the business to succeed. The business model as described here consists of the following basic elements:

- The profit structure of the business
- The potential for return on investment
- The inherent cash flow
- The availability of growth (in revenues and profit)
- The stability (predictability) of results

The business model also is highly dependent on the following two factors that characterize every industry to some extent:

- The degree of capital intensity of the business
- The economies of scale prevalent in the industry

The success or failure of the general manager will be determined in large part by his or her ability to manage the trade-offs inherent in the drivers of the business model to achieve the desired results. We discuss identified elements of the business model below.

The Profit Structure of the Business

The relationship between selling prices and costs determines the basic level of profitability attainable in an industry. A general manager may have the market power to charge premium prices that lead to advantageous profit margins on sales. In other situations, it may be impossible to differentiate a firm's product and the selling prices will be set in the marketplace. Profits for all competitors in such industries will then be determined by achievable costs. The profit structure is largely determined by the relationships among the following key attributes, which characterize the competitive arena:

- Pricing
- Costs and cost control
- Contribution to overhead and profit

Pricing

Prices are a primary determinant of the top line of the business's income statement, and pricing decisions are among the most important determinations the general manager makes. A conventional approach to pricing is to base prices on costs, with some level of markup incorporated to allow a profit to be made. Other basic principles related to the pricing of the firm's products or services are explored below.

PRICE LEVELS ARE INFLUENCED BY THE MARKETPLACE The general manager must analyze the prices charged by competitors, determine a response to those prices, and, finally, assess the reactions of customers to any pricing change implemented. Naturally, no firm aims to consistently sell goods or services at prices below its direct costs because the firm would lose money on every sale. In contrast, nearly all firms would enjoy a situation where the market permitted a high price relative to prevailing costs due to either cost efficiency or customer perception of product superiority relative to offerings of competitors. Recall that these two situations represent the benefits of competitive advantage. An astute general manager constantly monitors and judiciously tests the market to determine the most advantageous selling price in order to maximize profits over the long term. When the opportunity arises to charge premium prices, management should try to take advantage of the situation with all due haste, as the availability of such pricing opportunities normally attracts competition.

Referring to Exhibit 8-2, we see that JL Inc. is forecasting price increases greater than inflation (6 or 7 percent) for Product 1 and increases approximately equal to inflation (3 percent) for Product 2. The general manager of JL Inc. thus believes that pricing flexibility exists for Product 1 and the market price must be met for Product 2.

BEWARE OF AVERAGE PRICING   Managers should be careful in their pricing strategies when considering the notion of average pricing. When an "average price" is applied across the collective set of products or services, it results in the collection meeting some target profit level. Using this approach results in charging more for some items than prevailing costs would require and rejecting other orders that would be attractive at lower prices. If the costs of different products vary, average pricing will hurt the profitability of the total product mix. The average price is also relatively low for those products that have higher than average costs, thereby attracting less profitable volume. Use of average prices thus tends to erode a firm's competitive position at both ends of the pricing/cost spectrum.

CREDIT STRATEGY   A company's credit strategy is related to its pricing strategy, as the availability of credit influences the purchasing decisions of customers, including the prices they are willing to pay. In addition to deciding whether or not to issue credit—and if so, under what terms— management must also determine the credit risks that will be taken so that bad debt write-offs are contained within acceptable bounds and collection efforts are cost effective. Managers, however, should always be vigilant that credit facilitates sustainable sales practices; credit should not be used to meet sales growth targets or to meet unrealistic expectations.

Costs and Cost Control

THE COST STRUCTURE   A key attribute of the business model is the distribution of costs between those that are variable (directly related to transactions or volume) and those that are fixed (related to the productive capacity of the business). The greater the proportion of costs that are fixed, the greater variations in volume will affect profitability, thus making accurate volume forecasts crucial to success. The projected income statements for JL Inc. (Exhibit 8-5) show that the preponderance of costs are variable with low levels of fixed costs. This would imply that the company's profitability is not overly sensitive to volume changes.

A business model with prohibitively high costs usually results in lower sales and weak financial results for the organization. When this is the case, the marketplace has indicated that the firm is not cost competitive. JL Inc.'s performance indicators shown in Exhibit 8-8 indicate strong performance relative to all desirable performance measures, so there is no evidence that the company has cost problems. The nuances of the interaction of intended product or service quality levels and relative costs and prices are discussed in some detail later in Chapter 12.

COST CONTROL   Controlling costs has a direct effect on a firm's profitability, and crucial areas of cost control include efficiency, the rates of spending, and capital costs. Efficiency implies managing operations in order to consume the least possible amount of inputs—including purchased materials, energy, and labor—for a given level of output. Note that Exhibit 8-3, the unit cost forecast for JL Inc., shows labor requirements are expected to remain constant for Product 1 and actually improve (reduce) for Product 2 over the three-year planning horizon. This implies constant labor efficiency for Product 1 and improving efficiency for Product 2.

Spending is controlled by managing the rates (prices) paid for the required inputs, such as materials and labor, consistent with quality and skill requirements. Referring again to Exhibit 8-3, JL Inc.'s material costs, direct labor costs, and variable overhead costs are forecast to escalate 5 percent per year for each product.

Capital costs are minimized by effectively managing capacity (physical capacity and overhead costs), the credit function (receivables), and inventory, given the volume demanded by customers. The cash flow statements for JL Inc. in Exhibit 8-7 show additions to gross fixed assets approximately equal to depreciation over Years 2 and 3, with Year 1 showing $4 million in planned additions and only $2 million in depreciation, most likely to expand capacity to accommodate expected growth. Working capital (receivables plus inventories less payables) is forecast to grow in proportion to sales growth.

UNIT COSTS AND VOLUME VARIATION An effective cost accounting system can usually determine the direct cost of a unit of output with reasonable accuracy. For the price of a product, however, relevant overhead costs must also be considered. Cost accountants make strong efforts to allocate overhead costs as accurately as possible, but the resulting cost estimates are valid only for the prevailing allocation assumptions.

The primary challenge in setting price based on costs is to determine the volume on which to base the allocation of overhead costs. Higher estimates of volume will reduce the estimated overhead cost per unit, and lower volumes will increase the estimates. An important question for the general manager then becomes, "How much volume is needed to arrive at a competitive unit cost?"

ACCURACY OF OVERHEAD ALLOCATIONS Aside from the impact of volume variances, the choice of overhead allocation methods also creates costing problems. Popular ways of allocating overheads include the following:

- Occupancy costs for facilities are often allocated based on usage (square feet of space, for instance).
- Supervisory and administrative costs are usually allocated based on head count or payroll (because they are personnel driven).
- Selling costs are normally allocated based on sales volume (which assumes that all sales have the same selling costs).

For numerous reasons, use of these types of allocation has the potential to produce misleading cost estimates. Refinements may make the estimates more accurate. For instance, overheads may be divided into direct and indirect segments, per accounting guidelines, and the direct overhead of different locations may be allocated appropriately to the relevant sales or production volume. Separate departments may also have varying direct overheads, all with the intent of allocating overhead costs as accurately as possible.

THE VALUE OF VOLUME Rather than expending major efforts allocating overhead costs to lower levels of the organization, or to low-volume products or services, managers may find it more useful to think in terms of the incremental value of volume. A given amount of sales volume is more valuable to the firm if it produces a larger contribution (revenues minus direct costs), which may also be captured by the product's contribution margin (the percentage of revenues that is not attributable to direct costs). When price elasticity is present, unit sales for a given product vary with price and, consequently, the dollar value of contribution varies as well. As a result, the general manager must search for that combination of unit price and resulting unit volume that creates the greatest dollar contribution.

Contribution to Overhead and Profit

Management's use of the contribution concept minimizes the need for cost allocations. With this concept, instead of trying to determine the full cost of a product or service, management's goal becomes one of maximizing contribution. In adopting this approach, management recognizes that the total contribution must cover all overhead and capital costs before the business can become profitable. If the business cannot generate sufficient contribution, the overhead costs and capital costs must be reduced. The relationship between total contribution and total overhead costs (including capital costs) becomes a critical ratio in evaluating the profit potential of the business. Managers should be wary to avoid using contribution to improve returns on capital investments and should take a very strict, objective view on the economic costs of overhead expenses.

Generally Accepted Accounting Principles (GAAP) and the tax laws require that manufacturing overhead costs be included in inventory valuation for purposes of calculating taxable income, reinforcing the need for cost allocations. But managers cannot simply rely on accounting figures to assist in making managerial decisions. The contribution concept is an internal (to the company) management decision-making tool that requires skillful adjustment of accounting numbers to reflect economic reality.

The Potential for Return on Investment

The degree of capital intensity within a firm or an industry is defined as the amount of capital investment required to produce a dollar of sales. It is axiomatic that the greater the asset intensity of an industry, the more difficult it is to earn high returns on assets. Thus, companies competing in industries that are very asset intensive often attempt to offset this disadvantage by pricing to gain higher returns on sales (higher margins), negotiating with customers to secure progress payments, and securing high degrees of financial leverage (debt) in their capital structures.

JL Inc.'s projected balance sheets (Exhibit 8-6) and performance indicators (Exhibit 8-8) show a healthy asset turnover ratio and strong returns on assets, net assets, and equity. The return on equity is seen to be above 20 percent, placing JL Inc. in the range of companies that would be considered "premium." Note that the strong return on equity (greater than 24 percent) is forecast in spite of the expected accumulation of $31 million of excess cash over the three years. The excess cash contributes relatively low amounts to profit levels owing to the low rate of interest income (3 percent) earned on excess cash.

The Incremental Cost of Debt

In general, the greater the leverage (the ratio of debt to total capital), the higher the likely interest rate on the debt, since adding debt increases the financial risk of the firm. The example in Exhibit 10-1 illustrates the high cost of incremental debt for a hypothetical company as it moves toward a more debt-heavy capital structure. The cost of the additional $50,000 of debt is not 10 percent but 12.5 percent. After determining the incremental cost of the additional debt, the manager should compare that rate to the expected rate of return on the associated investment.

EXHIBIT 10-1   The Incremental Cost of Additional Debt

	Capital Structure A	Capital Structure B	Difference
Capital	$100,000	$100,000	$0
Debt	$25,000	$75,000	+$50,000
Interest Rate	5%	10%	5%
Interest Cost	$1,250	$7,500	+$6,250
Incremental Cost of Additional Debt			12.5%

JL Inc. enjoys the relatively low borrowing rate of 8 percent as a result of its strong balance sheet, which maintains a 35 percent debt-to-total-capital ratio. JL Inc.'s CEO would be on the lookout for growth opportunities, including acquisitions and other investment opportunities, in which to employ the accumulating excess cash to the greatest benefit of the company.

The Capital Structure

The distribution of the invested capital of a business between debt and equity defines the capital structure of a firm. The capital structure usually determines the allocation of income, risk, and control among the equity holders (shareholders in public companies) and debt holders. Without any debt, all income belongs to the owners; they take all of the risk, and they have all of the control. Creditors, who lend money to the firm, gain a share of the income, assume some of the risk, and through the terms of any exacting debt agreements, may assume some control. Owners obviously want to shift as much risk to the lenders as possible for the lowest cost (typically the interest rate), while conceding as little control as possible.

There are several important principles related to the funding of the capital structure of a business. First, operating cash flows should ideally be a reliable source of funding. A key strategic consideration is the portion of the cash flows that must be reinvested in the business to maintain or grow operations. As discussed briefly earlier and in more detail in Chapter 11, the operational cash flows will support a sustainable growth rate (or cash-balancing growth rate). This is the growth rate above which the business would need additional capital investment, either debt or equity. The methodology described in Chapter 11 allows for the calculation of the approximate cash available or required for any rate of growth.

An examination of the financial statements of JL Inc. reveals that the company has and is expected to maintain over the planning horizon a strong balance sheet and a financial structure that allows growth at the expected rate and the simultaneous generation of a great deal of cash.

Second, managing cash requires effective skills in forecasting cash flows, both inflows and outflows. The ideal is for a business to produce free cash flow, cash above the amount required for reinvestment (capital appropriations), debt service, and from which dividend payments may be made to

EXHIBIT 10-2   The Sources of Funding for Various Classes of Assets

Asset	Funding
Seasonal Working Capital	100% short-term debt
Permanent Working Capital	100% equity
Fixed Assets	New: 50 to 100% long-term debt
	Old: Move toward 100% equity

shareholders. As shown in JL Inc.'s forecast cash flow statements (Exhibit 8-7), the company expects to generate increasing levels of free cash flow over the planning horizon.

Third, the nature of the assets determines an appropriate type of capital structure. Short-term liabilities should be matched with short-term liquid assets. Longer-term assets should be funded with longer-term debt, when needed. This logic leads to the types of guidelines described in Exhibit 10-2. This is not an issue for JL Inc. because of its very strong balance sheet.

A vital concern for the management of any organization with leverage is whether the debt can be repaid in the normal course of conducting business. Seasonal working capital requirements should be self-liquidating at the end of the relevant season. Debt on fixed assets may be serviced with cash flow from depreciation tax benefits and/or earnings. Cash flow and the scheduled maturities of debt determine the amount of debt a business can afford. The coverage ratio of cash flow to debt service, which includes interest and principal, is critical to the survival of a business. Again, JL Inc. avoids these issues with its advantageous cash flows and capital structure.

The Cost of Capital

In nearly every business, the general manager must thoroughly understand the cost of capital, which is commonly recognized to consist of a weighted average of the cost of debt and the cost of equity. Financial texts provide extensive detail on this topic. The cost of debt is the interest rate the organization pays on its borrowings. Because interest expense is tax deductible, for a profitable business, the cost of debt is the after-tax interest rate. For an unprofitable business that is paying no taxes, the cost is the full, before-tax interest rate. As an example, the cost of debt for JL Inc. is .08 or 8 percent, the interest rate on its current debt and any new debt.

Determining the cost of equity is more complex. It is essentially the return that investors would expect in exchange for providing capital to a given company for a specified share of ownership, essentially their personal judgment as to the risk/reward relationship for the specific firm and its management. For example, the cost of equity might be the expected rate of return (15 percent) demanded by investors from the purchase of stock at the current market value.

The overall cost of capital for the firm is the blended (average) cost of debt and equity, based on the prevailing long-term capital structure. Management has a great deal of discretion as to how this somewhat arbitrary number (the cost of capital) is calculated. Management uses the cost of capital in evaluating the attractiveness of investment opportunities, such as new products, production facilities, and capital equipment. JL Inc. would enjoy a relatively low cost of capital, and its performance would lead to a strong rating by financial analysts.

The Inherent Cash Flow

We review below the results of JL Inc. to provide insights regarding the three remaining performance attributes: cash flow, growth in revenues and profits, and stability of results.

As we see from an examination of JL Inc.'s business plan, the numerous internal financial structures and competitive factors related to the company combine to produce expected cash flows adequate to finance the expected internal (organic) growth, including unit sales growth and price increases. In addition to funding expected growth, the expansive cash generation will lead to ever-increasing levels of excess cash available for further expansions of product lines or the acquisition of additional businesses. The general manager would not want to preside indefinitely over large cash balances that lower the returns of the company, and therefore would ideally search for more efficient avenues for deployment or return the excess cash to shareholders.

The Availability of Growth (in Revenues and Profits)

Unit sales for JL Inc. are expected to grow over the planning horizon by 15 percent per year for Product 1 and 10 percent per year for Product 2. Given the strong current and forecast financial performance of JL Inc., it is reasonable to assume that either JL is growing more rapidly than its market and is thus capturing market share from competitors, or it is growing at the market rate, maintaining share, and has no capability to increase share. In either case, because there is no financial impediment to further growth in the two current products, we may assume that the general manager must look elsewhere for additional growth. The general manager likely will find it a challenge to expand further without diluting some performance metrics, as the company currently is expected to grow sales by 19 percent, operating income by almost 50 percent, and net income by greater than 40 percent.

The Stability (Predictability) of Results

All of the financial statements developed in JL Inc.'s business plan reflect the successful operation of a growing, profitable, stable, and steadily improving organization, suggesting that the company is well managed. As we can see from JL Inc.'s projected balance sheets (Exhibit 8-6), the company's commendable success will be confronted by the growing need to find advantageous ways to invest the rapidly accumulating excess cash. This reinforces the strategic imperative that success is closely followed by its recurring challenges.

The Degree of Capital Intensity of the Business

As described above, JL Inc. does not appear to have any discernible problems with capital intensity. It has relatively favorable asset turnover ratios, low fixed costs, low borrowing rates that result from its strong balance sheets, and favorable and increasing profit margins.

Economies of Scale

This well-known concept from economics defines for any industry the demonstrated minimum size a business has to achieve to enjoy competitive unit costs, as well as the maximum size a business unit may reach before reverse economies (or diseconomies) of scale set in (unit costs rise with further increases in size). A firm will have difficulty competing effectively over the long term in an industry with pronounced scale economies if it operates at a smaller scale and thus has higher relative costs. The general manager must ensure that his or her firm has the requisite scale of operations to maintain an adequate business model. Economies of scale are discussed further in Chapter 13. JL Inc. does not appear to have any problems related to scale economies.

Summary

Understanding financial fundamentals is quite obviously a critical success factor for any general manager. Regardless of the CEO's background, he or she must be cognizant of the financial implications of the prevailing business model. The economic engine must function reasonably smoothly for a business to maintain viability and fulfill its mission over time. JL Inc. is currently benefiting from the strong "condition" and "momentum" created by its past successful strategies and strong current operations. In order to continue to grow and prosper, it must devise new strategies for gainfully employing its rapidly increasing base of assets and debt capacity.

DISCUSSION QUESTIONS

1. What is a business model, and what are its key elements?
2. Why is pricing strategy so important to profitability?
3. What are the elements of cost control?
4. What is meant by the incremental cost of debt?

11

THE RELATIONSHIP BETWEEN
CASH FLOW AND GROWTH[1]

A corporate manager attempts to achieve a pattern of improving operating results that are predictable from year to year. A number of different criteria are used to measure financial performance, including the levels of profit or cash flow and the growth rate of sales, assets, or profits. This chapter presents analytical relationships between a firm's growth rate and cash flow. These relationships provide tools that assist in the process of developing feasible, self-reinforcing sets of operating goals, and in making efficient trade-offs among competing objectives. The computing technology available today makes the generation of pro forma financial statements a straightforward exercise. For the purpose of strategic planning, however, it is often helpful to utilize the key quantitative relationships to provide rapid estimates of the likely major consequences of various strategic alternatives.

Projecting cash requirements is essential for developing a capital structure that assures adequate funds for a growing company. Too often, a firm that is growing rapidly and profitably will run out of cash. If a firm becomes illiquid, it usually has difficulty getting new funds and the cost may be very high. And, if it doesn't obtain the funds, it may have to declare bankruptcy to restructure its balance sheet.

The Relationship between Cash Flow and Growth for a Corporation

As an example, the firm with the following financial situation is approaching the end of an operating period and is planning for the next period. Exhibit 11-1 shows the expected end-of-period balance sheet and the anticipated income statement.

Using this example company, we develop the options available for cash flow and growth based on the following assumptions:

1. The firm maintains a constant debt-to-equity ratio.
2. The firm maintains a constant dividend-payout percentage.
3. Profit before tax, current assets, current liabilities, fixed assets, and other assets change with the growth rate in sales.
4. Depreciation is reinvested in fixed assets.

EXHIBIT 11-1   The Expected Balance Sheet and Income Statement

Expected Balance Sheet at End of the Current Period

Cash	$25	Accounts Payable	$50
Accounts Receivable	$75	Accrued Taxes	$50
Inventories	$75	Current Liabilities	$100
Current Assets	$175		
Net Fixed Assets	$200	Debt	$150
Other Assets	$25	Equity	$150
Total Assets	$400	Total Liabilities + Owners' Equity(OE)	$400

Expected Income Statement for the Period

Sales	$500
Cost of Goods Sold	$400
Gross Margin	$100
General and Administrative (G&A) Expense	$20
Interest Expense	$20
Profit Before Tax	$60
Tax	$30
Profit After Tax	$30
Dividends Paid	$5

Other Data Needed Are as Follows:
Depreciation rate = 10% of beginning fixed assets
Dividend-payout ratio = 16.67%

EXHIBIT 11-2   The General Form of the Cash Flow Statement

Cash-Flow Statement	
Profit after Tax	+
Depreciation	+
Change in Cash	−
Change in Accounts Receivable	−
Change in Inventories	−
Fixed-asset Additions	−
Change in Other Assets	−
Change in Accounts Payable	+
Change in Accrued Taxes	+
Dividends Paid	−
Additional Debt	±
Cash Flow	Total

The Cash Flow-Growth Relationship

If the firm grew with an actual growth rate,[2] G, in the next period, the general form of the cash flow would be as shown in Exhibit 11-2.[3]

With this cash-flow statement, we can develop a general expression for cash flow as a function of G, Equation 1.

$$CF = (EBIT - I)(1 - t)(1 - DPO\%)(1 + G)\left(1 + \frac{D}{E}\right) - NA_oG \qquad (1)$$

Where:

$$
\begin{aligned}
\text{Lowercase o} &= \text{Beginning-of-period value} \\
CF &= \text{Cash flow} \\
EBIT &= \text{Earnings before interest and taxes (previous} \\
&\quad \text{period; assumed positive)} \\
G &= \text{Actual growth rate} \\
I &= \text{Interest expense on beginning debt} \\
t &= \text{Tax rate} \\
DPO\% &= \text{Dividend-payout percentage; } 1 - DPO\% = \% \text{ of} \\
&\quad \text{Profit Retained} \\
NA &= \text{Net Assets} \\
D &= \text{Debt} \\
E &= \text{Equity (assumed positive)}
\end{aligned}
$$

This equation provides for the direct calculation of cash flow for any anticipated growth rate. Suppose we are interested in the cash-balancing growth rate (that is, the rate at which the cash generated would just equal the additional cash needed to finance the expanded operations).

Substituting the values from the example above yields:

$$\text{Cash flow} = 50 - 250G$$

Setting cash flow equal to zero, and solving for G:

$$0 = 50 - 250G$$
$$G = .20$$

Given the negative, linear relationship between cash flow and growth, we can graph a schedule for the firm:

Growth rate	−.10	0	.10	.20	.30	.40	.50
Cash flow		75	50	25	0	−25	−50	−75

These data are plotted in Exhibit 11-3.

It is apparent that if market conditions don't permit growth at the 20 percent/year rate, or if management chooses to grow more slowly, positive

EXHIBIT 11-3   The Relationship between Cash Flow and Growth

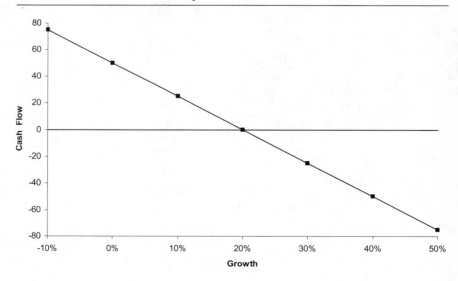

cash flows will result. At a 10 percent growth rate, a positive flow of twenty-five would be produced.

The Effects of Growth, Inflation, and Capacity/Demand Relationships

Recall the general cash-flow equation developed earlier (Equation 1):

$$CF = (EBIT - I)(1 - t)(1 - DPO\%)(1 + G)\left(1 + \frac{D}{E}\right) - NA_oG \qquad (1)$$

The growth rate, G, was assumed to be the composite of real growth in unit sales (labor-hours, tons, and so forth) and inflation or deflation (price changes). Further defining G:

$$G = [(1 + G_p)(1 + G_v) - 1]$$

Where:

G_p = Growth in prices
G_v = Growth in volume

Redefine NA_o as follows:

$$NA_o = FA_o + WC_o$$

Where:

FA_o = Beginning fixed assets
WC_o = Beginning working capital

Substituting in Equation 1:

$$CF = (EBIT - I)(1 - t)(1 + G_p)(1 + G_v)(1 - DPO\%)\left(1 + \frac{D}{E}\right)$$
$$- FA_o(G) - WC_o(G) \qquad (2)$$

In many businesses, the growth rate of working capital equals the growth in sales or $[(1 + G_p)(1 + G_v) - 1]$. In the short run, however, this assumption is not realistic in regard to fixed assets. Fixed assets tend to increase in discrete increments as capacity is expanded, not smoothly as sales increase. Thus, it is necessary to adjust the cash-flow equations to account for this circumstance if more precise cash flows are to be calculated in short-run situations. If a capital plan exists for the company, then the cash flow associated with the change in fixed assets, FA_oG, will equal depreciation (DEPR) less planned capital expenditures (PCE). When a capital plan exists, the general cash-flow equation then becomes:

$$CF = (EBIT - I)(1 - t)(1 + G_p)(1 + G_v)(1 - DPO\%)\left(1 + \frac{D}{E}\right)$$
$$+ DEPR - PCE - WC_o[(1 + G_p)(1 + G_v) - 1] \qquad (3)$$

Equation 3 can be altered to reflect the capacity/demand relationships faced by different businesses. The income portion of the equation would remain the same. The term $+ DEPR - PCE - WC_o$ $[(1 + G_p)$ $(1 + G_v) - 1]$, however, would become NA_o $[(1 + G_p)(1 + G_v) - 1]$ in the case of a rapidly growing business in which the firm is operating at capacity and the fixed assets must be expanded in proportion to sales growth.

In the case of an unprofitable business facing severe competition, excess capacity in its industry, and mature (slow-growth) markets, the firm might choose not to reinvest depreciation and might use negative growth rates to extract the working capital; this is known as a "harvesting" strategy. The asset portion of Equation 3 would become:

$$+ DEPR - WC_o[(1 + G_p)(1 + G_v) - 1]$$

In the case of an effective cash producer with a strong market position, the firm would use a "holding" strategy, reinvesting depreciation to maintain its position as a low-cost producer. In this case, the asset portion of Equation 3 would become:

$$+ DEPR - DEPR\ REINVESTMENT - WC_o[(1 + G_p)(1 + G_v) - 1]$$

In other instances, a firm might find itself faced with a need to expand capacity in large discrete increments or to rebuild its technological base. In this situation, the asset portion of Equation 3 would remain:

$$+ DEPR - PCE - WC_o[(1 + G_p)(1 + G_v) - 1]$$

The results for the four cases are summarized in Exhibit 11-4.

EXHIBIT 11-4   Expressions for Different Asset Strategies

Strategy	Cash Flow from Asset Changes
Growth	$-NA_o\,[(1+G_p)(1+G_v)-1]$
Disinvestment	$+DEPR-WC_o\,[(1+G_p)(1+G_v)-1]$
Holding	$+DEPR-DEPR\ REINVESTED$ $-WC_o\,[(1+G_p)(1+G_v)-1]$
Rebuild and General Case	$+DEPR-PCE-WC_o\,[(1+G_p)(1+G_v)-1]$

The Long-Term Cash-Balancing Growth Rate

Equation 1, the formula for the cash-balancing growth rate in the next planning period, can be modified to reflect longer-term trends based on historical rates of return and interest rates, resulting in Equation 4.

$$G^* = D/E(r-i)P + rP \qquad (4)$$

Where:

G^* = the long-term cash-balancing rate of growth

D/E = the debt/equity ratio

P = the percent of profits retained

r = the after tax, before interest return on beginning net assets

i = the after-tax cost of debt (on beginning debt)

Equation 4 is the well-known finance formula for calculating the maximum sustainable growth rate, given the previously stipulated assumptions about the relationships between sales, profits, and asset levels, and the following limitations. This formulation is based on the assumption that the fixed assets must grow at the rate of growth of sales, *and it thus treats only the case of a rapidly growing business operating at capacity (the Growth case in Exhibit 11-4).* This formulation also assumes that the firm has a return on beginning equity of less than 100 percent. A firm that is able to achieve a higher return will be able to finance any rate of growth through the use of internally generated funds. Each dollar increase in assets results in at least a dollar increase in funds available.

It can be shown that Equation 4 is equivalent to (return on equity) $x(P)$, or the "rate of retained earnings to equity."

Using the data from the example company,

$$G^* = \frac{(30)(1+G^*)(5/6)}{150}$$

$$150G^* = (30+30G^*)(5/6)$$

$$G^* = .20$$

Summary

This discussion has illustrated the relationships between cash flow and growth that follow from a base-year income statement and balance sheet. These tools of general guidance assist the strategic planner in focusing on the changes in cash flow from one year to the next, based on a firm's capital structure and return characteristics. A general expression for cash flow as a function of growth rate was also developed for several categories of market growth and capacity/demand relationships. The analytical relationships and their graphical formats allow planners to understand the fundamental relationships among cash flow, return on net assets, and growth rates, which determine the long-term profile of operating results. In fact, the more stable and profitable a business becomes, the more likely the relationships are to remain valid. Profit margins and asset levels stabilize as improvements in costs, receivables, inventories, and/or fixed-asset turnover reach operationally sustainable limits.

DISCUSSION QUESTIONS

1. Why is projecting cash requirements so critical in a growing firm?
2. What are the principal elements in the cash flow–growth relationship?
3. How does inflation affect the need for cash?
4. What is the capacity-demand relationship?
5. Should a general manager understand the firm's sustainable growth rate?

12

PRODUCT, MARKETING, AND PRICING STRATEGIES

Management Control

As described earlier, the control stage of the strategic planning process compares results with goals or targets and notes exceptions for corrective action. Control activities take place throughout the organization at an overall level, and within each functional department at a detailed level. At a profit-center level, the general manager must exercise control to ensure that the product, marketing/pricing, and manufacturing strategies are realistic and provide a framework for successful business operations. This process is described in some detail in Chapter 3 in the discussion of managing the functional interfaces and, in a broader context, in Chapter 10 as the business model.

A Cost Effectiveness Analysis

Management must have an orderly framework to help accurately assign responsibility for profit problems to the three functional areas. A graphical procedure illustrates an approach to this circuitous problem. A firm must view its products in comparison with competitors' products on scales of the cost to the customer and relative product effectiveness.

In Exhibit 12-1, the customer would prefer a product at point A to one at point B, because he or she would choose strictly on price if the products were considered equally effective. The customer would also prefer a product

EXHIBIT 12-1   Customer Preference Diagram

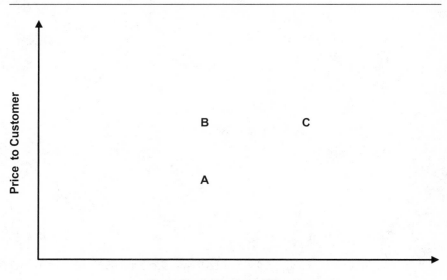

at point C to one at point B, because the more effective product would be preferred if the two products were equally priced.

Given that a product must meet common minimum standards of safety and reliability in every industry, a line should be added to represent the codes and standards that prescribe the minimum level of product effectiveness that can be marketed. There is also some minimum feasible cost at which any given level of product effectiveness can be delivered consistently, and this minimum cost increases as a producer markets a more effective product. These two considerations are shown in Exhibit 12-2.

The top-level planning and control sequence begins with the determination of the product, market, and pricing strategies.

- Does the management intend to be a leader or a follower in the market served?
- Will the organization work toward the marketing of a superior product that will sell at a premium price (the leadership role)?
- Is the product intended to be similar in effectiveness to competitors' products?

EXHIBIT 12-2   Effect of Manufacturing Constraints

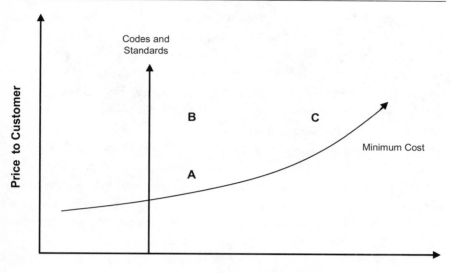

Perceived Product Effectiveness

- Does management intend to segment the market and seek a dominant market share of the differentiated segment, such as the discount-house segment, the low-priced segment, or the high-quality segment?

Regardless of the product, market, and pricing strategies chosen, the role of manufacturing or operations is to produce the designated product at a lower cost than that of competitors (further defined as "no profitable competitor can market an equivalent product at a lower price").

If management believes that product-line profitability is unsatisfactory, it must first determine the following:

- Is the product engineered to meet the strategic intent?
- If yes, is the marketing function effective compared with competitors'?

If the answer is yes to both questions, then resolution of the profitability problem will lie with manufacturing or operations and the management of costs and assets.

Problem: A High Cost Base

Exhibit 12-3 reflects the additional factors of production costs and product effectiveness. If a firm's product is intended to be similar in effectiveness to those of competitors, the firm faces strict price competition. Any operational inefficiency will lead to reduced profit margins. A firm with costs at point B in Exhibit 12-3 will obviously face reduced profit margins on sales when it must meet competitors' prices in the marketplace. If the firm attempts to maintain its profit margin on sales, it will be forced to sell at higher prices, and this will lead to a loss of market share.

Management can confirm or reinforce its suspicion of the existence of a high cost base or excess assets by comparing such aggregate performance measures as sales per employee, material costs or cost of goods sold as a percentage of sales, value added, and overall wage costs to those of competitors. In today's Information Age, numerous databases are available by subscription or without cost on the Internet to assist a firm in analyzing how its operating performance and level of capital investments compare with those of competitors.

EXHIBIT 12-3   Sources of Price Differences

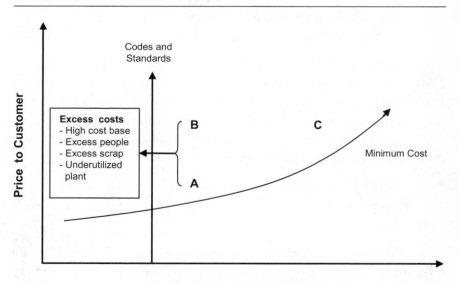

If the cost base is out of control, actions must be taken to correct the problem. An unacceptable performance level often leads to management changes. Providing the specifics for success is the job of middle management. In practice, top management can only evaluate results, approve or reject proposals, or change the managers involved. Otherwise, if top management is forced to resort to edicts, it is a sign of failure at the middle-management level.

Such edicts often take any of several unsavory forms, including:

- Large layoffs of salaried and hourly personnel
- Freezes on hiring to allow attrition to reduce the employment level (and wage costs)
- Mandatory reductions in inventory levels
- Freezes on capital expenditures

These painful actions are often seen by the workforce as unpopular manifestations of top management's authority when, in fact, they are brought on by failures at the middle-management, operational level.

To continue the discussion of the cost effectiveness analysis, problems with excess costs may also exist with a product intended for the high-quality, high-priced segment of the market. Exhibit 12-4 shows the results. The excess costs experienced at point D will reduce the profitability of the firm relative to that of competitors.

Problems: Overdesign and/or Overmanufacture

The organization that is pursuing a product-leadership strategy with the production of a superior product that commands a premium price may also face a second type of control problem. If the customers have difficulty accepting the product's superiority, then a situation exists as shown in Exhibit 12-5. The customer may not accept the use of extra quantities of materials, higher cost materials, superior facilities, or meticulous workmanship as proof of a superior product. If the product perception does not warrant a premium price, the overdesigned or overproduced product results in excess costs for the firm at point E. An equivalent product provided by a competitor whose costs are at point C will command that segment of the market. If the extra engineering, quality control, superior materials, and the like, designed and manufactured into the

EXHIBIT 12-4 Sources of Price Differences (b)

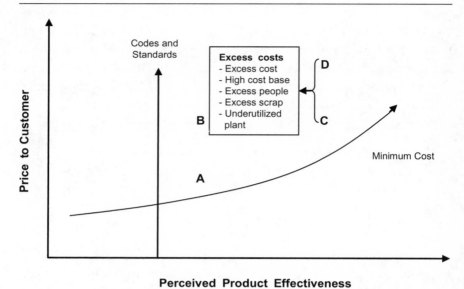

EXHIBIT 12-5 Sources of Price Differences (c)

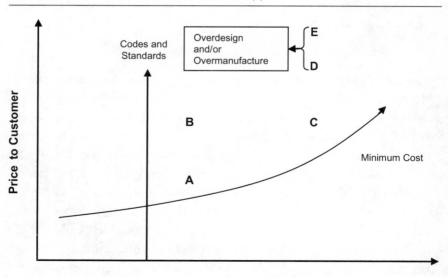

EXHIBIT 12-6   Sources of Price Differences (d)

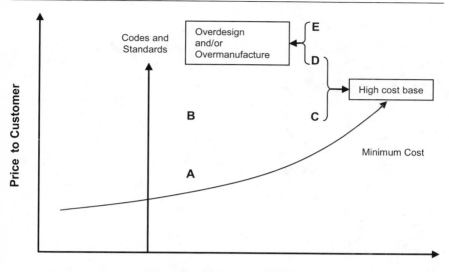

Perceived Product Effectiveness

product do not achieve perceived product superiority, then they are simply excess costs and must be eliminated.

The Most Difficult Situation: A Mix of the Two Problems

Finally, the situation may reflect a bit of each of these unfortunate situations. The company may face a mix of a high cost base confounded by overdesign and/or overmanufacture. The firm then faces the situation illustrated in Exhibit 12-6.

Management Action

The general manager must continually assess whether the causes of these problems are capable of being overcome by the management personnel in place or whether more forceful action is required. These judgments are made difficult by the lack of complete knowledge of competitors' costs and profits for a given product line, by the lack of specific knowledge of the marketplace on the part of the top corporate managers, and by a tendency of the operating managers involved to insist that the current team can make the necessary improvements.

In the long run, a firm must strive to deliver products that the customers want and for which they are willing to pay, produced at a cost lower than those of its competitors. Top-level problems such as these often must be corrected by drastic actions by senior management, including reorganizing, changing managers, mandating workforce reductions to bring productivity into line, and/or directing a change in product/market strategy. The importance of productivity improvement to effective competition is covered in Chapter 13.

Detailed Operating Controls

As stated earlier, when the product, marketing, and pricing strategies are properly synchronized with the cost base, a business is under "control" from a top-level standpoint. Management must then plan and control numerous detailed aspects of the firm's operations. The large number of related detailed measurements requires that operations managers have a special temperament to cope with them on a positive basis, since manufacturing or operations is the crucial hub of the control problem. In most businesses, the majority of the people, assets, and costs are managed by the manufacturing or operations organizations. Therefore, most of the control organizations, systems, and procedures are found in the manufacturing or operations function. Top managers realize that if they are to achieve outstanding profit performance relative to competitors, they cannot succeed with an out-of-control operations function.

Summary

At the profit-center level, an operating unit (division) must determine if it is in the right business with a correct strategic approach and with a reasonable possibility for success (an effective business model). No amount of lower-level skills, experience, dedication, or energy can compensate for "being in the wrong ballpark." The result will be similar to a forfeited ball game. On the other hand, when the broad strategic factors are in order, the managers at the operating level must still win the marketplace by "outexecuting" the competition.

DISCUSSION QUESTIONS

1. Why is it important for everyone in a business to understand the target market segment?
2. Is it preferable to have a high market share of the target segment or a given share of the total market?
3. How does the general manager pinpoint his or her organization's weaknesses?
4. How does a general manager with a liberal arts background identify such technical problems as overdesign or overmanufacture?
5. What is the result if the firm can lower the cost to the consumer of a premium product to equal the prices of competitors' less-effective products?

13

RELATING PRODUCTIVITY AND
FIRM GROWTH

The understanding, management, and improvement of productivity, and their relationship to competitiveness are compelling aspects of general management. Competing organizations often have access to the same or similar production technology, as well as the same or comparable supplies and suppliers of raw materials and finished parts. When a firm does have proprietary technology, it can have a significant competitive advantage. But, in most situations, competitive advantage results from neither the availability of technology nor the cost of purchased goods. A preponderance of the other noninterest costs—the remaining direct costs; sales, general, and administrative (SG&A) costs; other overhead costs; and corporate expenses—largely consists of the cost of people (employees). As a result, management of these costs provides opportunities for creating competitive advantages.

Several elements contribute to the relative cost of people, including wage and salary rates, benefit levels and costs, ancillary costs (for example, space, equipment, and travel), compensation other than wages and salaries, and, finally, the level of output achieved during the time people work. Together, these elements are among the most important aspects of competition in both manufacturing and service environments, with importance generally tracking the degree of labor intensity in a firm's products (cost structure). Naturally, then, these elements must be considered in developing a firm's strategy.

For most organizations, pursuing a strategy of cost leadership requires an organization-wide focus on employee productivity. Pursuit of either of the other two generic strategies—differentiation or focus—does not necessarily require such intense attention to labor productivity, but strong management of productivity, even in these cases, can lead to enhanced profitability and, expectantly, an enhanced market position.

In this chapter, the conceptual underpinnings of a strategic emphasis on employee productivity are addressed. The nature of the problem or opportunity is discussed, along with some well-known concepts related to the measurement of productivity and some new comparison processes to assist management in measuring the relative effectiveness of its firm at achieving outstanding levels of productivity. All-important behavioral aspects of managing the workforce are also addressed, including relevant, potential determinants of the inclination of employees either to resist attempts to improve productivity or to assist willingly and energetically in achieving productivity gains.

The Measurement of Labor Productivity

Early records of formal attempts to measure work in the interest of productivity improvement are found in the writings of Frederick W. Taylor, who originated time studies of work around the turn of the twentieth century.[1] These methods of work measurement were gradually introduced into a wide variety of production contexts, from job shops to assembly lines. Several systems for defining work and the time required to accomplish it were developed and refined, and over the years a variety of means of defining productivity and tracking its improvement have evolved and are used to this day.

The term productivity describes how well an organization converts its resource inputs into profit-generating outputs. Many measures of employee or labor productivity are used in assessing the performance of operations, firms, and economies. General managers have numerous choices for the measures of outputs (some measure of the goods and/or services produced) and inputs (some measure of labor used), which are employed as the numerator and denominator, respectively, of a ratio measure of labor productivity.

When examining the internal operations of a firm, managers might prefer to employ measures of activities for output: for example, the number of times an operation is performed, the number of products produced, the number of transactions completed, or the number of services delivered. One example of this type of measurement is a large bank holding company's use of *millions of transactions per full-time-equivalent employee per month* as the bankwide measure of productivity. Managers should be able to track chosen internal productivity measures over time and through acquisitions and divestitures in order to ensure that productivity continually improves.

When a firm formulates its strategic goals and objectives, and compares its operations to those of its competitors, managers must use broader measures. Data that report levels of transaction, service, or even production volume are not readily available in most competitive situations. Even when the production of automobiles is regularly reported in units, the number of units cannot be used as a measure of effective output for purposes of measuring productivity because of the major differences in cost and complexity among the different makes and models produced. As an enterprise-level measure of productivity, therefore, this chapter proposes the use of *revenues (dollars) per employee*. (When examining banking and financial-institution operations, the amount of total assets is substituted for revenues.) There are several advantages to using such aggregate measures.

The emphasis on productivity has traditionally been associated primarily with lower-level, direct workers. Such an approach works well and is fully appropriate for the managers of small, internal operations such as discrete production units, but in the strategic context, productivity should be considered as the relative level of effectiveness among competitors of all of a firm's employees, from the chief executive officer (CEO) to the lowest level. Employment level as a measure of input is advantageous at this enterprise level because it is comparable across industry players, it is uninfluenced by regional wage differentials, it avoids the need to account for compensation in addition to wages, and it is not affected by accounting allocations of employment costs.

For comparability, it is reasonable to assume that the tasks within a group of competitors are sufficiently similar that the ability to accomplish given levels of output represents equivalent demands for resource inputs. (We recognize, however, that exceptions can and do occur to this general assumption.) Some firms will simply be better at accomplishing these tasks. Similarly, firms may be advantaged or disadvantaged by regional wage differentials. Firms located in high-wage neighborhoods will face a tougher job of cost improvement, but the difference is similar to a rate variance in cost accounting as opposed to a usage variance. The firm that achieves an outstanding level of revenues/employee enjoys the higher level of productivity, regardless of the wage differentials.

Finally, the level of employment transcends a variety of corporate practices in regard to allocating the cost of employees to corporate or divisional budgets, to line or staff designations, or to definitions of direct versus indirect labor. The choice of the total number of employees as the measure of labor input nullifies these otherwise complicating factors. If management sets out to measure factory productivity, for instance, it may be deluded into believing productivity improvements are being achieved, when, in fact, computer software specialists to prepare computer instructions for automatic machines are being added at a rate faster than the reduction in direct factory workers. This illusion of improvement would occur if computer personnel were considered members of the corporate or indirect staff, rather than direct factory workers. All of these contradictions are avoided by using the total number of employees, from the CEO to the entry-level worker.

Having established the importance of labor productivity and a means of measuring it, we dedicate the remainder of this chapter to examining three concepts related to labor productivity. Two of these are familiar in the field of management: economies of scale, and the learning or experience curve. The third—called economies of growth—is a new concept that addresses the need for the continuous improvement of employee productivity.

Economies of Scale

Economies of scale have long been a staple of economics literature. This term has generally been used to describe the results of the process by which larger firms are able to spread their fixed and semi-fixed costs over a larger volume of products or services, leading to lower average costs per unit of output. In many industries, it was proven and widely understood that "scale" alone could provide a competitive advantage through lower average costs, exerting pressure on smaller competitors.

With scale economies, firms achieve economies in costs and productivity factors as size increases, and negative economies of scale may set in as organizations pass the most efficient (lowest cost/highest productivity) size. The result is the classical U-shaped curve of economic theory, which is sketched in Exhibit 13-1. Not all industries demonstrate diseconomies; for some, costs continue to decrease as volume increases. This trend is often made possible by the capability of computer-based information systems that assist in efficiently controlling larger and larger organizations.

Our focus on the number of employees as a single-factor productivity measure leads us to define and demonstrate the use of scale economies in this context. As a result, we refer to the related phenomenon as economies of scale in labor.

EXHIBIT 13-1   Economies of Scale in Labor: Ratio Model

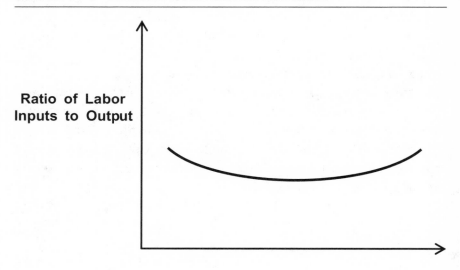

Learning Curve/Experience Curve Theory

In the 1930s, a manager at the Wright-Patterson Air Force Base in Dayton, Ohio, published a paper reporting a newly observed phenomenon—the learning curve.[2] Later applications of the concept were sometimes referred to as "progress functions" and "experience curves," with the latter finding prominence in the field of business strategy. The learning curve concept used mathematics to represent the observed improvement in production times as tasks were accomplished repeatedly. These improvements came to be expected in work settings involving repetitive tasks, and the standard formulations of the relationships between units produced and the rate of improvement in productivity became widely used in industry. Firms that were not able to achieve improvements found themselves at a severe competitive disadvantage.

The magnitude of the learning curve improvements was seen to diminish in a systematic way as the number of repetitions increased. Learning curve theory thus proposes a predictable relationship: a constant percent improvement in labor hours for each doubling of cumulative volume of output. In the language of the theory, an 80 percent learning curve denotes a 20 percent improvement for each doubling of cumulative volume. Improvement usually applies to the measure of productivity, for example, labor hours per unit of output, the labor cost per unit (in constant dollars), or the total variable cost per unit (in constant dollars). Transforming the units of both productivity and cumulative output into logarithms creates a linear relationship. Exhibit 13-2 presents a learning curve found in a large, U.S. service operation. The learning rate for this curve was approximately 90 percent.

In addition to ensuring that the productivity gains of the learning curve occurred, managers and strategic planners also have naturally attempted to influence the rates at which their firms captured these gains relative to their competition. To do this, they have focused on affecting the two factors upon which ongoing productivity gains depend—the learning rate and the cumulative number of products made or services delivered. Managers have endeavored to increase the slope of the curve (the learning rate), capturing more improvement with each doubling of the cumulative output of the organization, and they have aimed to move their organizations

EXHIBIT 13-2   Example of the Learning Curve in a Service Business

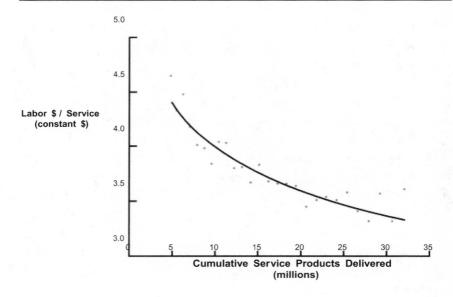

down a given curve faster by focusing on increasing production volume. In a competitive context, this latter activity regularly involves increasing market share at the expense of one's competitors. A common method of achieving this goal has involved cutting prices in order to take advantage of price elasticity.

Economies of Growth

A newer concept in productivity improvement, the phenomenon termed economies of growth,[3] provides an additional tool for general managers seeking a competitive advantage. This notion can be related to the fundamentals of learning curve theory and extends the previous notions regarding productivity to include the positive impact of the sheer growth of a firm on its prospects for improving productivity. Previous work established that the mere measurement of the work accomplished in a given time would improve productivity and that repetitiveness (accomplishing the same tasks over and over again) also enhanced productivity. Economists noted the effect of "scale" on output per worker, and scale economies became a readily understood means of achieving productivity advantages over competitors. Economies of growth draws upon these productivity relationships and describes a strong and statistically significant relationship between the growth rate of a firm and its productivity growth rate (or improvement in productivity).

The concept of economies of growth was recognized during an exploration of the differences between growing firms and stagnant firms in the context of the learning curve. In the specific organization studied, productivity improvement was occurring, following the general pattern of a learning curve, with the labor requirements per unit of output declining as the cumulative number of units completed increased. As the complement of workers in the organization accumulated experience, the number of labor hours required to perform each unit of service declined. This effectively increased the labor capacity of the group. Because the availability of increased demand existed for the product of this organization, the group was able to grow its production volume without a proportional growth in its workforce. Concurrently, the organization was able to capture the advantages of the reduced per-unit labor requirements, and because its operations were labor intensive, the firm benefited substantially over time from the resulting cost reductions.

The circumstances of this situation also bring to light the possibility of an alternative scenario—one in which the opportunity for growth is absent. In the case of the organization described above, stagnant growth could have come about as a result of a lack of additional demand or a lack of physical capacity. With the improvements in productivity described previously, management would have faced a situation of excess labor capacity. The resulting options for management would have included reducing the workforce or maintaining a constant workforce and foregoing the benefits of the reduced costs. If management elected to pursue the first of these options and proceeded with a reduction in workers, it would have effectively delivered the message that through performance improvement, employees had contributed to the elimination of some of their own jobs. In selecting the latter of the two options, however, management would have created the potential for idleness or underutilization of the workforce. Neither of the two options appears to compel a continuing pursuit of improvement on the part of the workers.

With consideration given to these alternative scenarios of productivity improvement under conditions of different growth rates, the relationship between corporate growth rate and the rate of productivity improvement in various industries of the U.S. economy was explored. The hypothesis, which has been borne out repeatedly, was that there is indeed a relationship between a firm's rate of growth and the rate at which its productivity improves. In particular, faster-growing firms enjoy, on average, faster rates of improvement in labor productivity. As noted, these competitive advantages have been termed economies of growth. A sketch of the basic growth economies relationship for a U.S. service industry is shown in Exhibit 13-3.

The premises of economies of growth include a number of reflections related to workforce motivation and human nature. First, growth creates a secure and stimulating work environment where additional workers are often added to meet growing demand. As a result, most employees do not fear being let go for lack of work. Second, workers and managers with growing workloads increase productivity by focusing on important tasks, shedding unnecessary activities, creating new ways of accomplishing more, and seeking best practices through shared learning across the firm. It

EXHIBIT 13-3   Economies of Growth

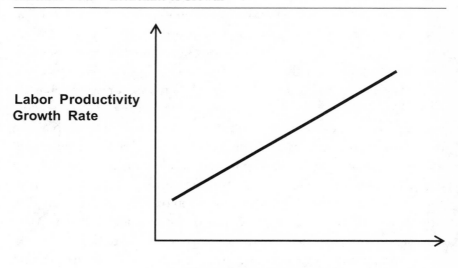

Labor Productivity
Growth Rate

Corporate Growth Rate

should be noted that in growth environments, productivity improvement and employment expansion can occur simultaneously; however, stagnant and declining environments can create resistance toward productivity improvement. In such environments, productivity improvement (as defined here) can occur only through declining employment rolls. In situations of stagnant or declining growth, productivity improvements would result in a need for fewer workers to accomplish a given amount of work. Acting in their own best interests, workers are likely to be reluctant to "downsize" themselves out of a job. Thus, productivity improvements are generally more difficult to achieve in operations with stagnant or declining output.

The dynamic situations accompanying acquisitions, divestitures, and organizational changes or restructurings create prime opportunities for firms to adjust productivity levels. In these circumstances, management often takes advantage of the period of corporate redefinition to reduce employment rolls. Frequently, this pruning occurs among the ranks of middle management, particularly in the case of mergers, where line workers are likely to be retained to maintain production and service levels.

In today's dynamic, worldwide competitive environment, America's economy continues a long-term shift toward services and away from manufacturing, spurred on by the growth in services. With this shift, the management of labor productivity has become increasingly important. It is recognized that labor productivity—and the related cost of people—is one of the dominant competitive arenas for the many firms striving to lower costs. In the next section, we explore the presence of economies of growth as a cross-industry phenomenon in America's largest firms.

Economies of Growth in the Fortune 500 Companies

With revenues as the measure of size and revenues per employee as the measure of productivity, growth economies have been found in numerous and diverse industries as well as the Fortune 500. Most recently, companies listed in the Fortune 500 for the year 2004 (published in April 2005) were examined, and strong economies of growth were found among the ranks of this set of large, U.S. firms. Exhibit 13-4 illustrates that the productivity growth rate over the five-year period examined (1999–2004) increased, on average, as the rate of corporate growth increased, and the

EXHIBIT 13-4 Economies of Growth in the Fortune 500, 1999–2004

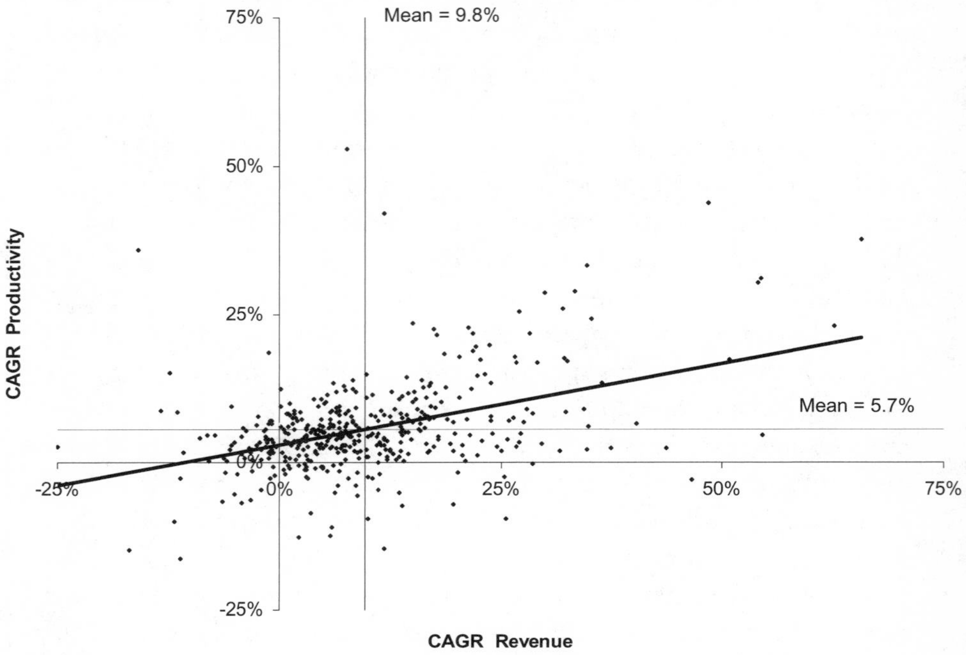

CAGR Revenue

linear relationship shown was very highly statistically significant. Interestingly, we have found significant economies of growth among the Fortune 500 in research that has spanned the past decade and covered approximately fifteen years of reported performance data. Additionally, we have examined two supplementary relationships of interest among the companies in the Fortune 500. First, we have intermittently found a significant relationship between productivity growth rate and market value (market capitalization) growth rate. For the most recent data, this relationship was statistically significant for the Fortune 1,000 companies, but not the Fortune 500. Second, as one might expect, we have consistently found a very highly significant relationship between corporate growth rate and the growth rate of market value, with market value growth rates increasing for larger corporate growth rates, confirming long-standing premises of the investment community.

The results cited from the Fortune 500 and 1,000 companies reveal insights into the critical strategic aspect of managing an effective workforce, with the obvious conclusion that in the mainstream of U.S. industry, those companies that manage the labor productivity of their organizations most effectively have a strong head start toward premium share prices and market value. For firms that already lead the competition in productivity levels, growth economies aid in distancing them further from the lagging competition. On the other hand, firms not taking advantage of growth economies will find themselves losing valuable ground in labor productivity relative to the competition. The relationships identified here reinforce the notions that faster growing firms should be able to capture strategically important efficiencies through more rapidly improving productivity, and more productive workers (and the anticipated lower costs) should contribute to increases in market capitalization and shareholder value. (An example illustrating these notions is presented later in this chapter.)

These conclusions regarding labor productivity reinforce one of the major strategic premises of this book, which is that in the long run, successful companies must manage the basics. Effective managers must have specific goals and objectives that all employees can understand; they must have in place viable strategies for achieving the goals; and finally, they must outexecute the competition. These precepts are the rules for engagement in all companies and industries, in the recent past and going forward. The management of labor productivity and its improvement is a critical element of execution for most firms in their quest for competitive effectiveness, and as such, it becomes a necessary component of a firm's strategic planning process. The cost of all of a firm's employees constitutes a common competitive battleground for the status of low-cost producer. Economies of growth are found when faster-growing firms demonstrate higher rates of productivity improvement than slower-growing firms. Thus, growth provides an advantage when economies of growth are present. This advantage of higher rates of improvement or growth in labor productivity aids firms in gaining on competitors in their quest for a more productive workforce and, consequently, lower costs.

The relationships presented in this chapter demonstrate the robustness of the concept of growth economies and their importance to managers throughout the U.S. economy. The next section provides a more detailed look at competitive analysis, along with other conclusions related to the crucial and strategic competitive factor of employee productivity.

Productivity and Competitive Analysis

Competitive analysis is critical for managers formulating corporate as well as divisional business strategies. In order to determine the best directions for their divisions and parent corporations, executives and planners must be aware of their competitors' performance levels as well as trends in their competitors' performance. Managers and planners also must be capable of critically assessing their own organization's performance, over time as well as relative to that of its competitive peers.

Competitive analyses are typically based on historical data, which allow managers to review how their firms have compared to competitors in the past. Current data are more difficult to come by, and future performance must be estimated. Managers and planners use the information gathered in the process of competitive analysis to set realistic goals and objectives and to develop strategic plans. Their analyses should focus on those performance measures that are central to gaining competitive advantage in the business's marketplace.

A Generic First Step

A straightforward first step in competitive analysis is to develop ordinal rankings of a group of comparable firms for each element in a set of given performance measures. For example, for an identified performance measure, such as revenues, the firms being compared should be listed in rank order, from the largest to the smallest. Listing the comparable firms in rank order on such variables as return on sales, gross margin percentage, asset turnover, and return on investment (among others) provides valuable comparisons. The development of such lists requires that a group of comparable firms must first be identified. Such a group might consist of firms in the same industry, or firms from different industries facing similar competitive environments. At least some of the firms examined should compose a competitive circle—businesses competing for orders in the same or overlapping markets. For the identified firms, performance measures vital to competitiveness should be tracked on a regular basis. These rankings aid managers in understanding how their firms compare to the competition, assist them in recognizing their organizations' strengths and weaknesses, and provide guidance in the goal-setting process.

Some managers demean this process and discount its results for failing to provide a rich review of the actual circumstances of the competitive environment. They have a valid point. More often than not, however, those who are most critical of the comparison process represent organizations ranking at or near the bottom of their peer groups. Strong organizations want to keep score and never lose sight of the necessity for continuous improvement, and managers of an organization cannot judge its improvement if they do not know its relative effectiveness.

The rank orderings of firms on any of the attributes of import may be refined slightly to aid in the goal-setting process. The list of ranked firms may be divided into four equal groups of firms, with each of the three separating values called a quartile. From the divided list, managers may readily determine the quarter within which their firms are positioned, as well as which competitors share situations similar to their own. A powerful motivator to which all members of the organization can relate is to have the goal of performing above the top quartile, or in the top quarter, for each of the key performance indicators of the firm and its industry. In the spirit of continuous improvement, after a level of performance in the top quarter is reached on any measure, the goal may be redefined to be ranked as first or second among the comparable companies. Upon achievement of this milestone, a manager may turn his or her attention to the performance of well-run businesses in similar industries.

Two-Way Performance Mapping

Two-way performance mapping is another general method of competitive analysis that may be used with any two performance measures. It allows managers to review their organizations' histories relative to those of their peers on the chosen two measures simultaneously. Mapping the two measures in a graphical format creates four quadrants into which the firms can be divided. The averages of the selected measures for a group of competitors provide straightforward and convenient dividing points for the quadrants. Managers should find it useful to determine how many and which competitors are above (or below) average, as well as their relative rankings on a given measure. An example of two-way performance mapping using rate of corporate growth and labor productivity growth for a sample industry is shown in Exhibit 13-5.

EXHIBIT 13-5   Two-Way Performance Map for Sample Industry

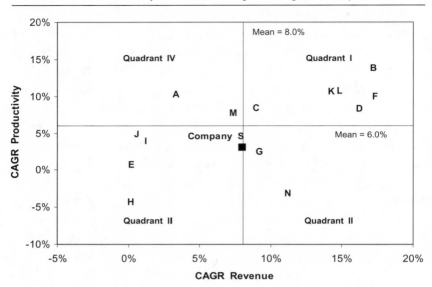

Managers would naturally want to position their firms in Quadrant I of the two-way map. Executives whose firms are not in this attractive position, however, may use the information on the graph in their goal-setting processes to attempt to move their organizations toward more promising competitive positions on these measures, with the ultimate aim of creating value for their shareholders.

The Impact of Productivity Improvement

As noted previously, managing productivity and its improvement can provide considerable benefits—or avoid significant disadvantages—for perceptive managers. A straightforward example of the potential impact of the management of labor productivity is provided in Exhibit 13-6 to illustrate the point.

The table in Exhibit 13-6 provides information on a sample firm (Company S) over a five-year period. We see that Company S grew from $2 billion in revenues (Year 0) to more than $2.9 billion in Year 5, while its workforce grew from 10,000 to 12,675 employees over the same period.

EXHIBIT 13-6   Impact of the Management of Labor Productivity

Company & Industry Growth Rates	5-year CAGR Productivity	5-year CAGR Revenue
Industry Average	6.0%	8.0%
Company S	3.0%	8.0%
	Year 0	**Year 5**
Performance History		
Company S revenue ($ Millions)	$2,000	$2,939
Company S employees	10,000	12,675
Company S actual revenue/employee	$200,000	$231,855
Potential Employment Impact		
Revenue/Employee if grew productivity at 6.0%	$200,000	$267,645
Anticipated employment if grew productivity at 6.0%		10,980
Difference in employees		1,695
Difference as a % of actual employment		13.4%
Potential Financial Impact		
Estimated cost per employee		$50,000
Pretax cost of additional 1,695 employees		$84,750,000
Corporate tax rate		35%
After-tax cost of additional employees		$55,087,500
Hypothetical Market Impact		
Shares outstanding		50,000,000
Savings/incremental earnings per share		$1.10
Company P/E multiple		12
Potential effect on stock price		$13.22

From the table, we may also note that Company S's sales grew at the average rate of the other firms in its industry, but its labor productivity lagged the average rate of its peers. Consider the effect this lower-than-average productivity growth rate had on Company S's earnings, as well as the potential effect it might have had on Company S's stock price.

To illustrate the impact of productivity performance, we begin by examining how many employees Company S would have had in Year 5 had the organization improved its labor productivity at the industry-average rate, assuming that revenues followed their actual pattern of growth. Exhibit 13-6 reveals this process. To arrive at the final figure, Company S's base-year labor productivity ($200,000 revenues per employee) was grown at 6.0 percent per year, the industry average, to arrive at a productivity figure for Year 5. Using this projected productivity figure and the actual Year 5 revenues, we are able to determine the expected number of employees. (Projected employees equal revenues divided by the projected productivity level.) The cumulative effect is sizeable, with the *difference* in employees accounting for more than one-eighth of the firm's workforce by Year 5.

A second step in examining the impact of productivity performance is to explore the potential effects the improved productivity growth rate would have had on Company S's earnings. Exhibit 13-6 also provides the details of one analysis of this question. An estimate of $50,000 pretax expense per employee is used in the analysis, and the financial effects are shown for Year 5. The calculation is uncomplicated: The number of employees that Company S would have avoided adding to its employment rolls by Year 5 (1,695) is multiplied by the assumed expense of $50,000 per employee to arrive at the total pretax savings that would have resulted from the reduced number of employees. The pretax savings are then converted to after-tax values using the assumed tax rate of 35 percent. These potential after-tax savings are calculated to be a substantial $55 million.

It is useful to extend the examination of the potential effects of the earnings differential to the firm's stock price. The after-tax savings must first be converted to a per-share value, based on the number of shares outstanding. In the example in Exhibit 13-6, we find that $1.10 per share in after-tax earnings could have been generated or saved in Year 5 under the scenario described. These incremental earnings per share may also be converted into potential or hypothetical stock price increases by considering Company S's price/earnings multiple. Using an assumed P/E multiple of twelve, Company S's stock price might have increased by as much as $13.22 had it managed its productivity as described.

Sensitivity analysis may be performed on any number of the assumed values in the example of Exhibit 13-6; however, it should be evident that the cost of failure to effectively manage productivity and its improvement can be considerable and even daunting. We have observed actual scenarios in which a firm's stock price was projected to double had the organization maintained a rate of productivity growth equal to the industry average over a five-year period, even with a P/E multiple well below the industry average.

Such dramatic results do not arise from a one-time slowdown in productivity improvement. They are the result of an ongoing pattern of poor performance that creates a widening gap between a below-average firm and the top performers over time. Firm S would not have had to cut employment over the five years to achieve the industry average productivity growth rate of 6.0 percent. Rather, the firm could have added employees, but obviously many fewer than it did. The next section of this chapter explores the relationship between job creation, firm growth, and productivity improvement in more detail.

As noted earlier in this chapter, management of the cost of people is one readily apparent area in which firms may achieve significant cost (and hence profit) differentials over less-disciplined competitors. Exhibit 13-6 demonstrates the relative potential effects using a cost per employee of $50,000, which represents the total cost per worker described earlier. Managers should develop a reasonable estimate of this cost to assess the full impact of their staffing decisions. Logically, more refined measures for pools of employees performing different roles within the organization can provide results more finely tailored to a firm's actual situation.

As one would expect, this concept of the cost of people is often extended to the realm of financial analysis. Many managers find the measure of the average cost of an employee a useful one for a variety of reasons, one in particular being a benchmark for investment and expense analysis. For example, managers might compare the cost of leasing a particular piece of equipment to the equivalent head count at the average cost per worker. Naturally, relevant employee costs are also included in investment decision analysis, with an average cost per worker a useful input. Later chapters address in detail financial topics related to the role of the general manager.

Economies of Growth and Employment Variation

Growth creates an environment in which organizations are able to increase employment while simultaneously improving labor productivity. As noted above, Company S could have achieved the industry average rate of productivity improvement while at the same time adding 980 employees over the five-year period we examined. Without growth, however, labor productivity improvements in any organization come about only through job elimination. As a general rule, a firm's productivity growth equals its revenue growth when employment remains constant. The following logic illustrates the interrelationships of revenue growth and productivity growth as they relate to job formation and job elimination.

The graph for the economies of growth relationship provides a means of quickly identifying firms simultaneously achieving gains in productivity and creating jobs. Productivity gains (in current dollars) are obviously occurring within firms plotted above the x-axis. Not quite so obvious, though, is that firms creating jobs are those whose revenue growth exceeds their growth in labor productivity. Exhibit 13-7 provides an example to illustrate this situation.

From a review of the scenarios in Exhibit 13-7, it is apparent that productivity growth equals revenue growth when employment is constant. Jobs are created (employment grows) when revenue growth exceeds productivity growth and, conversely, jobs are eliminated (employment declines) when productivity growth exceeds revenue growth. Addition of a line of constant employment—that is, a line where revenue growth rate

EXHIBIT 13-7 Economic Gains in Jobs and Labor Productivity: Alternate Scenarios Related to Employment Variation

	Year 1	Year 2	Growth
Scenario 1: Constant Employment			
Revenue ($000)	$1,000	$2,000	100.0%
Employees	10	10	0.0%
Productivity level (Revenue/Employee)	100.0	200.0	100.0%
Scenario 2: Job Creation			
Revenue ($000)	$1,000	$2,000	100.0%
Employees	10	11	10.0%
Productivity level (Revenue/Employee)	100.0	181.8	81.8%
Scenario 3: Job Elimination			
Revenue ($000)	$1,000	$2,000	100.0%
Employees	10	9	(10.0%)
Productivity level (Revenue/Employee)	100.0	222.2	122.2%

EXHIBIT 13-8   Regions of Job Creation and Elimination

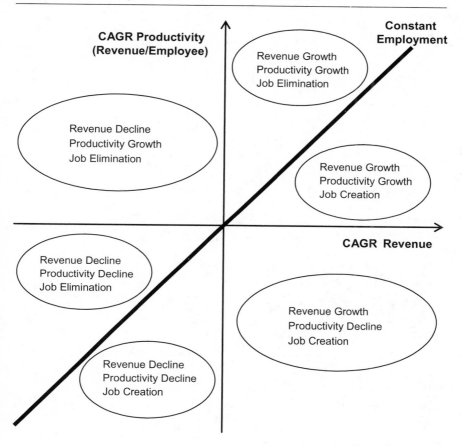

equals productivity growth rate—to the economies of growth axes leads to the graphic in Exhibit 13-8.

If we return to Exhibit 13-4, we may insert a line of constant employment on the Fortune 500 economies of growth graph to identify the distribution of firms between those in which jobs have been created and those where they have been eliminated over the five years examined. The intersection of the two lines creates four regions in the quadrant of the graph where all values of corporate growth rates and productivity growth rates are positive. Exhibit 13-9 shows these regions. It is intriguing to note that numerous firms fall within each region, with an abundance of them creating

EXHIBIT 13-9   Economies of Growth in the Fortune 500: Quadrant I (Limited View)

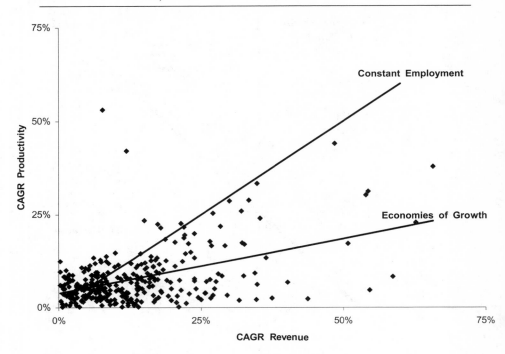

jobs, while a large quantity reduces its head count, and a portion of each outpaces the economies of growth line. From this graph, and others created similarly, managers may quickly assess the performance of their own firms as well as those of their peers, while visually determining whether each organization is expanding or shrinking its employment rolls.

Vignette 13-1 describes how one CEO took advantage of the hiring opportunities provided by growth to increase the diversity of his organization.

Revisiting the basic premises of economies of growth, we reiterate that growth as a rule creates a secure and stimulating environment for a workforce, and in growth environments, productivity improvements and employment expansion can occur simultaneously. Firms in this situation are those where the rate of corporate growth exceeds that of labor productivity. Conversely, stagnant and declining environments often produce an understandable resistance toward productivity improvements because they result in a need for fewer workers to accomplish a given amount of work. Most importantly, in firms where sales are not growing, labor productivity improvement can only occur through declining employment rolls. Many managers have found and take advantage of the fact that the dynamic situations accompanying acquisitions, divestitures, restructurings, and organizational change initiatives create situational opportunities for the adjustment of productivity levels.

Concluding Remarks

Earlier chapters establish the strategic importance of managing costs and the generic strategy of cost leadership. If a low-cost producer is defined as one for whom no competitor can deliver an equivalent product or service at a lower cost, it follows that effectively managing the cost of people is a prominent key to achieving this status since most other factor costs are similar for most competitors. The firm that manages its employees best in its quest for positive productivity differentials will have a head start toward achieving cost as well as profit advantages in the marketplace. The converse is obvious; the firm that is at a disadvantage with regard to employee costs will find it difficult to become or remain cost competitive. Such disadvantaged firms become likely takeover targets for the financially stronger competitors, who upon acquisition may apply their better systems for rapid gains and economies.

DISCUSSION QUESTIONS

1. Why is the productivity of a firm's workforce important strategically?
2. What factors influence employees' willingness to support efforts to increase productivity?
3. Why should measures of labor productivity include all of a firm's employees, as opposed to only the direct production workers?
4. How do growth economies differ from scale economies or learning curve effects?
5. What is the significance of strong growth economies among the Fortune 500?
6. What natural instincts cause some managers to resist detailed comparisons with competitors?
7. How might knowledge of economies of scale and growth relationships among competitors assist managers in strategic planning efforts?
8. How can two-way performance mapping assist a manager in understanding the competitive structure of his or her industry?
9. Why might managers want to know which competitors are creating jobs, which are eliminating jobs, and over what type of time frame?

14

RESIDUAL INCOME, EVA, AND CORPORATE CAPITAL CHARGES

Measuring the profitability and value of a business is very important because it is a key consideration when there is discussion of a merger or acquisition, when capital investment decisions are being considered, and in designing management incentive compensation plans. Investors have the same challenge when deciding whether or not to buy or sell a company's stock. General managers must regularly evaluate the performance of their operating business units, and that is the perspective on which we are focused in this chapter.

The efficiency with which a profit center (division or subsidiary) of a diversified, decentralized company employs its assets to generate profit is often measured by the company's return on net assets (RONA). Return on investment measures, ratios of profit to investment, are widely used as approaches to evaluating division performance. Alternative approaches evaluate division performance through various forms of residual income measures. Many well-run companies employ both measures, finding their positive attributes complementary. Both methodologies evaluate the financial performance of autonomous divisions or profit centers, with the specific aim of relating the earnings of a division to the investment required to generate those earnings. Residual income is measured in dollars, while return on investment is a ratio.

In 1993, *Fortune* magazine's cover story, entitled "The Real Key to Creating Wealth," announced the arrival of economic value added (EVA) as the performance measurement metric of the 1990s.[1] *CFO* magazine polled senior executives in November 1996 and reported that 30 percent had some form of EVA program in place and another 10 percent were currently evaluating the measure.[2] EVA generated a surge of related consulting, with numerous consultants promoting the latest performance measure. CFROI (cash flow return on investment), TBR (total business return), and SVA (shareholder value added) are just a few examples of the various acronyms devised for various versions of the residual income concept.

Are EVA and its derivatives really residual income repackaged for the more recent times? Mark Ubelhart, practice leader at the compensation consulting firm Hewitt Associates LLC, seems to believe they are: "The fact is, EVA, CFROI, and all the others are premised on fundamental economics that 20 years ago were called residual income."[3] Stern Stewart & Co., the apparent inventor of EVA, appears to agree. EVA was described in their literature as "the 'residual income' that remains after subtracting the cost of all capital (debt and equity) from after-tax operating profits."[4]

Residual income is a useful measurement tool for general managers, regardless of its origins. Every chief executive officer (CEO) should understand that the market rewards companies that not only produce profits, but also do so in a way that efficiently deploys the capital of investors. Managers focused on increasing residual income at the business unit level will typically make decisions that mirror those of an owner of the company. Residual income can be measured throughout the organization and align the actions of managers at all levels with the strategic objectives of the company.

The Definition of Residual Income

Residual income consists of the "profit" remaining after the suppliers of all of the resources that were consumed to generate revenues have been fairly compensated, including the supplier of the capital, the investor or the parent corporation. Residual income is calculated by assessing a corporate capital charge against the earnings of a profit center, which is subtracted from division income, to arrive at division residual income. The capital charge is calculated by multiplying the relevant investment base by a prescribed interest rate that reflects the required return to the suppliers of capital. Suppose, for example, that a division had a profit of $20,000 per year on an investment (net assets) of $50,000, and the company's cost of capital was 10 percent. The 10 percent capital charge rate would be applied to the investment base indicating a capital charge of $5,000. The capital charge would then be deducted from the division profit of $20,000 to yield a residual income of $15,000. In this example, the return on investment would be 40 percent ($20,000 profit/$50,000 investment). The residual income of $15,000 represents profit over and above the cost of the corporate capital investment in the division. The general manager could use either the 40 percent return on investment (compared to the 10 percent cost of capital) or the residual income (EVA) of $15,000, or both, as measures of division performance.

Some companies also evaluate division performance using the ratio of residual income to corporate investment. This return measure relates the "profit" remaining after all factor costs have been accounted for to the investment required to generate the profit. In the example above, the residual income return on investment (RIROI) would be the $15,000 (RI) divided by the $50,000 (investment), or 30 percent. This residual income return on investment is similar to traditional return on investment measures, with the added feature of the division having been explicitly charged for the cost of invested funds.

Components of Residual Income and Return Measures

The accurate assessment of division performance requires that the results reflect the total impact of the division management's decisions and include no allocated costs, revenues, assets, or liabilities from the parent. The estimation methods for each component of residual income or return on investment measures that conform to the above principle are discussed below.

The Investment Base

There are two issues related to the determination of the investment base. The first issue is to identify the line items from the division's balance sheet to be included in the investment base. The two most commonly used investment bases are net assets (total assets minus current liabilities) and corporate equity (total assets minus total liabilities). The second issue is to determine the dollar value to assign to each line item included in the investment base.

NET ASSETS Net assets are defined as total assets less non-interest-bearing current liabilities. The inclusion of a specific balance sheet account in the investment base depends on the degree of control division management exercises over the level of the account. Total assets are determined as follows: Cash should be included in the total asset base, but only in the amount necessary for ongoing operations. Any excess cash, above the minimum cash balance required for operations, is a corporate resource and the decision to leave it in the division's accounts rather than transferring it to a centralized corporate account is a corporate, not a division, decision.

Accounts receivable and inventories are usually entirely under the control of the division and vary with the level of business activity. For this reason, they should be included in the total asset base. If corporate policy affects the level of these assets, then appropriate adjustments must be made to approximate the levels of these asset accounts without corporate interference.

Fixed assets should be included in the total asset base, but adjustments may need to be made. In the case of more than one division sharing the use of an asset, the value of the asset should be allocated among the two or more divisions. Allocating jointly used assets, such as a shared office facility, is frequently based on each division's proportional usage.

Idle assets, which do not contribute to profits but are included in the investment base, reduce a division's apparent performance. These idle assets must be included in the investment base, however, if the division management has the option of disposing of them. If the corporation requires that the division retain the idle assets for some future use, then these assets should be excluded from the division's investment base.

The appropriate current liabilities to be deducted from total assets to determine the division's investment base are those that are under the control of division management, such as accounts payable. The selection of vendors and the negotiating power and skill of the division management determine credit terms and can significantly alter the price of purchased materials.

Short-term debt carried by the division should be excluded from the calculation of net assets. All debt is ultimately the responsibility of the parent corporation, which determines its appropriate financial structure. Whether the debt is carried by the divisions or by the parent corporation is not subject to the control of division management.

Any other current liabilities should be included in the calculation of the net asset investment base if they result from division operations, but should be excluded if they result from corporate policies or decisions.

The use of net assets provides a very useful, if not the best, measure of the corporate investment in a division. The evaluation of division performance based on net assets provides the proper incentives to division management to minimize the investment required from the parent corporation.

CORPORATE EQUITY   The use of a division's corporate equity as its investment base is equivalent to using a net asset investment base, unless the division has long-term debt on its balance sheet. An accurate evaluation of division operating performance is achieved by eliminating all division debt from the investment base and all interest expense from the division's income statement. The end result of this adjustment is that corporate equity and net assets are identical for the purpose of determining the division's investment base.

THE VALUATION OF ASSETS AND LIABILITIES   The assets and liabilities included in the investment base for a division are normally included at their book value in the division's accounts. The feasible alternatives available for fixed asset valuation are net book value and replacement cost. The use of the book value of assets may reduce management's incentive to make capital investments because new equipment must generate increases in profits to offset the increases in the investment base. In the short term, division management may attempt to improve performance by not investing in new capital projects.

The use of replacement cost as a basis for fixed asset valuation is intended to compensate for the effects of inflation. Current income may be related to an investment base that includes a high proportion of older fixed assets recorded at low historical costs and reduced further by depreciation. This situation would yield inflated returns compared to the same business with newer assets purchased at more recent prices. Valuing fixed assets at replacement cost would make the division's capital charge independent of the age of the assets, but practical problems accompany this approach.

Implementing replacement cost valuation methods requires extensive effort and much subjective judgment. Each asset must be evaluated separately, and determining a replacement cost may be impossible because of imperfect markets, specialized equipment, or changes in technology. The successful implementation of a replacement cost approach, while sound in concept, is prohibitively expensive and time-consuming. The values carried in the accounting records for assets are generally favored because they are objectively determined and readily available. The distortion to estimates of residual income caused by an aging asset base will be mitigated by the mix of ages of assets in an ongoing business brought about by the continuous investment in new assets.

For these reasons, net book value remains the preferred method for determining the value of assets for either approach to measuring profit center performance.

The Capital Charge Rate

The capital charge rate serves a dual purpose. It is used to determine the capital charge for the purpose of calculating residual income and it is (or should be) a market-based hurdle rate for new investment opportunities. A division manager evaluated on division residual income theoretically would accept any investment proposal with a higher rate of return than the capital charge rate because it would increase residual income.

If the division does not consistently earn sufficient profits to cover the costs of the investment, the corporation could improve overall results by selling or spinning-off the division. The challenge is how to set the capital charge rate such that the parent corporation is adequately compensated for its investment in the division and the division management is motivated to make strategically valid decisions in a variety of situations.

There are three philosophies on how to set the capital charge rate:

- Set the capital charge rate based upon the marginal cost of debt. This assumes that the operating results or liquidation of a division would provide funds that could be used to retire corporate debt.

- Set the capital charge rate based on the weighted average cost of capital for the corporation, with or without an adjustment to compensate for differing levels of risk between divisions or between the various assets within a division.
- Set the capital charge rate or hurdle rate to equal the target return on net assets desired by the CEO or general manager to have the company judged by the investment community to be a "premium company." This approach results in a charge rate consistent with the returns earned by the set of companies that command "premium" share price multiples.

At a minimum, a division must return the cost of the debt that could be eliminated if the business were to be divested. The next threshold that a division might be required to contribute would be its full share of the corporation's cost of funds, which would be the weighted average cost of capital adjusted for the division's risk level. The highest level of return a unit would be expected to achieve would be some arbitrary level associated with the goal of the firm to meet the expectations of the investment community for a "premium company."

The advantages of a capital charge rate based upon the cost of debt are:

- It is a minimum figure that allows positive residual income to be earned by a business that is struggling to improve and whose performance is approaching adequate levels. This will provide positive reinforcement for motivational purposes.
- The interest rate on corporate debt is known and understood by division managers. The capital charge assessed against a division is therefore easily explained and more readily accepted by division managers.

Using the marginal debt rate, however, would understate the required return of all investors in the company, and potentially lead general managers to make decisions that would destroy value for the equity holders.

There are three practical problems with assessing a capital charge equal to the cost of capital:

- The calculation of the cost of capital involves estimating the cost of equity. The cost of equity is the subject of considerable debate and may depend on subjective estimates that can lead to counterproductive internal squabbles and deflect effort from achieving the objectives that residual income reporting is designed to reinforce.

- The corporation's risk profile may differ considerably from a division's risk profile. Adjusting the corporation's cost of capital to account for a division's different risk level is subjective and/or complicated. Not adjusting for different risk levels among divisions is unfair, penalizing low-risk divisions and benefiting high-risk divisions.

- Assessing a capital charge rate equal to the cost of capital implies that a division that does everything required of it by the parent corporation will have a residual income equal to, or greater than zero. A residual income of zero may have a negative impact on division morale and motivation since its future may be in doubt.

If the general manager is judged on improvements in residual income (RI) rather than the level of RI, then the division's motivational issues will be mitigated, and the general manager will focus on improving the performance of the division.

There are major advantages to using a more demanding capital charge or discount rate after a firm is earning its cost of capital. Management can determine the level of return on investment consistent with the stature the firm wants to have within the investment community. As described earlier, a return on equity of 20 percent or greater may lead to share-price-to-earnings multiples of twenty to twenty-five or greater. A firm that prunes less-profitable stock-keeping units (SKUs), product lines, plants, or divisions may evolve into a leaner and more profitable smaller firm that enjoys a propitious share price multiple.

Net Income

In a diversified, decentralized corporation, the choice of methods for measuring the net income of a division is complicated by competing corporate objectives. Division net income should ideally reflect only those revenues and costs that are the direct result of division efforts and decisions, and should include few, if any, corporate cost allocations. Division net income would then be a measure of the division's true contribution to corporate profits.

The allocation of corporate expenses to the divisions reduces division profitability, cannot be controlled by division management, and might reduce the level of motivation. Substantial effort may be expended by division management to alter the allocation of expenses to their division, diverting effort from the primary task of improving the division's contribution to corporate performance. The allocation of corporate expenses to a division is proper when the divisions request the use of corporate resources and are charged for the quantity consumed. Many well-run companies, however, choose not to allocate corporate expenses to operating divisions. They choose instead to aggregate the earnings of the profit centers and then subtract corporate expenses to determine consolidated corporate net income.

The best measure of the contribution of a division to the corporation is profit before corporate allocations (including interest) and before tax, because it is unaffected by factors outside of divisional control. It may be advantageous, however, for corporate management to charge a marginal tax rate at the divisional level. The marginal tax rate provides a minimum estimate of the taxes the division would pay, assuming profitability.

Taxes should generally be excluded from the calculation of residual income, however, because the amount of the tax to be paid by a corporation is a function of overall corporate profitability, past corporate performance, corporate tax accounting policies, and prevailing tax rates. An exception to excluding tax effects from divisional performance evaluation logically applies to industries that qualify for special tax incentives, such as mining or oil exploration. It would be misleading to compare the performance of a division in the extractive industries to another division on a before-tax basis, without accounting for the special tax treatment.

A Corporate Example

Exhibits 14-1 to 14-4 provide a detailed example of the calculation of residual income for the XYZ Corporation, a diversified corporation with four operating divisions. The XYZ Corporation evaluates its divisions on

EXHIBIT 14-1 Balance Sheet

	Total	Div. A	Div. B	Div. C	Div. D	Corporate
	Year Ended 12/31/—($ in thousands)					
Assets						
Cash	$14,000	$1,000	$4,000	$500	$500	$8,000[1]
Accounts Receivable	$8,000	$4,000	$1,000	$1,000	$2,000	$0
Inventory	$40,000	$18,000	$7,000	$6,500	$8,500	$0
Total Current Assets	$62,000	$23,000	$12,000	$8,000	$11,000	$8,000
Fixed Assets	$50,000	$28,000	$6,000	$7,000	$6,000	$3,000[2]
Accumulated Depreciation	($15,000)	($8,000)	($4,000)	$0	($2,000)	($1,000)
Net Fixed Assets	$35,000	$20,000	$2,000	$7,000	$4,000	$2,000
Other Assets	$3,000	$2,000	$0	$1,000	$0	$0
Total Assets	$100,000	$45,000	$14,000	$16,000	$15,000	$10,000
Liabilities						
Accounts Payable	$30,000	$6,000	$8,000	$9,000	$7,000	$0
Notes Payable	$5,000	$5,000	$0	$0	$0	$0
Deferred Expenses	$3,000	$0	$1,000	$2,000	$0	$0
Total Current Liabilities	$38,000	$11,000	$9,000	$11,000	$7,000	$0
Long-term Debt	$20,000	$0	$0	$0	$0	$20,000
Owners' Equity	$42,000	$34,000	$5,000	$5,000	$8,000	($10,000)
Total Liabilities and Owners' Equity	$100,000	$45,000	$14,000	$16,000	$15,000	$10,000

[1]Represents $8,000,000 in cash held in centralized corporate accounts.
[2]Represents corporate headquarters land and building purchased at a cost of $3,000,000 with a current book value of $2,000,000.

the basis of residual income before tax using a net asset investment base and a capital charge rate equal to the interest rate on outstanding short-term debt.

- Exhibit 14-1 shows the balance sheets for the four divisions, corporate, and the total company.
- Exhibit 14-2 shows the calculation of the division investment bases for the four divisions.
- Exhibit 14-3 shows the income statements for the four divisions and the total company.
- Exhibit 14-4 shows the calculation of the division capital charges and residual income.

EXHIBIT 14-2   Calculation of Division Investment Bases

Year Ended 12/31/—($ in thousands)						
	Total	Div. A	Div. B	Div. C	Div. D	Corporate
Assets						
Cash	$14,000	$1,000	$1,600	$500	$500	$10,400[1]
Accounts Receivable	$8,000	$4,000	$1,000	$1,000	$2,000	$0
Inventory	$40,000	$18,000	$7,000	$6,500	$8,500	$0
Total Current Assets	$62,000	$23,000	$9,600	$8,000	$11,000	$10,400
Fixed Assets	$50,000	$28,000	$6,000	$7,000	$4,000	$5,000[2]
Accumulated						
Depreciation	($15,000)	($8,000)	($4,000)	$0	($500)	($2,500)
Net Fixed Assets	$35,000	$20,000	$2,000	$7,000	$3,500	$2,500
Other Assets	$3,000	$2,000	$0	$1,000	$0	$0
Total Assets	$100,000	$45,000	$11,600	$16,000	$14,500	$12,900
Liabilities						
Accounts Payable	$30,000	$6,000	$8,000	$9,000	$7,000	$0
Notes Payable	$5,000	$0	$0	$0	$0	$5,000[3]
Deferred Expenses	$3,000	$0	$1,000	$2,000	$0	$0
Total Current Liabilities	$38,000	$6,000	$9,000	$11,000	$7,000	$5,000
Net Assets	$62,000	$39,000	$2,600	$5,000	$7,500	$7,900

Investment Base for Calculation of Capital Charge

Adjustments
[1]Excess cash balances held by divisions were removed from division investment bases (net assets). Division B was holding $2,400,000 in cash above the minimum required to sustain normal operations.
[2]The gross book value and accumulated depreciation for the idle facility held by Division D were removed from the division's investment base. Division D wanted to sell the facility but corporate management requested they hold it for possible future use.
[3]The $5,000,000 in short-term notes payable held by Division A were transferred to the corporate accounts and replaced by corporate equity in the division when calculating net assets. All debt held by the divisions is the responsibility of the corporation and this debt was held by the division because of corporate policy.

Each of the exhibits is heavily annotated to indicate the series of assumptions that were made in the process of calculating the various elements of the residual income of the divisions.

The calculation of the capital charge utilized the investment base (see Exhibits 14-1 and 14-2) and the capital charge rate. The XYZ Corporation used net assets valued at net book value for the investment base for each division. The net assets value was used because it reflected the parent investment in each division and encouraged judicious management of current li-

EXHIBIT 14-3   Income Statement

	Total	Div. A	Div. B	Div. C	Div. D
			Year Ended 12/31/—($ in thousands)		
Net Sales	$450,000	$95,000	$200,000	$70,300	$84,700
Cost of Goods Sold	$280,000	$36,000	$160,000	$49,300	$34,700
Gross Margin	$170,000	$59,000	$40,000	$21,000	$50,000
Selling Expense	$40,000	$12,000	$5,000	$12,000	$11,000
General and Administrative Expense	$55,000	$17,300	$10,800	$8,000	$18,900
Interest Expense	$1,000	$1,000	$0	$0	$0
Contribution Margin	$74,000	$28,700	$24,200	$1,000	$20,100
Allocated Corporate Overhead	$32,000	$6,700	$14,200	$5,000	$6,100
Profit Before Tax	$42,000	$22,000	$10,000	($4,000)	$14,000
Taxes	$21,000	$11,000	$5,000	($2,000)	$7,000
Profit After Tax	$21,000	$11,000	$5,000	($2,000)	$7,000

Other Information

- XYZ Corporation divisions require between .5% and .8% of net sales as minimum cash balances.
- The interest rate on short-term debt is 15%.
- The interest rate on long-term debt which was acquired 12 years ago is 10%.
- XYZ Corporation's cost of capital is 20% before tax, 10% after tax.
- All divisions have similar levels of risk.
- Division D has an idle facility that produced a product no longer marketed by the division. This facility has a gross book value of $2,000,000 and accumulated depreciation of $1,500,000.
- The tax rate = 50%.

abilities as well as assets. Fixed assets were valued at net book value because the added effort and subjective judgments necessary to value fixed assets at replacement cost was not warranted for an ongoing business with a reasonable mix of asset ages. Idle plant and equipment, excess cash balances, and short-term debt held by the divisions were excluded from division investment bases because they resulted from corporate, not division, decisions.

The residual income represents the contribution each division made to overall corporate profit on a before-tax basis, after all factor costs incurred by the divisions were recognized. Each division was charged only for the costs subject to division control. Income reported by the divisions was included only to the contribution margin line in order to exclude corporate

EXHIBIT 14-4   Calculation of Division Capital Changes

Year Ended 12/31/—($ in thousands)					
		Div. A	Div. B	Div. C	Div. D
Net Assets (investment base)		$39,000	$2,600	$5,000	$7,500
Capital Charge at 15% (interest rate on short term debt)		$5,850	$390	$750	$1,125
	Total	Div. A	Div. B	Div. C	Div. D
Sales	$450,000	$95,000	$200,000	$70,300	$84,700
Cost of Goods Sold	$279,950	$36,000	$160,000	$49,300	$34,650[1]
Gross Margin	$170,050	$59,000	$40,000	$21,000	$50,050
Selling Expense	$40,000	$12,000	$5,000	$12,000	$11,000
General and Administrative Expense	$55,000	$17,300	$10,800	$8,000	$18,900
Contribution Margin	$75,050	$29,700	$24,200	$1,000	$20,150[2]
Capital Charge		$5,850	$390	$750	$1125
Residual Income Before Tax		$23,850	$23,810	$250	$19,025

Adjustments:
[1]$50,000 in depreciation expense on the idle facility held by division D has been excluded from the cost of goods sold.
[2]Interest expense associated with Division A short-term debt has been excluded as a corporate expense not subject to division control.

overhead expenses that were outside of division control (see Exhibit 14-3). Interest expense and depreciation on the idle facility were excluded from division expenses because these expenses resulted from decisions made at the corporate level.

The capital charge rate was 15 percent, the interest rate on the outstanding short-term debt. The 15 percent rate was used for two reasons:

- It represented the current cost of funds for further investment or disinvestment (within a reasonable range).
- Division managers readily accepted the current interest rate on short-term debt as a fair rate to be charged for the use of corporate funds.

The residual income, as calculated in Exhibit 14-4 for the divisions of the XYZ Corporation, reflects the results of division management's decisions and actions and is therefore a fair measure of division performance. Management actions that achieve the objectives of improved efficiency and profitable growth will increase division residual income and improve overall corporate performance.

Residual Income versus Return on Investment Measures

The primary objective of a division manager is to sustain a consistently outstanding return on invested capital and grow the business at a rate equal to or greater than market growth. The growth can be a combination of organic (internal) growth and the acquisition of other businesses. This is accomplished through the efficient use of resources (assets) and by increasing the size of the business through profitable expansion in existing and new markets. Residual income and return on investment measures are both designed to connect profits to the assets employed.

The advantages of return on investment measures are:

- They provide a common denominator for divisions whose investment bases vary. They measure the efficiency with which a division uses its assets, independent of the size of the investment base.
- They are familiar concepts in widespread use. Shareholders, security analysts, and business periodicals routinely use return on investment ratios to compare the performance of companies and industries.
- They are directly comparable to the company's return on investment objectives.

Measures of return on investment have one major disadvantage. Under certain circumstances, if a division's return on investment is not compared to a required return or hurdle rate, a division general manager may seek to improve his or her overall return on investment by not investing in, or even liquidating lines of business that offer attractive returns. Any line of business that yields a return less than the current average return (for all other lines of business) reduces the overall return on investment. The general manager could thus increase the division ROI by liquidating the below-average lines of business.

The current dominance of return on investment measures for division performance evaluation results from the entrenched position of return measures in the financial community and the added complexity of residual income calculations.

Summary

Residual income and return on investment measures are effective management control tools because they measure performance in regard to the primary objectives of a general manager, which are to sustain a consistently outstanding return on invested capital and continually grow the business at a rate equal to or greater than market growth.

The effective use of residual income and return on investment performance measures requires that two of the key components of the calculations—division income and the investment base—be controlled by division management and exclude all corporate allocations. A third component of the residual income calculation—the capital charge rate—should reflect management's judgment as to the best means to align the interests of division general managers with the objectives of corporate management. These approaches to performance measurement enhance the corporate objective of steering division decisions in an environment of decentralized management, and if used appropriately, provide alignment between managers and owners.

DISCUSSION QUESTIONS

1. What led to the intense interest in EVA in the 1990s?
2. Should assets be valued at replacement costs?
3. How should the capital charge rate be determined?
4. How should a general manager choose between EVA and ROI measures?
5. Why are ROI measures more widely used?

15

THE ALLOCATION (REDEPLOYMENT) OF CAPITAL (CASH)

The allocation of available and anticipated levels of cash to strategic and operational initiatives constitutes one of the most important duties of the general manager. A firm begins competing with a prescribed capital structure, normally consisting of a combination of debt and equity. Throughout this book, the examples have stressed the great strategic value attributable to a strong balance sheet. There is, of course, a wide diversity of opinion about the definition of a "strong balance sheet." For the purposes of this book, we assume that a (book value) debt to capital ratio of .35, which corresponds roughly to an AA (double A) bond rating, would be recognized by most authorities as constituting a strong balance sheet.

Assume that a firm begins its corporate life with such a balance sheet. From the beginning, the general manager must make strategic decisions about deploying the available cash among such possible uses as purchasing plants and equipment, acquiring raw material and purchased parts inventories, and financing finished goods inventories and accounts receivable. As operations commence, the firm experiences increases in the amount of available cash as a result of:

- Cash flow from operations,
- The raising of additional equity, and
- The availability of additional debt, made available by earnings retained that increase both equity and debt capacity, given a target debt to capital ratio.

The chief executive officer (CEO) or general manager must then deal with a myriad of possible uses for the existing cash. Some of the available cash will be allocated to alternative uses within the various businesses in which the company currently competes. Such uses include:

- The allocation of cash to a variety of capital projects,
- The repayment of debt,
- The payout of dividends, and/or
- The repurchase of outstanding shares.

The general manager may also choose to restructure the company through the process of entering new businesses and exiting others by:

- The divestiture of current businesses, and/or
- The acquisition of additional businesses.

The general manager must continually make decisions regarding the allocation of the available cash to these and other possible uses. Further, these are among the most crucial decisions the general manager makes.

Cash Flow from Operations

This is the cash flow (positive or negative) that results from a period of operations (a month, a quarter, or a year). As we discuss in some detail in Chapter 11, there are differences among companies in their propensity for generating or using cash. In fact, given a company's forecast income statement, balance sheet, and expected growth rate, its inherent cash-flow-generating characteristics can be calculated. This is an important attribute of any firm, since few firms generate exactly the amount of cash needed for ongoing operations.

Capital Budgeting and Strategic Planning

The corporate form of business organization is especially effective at aggregating large amounts of capital, allowing firms to undertake major projects. Organizations are intent upon increasing shareholder value by investing in initiatives with returns higher than the firm's cost of capital. The greater the number and variety of proposed projects whose estimated returns exceed the cost of capital, the more difficult the task of the corporate officers who must allocate the available capital among its numerous businesses and initiatives. The final set of approved projects is commonly referred to as the firm's capital budget. Viewed from the outside, the most tangible information about a company's intentions and strategy is reflected in its allocation of its available capital funds. Divisions, product lines, or projects that have less strategic importance to a company normally receive little or no funding.

The capital budgeting process is concerned with long-term investments that require extensive commitments of funds, such as land, buildings and facilities, equipment and machinery, vehicles or aircraft, and information technology undertakings. It is concerned not only with physical assets that are capitalized in the accounting sense but also with issues that are linked to an organization's strategic plan, such as the funds allocated for research and development spending or business combinations and divestitures.

In theory, the capital budget is inextricably linked to an organization's strategic objectives and planning goals. A company's strategic objectives are usually expressed in general terms. Concrete and attainable goals are then derived as part of the strategic plan. These goals are typically defined in the strategic plan in terms of return on assets, market share, or profitability. The investments that a company chooses to undertake from a range of potentially profitable opportunities have to be consistent with the company's strategic objectives and planning goals.

In practice, however, the link from investment proposals to strategy is often weak or even nonexistent. The capital budgeting process may, in fact, impede or complicate strategy formation.[1] This anomaly comes about from the dichotomy that proposals for capital spending most often originate at lower levels in the organization based on perceived needs at that level, without the corporate strategic perspective. It should be noted, however, that small projects can sometimes bubble up through the organization, form patterns, and eventually change the very strategy of a firm. This might be termed the inevitability of gradualism. The invention of the Post-it notes within 3M Corporation is a case in point, since this blockbuster product emanated from deep within the organization from the efforts of a single individual.

Types of Capital Investments

Capital investments can be classified in a number of ways. One method of classification is by the form of benefits the organization is expected to receive (or lack thereof), as follows.

Obligatory

These investments are either dictated by law or required for replacing currently needed, nonfunctioning assets. The Americans with Disabilities Act (ADA) Standards for Accessible Design, for example, require work areas to be designed and constructed so that they are accessible to individuals with disabilities. Increasingly stringent environmental regulations also drive corporations to increase spending to control pollution. Obligatory investments typically do not generate a positive return on investment in the strict economic sense, but they may be necessary in order to continue operating a given facility.

Financial justification does not normally enter into decisions about obligatory projects, but they may command a significant amount of available funds, depending on the specific industry.

Cost Reduction

The experience curve, when it exists, describes an inverse exponential relationship between the costs incurred and the cumulative volume of products or services produced. In simpler words, as experience increases with cumulative increases in production, costs usually decline systematically. This phenomenon is evident in many manufacturing and service industries, and is especially apparent in the semiconductor industry, where chip costs, and thus prices, have declined by 48 percent a year over an extended time period.[2] In order to benefit from the declining costs and retain their cost leadership positions, companies have to invest in new production facilities and technologies. Such investments border on being necessitated by the strategic position of the company and the industry within which it competes.

Targeted productivity improvement programs, such as business process reengineering or information technology initiatives, are undertaken to provide an overall reduction in relative operating costs. Wal-Mart's recent decision to replace bar codes with radio frequency tags on products is expected to realize annual cost savings in the range of $1.3 billion to $1.5 billion, based on 2002 sales levels.[3] Many organizations implement enterprise resource planning (ERP) solutions to streamline operations and increase supply chain efficiencies in order to lower costs.

Firms often want projects of this type to have estimated future returns on investment of 40–50 percent. This is partly caused by a frequent tendency for project sponsors to systematically overstate the expected returns.

New Products and Services

Products in the pioneering stage are usually characterized by negative or low profitability and large investment requirements. These investments create future options for management to expand or contract production, based on characteristics of the product life cycle. Research and development budgets in pharmaceutical firms and other risky businesses fall into this category.

Technology companies that are highly dependent on the rate of innovation to compete have to be especially mindful of managing the resource allocation process and criteria for funding proposals. Innovation proposals that are sufficiently funded may succeed. Lower-priority proposals will starve for lack of resources and have little chance of success. The expected returns on investment for such projects are frequently 30 percent or more, partly to mitigate the considerable risk required in bringing new products and services to market.

Growth within Current Businesses and Products

Companies that adopt a growth strategy would normally want to grow their net assets consistent with the expected market growth rate. Knowledge-intensive organizations may have to increase capital spending in research and development, beyond the growth of physical assets. Conversely, investment needs classically decline as product lines mature.

Capital projects designed to expand capacity for organic growth of existing products and services involve less risk and would normally be expected to project returns greater than the cost of capital or the company's strategic return goal.

Product or Service Differentiation

In most markets, products or services that are differentiated by unique features or quality are able to generate excess returns in the long term. To attain such an enviable market position, companies usually must invest heavily in research and development, production processes, and advertising and marketing to create barriers of entry for their competitors. When Gillette launched the Mach3 razor, it had invested $750 million in custom machinery and production facilities and planned to invest another $300 million in the initial marketing program. Gillette's goal was to make the Mach3 a long-lived, cash-producing, consumer product.[4]

Such projects carry somewhat greater risk than those for organic growth, so most companies would want expected returns to be significantly higher than the cost of capital, often 25–30 percent.

Discretionary Investments

Discretionary investments are not mandatory to a firm's survival. Customer relationship management (CRM) software packages, corporate aircraft, and most information technology spending fall under this category. Corporations also invest in such discretionary activities as gymnasiums, running tracks, company-funded cafeterias, contributions to charity events in the communities in which they are located, and numerous other activities felt to be in the best interests of the shareholders.

Such expenditures are not expected to provide easily identifiable economic return to the company.

Analyzing Proposals for Capital Expenditures

Each organization has its unique approach to analyzing, measuring, and selecting capital investment projects. All new managers, including graduates of business schools, have to learn and adapt to their employer's approach, while grasping the strengths and weaknesses of the logic and techniques used. Some frequently used tools and techniques for analyzing capital expenditure proposals are described briefly here, in the context of the understanding required by a general manager. A reader interested in more detailed presentations of these techniques should consult appropriate accounting or finance texts.

Net Present Value (NPV) of the Discounted Cash Flows (DCF)

This is the most widely used method for evaluating capital projects. The investment is evaluated by summing the present value of cash outflows required to support an investment with the present value of cash inflows generated by operations of the resulting project. While it is the most commonly used analytical approach, there are challenges related to the determination of appropriate terminal values (future cash flows beyond the planning horizon) and the appropriate discount rate.

Internal Rate of Return (IRR)

The internal rate of return is defined as the discount rate that results in an NPV of zero. The IRR is a widely accepted method for comparing projects, since the IRR of several projects competing for funding can readily be compared to each other and to the company's cost of capital or hurdle rate.

Payback Period

The payback period refers to the time required until cash inflows equal cash outlays. While it is easy to explain and compute, the measure ignores cash flows beyond the end of the payback period. The typical payback period used to evaluate projects is between two and three years, which usually corresponds to a return on investment of 35–50 percent. Managers may employ this approach for lower-level projects because most people readily understand it. CEOs use this approach because of the pressures they are under for short-term results. They can rarely take a chance on a project with a very high potential NPV or IRR, but which will be cash flow negative each year, say, for the first seven years.

A Typical Capital Budgeting Process

Capital budgeting (developing the list of projects to be recommended to the board of directors) usually has to be completed in the third quarter of a company's fiscal year so that the projected capital base (assets)

EXHIBIT 15-1   A Typical Process for Capital Budgeting

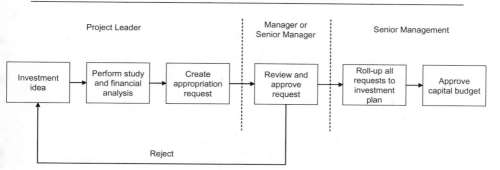

can be fixed before the other budgets are finalized, thus locking in the return on net assets (RONA) and return on equity (ROE) estimates. In order to complete the process in the third quarter, the identification of potential projects and the analyses of their pros and cons will have taken place even earlier in the fiscal year. Most companies of any size have formal processes that prescribe the required dates for these analyses to be completed.

The capital budgeting exercise can take a top-down or bottom-up approach. Most organizations utilize processes that are a combination of the two, with much negotiation and compromise along the way. As noted before, in practice, it is more of a bottom-up approach than top-down. A typical bottom-up process is shown in the diagram in Exhibit 15-1.

Approval of the capital budget is separate from the approval of the individual projects. Detailed analysis and planning must occur in order for individual projects to be recommended by the appropriate managers. As we explain herein, the total amount of capital requested by the operating units will invariably exceed the cash available to fund them. The process of deciding which projects will be funded involves a strategic point of view not available to lower-level managers. These strategic choices determine the long-term future of the company.

Consider a corporation with a total current cash flow of $550 million available for funding capital projects. Let us assume that the following proposals (listed by category in Exhibit 15-2) for capital expenditures have been submitted to corporate headquarters. Each proposed project is accompanied by analyses that show the project meets the corporate return criteria for its particular category of capital investment.

EXHIBIT 15-2   Capital Requests, by Type, Funds Requested, and Number of Projects

Type	Amount	Number
Obligatory	$25M	11 projects
Cost Reduction	$300M	131 projects
New Products	$275M	22 projects
Growth	$100M	41 projects
Differentiation	$250M	67 projects
Discretionary	$50M	78 projects
Total Requests	$1B	350 projects

The key question for the corporate office is how to choose the projects that will be funded with the expansive but still limited available funds ($550 million cash flow claimed by 350 requests totaling $1 billion), given that each project has been estimated by the responsible operating managers to meet the financial return criteria for its class of projects. Each type of project is intended to make a distinct contribution to one or more of the strategic and operational goals of the corporation. The choices made in this selection process will clearly structure the company's future. The CEO and his or her staff must ensure objectivity as they choose among the alternatives. The example illustrates the level of difficulty that is inherent in these choices.

It is very unlikely that the options perceived to be most important to the operating-level managers could smoothly fit with the strategic direction desired by the general manager. The more clearly the corporate strategy is articulated for all to understand, however, the more likely it is that the proposals from the operating units will mesh with the corporate goals and objectives.

Finally, measuring and controlling the progress of spending and completion are essential aspects of the capital investment process. Modern information systems allow projects to be monitored to ensure that specified financial and operational milestones will be met as funds are spent. They can also ensure that the total commitments for each project do not exceed the allocated capital budget.

Additional Uses of Cash

As described above, the general manager has several other uses for available cash over and above the amounts allocated to capital projects. He or she may choose to pay down outstanding debt or return some of the cash to shareholders through the payout of dividends or the repurchase of outstanding shares. The payout of dividends has become more attractive recently as a result of lower U.S. federal tax rates on dividend income for the recipients. Share repurchases, in theory, increase the value of the shares of the remaining shareholders but do not affect the total market capitalization of the firm. Share repurchases are discussed in detail in Chapter 16. When excess cash exists, general managers frequently use both of these methods to return some of the cash to shareholders, thus increasing shareholder value. Excess cash is defined as the cash remaining after funding all of the identified and selected investments that meet the strategic risk/return objectives of the firm, while maintaining the firm's target debt-to-capital ratio.

The Redeployment of Cash through Restructuring

There are situations in which the returns available from continuing current operations and the identified investment opportunities available within the current portfolio of businesses do not meet the return and/or the growth requirements of either the company's strategic plans or the expectations of the investment community for a "premium" company. In such cases, the general manager often seeks to redeploy the firm's capital (cash) into more attractive alternatives through a process of divestitures and acquisitions. This process is illustrated by Vignette 15-1, which describes the restructuring of PepsiCo, Inc. through the divestiture of its restaurant businesses and the subsequent acquisition of the Quaker Oats Company.

Summary

The actions of the general manager in allocating cash to various competing uses structure the company in the long run. These actions vary

VIGNETTE 15-1

A Successful Strategic Corporate Restructuring

The Issue

A major consumer goods company, PepsiCo, sought to complete a significant restructuring in order to continue to grow more profitably in a spirited competitive environment. In such situations, management must recognize the need or opportunity at hand and develop a recommended solution. As part of this process, senior management must present its recommendations to the board of directors. The board must come to understand the problem or opportunity and consent to management's recommendations before such action is taken.

The Situation

PepsiCo enjoyed a strong position in its industry, with a focus on both convenience foods and beverages, after emerging from a three-year restructuring effort. The company maintained dominant market positions in three key product areas: salty snacks (number one worldwide), beverages (number two worldwide), and branded juices (number one worldwide). Further, PepsiCo led the world in brand recognition with fifteen brands that generated more than $500 million in revenues per year each, including eleven brands that generated more than $1 billion each in revenues. A powerful distribution network augmented the marketing of this impressive portfolio of products worldwide.

The major restructuring of this company began in 1996, when management recognized the lack of strategic fit between its restaurant businesses and its other businesses. Management recommended and the board approved the spin-off of Pizza Hut, Taco Bell, Kentucky Fried Chicken, PepsiCo Food Systems, and several other non-core U.S. restaurant businesses into Tricon Global Restaurants. In 1998, PepsiCo completed the acquisitions of Tropicana Food Products and The Smith's Snackfoods Company (TSSC) in Australia. In addition, acquisitions and investments in unconsolidated affiliates, various bottlers, and other international salty snack food businesses brought the aggregate cost of acquisitions to $4.5 billion in cash in 1998. The company also completed a spin-off of bottling operations through an initial public offering (IPO) and completed a major acquisition of Quaker Oats.

The Results of the Actions of the CEO and the Board

The strategic moves to restructure the company through acquisitions and spin-offs (divestitures) led to a dramatic improvement in the company's financial results over the next five years. Results for the years 1996 and 2001 are shown in Exhibit 15-3.

(continued)

EXHIBIT 15-3 A Successful Strategic Corporate Restructuring

	PepsiCo's Transformation[1]	
1996	*Measures*	*2001E*
$31B	Revenues	$27B
12%	Operating Profit Margin	16%
$1.22	EPS	$1.66
$1.4B	Operating Cash Flow	$2.5B
15%	Return on Invested Capital	26%

[1]PepsiCo Presentation to the MS Global Consumer Conference, November 7, 2001.

New strategic initiatives included focusing on convenience in beverages and snack foods, completing the integration of Quaker Oats, leveraging existing broad distribution channels, and maintaining a balanced brand portfolio in the targeted market segments. The products were balanced as to demand at specific times of the day, consumer age groups, and states of consumer need (healthy versus indulgence).

The Point

As a result of these strategic initiatives, the board and management of PepsiCo completed a major restructuring of the company during a period of transition to a new CEO. These results speak well for the environment in which the board and the CEO could work together to reposition the company in a major way. The restructuring involved pruning away less-effective businesses (in terms of growth potential and returns on capital) and left a smaller but richer mix of businesses for the future.

from numerous, smaller-scale investments in various categories of operational projects to major, strategic moves that dramatically redeploy the company's capital through acquisitions and divestitures. The uses of cash by the general manager determine the long-term fate of the company.

DISCUSSION QUESTIONS

1. What are the major sources of cash for a company?
2. What are the major uses of cash for a company?

3. How should the sample company decide which capital projects to fund?
4. How can a general manager defend discretionary projects that may appear to shareholders to be "perks"?
5. What role does cash play in the restructuring of a company through acquisitions and divestitures?

16

SHARE REPURCHASES[1]

Share repurchases have become a widely used strategic tool for U.S. corporations (see Exhibit 16-1). This chapter explores the reasons why corporations repurchase shares, how share repurchase plans are implemented, and the implications of those plans.

Reasons for Share Repurchase

There are four key reasons a company repurchases its outstanding shares:

- To return excess funds to shareholders
- To increase the proportion of debt in the company's capital structure
- To signal the management's confidence in the company's stock to the financial markets
- To mount a corporate takeover defense

Companies also may choose to buy back shares in order to have them available for subsequent issue within employee benefit plans or to lower the costs of servicing shareholders,[2] but this chapter focuses on the four principal objectives cited above.

Return Excess Funds to Shareholders

A shareholder invests in a company and expects a certain return from the investment. This return is often measured as return on equity

EXHIBIT 16-1   Announced Share Repurchases in the United States

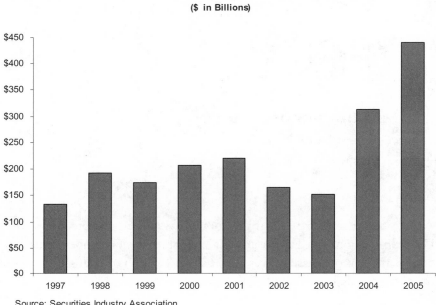

($ in Billions)

Source: Securities Industry Association

(ROE) or return on net assets (RONA). If the company is not employing its invested capital in a way that achieves the expected return, then the shareholder will likely sell his or her shares or demand that the capital be returned so that it can be invested elsewhere for a higher return.

Companies strive to achieve the returns expected by their investors, both in level and in consistency. To do so, a company might turn down new business opportunities that are expected to generate lower returns. Consider, for example, a company that has a strong balance sheet, consistently large annual cash flow, and an average RONA of 15 percent. If the company identifies a new product line that is likely to achieve a RONA of 10 percent, it might be tempted to pursue the new line if the company has excess cash. By pursuing the new line, however, the company would dilute its aggregate RONA. The shareholders, whose desired return on net assets was 15 percent, would prefer that the company return the excess cash to the shareholders and let them reinvest their capital in a different investment that would provide the desired 15 percent return. It is precisely this situation that drives companies with a strong balance sheet, solid cash flow, and a lack of compelling new investment opportunities to undertake share repurchase programs.

Share repurchases clearly are not appropriate for companies in all stages of the business cycle. In fact, share repurchase programs are typically pursued by more mature companies in low- to medium-growth industries. Younger, higher-growth companies are usually cash-short and can internally generate higher returns for any available capital. Thus, from a more macroeconomic perspective, share repurchases enable capital to be transferred from old-line companies to newer ones. As Harvard Business School professor Marc Bertoneche states: "Buy-backs are therefore an essential part of the process by which capital is recycled from mature companies with limited investment opportunities to young businesses with huge growth potential and enormous financing needs."[3]

But there are other ways to return excess cash to shareholders than through share repurchases. In fact, year after year, companies distribute billions of dollars to investors through regular and special dividend distributions. So why should a company choose to repurchase shares instead of issuing dividends? Primarily because the process of repurchasing shares is accretive to the remaining shareholders, increasing the value of their shares.

Given the benefits shareholders receive from repurchases, one might expect companies to choose to distribute cash in the form of repurchases instead of dividends. This is not the case, however. Most companies that institute share repurchase programs continue their dividend payments.[4] Investors often choose to buy the stock of a particular company because of the expected regular income that the shareholder can expect from dividend payouts. If a company were to halt its dividend payments, those investors would be upset about the loss of dividend income. To avoid upsetting shareholders, most companies continue to pay their regular dividend and opt to use repurchases for larger, perhaps irregular cash distributions. If a company has an unusually large amount of excess cash, the general manager may be reluctant to set an expectancy for higher dividends in the future and therefore choose not to increase dividend payments.[5]

Increase Proportion of Debt

When companies decide to increase the proportion of debt in their capital structure, they often use share repurchases to make the change.[6] As William Sihler explains: "the generation of excess funds indicates that excess capital is available to the company and that the organization can lower its capital costs . . . by decapitalizing. Whether this is done by reducing debt or equity, or some mixture of the two, depends on a determination of the appropriate capitalization for the company."[7] In most instances, companies choose to increase the proportion of debt in their decapitalization process.

Signal Management's Confidence in the Stock

Stock repurchases may also be used to signal a manager's confidence in the future of the company. For example, stock prices plummeted on Black Monday, October 19, 1987, and the next day many companies announced large share repurchases. Citicorp was the first to announce a share repurchase plan of $250 million, but many other companies quickly followed. In fact, within two days of the crash, firms announced a total of $6.2 billion in share repurchases as management and boards attempted to regain market confidence.[8] To emphasize the commitment of the board and management to the company's future, senior managers and directors usually hold onto their stock when companies offer to repurchase their shares at a premium price.[9] Were either party to sell, the financial markets would invariably interpret this as a vote of "no confidence" in the company's future. Insider sales in general, unless planned and disclosed well in advance, are almost universally frowned upon by capital markets.

Deter a Takeover Attempt

A company may choose to use share repurchases to deter a takeover attempt. Share repurchases protect a company from a hostile takeover in the following three ways.[10] First, the repurchase may persuade shareholders not to tender their shares in a takeover. Second, the share repurchase alters voting rights within a firm, making it more difficult to acquire the firm. Third, a repurchase removes the shareholders with the lowest reservation prices, thereby making it more expensive to buy the remaining shares.

Methods for Share Repurchase

There are three principal ways to repurchase stock.[11] The most common approach is for the firm to announce that it plans to buy its stock in the open market, similar to any other investor. Alternatively, a company can buy back a stated number of shares at a fixed price, which is typically set at about 20 percent above the current market level. This method allows individual shareholders to choose whether to accept the premium offer. Finally, a company can undertake a share repurchase via direct negotiation with one or more major shareholders. The most notorious examples of these negotiations are greenmail transactions that occur when the target of a takeover attempts to buy off the hostile bidder by repurchasing any shares that the hostile party has acquired.

Market Reaction to Share Repurchases

When a share repurchase is announced, the market tends to react positively, and the share price usually rises, but this rise is to be expected. By reducing the number of shares outstanding through a share repurchase, the company lowers the denominator in the earnings per share (EPS) calculation, thereby increasing EPS (see Exhibit 16-2 for an example). Because the performance of the company has not materially changed with the share repurchase, it is reasonable to expect the market to apply the same price/earnings (P/E) multiple to the EPS. Also, since the post-repurchase EPS is higher, the share price should rise accordingly. The fundamentals of the company have not changed, so the total market value or market capitalization (share price times the number of shares outstanding) should remain the same.

Notwithstanding that logic, the financial markets may reward a company's announcement of a share repurchase with a slight extra increase in share price. A study by Comment and Jarrell of the announcements of open-market repurchase programs found that, on average, the programs resulted in an abnormal price rise of 2 percent.[12] One explanation for this extra increase is that investors are pleased with management's decision to pay out the excess cash rather than risking it on less-profitable investments.[13] Investors are apparently willing to pay slightly more for strong management decision making.

A Methodology to Evaluate the Impact of Share Repurchases on Share Price

Assume, for example, that a company announces a five-year share repurchase program and intends to use $50 million in excess cash to repurchase shares on the open market each year. The current share price is $30 with ten million shares outstanding, and the stock trades at a 10.0x price-to-earnings multiple. The company expects to earn $33 million in net income next year, and an additional $3 million each subsequent year.

Exhibit 16-2 details the conceptual impact of a share repurchase program on share price within the first year. Management is often interested, however, in forecasting the potential share price impact of announcing and implementing a longer-term share repurchase program. One can either solve for the expected ending share price iteratively or by means of an analytical model. The iterative process is shown in Exhibit 16-3. The company should be able to repurchase 1.46 million shares at an average share price of $34.31, based on a share price of $38.63 at the end of the second year.

EXHIBIT 16-2   The Impact of Share Repurchases on Share Price
(one-time repurchase at fixed price)

Before Stock Repurchase	
Net Income	$30,000,000
Shares Outstanding	10,000,000
EPS	$3.00
P/E	10x
Share Price	**$30.00**
Market Capitalization	**$300,000,000**

After Stock Repurchase	
(Assume company bought 1,666,667 shares at $30 each)	
Net Income	$30,000,000
Shares Outstanding	8,333,333
EPS	$3.60
P/E	10x
Implied Share Price	**$36.00**
Market Capitalization	**$300,000,000**
Increase in Share Price	20%

EXHIBIT 16-3   An Iterative Process for Determining Share Price and Shares Outstanding (in successive years)

PAT (yr. 0) =	$30,000,000
Excess Cash =	$50,000,000 each year
Share Price =	$30.00
Shares Outstanding =	10,000,000
PAT (yr. 1) =	$33,000,000
Natural Equity Price (yr.1) =	$33.00
Average Buyback Price =	$31.50
First Iteration	
Shares Repurchased =	$50,000,000/$31.50 = 1,587,302 shares
Original EPS (yr. 0) =	$3.30/share (P/E = 10)
Tentative New EPS =	$33,000,000/(10,000,000 − 1,587,302) = $3.92
New Share Price =	$39.23
Actual Average Price of Shares Purchased =	(39.23 + 30.00) / 2 = $34.61
Second Iteration	
Shares Repurchased =	$50,000,000 / $34.61 = 1,444,535
New Shares =	8,555,465

Note: If this iterative process is continued to its asymptotic conclusion, the result is an average share price of $34.31, a final share price of $38.63, and a terminal shares outstanding of 8.54M shares.

The method outlined allows one to estimate iteratively the number of shares likely to be repurchased and the expected ending share price. The number of shares likely to be repurchased and the expected ending share price that should result from the implementation of a share repurchase program can be calculated directly using the formula in Exhibit 16-4.

As with the iterative approach, having calculated the expected ending share price, it is straightforward to find the likely average share price during the year of $34.31, resulting in the repurchase of an estimated 1.46 million shares. We want to emphasize that the actual results of any share repurchase program will be affected by many unpredictable factors. The approach described here provides a useful conceptual tool for general managers considering share repurchase programs.

EXHIBIT 16-4   A Formula for Calculating Share Price after Repurchase

$$Y = \frac{-[(S \times P) - 2C - (PE \times NI)] + SQRT\{[(S \times P) - (2 \times C) - (PE \times NI)]^2 + 4 \times S \times (PE \times NI \times P)\}}{2 \times S}$$

Where:

> Y = Share Price at the End of the Next Period
> P = Current Share Price = $30
> C = Excess Cash = $50M
> S = Current Shares Outstanding = 10M
> PE = Expected P/E Multiple with Share Repurchase Program = 10
> NI = Forecast Net Income Next Period = $33M

This formula is derived in the Technical Note referred to in note 1. Substituting the values for the previous example into the formula:

$$Y = \frac{-[(10^*30) - (2^*50) - (10^*33)] + SQRT\{[(10^*30) - (2^*50) - (10^*33)]^2 + (4^*10^*10^*33^*30)\}}{2^*10}$$

$$Y = \frac{130 + SQRT((-130)^2 + 396000))}{20}$$

$$Y = \frac{130 + 642.57}{20}$$

$$Y = \$38.63$$

The iterative methodology and/or the formula can be used to forecast the share price effects of a share repurchase program over time. Exhibit 16-5 shows the results of extending the example for five years.

Conclusion

Vignette 16-1 describes a company's recent experience with a share repurchase program over a five-year period. This example illustrates the application of these methodologies to the activities of an actual company.

General managers should consider implementing share repurchase programs in several situations, including times when the manager feels the stock is undervalued, instances when there are excess funds and there is a dearth of attractive internal investment opportunities, and situations when the manager must defend against corporate takeovers. As previously

EXHIBIT 16-5   The Effects of a Long-Term Share Repurchase Program

With Stock Purchase Program						
	Year 0	Year 1	Year 2	Year 3	Year 4	Year 5
Revenue	$500	$550	$600	$650	$700	$750
Net Income	$30	$33	$36	$39	$42	$45
Excess Cash	$50.00	$50.00	$50.00	$50.00	$50.00	$50.00
Shares Outstanding	10.00	8.54	7.40	6.48	5.73	5.11
EPS	$3.00	$3.86	$4.87	$6.02	$7.33	$8.81
P/E	10.0x	10.0x	10.0x	10.0x	10.0x	10.0x
Share Price	**$30.00**	**$38.63**	**$48.67**	**$60.20**	**$73.30**	**$88.06**
Average Share Price		$34.31	$43.65	$54.43	$66.75	$80.68
Shares Repurchased	—	1.4571	1.1455	0.9186	0.7491	0.6197
Market Capitalization	**$300.00**	**$330.00**	**$360.00**	**$390.00**	**$420.00**	**$450.00**
Without Stock Purchase Program						
	Year 0	Year 1	Year 2	Year 3	Year 4	Year 5
Shares Outstanding	10.00	10.00	10.00	10.00	10.00	10.00
EPS	$3.00	$3.30	$3.60	$3.90	$4.20	$4.50
P/E	10.0x	10.0x	10.0x	10.0x	10.0x	10.0x
Share Price	**$30.00**	**$33.00**	**$36.00**	**$39.00**	**$42.00**	**$45.00**
Market Capitalization	**$300.00**	**$330.00**	**$360.00**	**$390.00**	**$420.00**	**$450.00**

VIGNETTE 16-1

AutoZone, a specialty retailer of automotive parts and accessories, has aggressively repurchased its own shares since fiscal year 2000. In the late 1990s, the
company implemented a strategy focused on operational improvements designed
to enhance profit margins and generate free cash flow. As the company began to
generate cash flow in excess of its operating needs, the board of directors author-
ized a share repurchase program to return excess funds to shareholders and lower
its cost of capital by increasing the proportion of debt in its capital structure.

From the end of fiscal 2000 through 2005, AutoZone reduced its overall
share count by 34 percent as it repurchased a total of 54.2 million shares at an aggregate cost of $3.2 billion. The company's total capital (debt plus equity) in-
creased slightly from $2.2 billion to $2.3 billion while the proportion of total
debt to capital increased from 56 percent to 83 percent. However, total debt to
(continued)

VIGNETTE 16-1 *(continued)*

earnings before interest, taxes, depreciation, and amortization (EBITDA) declined from 2.0x at the end of 2000 to 1.6x in 2005.

Over the same period, AutoZone grew sales and net income at compound annual growth rates (CAGRs) of 5 percent and 17 percent, respectively. As a result of the additional effects of the share repurchase program, the company generated an EPS CAGR of 29 percent. The company also improved return on assets (ROA) from 8 percent to 14 percent and ROE from 27 percent to 147 percent while maintaining the only investment grade credit rating in its industry. The company provided shareholders with an average annual return of 33 percent with very little multiple expansion awarded by the investment community.

Addendum: AutoZone—Applying the Iterative Methodology

Exhibit 16-6 should be analyzed in conjunction with Exhibit 16-5. Assume that AutoZone's board of directors asks you to present the merits of a five-year share repurchase plan. Using the iterative methodology for projecting the long-term

EXHIBIT 16-6 AutoZone Projected Share Prices, with Repurchasing

Model Year	0	1	2	3	4	5
Fiscal Year	2000	2001P	2002P	2003P	2004P	2005P
With Share Repurchase Program						
Revenue	$4,483M	$4,818M	$5,216M	$5,457M	$5,637M	$5,711M
Net Income	$268	$271	$410	$506	$540	$575
Cash Used for Share Repurchases		$366	$699	$891	$848	$427
Shares Outstanding [1]	133.87	118.70	99.35	83.79	72.62	67.86
EPS	$2.00	$2.29	$4.13	$6.04	$7.43	$8.47
P/E [2]	11.3x	11.3x	11.3x	11.3x	11.3x	11.3x
Projected Share Price	$22.52	$25.75	$46.48	$68.09	$83.76	$95.48
Average Share Price		$24.14	$36.12	$57.29	$75.92	$89.62
Shares Repurchased		15.1674	19.3531	15.5554	11.1706	4.7631
Projected Market Cap	$3,015M	$3,057M	$4,618M	$5,705M	$6,083M	$6,479M

EXHIBIT 16-6

Model Year	0	1	2	3	4	5
Fiscal Year	2000	2001P	2002P	2003P	2004P	2005P
Without Stock Purchase Program						
Shares						
Outstanding	133.87	133.87	133.87	133.87	133.87	133.87
EPS	$2.00	$2.03	$3.06	$3.78	$4.03	$4.30
P/E	11.3x	11.3x	11.3x	11.3x	11.3x	11.3x
Projected						
Share Price	$22.52	$22.84	$34.49	$42.62	$45.44	$48.40
Market Cap	$3,015M	$3,057M	$4,618M	$5,705M	$6,083M	$6,479M
Actual						
Share Price[3]	$22.52	$46.20	$72.35	$91.80	$74.06	$94.50

Notes:
1. Represents weighted average fully diluted shares outstanding reported in fiscal 2000.
2. Assumes that P/E multiple remains constant from fiscal year end 2000.
3. Reflects the actual closing share price on the last day of each fiscal year.

Sources: AutoZone public filings, Yahoo! Finance.

impact of a share repurchase program on AutoZone's share price, your analysis would be similar to that in Exhibit 16-6.

As shown, AutoZone's share price at the end of fiscal 2005 would have been projected to be $95.48 if the company implemented the proposed share repurchase program. This represents a compound annual return of 33 percent to AutoZone shareholders. If the board chose to let the cash balance grow rather than repurchase shares, then the share price would have been projected to be $48.40, representing a compound annual return of 17 percent to shareholders.

In reality, AutoZone's share price reached $94.50 at the end of fiscal 2005. While the iterative methodology is an effective tool for assisting in the management decision process, the fact that the actual closing share price was within $1.08 of the projected figure is largely a coincidence. There are many other macroeconomic and company-specific factors that contribute to share price performance over an extended period of time. It is clear, however, that the aggressive share repurchase plan implemented by the board of directors generated significant value for AutoZone shareholders.

demonstrated, while share repurchases will often increase equity returns, they do not typically change the overall valuation of the firm.

DISCUSSION QUESTIONS

1. What are the reasons for share repurchases?
2. What are the benefits to the shareholder?
3. Under what circumstances is it prudent to increase leverage by purchasing shares?
4. What are the methods of share repurchase?
5. How can the impact of share repurchases on stock price be evaluated?

IV

GENERAL MANAGERS
TAKING ACTION

The general manager is faced with the challenge of converting the previously developed plans into action—to make the right things happen, and to accomplish them effectively. No matter how brilliant the strategies are or how well they have been planned, at the end of the day, management must take actions that produce the desired results.

Part IV begins with Chapter 17, "Making Effective Decisions." The effectiveness of the leader determines how well an organization functions. The most successful leaders are prone to action, since meeting goals and operating effectively require strong management. General managers must exhibit the combined skills of leadership and management in order to fulfill their responsibilities to take actions that generate positive results for the firm.

Chapter 18, "Organizing and Aligning," discusses the inherent nature of the work of a business that must be reflected in the organizational structure. The appropriate structure must reflect the size of the company, the type of work, its growth rate, the complexity of its product lines, and the number and geographic locations of its operations and customers. The organizational structure defines the authority relationships and related responsibilities that establish the chain of command. This structure is a prerequisite for effective control and accountability.

Chapter 19, "Staffing," covers the need to get the right people into the right jobs—which is one of the most important ways that leaders impact their organizations. The employees, from the hourly workers to the general manager, are essential strategic resources. No principle of management is more important than "getting the right people in the right jobs." The appropriate people create opportunities and resolve problems—the wrong people create problems.

Chapter 20, "Integrating," covers the all-important integration of the organizational units and their staffs into a smooth-functioning whole. Bringing about this coordination and essential collaboration of the employees is one of the major challenges facing a general manager. The topic of integration can be examined from three perspectives: the management of integration of the functional departments within a single business; the integration of the activities of separate strategic business units within a diversified, decentralized parent company; and the integration within companies that have evolved to employ vertical (forward and backward) and/or horizontal integration.

Chapter 21, "Executing," discusses the requirement that management must, above all, innovatively execute the detailed plans developed in Part II. This means effectively creating a demand for what the firm does (marketing) and delivering what the firm has promised (operations). As with any trip undertaken, the firm must be carefully steered in order to stay on course. Despite the intrusion of numerous perturbations along the way, the general manager must cope with the impeding forces and repeatedly return to the appointed course. The prize (success) goes to the leader who runs the course best, since unplanned events impact the lives of all competitors.

In summary, Part IV is focused on the successful implementation of the plans developed in Part II. In every industry, some general managers "outexecute" the competitors, even though many complicating factors affect all "players in the game."

17

MAKING EFFECTIVE DECISIONS

In Chapter 3, general managers are described as serving as both leaders and managers, which are important and different, but complementary, roles. Contemporary management literature includes many definitions of leadership and management and discussions of the distinctions between the two terms. Our understanding of these terms is explained in Chapter 3 and is restated here. Managers are focused on the present, assuming responsibility for profit and loss and managing the functional interfaces. Leaders are seen as having a focus on the future and defining the need for and the desired pace of change. Leaders determine where the organization should go, and create the strategies for getting there. The strategies must be well executed, however, for the business to be successful. Execution via aiming to meet goals and operating effectively requires strong management. General managers must manifest the combined skills of leadership and management in order to fulfill their responsibilities.

General Managers Make Decisions

As described in Chapter 5 and shown previously in Exhibit 5-1, the most important manifestations of the authority of general managers are the decisions they make in choosing a course of action; thus, making decisions is a definitive first step in taking action. There are a number of approaches a general manager may pursue in making decisions. The approach typically varies with the situation, which may range from encompassing a clear course of action (unambiguous) to involving a great deal of risk and uncertainty, although for general managers, most significant decisions are made under conditions of uncertainty. Various situations are summarized here to provide a preamble to the discussions of the general management environment that follow:

- When the facts are clear and complete, and any reasonable person would choose to pursue the most logical course of action, the choice of the course of action is best described as a conclusion rather than a decision. For example, a company would conclude that it is necessary to invest in the installation of an environmental control system if federal law required the installation and the plant would face closure if it did not comply.

- Certain other, lower-level, often repetitive situations for which the data are available may be analyzed using well-known optimization procedures. Again, with a given slate of known facts, the optimization procedure may be employed to determine a best approach given the inputs used. One example involves determining the optimum production sequence for a manufacturing facility. Another example encompasses the determination of the optimum mix of petroleum products to be derived from a given batch of crude oil. The goal of optimization normally is to maximize the contribution to profit and overhead by implementing the optimum result.

- In certain situations, when the likely reaction of competitors cannot be known, management may choose to adopt the "mini-max principle" from game theory. The course of action chosen under this approach is conservative in that the firm, in the end, will be guaranteed some minimum level of profit (or maximum level of cost) regardless of actions taken by the competitor(s). An example might be the submission of a bid for a one-time project. The bid price and contract terms would be such that the firm would make some minimum amount of profit if the bid were successful, regardless of the bids of competitors.

- Another approach to uncertainty involves the use of statistical decision theory. With this approach, management assumes that the observation of some extremely unlikely event lends credence to the strong likelihood of some outcome in which it is interested. For example, if any of us flipped a coin (*assumed* to be a fair coin) six times and observed the result each time to be heads, it would be reasonable to assume that the coin was not a fair coin because of the very small probability (less than 2 percent) of observing the same result six consecutive times.

- Finally, we come to the realm of the general manager—the subjective, nonquantifiable, ambiguous situations with which the general manager continually copes. These situations are characterized by the following complications:
  - *Lack of information*—General managers rarely have all of the information they would like before making complex decisions. Instead, they must move ahead using their best estimates and employ ways to account for uncertainty and risk.
  - *Data inaccuracies*—Numerous inputs to managerial decisions, such as forecasts, are well understood to be fraught with uncertainty, if not error. Managers should thus focus on how much error is implicit in the data and/or the analysis.
  - *Competitors' actions or reactions*—The general manager can never fully know the intentions or actions of competitors, except after the fact. For example, if a general manager decided to reduce the prices of the firm's products, competitors' reactions would only be known with certainty after they unfolded. Decisions likely to provoke competitive response embody a great deal of risk and must therefore be approached with caution.
  - *Ability of the firm to execute the chosen course of action*—A general manager should take care to understand and carefully consider the capabilities of his or her organization before making major decisions. For example, a general manager might decide to launch a new product on a very tight time schedule that his or her marketing and manufacturing organizations simply cannot meet for a myriad of reasons. In such a situation, a great deal of money may be spent on promotional activities only to find that the product is not available. These are the risks attendant to failing

to understand clearly the capabilities of the general manager's organization.

The rest of this chapter discusses the importance of integrating the general manager's values, skills, and experience with the demands of a variety of decision situations.

The Fit between the General Manager and the Situation

Situations vary widely, and management skills and styles do as well. It is axiomatic that there must be a fit between the demands placed on the general manager by the situation and his or her skills and style. If there is a poor fit, the enterprise may be disadvantaged, and possibly even put in jeopardy.

Characteristic Managers

Each of us has a distinct personality combined with an accumulation of skills and experiences. We all have our characteristic strengths and weaknesses, of which we should be aware. Successful general managers understand their capabilities (acquired from skills and experiences) and seek tasks that exploit their strengths. They also know how to compensate for their weaknesses by surrounding themselves with people who have complementary talents.

Lawrence M. Miller has described a number of types of general managers. He uses interesting, descriptive titles to characterize the behavior of each type of manager.[1] We summarize these below, for they provide useful insights into the necessary fit between a certain type of general manager and his or her situation. According to Miller:

- *Prophets* are the visionaries who create the new ideas. Every business can benefit from a visionary perspective. Prophets, however, may or may not have the ability to bring their ideas to fruition and to manage the resulting businesses. An unfortunate result ensues when a prophet with a good idea does not recognize his or her limitations and refuses to let someone else manage its success. A general manager who is a visionary must therefore be able and willing to collaborate with others who may be more capable of turning his or her visions into reality.

- *Barbarians* are those managers who know how to take charge personally and to make things happen. They rule by the force of their personalities along with solid economic instincts and strong management skills. They are best suited to companies that are small enough to provide limited spans of control, and they also perform well in start-ups and in turnarounds. They may encounter trouble, though, when they are unable to maintain an intimate knowledge of what is happening and must delegate.

- *Builders* are best suited to growth situations. While they may have the drive of the barbarian, they know how to attract and develop outstanding talent. They are able to organize subordinates into effective teams and excel at delegating authority to those willing to take on responsibility.

- *Administrators* bring order out of chaos. They know how to build business systems and procedures so that the "buses run on time." They are very valuable in rapidly growing businesses where control can easily be lost. Good administrators realize that they exist to support the line managers.

- *Bureaucrats* can be seen as administrators who have gained too much power. They consider rules and processes as the end results, and do not see themselves as accountable for failures if they faithfully enforce the rules. They see the line managers as people to control, not to support. A comfortable environment for a bureaucrat is a large, complex, highly centralized organization. Bureaucrats are not especially effective as general managers because they do not make things happen or bring about change.

- *Aristocrats* are people who have inherited their positions based on some criterion other than merit. Their positions may result from nepotism, seniority, or some favored relationship. They do not focus on what they can do for the organization but rather what the organization does for them. An effective general manager who achieves great success and begins to believe he or she is entitled to extensive benefits, even in retirement, is thinking like an aristocrat.

- *Synergists* are the ultimate general managers. They combine the best of the prophet, barbarian, builder, and administrator. They are the natural leaders of large, complex organizations.

A General Manager Must Learn and Grow

As they progress through their careers and encounter various circumstances, general managers need to expand their skills for the various roles they must play. To do so, general managers should realistically assess the skills and experiences that led them to their current positions and systematically broaden their repertoires to enhance their chances for success. An introspective person who has the humility and self-confidence to admit to and confront his or her shortcomings may be able to perform this task, but this activity is difficult for many. One of the characteristics of very effective general managers is that they recognize that they are not perfect and constantly aim to improve their game. Vignette 17-1 illustrates how general managers must learn and grow over time.

Situational Fit

One characteristic not mentioned by Miller is the ability of the general manager to create and manage change. Effective change agents require the personal characteristics of both *prophets* and *barbarians,* but when change has to be brought about on a large scale, a *synergist* is required.

Thus, when a general manager is being chosen, the members of the board of directors and any senior management involved should understand the state of the business and the type of general manager needed. The candidate general manager should also understand the situation of the business to determine if there is a fit with his or her style, skills, and experience.

A number of variables determine the type of general manager who is needed in a particular situation, including the following:

- Size of the organization
- Maturity of the organization
- Scope of the organization
- Nature of the work and the workers

VIGNETTE 17-1

One of the great stories of change is that of Ralph Stayer, the owner and chief executive officer (CEO) of Johnsonville Sausage in Johnsonville, Wisconsin.[2] Ralph began running the family business in 1975, at which time sales were $4 million. By 1980, sales had reached $15 million, with a return on equity of 18 percent. The business was growing and profitable, but Ralph did not like what he saw happening. He was a classic *barbarian*, making all of the decisions, but the growing span of control was diluting his effectiveness. He felt the quality of the company's product was slipping and no one cared. An attitude survey suggested that employees of the company were just even with the national average on a measure of positive thinking.

He concluded that the organization reflected his style, and for the organization to change, he had to change. He had to develop for himself a new model of managerial performance. To do so, he went to seminars, read widely, and hired an effective consultant. He came up with a new management model, and began the process of implementing it. In effect, he wanted to become first a *builder* and then a *synergist*. It was a long, slow process, which he found very difficult.

Among the necessary changes was the need for Ralph to learn to delegate, which meant that he needed people to whom he could delegate. He made some key staffing changes and began to train employees and change structures and systems to support a more decentralized management style.

By 1985, sales had grown to $50 million, and the return on equity to 27 percent. By 1990, sales reached $100 million. During this period, Ralph spent a lot of time consulting for other firms, and in 1991 revenues did not grow. He recognized a connection, and once again focused intently on running the company. In 2004, Johnsonville Sausage became the number one sausage brand in America.[3]

Ralph, the natural *barbarian*, had to reinvent himself in 1975, and again in 1991. He also learned to lead and manage an ever-larger business as it grew over the years.

- Organizational structure
- Condition and momentum of the organization

Each of these variables is discussed below.

SIZE OF THE ORGANIZATION The table in Exhibit 17-1 shows the spread in the size of firms in the United States in 2001. More than 98 percent of the firms had fewer than one hundred employees, but they employed only 35 percent of the total workforce. Only 1.66 percent of the firms were medium-sized (100 to 999 employees), but they had almost 20

EXHIBIT 17-1   Employment Size of Employer Firms (2001)

Number of Employees	Number of Firms	Percentage	Total Employees	Percentage
Small Firms				
0	703,837	12.44%	0	0.00%
1–4	2,697,839	47.68%	5,630,017	4.90%
5–9	1,019,105	18.01%	6,698,077	5.80%
10–19	616,064	10.89%	8,274,541	7.20%
19–99	518,258	9.15%	20,370,447	17.7%
Total Small Firms	5,555,103	98.18%	40,973,082	35.6%
Medium Firms				
100–499	85,304	1.51%	16,410,367	14.3%
500–999	8,572	0.15%	5,906,266	5.1%
Total Medium Firms	93,876	1.66%	22,316,633	19.4%
Large Firms				
1,000–1,499	2,854	0.05%	3,474,455	3.0%
1,500–2,499	2,307	0.04%	4,419,771	3.8%
2,500–4,999	1,770	0.03%	6,063,596	5.3%
5,000–9,999	934	0.02%	6,456,068	5.6%
>10,000	930	0.02%	31,357,579	27.3%
Total Large Firms	8,572	0.16%	51,251,805	45.0%
Total All Firms	5,657,774	100.0%	115,061,184	100.0%

Source: U.S. Census Bureau: Statistics of U.S. Businesses, 2001.

percent of the workforce. The large firms (1,000 employees and above) were only 0.16 percent of the total number, but they employed 45 percent of the workforce.

Because every firm must have a chief executive officer (by some title), there are many more CEOs of small firms in the United States than of large firms, each of whom is a general manager. Large firms, though, have more strategic business units and divisions, especially in decentralized organizations, and as a result, they employ many more general managers per firm than the smaller firms. Assume that we would like to estimate how many general managers are employed in medium and large firms. If we assume that a general manager is needed, on average, for every 250 employees in the medium firms, and for every 500 employees in the large firms, we may conclude that the medium and large firms employ more than 200,000 general managers.

The size of a firm is relevant to the general manager's role for a range of reasons, primarily span of control and magnitude of resources. As firms become larger, managers must increasingly delegate to subordinates. No matter how brilliant a hands-on manager is, a firm most often reaches a size where others must become involved. As growth occurs, the general manager must then learn to work through others. This delegation of authority means that the general manager can no longer rely on first-person contact with all or most of the activities of the organization to gain an understanding of the status and operations of the business. As a result, the organization must develop effective information systems to keep executives informed.

The second primary issue related to size is that of resources. As the scale of an organization increases, it is much more likely to be able to afford management talent, both in numbers and skills. In effect, the organization generates the monetary resources to hire more professionals and pay them more. They, in turn, often contribute to the generation of more sales.

For these reasons, and many others, the general management responsibility in a small firm is different from that in a large firm. A small firm has essentially the same functions as a larger firm, but on a smaller scale. Without adequate scale, managers in smaller firms must cover broader and more diverse ranges of responsibilities.

Consequently, the smaller the firm, the more versatile the general manager needs to be. The general manager of a smaller firm traditionally will be more involved in the details of more facets of the ongoing activities. People who have been successful in larger firms do not necessarily fare well as general managers of small firms; frequently, they have a lot to learn. In larger firms, the scale and resources support the hiring of more specialized employees, whereas in smaller firms, executives often must cover a range of responsibilities themselves.

Nonetheless, bright, hardworking individuals with strong management instincts are requisite to the successful management of any business, regardless of size.

MATURITY OF THE ORGANIZATION Maturity refers to the position of the organization in its life cycle. Like many elements of strategy, the life-cycle stage in which a business operates influences the demands placed on the general manager.

An organization in its start-up phase usually requires a general manager capable of dealing with a dynamic, often chaotic, situation. The general manager of a start-up business must respond to the strategic imperative to generate volume as rapidly as possible while building capacity capable of handling the generated volume. Capacity encompasses both facilities and personnel, as well as the infrastructure needed to support them. All of this must be accomplished within the constraint of the available financial resources, which the general manager most likely will need to arrange. In particular, the general manager must ensure that the business does not run out of cash before it establishes a positive cash flow. Many businesses fail simply due to undercapitalization. Financial problems arise for a range of reasons, most commonly because the planning was faulty (which is common given the uncertainty of new ventures), or sources of cash—such as venture capital or bank financing—dried up.

If a business survives its start-up phase, its general manager must be prepared to manage sudden rapid growth when it occurs. The general manager will need to adopt both a short- and a long-term perspective to rapid growth. The longer-term perspective is to understand how long the buildup in demand might last and approximately how large the business might eventually become. Care must be taken to balance demand for increasing capacity with the risk of overinvesting and developing excess capacity when the demand ceases to grow. In moving out of the start-up phase, the *barbarian* needs to evolve into a *builder*. If that transformation is not feasible, a change in general managers is required.

During this growth phase, effective administration is also crucial. It may not provide profitability, but its absence can result in the failure of the business. At some point, therefore, and better early than late, an effective administrator must join the management team. Functional management usually fulfills this role at an early stage of the organization's development.

Administration of the details of a rapidly growing business tends to bridge the long- and short-term perspectives required of the executives of the business. The short-term emphasis of the general manager typically encompasses maintaining schedules, quality, and efficiencies so that products are delivered in a timely fashion and customers are satisfied. These duties require a general manager who is strong in operations. As the business grows, though, the demands of the general manager's position will as well. In response, the general manager must be able and willing to delegate operations effectively to other managers. As demonstrated, growth typically brings the need for change of various sorts, and the successful general manager must be adept at sensing the need for change and responding accordingly.

If an organization reaches a profitable and stable maturity, the pace of change slows. An experienced workforce will be in place supported by an effective infrastructure. For many organizations, particularly those with a strong brand or patent protection, the temptation to relax grows strong, and general managers may become complacent and organizations bureaucratic. At this stage, some general managers become very good at reducing costs and increasing productivity (via continuous improvement). In these situations, it is not unusual to see an *administrative* personality promoted to the top job. This is the classic default choice of maintenance over initiative.

The danger for a mature company is that it might get "stuck in the box." This situation occurs when growth has slowed because the market growth has slowed, and the business is not gaining market share. In essence, a successful strategy has run its normal course. To find continued success for the organization, the business now requires a general manager who understands the necessity of identifying and exploiting available entrepreneurial opportunities.

When a business's market is mature, incremental growth above the level of market growth can only result from gaining market share from competitors. Such businesses need general managers who are strong marketers and innovative product developers. The business may want to gain market share by the acquisition of other businesses, which requires an entirely different skills set. The general manager must be able to consummate attractive deals, and of equal importance, know how to integrate them into the current business and manage their operations effectively. The *synergist* is best equipped to provide these skills and carry out these demanding tasks.

Diversification into new businesses is another method of growth and may involve extending the business's value chain via a vertical integration strategy. Many of the natural resource businesses, such as paper and oil, have followed this strategy. Diversification may be related to the organization's current business, as is often the case with integration, or unrelated, where organizations move into businesses outside their industry. To be an effective manager of change through diversification, a CEO must be adept at integrating acquisitions, as well as delegating authority to well-chosen general managers.

SCOPE OF THE ORGANIZATION The scope of an organization refers to the breadth of its product lines and the number of production and sales locations. Single-product companies in one location are much simpler to manage than companies producing an expansive range of products with a wide geographic dispersal of plants and service or sales offices. *Barbarians* are good at managing smaller, less-complex organizations. As businesses become larger and more complex, *builders* and then *synergists* fit better.

NATURE OF THE WORK AND THE WORKERS The kinds of challenges that confront a general manager are strongly influenced by the nature of the work of the organization, and the resulting characteristics of the workforce. Creating software programs for Microsoft is very different from making steel products in Nucor's minimills. A long list of industries could be cited—retailers, manufacturers, professional firms (lawyers, doctors, accountants, and engineers), schools and colleges, hospitals, and nonprofit agencies—each of which has its individual management challenges. Thus, the nature of the work influences the necessary characteristics of the general manager. As noted earlier, both parties should investigate the fit when involved in the process of identifying a new general manager. A similar process should occur in the performance reviews of incumbent general managers as well.

ORGANIZATIONAL STRUCTURE The nature of the work and the strategy of an organization should be aligned with the organizational structure. Decentralized structures demand more independence on the part of the general managers, while, conversely, more centralized structures require greater adherence to corporate direction. As work has become more knowledge-based (requiring on-site judgment and expertise) and more widely spread out in location and across time zones, businesses are moving toward flatter organizations with more decentralized decision making.

EXHIBIT 17-2   The Need for Change

		Condition	
		Strong	*Weak*
Momentum	*Improving*	Continue on course.	Stay the course only if the pace of improvement is rapid enough to salvage the condition.
	Declining	Management must address issues. Urgency depends on the rate of decline.	Situation must be turned around. A sense of urgency is required.

CONDITION AND MOMENTUM OF THE ORGANIZATION The condition of a firm is defined here as how effectively it is currently operating, while the momentum of the same firm describes whether it is improving, stable, or declining in the effectiveness with which it functions. This classification may be applied to the functional areas of the firm, as well, by determining, for example, answers to the following questions: How strong is the firm's position in the market, and is it improving or declining? Are the firm's operations currently effective, and are they improving or declining? Does the organization have the right people in place? Is the capital structure strong or weak? Are profits solid, and what are their trends?

The general manager's options for the pace of change may be summarized by the information within the matrix in Exhibit 17-2.

Strong conditions usually provide time for the general manager to correct negative momentum. The weaker the condition, the more urgent it is to take corrective action to reverse negative momentum. When the condition in a declining situation is critical, aggressive corrective action is required. This situation provides the ideal arena within which the *barbarian* may excel. The *builder* and *synergist* are most effective within improving situations.

Setting the Tone

The tone of an organization is set at the top. What the general manager and senior management do creates a standard for the employees of the organization in terms of desirable and undesirable values, attitudes, and behavior. The general manager is responsible for ensuring that the members of the management team carry the desired tone to their subordinates, and all employees, including management, should be held accountable for the values, attitudes, and behaviors they display in the workplace.

The tone set at the top should be company specific, industry specific, and culture specific. Thus, the tone is influenced by the environment in which the organization operates. The prevailing environment might create conflicts with the leader's values, resulting in difficult ethical dilemmas, particularly when executives are stationed in cultures very different from those of their homelands. Even within a home country, however, cultural differences exist among industries and geographic regions. Consider the ethical challenge posed by the situation in Vignette 17-2.

VIGNETTE 17-2

The new CEO of a car wash corporation put down the telephone after speaking with the company's lawyer. Having just taken over after being hired by the owners of the company, he wanted to play "by the book." Earlier that day, his real estate broker had called him on behalf of the owner of his organization's principal competitor, another car wash company. The competitor wanted to meet with the CEO to discuss "how best to divide up the market so that we are not tripping over each other."

The CEO's lawyer, who was also an investor in the business, told the CEO that the comment sounded anticompetitive (which the CEO recognized as illegal), although it was likely no one would find out about the conversation. The CEO knew that the competitor was currently looking at various sites, including one near his organization's best store. Typically, when two car washes opened in close proximity to one another, results for both suffered, and one inevitably failed. The CEO was left to determine whether he should go through with the proposed meeting.

Absorptive Capacity

Absorptive capacity is a concept related to the ability to adapt to a rapidly changing environment, hence the ability to learn. It refers to the value a firm places on new ideas, its ability to acquire new knowledge, and, finally, its ability to absorb the new knowledge and act upon it. The absorptive capacity of a firm will reflect the interests of the general manager in acquiring new knowledge and learning to use it effectively. Some general managers are satisfied with the status quo, or think that they must stay focused by "sticking to their knitting." In the short run, this attitude may be a virtue, but in the longer run, the general manager may be disadvantaged by not placing an appropriate emphasis on learning and improving.

General managers who want their organizations to take action through innovating and adopting new concepts and ideas must value a diversity of viewpoints and complementary talent. They must also develop the means of identifying and evaluating new concepts, which frequently requires having strong personal relationships with those who are creating the knowledge. In this and numerous other ways, the personal connections of the CEO can be very important to the continued success of a firm. The importance of learning and innovating is discussed further in Chapter 23.

Communicating

The term communicating usually connotes the delivery of information to others, but in order for communication to occur, reception must also take place on the other end. Thus, general managers participate in communication by speaking as well as listening. Effective general managers listen to what others are saying to them through their words and their actions, and notice, too, what is *not* being said and done.

These general managers make great efforts to create opportunities and build relationships that give them timely access to customers, employees, competitors, suppliers, owners, and others who may influence their businesses. They skillfully ask probing questions about relevant topics and carefully analyze the information they collect, searching for patterns and trends. They learn not only what is effective but also what is ineffective.

They also recognize that the more subordinates are included in the decision-making process, regardless of the outcome, the more they are apt to accept and execute it. Inclusion involves the sharing of information—or communication.

After a decision has been made, it should be communicated to those who will be affected by it. This communication may be done in person one-on-one, in small groups, or in large groups, depending on the nature of the decision and/or the information. Decisions may also be disseminated through a variety of media outlets. If there is a culture of openness and trust in the organization, managers will find it easier to communicate, even when the message is unpleasant or difficult. If, however, an adversarial or distrusting relationship prevails, managers are likely to find that the effective delivery of a message can be very difficult. The long-term difficulties brought on within an entire industry by lingering adversarial relationships are described in Vignette 17-3.

VIGNETTE 17-3

A classic example of a dysfunctional relationship has prevailed for decades in the U.S. automobile industry. Early in its development, labor found it necessary to organize into a strong union, and an adversarial relationship developed. During the heyday in the 1950s and 1960s, there was industry-wide bargaining. Because the top three manufacturers all had essentially the same labor contract and thus the same labor costs, they learned to compete on product design and marketing efforts. They were willing to give major concessions to the unions because they were very profitable and wanted labor peace. They also had virtually no competition from outside the country.

As the Japanese brought better products to market at lower prices, the American manufacturers steadily lost market share. The most effective reaction to this competition would have been for labor and management to confront the threat as a partnership, working to improve quality, increase efficiencies, and decrease costs. Communication of this obvious message somehow failed between the leadership of the automobile companies and the labor union leaders. Why do these parties continue to act in an adversarial way that is inconsistent with their mutual best interest? There is not a simple answer to this question, but clearly a lack of trust plays a major role. They may come together ultimately in response to crisis, but only after losing share and profits for decades. In the end, a failure to take action will have been the cause of severe economic decline, if not failure.

Communication is a first step in the process of implementing strategy—taking action to bring about the desired future for the organization. There should be an ongoing process of listening to, working with, and openly providing information in the context of positive, trusting relationships. The communications process needs to be well conceived, systematically planned, and well executed. While some of the best communication efforts can result from spontaneous interactions, many organizations employ a communications plan to ensure orderly and timely dissemination of information.

Managing Change

Managing change is often a challenging task for general managers, primarily because people resist change for a variety of reasons. Inertia, the tendency to continue with the status quo, is well known to be a powerful force. One way of dealing with inertia is to impose a structure such that the decision to do nothing is a deliberate one rather than a comfortable default. When faced with a need to make a decision, employees should find maintaining the status quo listed as an alternative that has to be justified in terms of pros and cons, as with the other options.

There are those who have a vested interest in maintaining the status quo and believe they can only lose with change. There are those who are comfortable with the familiar, and choose not to visualize the benefits of any proposed change. Many individuals are so averse to risk that they simply fear the unknown, regardless of the prevailing facts; others are simply too lazy to make the effort to adjust to the demands of a new situation. A general manager must assess the situation and the most likely future, define the need for and pace of desired change, and consider the probable resistance. The risks of proposed changes must be well understood and openly acknowledged. The change agent may know change is required but not be clear about what action is to be taken. Any resulting ambiguity will increase or reinforce resistance.

Consider the following four levers that provide impetus for change: (1) catalysts for change; (2) power and persuasion; (3) systems, structure, and staffing; and (4) changing the people. The first of these levers is a catalyst for change. As discussed in Chapter 5, three possible catalysts for change include crises, visions, and philosophies of continuous improvement.

A second lever involves the use of power and/or persuasion and addresses managing the consequences of not making desired changes. This lever may range from recognition and promotion (incentives) to termination (penalties). The use of power to get results is perceived negatively by many today, with persuasion a preferred alternative. The reality is that persuasion, while often preferable, is much more effective when backed up by power.

A third powerful lever is to change the systems, structures, or staffing of the organization. The systems—such as promotion, compensation, and communications—are powerful shapers of behavior. Changing organizational structures likewise influences behavior, particularly through reporting and authority structures. Systems and structures must align with strategies if they are to be executed effectively. Staffing changes refer to shuffling individuals among the positions identified in the organization chart. Changes in title, supervisors, and direct reports could serve as strong influencers of change, particularly when they affect perceived status within the organization.

Perhaps the most effective lever for change is to change the people (by influencing their attitudes and actions), or change the people (through reassignment or separation). People may either be changed by the other levers, or the general manager may move them out of the organization and find new people.

General managers may expect varying levels of resistance to change within their organizations. Most organizations will have some complement of employees who are eager to implement change, with the inventors and innovators leading the way. Some others will embrace suggested change enthusiastically. These two groups together must lead the charge for change. As changes become proven, additional employees will follow willingly and others reluctantly. A hard core of employees, though, can be expected to oppose nearly any change.

In an organization that must change constantly to remain competitive, the general manager will need to attract a population made up entirely of those who are comfortable with change. A strong culture of embracing change will naturally help attract and retain like-minded employees.

Summary: A Management Model for Taking Action

A general manager who wants to be action-oriented should adopt an effective management model. Some version of the following attributes and actions will enhance the likelihood of success:

- Select a good business, and be willing to get out of poor businesses. Fix them, sell them, or close them.
- Know the business. If the general manager does not have market- and industry-specific knowledge, he or she must be surrounded by people who do.
- Put the right people in the right jobs.
- Negotiate mutually agreeable goals, strategies, and performance standards with subordinates.
- Communicate relevant information in an atmosphere of openness and trust.
- Align the interests of all employees with those of the owners.
- Let subordinates do their jobs, but in delegating, the general manager should not abdicate management's responsibilities.
- Both subordinates and the general manager should be aware of the situation of the business and the environment. They should hold themselves and one another mutually accountable.
- General managers should deal appropriately with opportunities and problems.
- The general manager should know when to intervene in subordinates' activities. He or she should do so when the subordinate:
  - Does not recognize or understand the problem or opportunity
  - Does not have a plan for dealing with it
  - Is unable to execute the plan

Action on the part of the general manager and the employees of the organization is the only avenue to the implementation of strategies and achievement of goals. In Chapter 18, we discuss issues related to organizing and organizational structure.

DISCUSSION QUESTIONS

1. Why is the fit between the general manager and the situation so important?
2. What factors influence the type of general manager needed?
3. What are the four levers that provide an impetus for change? Are there others?
4. Why is it important for a general manager to take action?
5. What are the risks associated with inaction?

18

ORGANIZING AND ALIGNING

Organizing has deep anthropological roots. Over time, human biological and social needs to organize expanded to include political and economic motivations. Initially, the military, the church, and the temporal powers (usually city-states or countries) were the only entities large enough to be faced with critical organizational challenges. This began to change with the Industrial Revolution in the latter half of the eighteenth century, during which larger, more complex businesses were created. The need for organization in commerce and industry became increasingly more important during this era.

In 1962, Alfred D. Chandler wrote *Strategy and Structure: Chapters in the History of the American Industrial Enterprise*.[1] The book revealed how the seventy largest corporations in America up to that time had dealt with a single economic problem: the effective administration of an expanding business. Chandler's principal point was that the strategy of a company must drive its organizational structure.

It is implicit in Chandler's reasoning that there is an inherent nature to the work of a business, and its organizational structure must reflect that nature. The appropriate structure must reflect the size of the organization, the type of work, its growth rate, the complexity of its product lines, and the number and geographic locations of its operations and customers. The globalization of the economy has only further complicated the issue, as has the ever more rapid pace of change across the entire commercial land-scape. Following Chandler's approach, the general manager should not set an organizational structure in place until he or she has settled on a strategy. It follows that if the general manager changes the strategy, the structure must be rethought.

A fundamental purpose of an organizational structure is to define the authority relationships and related responsibilities in an organization in order to establish the chain of command. The resulting "structure" permits effective control and accountability.

Governance Structure: Centralization versus Decentralization

In the discussion of governance in Chapter 2, we note that, as with other structural decisions, the firm's governance must align with the strategy and the nature of the organization, the context within which the organization operates. The cornerstone decision in designing the organizational structure for a business is the extent to which it should be centralized or decentralized. There are pros and cons for each approach.

The advantages of centralization are economies of scale and specialization in certain key functions. Many things may be accomplished more effectively, less expensively, and with greater control in a centralized organization. Problems related to centralization include the loss of flexibility, less contact with events at the operating level, and the possible development of inefficient bureaucracies. The advantages and disadvantages of decentralized organizations are the inverse of those of the centralized organization. Decentralized organizations are apt to be more flexible, but may have limited ability to take advantage of economies of scale, and coordinated decision making may be more difficult.

To determine which is better in the business world, one must consider the nature of the business and its strategy.

Common Organizational Structures

The Simplest Structure

When a business or an operating unit is very small and managed by a single individual, its structure is likely to be similar to the radial

EXHIBIT 18-1   The Simplest Structure

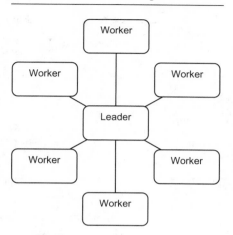

design depicted in Exhibit 18-1. The leader has direct, individual contact with each of the subordinate workers.

The building blocks of any organizational structure are teams or work groups, which typically operate in some variation of a radial structure. One goal of an organizational structure is to ensure that these teams operate effectively and that their efforts are coordinated with those of other teams to create an efficient organization.

A Functional Organization

As described in Chapter 2, the most prevalent form of organization for a business is a functional structure because it is most applicable to a large number of small businesses as well as most profit centers (divisions) of large diversified, decentralized companies. A functional organization usually denotes highly centralized control of the business in which:

- The marketing and sales of all the firm's products are the responsibility of a marketing manager, whose department generates the company's revenues;
- A manager of manufacturing or operations is responsible for the production of all the firm's products;
- The engineering and finance functions are similarly housed centrally.

EXHIBIT 18-2   A Functional Organization

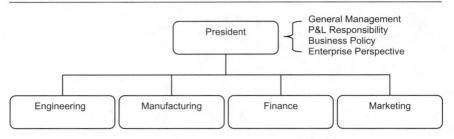

An organizational chart for a functional organization is shown in Exhibit 18-2.

The responsibility for profits in a functional organization clearly resides with its general manager, who must rely on a combination of sales efforts to produce revenues and expense budgets to control costs and to provide a total result that generates a profit for the operation.

At some point, the size and number of organizational layers requires a more complex structure. The general manager may formalize the delineation between line and staff positions, as shown in Exhibit 18-3. Each of these organizational blocks can be further subdivided as management sees fit. The manager of marketing might become a line position, for instance, if he or she also has responsibility for sales. As the layers of management within both line and staff functions proliferate, the higher-level managers become progressively more removed from the frontline workers.

EXHIBIT 18-3   A Functional Structure with Line and Staff Delineations

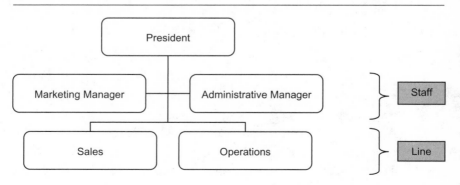

A Diversified, Decentralized Organization

It is clearly difficult for functional organizations to be responsive to a variety of customers in different markets from a centralized facility. The need to service customers has led many companies to decentralize the management of the enterprise into a number of profit centers, which then tend to be functionally organized. In such an organization, the responsibility for conducting the firm's business in a segment of the company's markets is delegated to a profit center manager and his or her staff. The parent company's chief executive officer (CEO) or general manager determines the broad direction for the company and sets goals and objectives for the divisions. The basic responsibility for profits resides within the divisions, and the overall company profitability is a sort of weighted average of the results of the divisions. The organization chart for a diversified, decentralized company is shown in Exhibit 18-4.

A Project, Product-Line, or Matrix Organization

As described in Chapter 2, companies or divisions that engage in long-running projects, or that have several different product lines within a profit center, may employ project, product-line, or matrix organizations. In such organizations, managers are designated to coordinate the activities of the functional managers for a given project or product line. For instance,

EXHIBIT 18-4   A Holding Company with Business Units

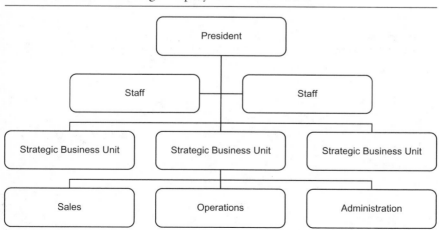

how do marketing, engineering, and manufacturing work together to create and introduce a new product? The functional managers may not want to give up control of their functions, but the general manager realizes that their efforts must be focused and coordinated to bring about the desired new product introduction.

These managers report to a general manager and are expected to plan for, coordinate, and monitor functional operations in order to ensure the profitable operation of their product line segment of the business. One common form of matrix organization is depicted in Exhibit 18-5.

Project-Oriented Organizations

Project-oriented organizations are similar to matrix organizations, except that the project structures are temporary in that they exist only for the life of the project. One example is the structure established by a general contractor in the construction industry who uses numerous subcontractors to complete the construction of a school or shopping center. Many organizations also use cross-functional task forces to manage specific projects that disband when the projects are completed.

The Marketing Organization

Organizing the marketing and sales effort is critical, regardless of the form of organization of the business. The business exists to serve a customer, and the marketing function must be organized to maximize customer relationships. While marketing functions are crucial every-

EXHIBIT 18-5 A Product-Line or Matrix Organization

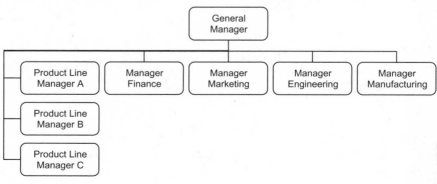

where, this discussion is limited to the challenges facing a single business or strategic business unit. The challenges of cross-selling and joint marketing efforts between strategic business units are discussed in Chapter 20, "Integrating."

The most common organizational schemes for sales forces are:

- *By geographic market:* The sales force is assigned geographic territories.
- *By customer type:* The sales force is organized around specific types of customers who have distinctive needs. For example, air conditioning equipment is sold through different marketing channels for residential and commercial applications.
- *By product:* The sales force is organized around products or brands.
- *By production facility:* Each production facility has its own sales force.
- Some combination of the schemes described above.

Global Strategies and Structures

The number of companies participating in global business is growing steadily. Global strategies include:

- Supporting a primarily domestic strategy that does not require overseas investment
  - Importing raw materials and equipment
  - Importing products for domestic sales
- Exporting products made domestically to foreign markets
- Investing in businesses overseas
  - Manufacturing overseas for importation to the domestic market, usually to gain a comparative (cost) advantage
  - Manufacturing overseas for sales in the local country or other countries, utilizing superior technology

Regardless of a firm's strategy for participation in globalization, the appropriate organizational structure must be determined after the strategic decisions are made. For instance, if a firm is selling overseas, management must decide between a multicountry organization and a global organization.

A multicountry strategy results in the organization operating within each nation (or sometimes groups of nations) as a separate strategic business unit. The advantage of this structure is that the business may focus on the local situation. A global strategy operates as one business unit (profit center), requiring worldwide functional coordination.

A concern for any complex marketing and sales organization, whether domestic, multicountry, or global, is the potential for multiple access points for customers. When customers (typically other businesses) may enter into arrangements with different parts of a sales organization (where each part is likely compensated based on sales figures), it is possible that the organization may enter into competition with itself. Savvy customers will take advantage of the potential to gain cost concessions from one part of the organization and use them to gain even further concessions from another. Sales and marketing managers must develop systems or structures to impede such behaviors.

Alignment

A second facet of organization that requires general management oversight is the alignment of the firm's infrastructure, business systems, and culture with the business strategies.

Infrastructure

Infrastructure is too often taken for granted as long as it functions reasonably well. For instance, it is customary for us to assume that the lights will come on, the water will run, the plumbing will function, and that there will be good roads for transport. If the elements that make up a supportive infrastructure are not in place, all other activities are at risk.

This is true within businesses as well. Supportive infrastructures must be in place with sufficient capacity to support the needs of the business, and their existence must not be taken for granted. In addition to utilities, the necessary facilities must be available in the right places to support the firm's strategy. If a firm outgrows the existing infrastructure, or management fails to maintain it or permits it to become obsolete, the firm will eventually encounter severe operating problems. Because infra-structure must be in place in advance to support growth or changes in strategy, expected future needs must be anticipated. A substantial lead time is often required to provide effective infrastructure as revenues increase or existing strategies change.

A major requirement of properly managing infrastructure is preventive maintenance. Preventive maintenance may range from properly servicing equipment to regularly refurbishing buildings. The temptation with preventive maintenance is to defer it in the short run because of operating pressures or financial constraints. As the oil filter mechanic says, "Pay me now, or pay me later," and the price tag later is usually substantially more than the cost of effective preventive maintenance programs.

Systems

Systems are similar to infrastructure in that they are essential supports for operations. A number of businesses have made certain systems central to their strategies. Key systems include the following:

- Planning and Budgeting
- Finances
- Human Resources Management
- Management Information Systems
- Operating Requirements
  - Communications
  - Customer Service
  - Management Control
  - Quality Assurance
  - Scheduling
  - Inventory Management

Most of these systems areas have been mentioned previously and several are explored in later chapters. All systems of the organization should be aligned with the strategy to enhance the likelihood of successful implementation.

What does aligning systems with strategy mean? In general, it refers to designing or altering systems so that they are oriented toward supporting the major thrusts or purpose of a strategy. Aligning a system with the organization's strategy should be based on an understanding of the system's role in the organization (most systems serve multiple functions), that is, what it does or should provide. Because systems serve numerous constituencies within the organization, alignment of systems with strategy should take into account the values of the general manager, functional managers, and system manager regarding how a system might best be designed to support the strategy and the achievement of the organization's goals.

Consider an organization whose mission is to become a world-class manufacturer and whose strategy calls for delivering high-quality products using lean production techniques. As an example of alignment within this organization, the billing portion of the financial system would be required to generate invoices daily for delivered products if this system were to be aligned with the principles of lean (just-in-time) manufacturing. Naturally, the information system would have to capture daily shipment data and make it accessible to billing. The implications could be extended further, as well as broadened to encompass other systems. From this very limited example, we see that aligning systems with strategy is a far-reaching exercise within an organization, and one that requires the thoughtful participation of a broad base of management.

Culture

The alignment of the organization's culture with the nature of the business and its strategy is among the most important requirements for sustainable success. Culture is pervasive in shaping how an organization performs, and consists of a complex set of values, attitudes, and behaviors. Some refer to culture as the informal organization. Very difficult conflicts may develop if the culture of a business is not aligned with the formal organization and its systems.

Corporate cultures necessarily reflect the collective cultures of their employees. In the United States, cultural differences within organizations are influenced by the region of the country where the firm is located, as well as whether it is in an urban or rural setting. These cultural differences are typically even greater across countries.

Cultures, like managers, may take on a wide range of attributes. They may be energetic and action oriented or sluggish and reactive, open and focused on the best results for the organization or guarded and protective of turf. Cultures may vary by division or function, and they may also be stratified into formal or informal classes, such as professionals and hourly workers, scientists and business professionals, old guard and new guard. Cultures may also be political, with workers organized into cliques that compete for power. Cultures found in government, academia, and large corporations may be bureaucratic, focusing on process and power. Some cultures are meritocracies while others favor nepotism and cronyism.

A wide variety of cultures has been successful across different organizations, often depending on the situation, which includes the type of work done, the nature of the workers, and the management style of the leaders. In today's world of knowledge workers and flatter organizations, there has been a gradual shift toward more collaborative cultures in which decisions are more participative, and the workforce is seen as a group of important stakeholders and professional colleagues.

Successful businesses tend to display a number of common cultural characteristics. General managers need to understand what these characteristics are, and how to bring them about if their organizations lack them. The cultures of successful businesses tend to include an emphasis on:

- Integrity
- Trust and loyalty
- Shared values
  - Respect for and valuing of all employees
  - Fairness
  - Shared goals
  - High standards of performance
  - Embracing change
- Esprit de corps

Integrity is the cornerstone of a positive culture and cannot be negotiable. To the degree that everyone in an organization is not honest and forthright in his or her views and behavior, the organization suffers.

Intellectual honesty is a closely related trait—the ability to see one-self and situations objectively, and then to act accordingly with consistency.

A culture of integrity begins at the top of the organization. Senior management must establish a set of shared values that embraces integrity as much as any other trait. Top management must also set an example for disciplined behavior that demonstrates integrity, remaining open and honest in their dealings and assessments, particularly when they have made mistakes. Management must also establish consequences for breaching these and all standards. As pointed out in Chapter 19, assessing individual employees on how well they demonstrate the values of the organization is an effective technique in establishing and maintaining a culture.

Other significant shared values of successful organizations are the valuing and fair treatment of all employees along with that of getting the job done well. In today's environment of rapid and certain change, a culture where change is embraced as a challenge rather than feared or resisted provides a greater likelihood of success.

An overriding characteristic of many successful cultures is a widespread esprit de corps, which typically may be recognized as shared pride in the organization and its work and commitment to its goals and objectives. Some might characterize this shared spirit as that of individual players working together to create an outstanding team.

Creating Cultural Change

It is imperative that a firm's culture change and adapt to align with the firm's strategy, with the realistic understanding on the part of management that dramatic changes in culture will likely come about very slowly. A first step in changing culture is understanding the existing culture and its strengths and weaknesses. As with every aspect of the business, management should aim to preserve and build on the obvious cultural strengths and neutralize the weaknesses.

The general manager may take some dramatic steps in initiating cultural change, such as terminating problem employees. This action not only removes the specific problems these employees bring to the organization, but also sends a clear signal to the rest of the organization. Removing employees from or ushering employees out of the organization sends a powerful message to those remaining in the workforce.

Many of the changes toward a new culture may be more symbolic. For example, the leaders may gradually remove status symbols that are counterproductive. In one company, middle managers coveted reserved parking places so much that a visiting customer was asked to move her car. The CEO used that opportunity to remove all parking places reserved for these managers to the great pleasure of the rank and file.

Cultural change should be guided by a long-term vision articulated by the general manager. The management team may then devise steps to move the organization toward this goal. The prevailing culture of the organization will be influenced by the ways in which the general manager and the management team make decisions, whom they hire and promote, and the behaviors they choose to reward and punish. In addition to these actions, management will need to convince the workforce that its members are trustworthy, committed, and care about the employees. The members of management must be cognizant of the reality that if they are to lead the organization to a new place—both strategically and culturally—they will need to demonstrate change individually and collectively. If they fail to do so, it is very unlikely others will change, and equally unlikely the organizational culture will change as they envisioned.

Summary

This chapter discusses the various forms of business organizations and the need to ensure that the organizational structure is aligned with the strategy. For companies to be successful, the supporting infrastructure, systems, and culture must also align with management's strategy. In the next chapter, we explore issues of staffing the organization to enhance the likelihood of business success.

DISCUSSION QUESTIONS

1. Why is the form of organization important to a business?
2. Which form of organization provides the best experience base for those aspiring to be general managers?

3. Why is the alignment between the organization and systems so important?
4. What role does culture play in implementing change?
5. Why should an aspiring general manager seek experience in at least two functional areas?

19

STAFFING

A general manager must realize that the likely effectiveness of even the "ideal" strategy and its related plans is dependent on people and how they perform. Personnel, from the hourly workers to the general manager, are therefore essential strategic resources.

Every general manager must recognize that there are limitations on his or her effective span of control, and must therefore learn to delegate the authority for certain actions to others. The act of delegating requires that those to whom the authority is delegated be competent to assume responsibility for achieving appropriate results in a timely way. Few, if any, principles of management are more important than "getting the right people in the right jobs." The right people create opportunities and solve problems—the wrong people create problems. Vignette 19-1 describes one chief executive officer's (CEO's) approach to identifying the right—and wrong—people within the organization.

VIGNETTE 19-1

One very successful CEO used a scheme involving green dots and red dots to classify his firm's employees. The green dots were labels for people who made things happen, and the red dots for those who impeded progress. The green dots created energy and the red dots drained energy. The CEO aimed to have a staff composed of green dots, and took action to make this goal a reality.

A useful metaphor for the general manager is a casting director. There is a play to be acted—a job to be done—both of which require a number of roles. The success of the metaphor begins with how well the actors are suited to their roles. The metaphor includes how well the actors learn their parts and come together as an ensemble. The casting director then becomes the director of the production, just as the general manager becomes the manager of the business.

Another metaphor for the staffing needs of filling a business is the roster of a professional sports team. Each team is made up of specific positions and the players' skills and experience are matched with the needs of those positions. The players compete to make the team at each position and every season. The idea of the way that players are terminated when they are no longer competitive may seem harsh in the business world, but it is common practice in the world of professional sports. While its application may be subtler, the principle remains—the general manager needs the most effective people he or she can hire to become as competitive as possible. This process is discussed in another venue in Vignette 19-2.

General managers can learn from these metaphors and develop systems for management development that effectively serve the needs of the firm.

VIGNETTE 19-2

Organizations that continually get the best people don't acquire them by accident. These organizations follow very systematic processes. The military provides an example. The leaders know the kind of people they want, how many they need now, and how many they will need in the future. They carefully recruit and screen for people who have the requisite qualifications. After the recruits are on board, they are trained relentlessly and then placed in positions that align with their individual skills. As personnel demonstrate their potential for more responsibility, they are assigned to a variety of jobs that broaden their experience base.

Performance is carefully monitored and promotions are based on merit and multiple evaluations. Each stage of promotion is competitive so that only the best make it to the next, higher level.

Determining the Needed Talent

The task of determining the talent needed within an organization requires an assessment of the skills needed as well as the quantity. A company must have enough capacity to produce the output to which it is committed or where it is forecast, which includes facilities as well as people who have the skills and experience to complete the work correctly, efficiently, and on time.

The Right Number of People

Virtually every operation may be examined to compare the desired throughput to the available capacity. Typically, there are two factors that limit capacity—the physical capacity of the production operation and the workforce capacity. Physical capacity may be defined as the maximum number of units of output that a fixed asset can produce when it is running as much as possible, usually twenty-four hours a day, seven days a week, and 365 days a year. The workforce capacity, when tied to the asset, consists of the production during the hours that the fixed asset is staffed.

If the required work of a business or some process is being completed on time at acceptable quality levels, the workforce has enough people. There may even be too many, if the operation is inefficient. Inefficiencies may be caused by obsolete equipment; poor training, motivation, or supervision of the workers; or weak processes or systems. When the organization has trouble meeting delivery schedules, the tendency is to respond by hiring more people and/or buying more equipment. This step should not be taken, however, until the general manager is satisfied that the existing capacity is being used efficiently. Alternative steps that could be taken to gain additional capacity include reengineering the processes, retraining the people, and procuring more efficient equipment. Vignette 19-3 describes the approach one CEO took to repeated requests for additional capacity in the support workforce.

In for-profit businesses, inefficiencies will normally adversely affect margins and/or prices. When charging market prices, an inefficient organization will typically have below-average margins. If too many employees are the cause of the inefficiencies, management will need to find ways to increase volume or reduce the workforce to restore productivity to appropriate levels.

VIGNETTE 19-3

The general manager of a division of a diversified company managed an exemplary business by any standards. The business was very profitable compared to similar companies, and the quality of the product was unequalled in the industry. Customers were very happy with the timely deliveries, and the parent company was very pleased with the performance of the business in all respects. In fact, the division manager was considered a likely successor to the CEO of the parent company.

The general manager was troubled, however, by persistent urging from some of his functional managers to enlarge the indirect/overhead workforce. It seemed that every manager of a staff department was seeking to hire additional people.

The general manager was slow to respond to these requests, primarily because when he took a walk around the offices each day, he never failed to find people reading books, making obviously personal phone calls, or just socializing with coworkers. He grew determined not to add any additional staff or overhead people to the payroll until he was satisfied that the existing workforce was fully utilized performing essential work.

The pressure from the middle managers built steadily as the level of direct work grew. Middle managers simply could not understand why the salaried workforce was not allowed to grow proportionally with the direct workforce. The general manager sought the advice of a consultant, whose advice was to simply ignore the requests. The circumstances did not seem to support the hiring of additional staff as long as the present staff was not fully utilized.

The general manager discarded the employee requisitions and subsequently told his staff that he would not authorize further hiring until his random walks through the facility convinced him that the existing staff was fully utilized. The plant continued to operate ever more profitably for the next two years, expanding the direct workforce to three full shifts without adding a single salaried worker, except to replace any who left voluntarily. The profit level of the business grew steadily and the general manager was promoted to CEO of the parent company at the end of the two-year period.

Understanding capacity utilization also requires the identification of any bottlenecks or variations in work flow. Bottlenecks occur when one part of a multistep process has too little capacity. To maximize throughput, management must balance the capacity at each stage of the process and ensure the capacities are adequate to meet the demand.

Uneven demand also reduces throughput because an operation must have enough capacity to handle the peak demands. This results in periods of underutilized capacity when demand is weaker. Uneven work flows may reflect seasonal demand or different patterns during the weeks of a month or days of a week. Some restaurants catering to businesses might have peak workloads at lunchtime during the workweek. Others catering to a different clientele may have peak hours at dinner on weekends. Accounting firms have seasonal peaks during year-end audit and tax seasons. The "fire department" syndrome describes a workload pattern that results from unpredictable demand.

One approach to managing gross mismatches between capacity and demand is to price the product or service to absorb the excess costs associated with the idle time. A second management approach is to find ways to generate off-peak volume to better balance the load and generate additional revenues. A fire department may take on the emergency ambulance service, for instance, to utilize capacity more fully. Similarly, an essential part of the strategy for the *USA Today* newspaper was the profitable incremental utilization of time available on printing presses that the company already owned around the country to produce the paper.

Management may also mitigate the problem of matching supply and demand by building flexible capacity. In most situations, management should prefer to allow labor to fluctuate with volume rather than trying to adjust buildings or equipment. One example of this approach may be found in the construction industry, where companies employ subcontractors that are hired by the project and construction workers who are hired by the day. Some businesses use at-home workers, known as "cottage workers," who do not require space and can provide an effective means to deal with spikes in volume. Still another way to provide flexible capacity is to use overtime to meet the peaks in demand. With overtime, the workforce remains unchanged while its capacity fluctuates within a defined range.

The Right People

Along with ensuring a proper level of labor capacity, managers must also have people with the necessary skills and training to produce the products or services of the business efficiently and within quality standards. The general manager must identify and hire the right people to fulfill these roles. For most organizations, the right people are those who share the values of the organization, have the requisite skills and/or the capacity to learn, have an interest in the work of the business, have the capability to take responsibility, and function with reasonable independence while being good team players who interact appropriately.[1] This is especially true when a new strategy is being implemented.

Understanding the kinds of people needed begins with a detailed understanding of the activities that must be performed, and the skills and knowledge required for performing them. The more complex the work, the more a firm needs a workforce of specialists. The more limited a firm's resources—in a small business, for instance—the more versatile the employees must be. Businesses grow and change over time, frequently requiring new or different skills in their workforces.

The right people are defined, however, by more than their skills. A firm should want a workforce consisting of people who are honest, have a strong work ethic, and can work effectively with others. The right people are ideally interested in the kind of work in which the firm engages and are committed to the organization. This is illustrated further in Vignette 19-4.

The Future

Assessing the number and kinds of people currently needed is relatively straightforward because management knows the specifics of the production. It is more complicated, however, to attempt to forecast more distinct future needs. The general manager must understand the lead times required to change the firm's capabilities or increase its capacity. It is very important to add capacity at the correct pace to lead growth effectively. If the incremental capacity is added too early, the business will maintain an

---

VIGNETTE 19-4

One very successful small business manager (his company had about $20 million in sales) had a criterion that no one with an "attitude" could work at the firm. His definition of an attitude was very broad. It included people who were moody or uncooperative; unable to relate to others; had a "chip on their shoulder"; and generally were not there because they wanted to be, but because they needed the job.

investment that provides no return. If the capacity is not added in a timely manner, the business will experience a lost opportunity and risk a negative market reaction if demand materializes and cannot be met.

A firm's competencies must align with the needs of the customers the firm chooses to serve. The general manager must clearly understand and identify the competencies that are and will be core to executing the firm's strategy, and among those, the ones intended to be distinctive as the firm seeks a competitive advantage. If the firm attempts to improve or change its strategies, the critical success factors may change and, hence, the requisite competencies. This will likely require that the firm rethink the kind of people it will need.

Dealing with Employee Turnover

Employees who leave an organization obviously must be replaced unless the firm is downsizing or changing its strategies. Most companies are able to predict normal attrition—retirement and employee turnover— with some accuracy. Organizations should have a formal process to regularly make these forecasts and establish plans for addressing turnover.

Unforeseen events can bring about abrupt departures at any level of an organization. Management should take care to identify the key jobs within the firm and ensure that plans are in place to handle normal attrition and to provide backups in the case of unexpected departures. Depth of talent also provides management with more competition and flexibility when promoting people.

Turnover may be a positive or negative event for an organization depending on who is leaving and why. If the culture of an organization is such that it creates dysfunction in ways that lead to employee dissatisfaction, the tendency will be for those who are able to leave to do so. Naturally, the best people will have the most options available to them and likely will be among those to depart, leaving behind the weaker people and those who thrive in the unpleasant environment. Turnover can be positive, though, if it weeds out these weaker performers. Bringing in new employees, particularly managers, with new ideas and skills will often strengthen organizations. Management should try to assess why so many weak people were hired in the first place and make appropriate changes to remedy the situation.

Companies that are faced with a need to downsize may sometimes achieve their objectives by being patient and letting normal attrition reduce the workforce. The task of anticipating needs is more difficult, though, when a company is growing. The management of a growing business will need to project its rate of growth and the likely accompanying workforce requirements. In growth situations, management must hire to replace those lost to attrition along with those to accommodate growth. For some organizations, this can mean hundreds of employees per month.

Dealing with Labor Unions

Historically, labor unions grew in response to abuses by management in imposing low pay and poor working conditions, and the resulting relationship between unions and management was inherently adversarial. As unions gained more power, they used it, they perceived, to protect the workers. Over time there was a strong tendency on the part of the unions to negotiate work rules and perquisites that worked against the efficiency of the organization. The world has changed since unions began, and the role of unions has had to change as well, as demonstrated in Vignette 19-5.

The forces changing the role of unions include:

- The industrial development of regions that do not have a tradition of unions
- The changing nature of the workforce as the number of knowledge workers grows
- The globalization of the economy
- The evolution of more enlightened managers whose human resource practices make unions less and less necessary

Every business should treat its employees fairly, pay them well in light of competitive realities, and provide favorable working conditions. These approaches are advantageous both economically and ethically. If a company's employees choose to organize, every effort should be made to work in partnership with the union for the common good of the business.

A leading manufacturer of specialty steel tubing enjoyed worldwide prominence in its industry. The firm's product was the industry leader in quality, commanded premium prices, and was requested by customers for especially difficult applications. The company had a long relationship with a prominent labor union and had been generous in its approach to wages, working conditions, and fringe benefits.

The company's dominant market position was abruptly interrupted when a foreign competitor built a steel mill with monthly capacity for the specialty tubing equal to the company's annual capacity. The foreign company, which enjoyed a 30 percent cost advantage as a result of lower wages and economies of scale, soon took to market a specialty steel tubing product that demonstrated metallurgical quality equal to the company's at significantly lower prices. The company's longtime industry dominance was clearly threatened.

The board of directors and the CEO devised a plan of reaction that included a very large capital investment that would match the foreign competitor's economies of scale. To be competitive, given the competitor's lower wage rates, the company also needed concessions from the union on wage rates and costly work rules.

The union leaders balked at the plan immediately and forcefully. They had no desire to give up benefits that had been won over decades of negotiations. The company sent notices to the homes of the workers and published in the press the plan for the large capital investment. The union was unmoved. In the total union workforce of three thousand workers, eight hundred members included in the negotiation were gate guards, janitors, inventory clerks, and similar workers, who were earning the high pay associated with making steel. The town where the facility was located had, at the time of this disruption, an unemployment rate greater than 20 percent.

Nevertheless, the workers voted to reject the company's offer and, as a result, the plant was shut down.

If the union leadership insists on maintaining an adversarial relationship, the company's management must resist demands that would make the business noncompetitive. Management also should ask itself whether it is doing anything to lead the workers to think that it is not interested in them. Businesses that treat their employees properly do not usually have labor problems, union or no union.

Recruiting

After the number and kind of people needed have been determined, management must assess the labor markets and develop strategies to attract qualified applicants in numbers sufficient to meet the firm's needs. The degree of tightness of labor markets, and hence the competition for people, varies widely by both the type of worker and geography. The available labor pool may also reflect both the firm's reputation as an employer and the attractiveness of its industry.

When the number of workers exceeds the number of jobs, recruiting is less taxing than otherwise, except that each firm wants to ensure it is attracting the best prospects. In tight markets, companies must be very innovative in the ways they attract newcomers. Management must decide whether it wants to hire "good athletes" with no experience but strong potential and train them, or whether it wants to hire experienced people who may require little or no training.

Experienced workers are typically found at other companies in the same or related industries. There are drawbacks to raiding other companies for talent, though, as it can result in a wage war not unlike a price war. While people will change jobs for increased pay, it helps any company to be perceived as a better place to work than competitors and as providing greater opportunity. People in companies in the same industry tend to know one another, and this network may be used to identify and/or evaluate potential employees.

If a firm is seeking "good athletes," its approach to recruiting may include maintaining good contacts with high schools and colleges, and participating in their on-campus recruiting and placement programs. In addition to full-time jobs, many students desire part-time positions or internships, which can be mutually beneficial without a lasting commitment. Strong training programs are frequently attractive to student prospects, who desire to remedy their lack of experience.

Friends and family of current employees may serve as effective sources of talent. Some businesses have a tradition of hiring family members, while others simply will not. There are pros and cons to this issue, and consequently it should be approached carefully. Attracting people from other industries provides another means of securing talent. If people have achieved success in other industries, they often will bring their experiences to a new situation and make significant contributions. Vignette 19-6 describes an effective approach to attracting workers from another industry.

Using Headhunters

Many firms utilize employment agencies or executive search firms to find new employees. These agencies can be very useful, especially when they specialize in some functional area or industry. The people most desired by a firm often are not looking for a new job, and so must be identified by some means. The most effective search firms use a disciplined approach that begins with identifying the characteristics desired in a recruited person and then finding people who fit the profile.

Some firms charge the applicant a fee, while others require that the employer pay the fee, which is a very important aspect of the mutual relationship. The search firm should realistically be considered to be "working for" the payer of the fee. Search firms often are expensive, and many of the people they identify may not have been thoroughly investigated. This is especially true of candidates identified by firms that charge contingent fees, that is, fees paid to the agency only upon successful placement of the employee. Such a pay scheme may induce a placement firm to be overly motivated to place a candidate. The employer, on the other hand, bears the risk of such placements because the company will not be compensated for any disruptions caused by bringing in the wrong person.

Advertising

Many businesses use media to advertise their needs for people. The media employed usually include local newspapers and industry publications. More recently, Web-based employment sites have become popular as has posting employment needs on the company's Web site. The problem with advertising is that it may generate many applications from individuals who are not qualified. The administrative task of reducing the large number of applicants to a smaller pool of qualified people can be daunting.

Hiring

After the identification of candidates, the process of hiring must be determined, including identifying who will make the decision and how it should be completed. In smaller businesses, hiring is frequently a very informal process in which the owner or a manager uses his or her personal judgment to make the decision. It often is influenced by relationships or recommendations from other employees, relatives, or friends. Nepotism is not uncommon.

As businesses become larger, the hiring process becomes more formal. At some point, a personnel department administers the process. The pool is reviewed and the qualified applicants are identified, with care taken to ensure compliance with all equal opportunity regulations. Personnel professionals conduct interviews; administer personality, intelligence, and/or skill tests; make reference checks; arrange physical exams and/or drug tests; and conduct background checks for credit, criminal, and/or other legal problems. The hiring agents involved typically examine attitudes as well as abilities. Unfortunately, a personnel department may on occasion grow into a bureaucratic operation that puts more emphasis on process than getting the right people, and its employees may guard their power zealously.

Members of the personnel department may make the actual hiring decision, or they may forward the qualified pool of applicants to the manager who will be the supervisor of the employee for interviews and the hiring decision. Some firms use multiple interviews with an individual, often in a variety of business and social settings. For some high-level, critical jobs, the candidate's spouse may be part of the process, especially if a geographic move is involved.

An interesting innovation is the use of team members to interview applicants and assist in making the hiring decision. These are the people with whom the individual would work if hired. In these cases, the person hired often faces a probationary period, at the end of which the members of the team help decide whether or not permanent employment should be offered.

A dual agenda prevails in the hiring process. While the firm is trying to ascertain whether the applicant is suitable, management is simultaneously "selling" the person on the job and the company so that if an offer is made, he or she is more apt to accept. This approach is more likely to be the case when the applicant is a very attractive prospect who has other options from which to choose.

As a rule, it is advantageous to wait to find the right person. In fact, some say when in doubt, do not hire.

Negotiating the Terms

After members of management decide that they want to hire an individual, the organization will extend an offer. For many lower-level jobs, the terms may be standard and not subject to negotiation. With very attractive candidates who have the requisite experience, though, especially in a tight labor market, some negotiations will usually be required before the deal is closed.

For nearly all positions, negotiations will be limited by the terms of employment for existing employees. While the firm must compete for talent in the external market, care must be taken to maintain internal parity. If management finds that the firm is not competitive in the marketplace for talent, the implications this has for the firm's entire salary and benefits structure should be considered. For instance, a remote location may be unattractive to potential hires and, as a result, the company might have to pay a premium wage to attract strong people.

Employees may be hired without a contract, in which case they are subject to dismissal at the will of the employer. Alternatively, they may be hired subject to a union agreement, or they may be signed to a personal contract. Personal contracts are typically needed when the term of employment is important, or when the firm wants to protect intellectual property or institute a noncompete agreement. Terms also normally include a detailing of the employee's severance package and the terms under which it is valid. Personal contracts are substantially more binding on the company in general than on the employee.

Reducing the Workforce: The Most Difficult Management Task

In spite of the best intentions of management and the most careful adherence to effective management practices, the general manager will occasionally have to separate someone from the organization for reasons other than lack of work. The management author Jim Collins, in his popular work *Good to Great*, describes this act as getting the wrong people off the bus. These actions should be taken soberly and decisions made as objectively as possible. The employee may have violated some company policy, or may be considered a "red dot" (described in Vignette 19-1), when management has committed to creating an organization of "green dots." A variety of situations arise in which management decides that someone should leave the organization. It is important that such situations are seen as being handled fairly and compassionately by all in the organization.

Training and Development

After an employee joins the firm, management must initiate the training the individual requires to do the job for which he or she has been hired and to acclimate to the system and culture of the organization.

Indoctrination

The starting point for training is indoctrination. In small firms, it may be just learning to fit in and building relationships with current employees. They pass along the "dos and don'ts" of the company by word of mouth and indoctrinate the new employee into the informal network of the organization. In so doing, they may reveal how things are really done, how people really think, and what behaviors are acceptable and unacceptable.

Many companies set up a "buddy system" to help a new employee fit in. The buddy explains the day-to-day operations and tries to make the new employee feel welcome and at home. Unfortunately, some companies have closed cliques that will not accept new people until they have been vetted or even initiated in some informal, cultural sense. Larger companies can have very formal indoctrination systems. These may include programs or courses lasting from a few hours to several days, in which the business, its policies and procedures, and its culture and values are described. Bill George, former chairman and CEO of Medtronic, in his book, *Authentic Leadership,* describes a "Mission and Medallion" ceremony in which he participated at Medtronic. At the end of this meeting, every new employee was given a bronze medallion symbolizing the company's mission.[2]

On-the-Job and Formal Training

On-the-job training is by far the most common method of training used in industry. The advantage of this approach is that a person works and learns at the same time. This practice stems from the craft approach to developing the skills of apprentices. The disadvantage is that it is an inefficient way to learn. It also simply teaches existing practices, both good and bad. The senior persons doing the teaching are generally not trained as teachers and may not have the patience and motivation to provide the apprentice with appropriate guidance and an effective learning experience.

At a minimum, on-the-job training should be supplemented with formal training by knowledgeable instructors. Sound training begins with a formal course in which the individual learns the basic principles of the subject. Then, further on-the-job training provides the practical experience that develops necessary ancillary skills. The medical model provides a good analogy for this sequence of training steps. Doctors go to medical school to learn the basic principles of medicine and then move into internships and residency programs to build experience and expertise in a selected specialty area. They typically spend several years learning their specialty, during which they gradually practice the medically necessary skills under supervision.

Career Management

General managers should work to create logical career paths for their employees. Entry-level jobs develop their basic knowledge and skills. As they become competent at their assigned tasks, they are taught to work effectively on teams or in groups. Some individuals make progress on technical tracks—they build expertise as salespersons, technicians, engineers, and the like. Others receive management training as team leaders, and then advance to higher-level management positions. Exceptional people are identified and moved ahead further and faster.

Companies that make an effort to develop the skills and competencies of their people receive many benefits. People are not only more competent in their current jobs, but also preparing for advancement, which provides the company with a talent pool that creates management depth. Exceptional people who sense opportunity are more likely to stay with their employers. As we have emphasized, the management and retention of talent within the organization is crucial to its sustained success.

Performance Measurement

Effective staffing and career management require that a business manage performance, both individually and collectively. Every individual, at every level, should have personal goals, regular feedback, and periodic performance reviews. Vignette 19-7 describes the value of regular performance appraisals.

A number of companies have reported using a two-way table to evaluate the performance of employees in combination with their demonstrated values. This approach evaluates not only the results achieved by an employee, but also whether he or she demonstrated commitment to the organization's value while working. Because the values of most organizations include activities and attributes that create a positive working environment and contribute to the success of the business, management's desire to evaluate employees on demonstrated values is logical and reasonable. A common approach to classifying employees based on their performance and commitment to values is shown in Exhibit 19-1.

Vignette 19-8 describes how one company dealt with a difficult division general manager.

A trucking company was having trouble with efficiency on its loading dock. It was much more profitable for the organization for the workers to consolidate shipments whenever possible, but they were doing so only 40 percent of the time. Management explored how to get them to raise that percentage, and in the process, engaged a consultant to recommend a solution. The consultant determined that the people had the training and skills to do the work. When it was suggested that the workers be given some sort of economic incentive, the consultant thought that such a move would not help.

The consultant recommended that all workers be given scorecards on which they recorded their work, showing the number of consolidations. Several times a day, the supervisor would walk around looking at the cards, praising those who were getting good results and making no comment to those who were not doing well. This selective, positive feedback, combined with recognition, produced immediate and lasting results.

At the heart of this approach to evaluating performance and commitment to values simultaneously is the recognition that a firm should be committed to dealing with problem people. Management must be firm, but fair. Sometimes a difficult person is so productive and valuable, that management will tolerate less-than-desirable behavior. This action sends a message to employees, and eventually the solid employees who are forced to interact with the difficult person leave the organization. The loss of effective people, in the end, may far outweigh the value of retaining the difficult individual.

EXHIBIT 19-1   Classification of Demonstrated Values and Performance

		Performance	
		Good	*Poor*
Values	*Good*	Recognize solid performance; Identify as candidate for promotion	Provide another opportunity; Train or transfer to a better fit
	Poor	Counsel and supervise closely; If no improvement, terminate	Terminate

VIGNETTE 19-8

A division general manager was successful by every measure used by the corporate office to judge performance. He was considered highly effective and might have been a candidate for the CEO position, had an opening occurred. On the other hand, he was a "red dot." He was arrogant, treated his subordinates with contempt, blamed all problems on someone else, and employees found that dealing with him was generally difficult. The corporate CEO was engaged in succession planning and sent a consultant to evaluate the division general manager as a possible candidate for the CEO position. The division manager was true in form, and the consultant was unimpressed. When the visit was concluding, the consultant gave the classical "red dot" manager a bit of unsolicited advice.

He told the division general manager, "Dave, you can be difficult as long as your results are strong." The division manager promptly discounted the advice. Approximately two years later, the industry his business served experienced a decline, and the financial performance of his division was negatively affected. Dave was terminated and new leadership was sent to run the business.

Personnel Administration

The staffing function should be supported by effective personnel administration. A number of key activities must be provided by this important function.

Personnel Actions: Hiring, Promotion, Discipline, and Termination

A business is well advised to maintain policies and procedures for all personnel actions, with clear responsibility and accountability articulated. The organization's personnel officer should provide oversight to enforce the policies and procedures. Many personnel problems are created by managers or supervisors who are lax with or actually violate the prevailing rules. Allowing such behavior will likely have a negative impact on morale and, in the extreme, create legal liabilities.

Personnel Records

Organizations must maintain a complete, up-to-date personnel file on every employee. The file begins with the employee's application and any character or professional references. Personal information should be current, including addresses, next of kin, and so forth. All pay increases, promotions, and transfers should be recorded. Any elections regarding benefits also should be in the file. Performance reviews and any disciplinary actions should also be preserved in the file, which are particularly important when employees contest the results of disciplinary action or termination, often alleging discrimination and/or wrongful discharge. Actions that are not supported by records of timely warnings often are overturned by the courts.

Compensation Systems

An organization's approach to compensation should encompass systematic ways of maintaining external parity in compensation with the marketplace, and internal parity based on responsibility and performance. A major decision in structuring a compensation package is how much of an employee's compensation should be fixed, and how much should be at risk. At-risk compensation (awarded only when certain performance hurdles are met) may be based on individual productivity and/or results for team, division, and company performance. Sales commissions and piecework pay are common in many industries. A distinction should be made between individual or team incentives directly related to performance, and profit sharing and bonuses that are not based on individual performance, but on company performance.

Incentive or at-risk compensation can be short term and/or long term. Long-term incentives are associated with higher-level managers who are able to influence longer-term results. Other managers and employees generally have a higher proportion of incentive compensation as short-term awards. In any case, awards should be tied to desired behaviors and results, and should support the alignment of the interests of the employees with those of the owners. Vignette 19-9 describes how one company sought to align the interests of employees with those of the company.

Compliance

An important function of personnel administration is ensuring compliance with the wide variety of current laws and regulations. Compliance, at a minimum, requires substantial paperwork and record keeping for various levels of government as well as federal, state, and local agencies

VIGNETTE 19-9

Northwestern Mutual Life Insurance Company set its sales agents up as independent businesspeople who personally covered all of their expenses and worked solely on commissions. People at the headquarters, though, were paid competitive salaries, but had no access to wage incentives. The company felt that it could measure the performance of the headquarters staff only over the longer term. Short-term incentives might result in relaxing underwriting standards in order to generate more business, which in the long term would hurt the company. Similarly, taking more risk in the company's investments could increase interest income, but this step would also put the company at risk for greater losses. In either case, the results of the actions might not be known for years.

and boards. All personnel offices should have employees with expertise in regulating compliance measures.

Certain types of discrimination are illegal in the U.S. workplace, including discrimination based on race, gender, religion, national origin, age, sexual orientation, and disabilities. Common sense and enlightened self-interest should lead one to accept the principle that all people should be treated fairly. The Equal Employment Opportunity Commission (EEOC) administers discrimination laws.

While the result of equal opportunity laws has been generally positive, these laws have created some problems. One problem for the employer is that an employee who is not performing well, not conforming to the company's rules, or is behaving badly may claim discrimination when criticized or disciplined. Avoiding these unjustified claims requires strict and uniform adherence to procedures and record keeping. Documentation is critical in this and nearly all other compliance-related issues. Among these, compensation laws also deserve close attention. Administered by the U.S. Department of Labor, these laws set minimum wages, define labor categories, and establish the hours an hourly employee is allowed to work, after which overtime pay is required.

Still another set of laws deals with safety. These are referred to as OSHA regulations because the Occupational Safety and Health Administration administers them. These regulations have also addressed important issues, such as employment of children and illegal immigrants. The Employee Retirement Income Security Act (ERISA) deals with benefit plans. While some of these laws exempt small businesses, it is essential that a general manager understands them, and ensures that the business has the administrative and training practices in place to guarantee compliance.

Employee Relations

Employee relations are among the most important functions of personnel administration. They encompass far more than simply having clever communications programs and feel-good events, although these can be worthwhile. Instead, employee relations should address and aim to bring about the kind of workplace that management desires. This endeavor usually requires building and supporting a culture that is based on mutual trust, respect, and support throughout the organization, and uniting employees in the pursuit of the organization's goals.

Compensation practices are important, but are seldom the most important force in maintaining good employee relations. Training, maintaining positive working conditions, and providing appropriate recognition for performance and commitment are some important ways to build an effective workforce.

Some organizations designate formal or informal ombudspersons to aid in problem resolution. These individuals are outside of the normal chain of command and proactively monitor policies and procedures that affect employees. Ombudspersons are also available to employees who have complaints or need help, professionally or personally. Because they are outside the normal chain of command, employees need not fear retribution when approaching ombudsmen with concerns about managers or supervisors who behave unfairly or inappropriately.

An open-door policy within an organization often works well to encourage positive relations. With such a policy, employees are permitted to see, or make appointments to see, anyone at any time without asking permission from a superior. One might think that this approach would invite trouble. While there may be some individual abuses, such a policy actually assists many organizations in avoiding or halting problems before they get out of control.

In recent years, the use of Web pages has become an excellent two-way tool as another avenue of communication. The publicity of whistle-blowers has resulted in the use of hotlines managed by independent third parties that protect employees, and aid the organization in uncovering wrongdoing. In addition to these approaches, companies have established other diverse avenues of communication, all with the intent of bettering the organization and enhancing the cohesion of the entire workforce.

Some will dismiss a managerial emphasis on employee relations as soft and unessential. Sound employee relations, though, combined with high performance standards, contribute to the establishment of a high-performing organization.

Summary

This chapter discusses numerous aspects of the staffing challenge, including the approaches an organization must take to organizing its team of workers and aligning their actions with the aims of the business. A successful company must:

- Continually assess its staffing needs
- Identify the best set of available job candidates
- Attract the best candidates to the firm
- Provide long-term career opportunities
- Maintain strict but fair performance evaluation systems
- Remain vigilant about compliance with laws and regulations
- Establish sound employee-relations practices

From the entry-level employee to the general manager, the composite character of a company is determined by the values, actions, and work ethic of each member of the team.

DISCUSSION QUESTIONS

1. Why is the metaphor of a casting director appropriate for the role of a general manager?
2. Why might an organization have too many people and what should a general manager do about it?
3. How does an organization determine the kind of people it needs?

4. Why is staffing so important to a firm?
5. How does a company go about getting the right people? How does it keep them?
6. What is the role of personnel administration?

20

INTEGRATING

An organization is a collection of many parts that must operate in a coordinated way to function effectively as an integrated whole. Bringing about this coordination and essential collaboration between and among the parts of a business organization is one of the major challenges facing a general manager. When these tasks are not done skillfully, severe operating problems may occur, accompanied by weak results and ongoing disputes among functions and groups within the organization.

Business integration occurs on various levels. Three primary levels of integration include the following:

- Integration of the functional activities within a focused business activity: This has been referred to earlier as managing the functional interfaces.
- Integration of the activities of separate strategic business units (SBUs) under the same corporate parent: This task may vary from implementing no perceived integration to creating interactions that require close monitoring.
- Vertical and horizontal integration: This technique is used in various industries.

Integration within a Single Business

In a small business, integration is not a major issue. Decision making falls to the general manager who manages all of the functions directly and is, in effect, the integrator. This concept is displayed in Exhibit 18-1. As businesses grow, they tend to be organized around specialized functional responsibilities that, in turn, evolve into natural groupings of teams and departments. The activities of these units create predictable and natural conflicts as they interact with each other. The leaders of these various functional units must manage the interactions between the departments and teams. It is the responsibility of the general manager, though, to coordinate the interactions between the functional organizations to best serve the interests of the entire organization.

The leaders of the subordinate units naturally see the business from their individual perspectives, and as a result, they may reasonably differ in their opinions of what is best for the organization as a whole. For some, loyalty to their unit overrides their loyalty to the larger entity, and they do not instinctively consider what is best for the overall organization. As a result of such parochial thinking, these subordinate managers dedicate themselves to protecting their turf.

There is a natural tendency for business organizations to operate in functional silos, a form of vertical isolation. The central goal of integration is to overcome these boundaries between and among the various units to improve the results of the overall organization. The general manager is driven to achieve cross-functional coordination and collaboration because the successful implementation of most strategies is dependent on the integrated actions of the various functions of the business. As a primary— and mandatory—step in the process of integrating functions, the manager of each functional organization must understand and support the larger picture of the whole organization and operate his or her function within the context of its overarching goals.

As discussed in previous chapters, matrix organizations as well as flatter organizations are often effective in helping overcome some of the interface problems inherent in functional organizations.

The internal customer is also useful in managing the integration of the functions. Every unit in an organization should understand what impact it has on other units, including how, when, and to whom it provides (or should provide) critical information, services, and/or goods. These internal relationships should function with the understanding that in every interaction, one party is a customer to be served and pleased.

The Functions

As described in previous chapters, three line functions—marketing (creating demand), engineering (product and process design), and production/operations (providing the goods or service)—are present in most single businesses. The concept of a production function, for example, is readily understood in a manufacturing business, but other types of business—distribution and service, for instance, or even education—also have operations functions that are comparable to the production function in a manufacturing business. The operations function encompasses those workers building a product or delivering a service to the organization's customer. In an educational institution, teachers would be part of the operations function.

Businesses typically encompass three support functions—human resources, information systems, and finance. The need for an effective administrative function is embedded in all six of the other functions. For each of the functions, employees require different skill sets and expertise to achieve outstanding results.

The Functional Interfaces

Here, we explore salient issues in managing the interfaces between various pairs of functions.

The Interface between Marketing and Production/Operations

In the short run, marketing must sell the products or services that the production or operations function produces. This activity requires managing throughput volumes and product mix such that the best use is made of the capacity, resources, and competencies of the production/operations function.

Marketing can wreak havoc if it sells products that are incompatible with the capability of the production/operations function. If the organization attempts to fill such orders, customers almost certainly will be disappointed with the product, or the production/operations processes likely will be disrupted and become inefficient and unprofitable. It is possible that engineering will be called in to attempt to remedy the situation, causing further disruption within the organization. If marketing has found a mismatch between its firm's offerings and what customers want and can obtain from competitors, the organization should determine if it needs to revisit its strategy and functional strategies before moving on to rethink its production capabilities.

The purpose of this assessment is to have management determine whether a shift in strategy is required to serve customers differently. Organizations may easily move off their strategies and away from their goals when they respond automatically to their marketing departments' perceptions that they need to revise product offerings and corresponding production capabilities. In some cases, the general manager will decide to stay the course, believing the new products to be outside the organization's strategy. In others, the general manager will find the products themselves to be consistent with the strategy and authorize necessary changes. The final scenario involves recognition that the competitive environment has shifted, and in order to remain competitive, the organization must adjust its strategy. In this final situation, the organization should follow the procedures it has in place for contingency planning and strategy reassessment outside the normal planning cycle. If no such procedures exist, the management team or an ad hoc strategic planning team should draft them and add them to the organization's planning system.

In the long run, the production function must have the capacity and competencies to produce what the customers want to buy at costs lower than those of competitors for comparable products. In short, the strategic challenge for the organization is to create production capabilities within the business that are competitive in the marketplace in terms of product characteristics and price, and the operating challenge is to utilize effectively the capabilities and capacity created.

Assuming that there is a solid alignment between production/operations capabilities, capacity, and market demands, the operational interfaces can still be very complex if the organization produces and delivers numerous products (goods and/or services), or if the products have complex specifications and/or critical delivery requirements.

A manufacturing plant would normally value a simple product mix with a very standardized product that could be produced in run lengths or lot sizes that fit with the economics of the operation. These circumstances often bring about the smoothest operation and result in the lowest costs. Marketing might find it easier, though, to sell a more customized product, with faster delivery times. A strategic issue that must be resolved is the degree of specialization that will prevail. Managers must determine whether the organization will be specialized, and likely more cost competitive, or more flexible. These considerations tie back to strategic choices regarding pursuing cost leadership or differentiation. Either strategy may lead to success, but being caught in the middle (called waffling) seldom works. Clarity of choice and execution should be present in the objectives and strategies of marketing and production/operations and their integration.

In many businesses, the sales representatives perform the customer service function. Due to the nature of this task, the customer service/sales representatives must coordinate with the production function. In other companies, an important integrating element is a customer service department whose responsibility is to determine and anticipate what the customer wants and needs, understand the capabilities of the manufacturing plant or service operations, and bring about satisfactory solutions to meet customer requests. The customer service representative then delivers a production order to the plant and coordinates the production to meet the required or promised delivery date.

Typically, both the marketing and production functions have an interest in supervising the customer service department. Most plant managers would desire this supervisory role in order to control the orders coming into the plant. Similarly, most marketing managers would want the same role in order to: (1) manage the quality of customer relations, (2) coordinate and integrate the activities of the salespeople and the customer service people, and (3) provide overall seamless account management. Effective customer service requires both perspectives for excellence. Customer service is often organized as a separate function reporting to the general manager and on the same level as the sales and production functions in businesses in which customer service is a critical success factor.

The Interface between Marketing and Engineering or Research and Development (R&D)

The interface between marketing and engineering or research and development (R&D) involves designing goods or services that meet the needs of targeted market segments. The more innovative the products or services, the more the business may be able to differentiate its offerings from those of competitors. Successful high-tech businesses such as drug manufacturers or electronics firms thrive on R&D and may spend a large portion of each sales dollar on creating new and better products. Other businesses may spend more than competitors in a quest to establish a brand. A challenge in integrating these two functions comes in economically matching the characteristics of new products to marketing's perception of needs and desires. Further complications may arise when the production function steps in to produce new products, as discussed below.

The Interface among Marketing, Engineering, and Production/Operations

In well-integrated organizations, the marketing, engineering, and production functions must work very closely to create products that are attractive to the market and yet can be manufactured satisfactorily in terms of speed, economy, and quality. Designing goods or services that cannot be produced efficiently will not aid the organization. Conversely, designing products or services that won't sell, even though they can be produced efficiently, is equally problematic and fraught with financial risk.

Such challenges have been observed in creative industries such as construction, home decorating, and printing. Architects and graphic designers are notorious for creating designs that cannot be produced efficiently. While some creative geniuses may depend on others to solve the production problems, truly effective design personnel also have the engineering or technical knowledge to make their ideas practical without destroying their creative content or uniqueness.

The Interface between Engineering or Research and Development (R&D) and Production

Research and development that is related to production is commonly referred to as engineering and is focused on product and process design. Engineering design efforts can be intended to improve existing products or processes, or to produce the current products or services better, faster, or more efficiently. These efforts may also be intended to develop new processes, either for improving the production of existing products or for new products. All such engineering efforts typically require use of the production facilities for test and experimentation. This need necessitates coordination and appropriate capacity planning.

When integrating engineering and production, the organization also should address the issue of parts commonality. When designing (or redesigning) products, engineering should work to maximize the use of the same parts within and across products, and minimize parts variety within the organization. This action will reduce complexity within production, as well as the purchasing function.

The Interface between Support Functions and Line Functions

It is important that the organization's support functions be closely integrated with the line functions. Without close coordination, managers of support functions may develop policies or practices that disrupt the essential activities of the line functions.

While the personnel of support functions bring to the organization special expertise in their fields, they should not develop systems or policies without the close collaboration of committed and informed users. Some companies find that line managers do not have the interest, time, or skills to participate actively in designing new systems or procedures. The line managers defer to the support specialists, who design the needed systems and then find that the systems are not what was needed or desired. This failing is often the case when new management information systems are being developed.

We discussed the human resources function (HR) earlier and the importance of its support of the line functions. The HR function is critical to getting the right people into the right jobs, ensuring their training and development, and administering appropriate evaluation and compensation systems. The HR function also plays a key role in designing and executing systems for performance measurement.

The information technology function provides the line functions with the data processing tools, communications capabilities, and specific information they need to support their work. Some goods and services provided by this function must be highly specialized and embedded in a line function, while others are company-wide utilities operated by the support function.

The finance function provides a range of services to the organization. One service is the provision of reports and period-ending financial statements that mirror the physical flows of products and services through the business to customers, providing a type of scorekeeping function to the line departments and the general manager. Finance also works to focus the attention of the line functions on the profit structure of the business. Department personnel pursue this aim through actions to ensure that the intended relationships among costs, prices, volume, and capacity are understood and proactively managed within the line functions to produce the desired results. Finance must disaggregate the business by profit center, by product, and by customer to understand where the business is making and losing money, and to ensure that appropriate actions are taken to solve problems and pursue opportunities. Finance also manages the economics of investment decisions regarding inventories, fixed assets, and projects of all kinds to ensure that the intended results will meet specified cost/benefit criteria.

One can easily imagine the potential for conflicts between the financial and line personnel as they are confronted with economic realities that may force unpleasant or difficult decisions. Further conflicts often emanate from difficulties in projecting the future economic impact of alternative decisions. Once again, we note the importance of intellectual honesty here in making projections as well as decisions. This fundamental issue of forecasting the future impact of current decisions should influence the finance specialists to go beyond accounting conventions to understand the drivers of costs, volume, and profits.

Accounting numbers are too often assumed to have an accuracy that is not justified. Accounting results are based on many judgments that might conform to generally accepted accounting rules but might not reflect the prevailing economics in a dynamic situation or even the managerial perspective necessary for more accurate decision making. For example, projections of volumes are based on expected or forecast price levels and judgments about the elasticity of demand in the market to price changes. Such projections, while the organization's best estimate, are rarely perfectly accurate.

The support functions should assist the line managers in understanding how to use their specialized services and make maximum use of the available tools and services they offer. In order to bring this about, support function personnel should maintain effective skills and knowledge related to their specialties, develop and maintain strong working relationships with the personnel of the line functions, and remain apprised of the operations of the various functions in carrying out their responsibilities.

Administration and All Functions

Some administrative functions are performed best within a functional area. Others may be centralized in a shared services model because of specialized knowledge and economies of scale. Trade-offs arise, though, in choosing which approach to implement for a given function. For example, credit management is an important part of many customer relationships, and thus may reasonably be assigned to the marketing organization. On the other hand, credit approval and collections require very specialized skills and should be tightly controlled. Centralizing credit management in a shared-services unit is often very effective, provided personnel are sensitive to customer relations considerations in their operations and in the decisions they make. While marketing managers might have a tendency to relax credit standards to achieve greater volumes, strict credit analysts might put off customers, which could result in depriving the business of profitable volume. An effective balance must be found in this trade-off, regardless of the placement of the credit management function within the organizational structure.

Purchasing is another administrative function that is frequently centralized. Economic benefits typically result from consolidating volume to leverage purchasing power, usually in the form of volume discounts. Additional benefits may come in the form of joint advertising deals with customers, preferential product placement in retail establishments, and dedicated account managers. The downside to centralized purchasing is that brand and product decisions may be made by employees far removed from their use, and often based solely on price. A number of large companies use their marketplace clout to purchase very aggressively. Some have accomplished this very successfully, while others have destroyed valuable relationships with suppliers.

Companies centralize other administrative functions as well, including accounting, insurance, pension management, payroll preparation, and cash management, primarily because they may be accomplished better and less expensively by specialists.

Integration among Strategic Business Units

An integration strategy is appropriate when operating and/or marketing synergies are perceived to be available or when a general manager thinks integration is the most feasible path to continued growth—often related to the execution of an acquisition strategy. If a diversified, decentralized company operates through a number of strategic business units, it has a different set of integration challenges, unless it manages the businesses as diversified stand-alone entities that have very little or no interaction with one another. If, however, the company is pursuing an integration strategy—either vertical or horizontal,[1] it must determine the rules that govern how the SBUs interface with each other. Such a strategy is usually driven by some expectation of potential synergies among and between the business units. Vignette 20-1 describes a major public company's effort to vertically integrate.

Managing the integration of acquired companies is a serious challenge for the general manager. If the acquisition is to be merged into an existing company, management must carefully address issues related to combining cultures and workforces, standardizing systems, selecting leaders (there are inevitably going to be winners and losers), and managing resource consolidations to achieve projected cost savings. This must all be done while preserving the customer base—or at least that portion of the customer base that the acquirer wants to keep.

VIGNETTE 20-1

PepsiCo was pursuing a strategy of vertical integration when it entered the fast-food restaurant market by buying into its distribution network. An obvious benefit of controlling the retail outlets would be the demand generated for its soft drinks and snacks. It became apparent over time that the situation complicated efforts to sell to other fast-food firms that recognized PepsiCo as a competitor, and the impact on PepsiCo's results was not advantageous. For this and other strategic reasons, PepsiCo eventually divested its fast-food businesses.

If the acquired company is to continue as a separate strategic business unit or profit center, but is expected to buy from or sell to sister businesses (or to cross-sell with them), the rules regarding transfer prices, delivery commitments, and quality need to be specified and the incentives aligned.

Some very successful companies have employed diversified, decentralized operations for decades. Most of these successful companies follow a few straightforward rules that govern the integration (or relative independence) between and among the business units. The following rules characterize at least some of these relationships:

- Each business unit is expected to achieve outstanding financial results as compared to a set of peer companies.
- Each business unit is free to purchase products or services from other (internal to the company) business units at their discretion given prevailing costs, quality, and delivery realities.
- Business units may be afforded the same margins on internal sales that they earn on outside sales.
- If a business unit is purchasing more than half of another (internal) unit's output, the "customer" business unit may subsume the supplying business unit. Thus, a business unit must profitably sustain more than half of its sales to outside customers in order to remain an independent business unit.

These rules, though not universally applied among diversified, decentralized companies, represent the kind of thinking that the general manager must embrace if the chief executive officer (CEO) of the parent company and the general managers of the business units are committed to our system of free enterprise and competition. Attempts to force integration (often called synergies) are frequently counterproductive.

Integration within Industry Structures

Vertical and horizontal integration have shaped the competitive structure of numerous industries. Different industries have used vertical and horizontal integration in varying ways, reflecting the economics of their value chains and the strategies individual companies have chosen. We have selected a few industries to illustrate how industry structures have evolved over time as a result of economic factors and competition. The "invisible hand" described by Adam Smith, eighteenth-century economist and philosopher, and mentioned earlier has led to the development of these structures (means to compete) without coercion or policy inducements.

As you read these descriptions of industry structure, note the forces that have shaped the structure, particularly economies of scale. Where economies of scale are present, there is a greater tendency toward vertical and horizontal integration. The general manager should understand the economic characteristics of his or her industry and how they shape the strategic alternatives of the competitors.

We recognize that reasonable people naturally could differ in their conclusions about the degree of vertical integration characterizing the industries described here. It is also true that the degree of vertical integration varies by company within most industries. This variation reflects the gradual development over time of the strategies of each company and the predilections of each CEO as they seek competitive advantages in various ways. We offer these examples to show the general long-term effects brought about by industry-wide economic forces. Each general manager must assess the best course of strategic actions for his or her company to compete, while recognizing the industry realities reflected in the positions of competitors.

The Papermaking Industry

Paper companies have traditionally vertically integrated backward through pulp making and harvesting to the owning of timberlands, through which they ensure access to a steady supply of raw material. In recent years, many paper companies have been selling their timberlands and purchasing raw materials on the open market because of the low return on the capital invested in timberlands. They may use their own crews to harvest the timber, or this activity may be outsourced. While most paper mills make their own pulp (from which paper is made), there are companies that make pulp to sell into what is a global market.

Papermakers have used two forms of distribution—direct selling to large customers and an independent merchant system for the broader market. In recent years, some companies have vertically integrated forward by buying the merchants. They use the merchant system to provide just-in-time inventory management as a way of differentiating their products and services in what could otherwise be a commodity market.

Some paper companies have vertically integrated into a number of product lines, such as packaging, napkins, and tissue. Distribution to the consumer varies widely depending on the product, and the integrated companies have not taken on this activity. Recycling has an independent value chain in which raw material is provided to specialty mills for use in the manufacture of certain types of paper products.

The Oil Industry

The oil industry begins with large-scale searches for oil deposits, continues with extraction where the oil is found, and follows with the shipment of the crude oil around the world to refineries in markets where it is consumed. The industry is virtually totally integrated down through the local filling station for gas. It is among the most vertically integrated of all industries at every stage of production and distribution.

Motor Vehicle Manufacturing Industry

There is an interesting dichotomy in the motor vehicle industry in that some companies are highly vertically integrated while others are substantially less so. Many motor vehicle manufacturers engage in very profitable consumer financing. The dealer networks are tightly controlled franchises that give the manufacturer many of the operational benefits of ownership while they avoid the financial risks which can be best managed by local entrepreneurs who are in touch with the local markets. Manufacturing, advertising, and financing have economies of scale, whereas selling and servicing currently have virtually no such economies and are best accomplished in a more flexible and responsive environment.

The Computer Industry

The computer industry has experienced an interesting shift away from vertical integration over its life span. In the 1970s and 1980s, IBM was highly vertically integrated. With the advent of the personal computer, however, the major components came from independent suppliers. Microsoft dominates the software industry—both operating systems and application software. Intel is the major chip producer. In fact, those brands have nameplates on the equipment alongside the name of the computer manufacturer, which is today primarily a product designer, assembler, and marketer. Even distribution varies. Dell and Gateway sell directly to the consumer, eliminating the middlemen, and are thus vertically integrated, whereas other major manufacturers still go through traditional retail channels.

The absence of vertical integration has characterized the broader electronics industry throughout its life of several generations. The relative independence of sequential stages has allowed the rapid inclusion of the latest developments in component parts by the assemblers of final products. This nonintegrated industry structure has helped the electronics industry achieve cumulative growth rates far above those of other industries for more than fifty years.

The Real Estate Industry

The real estate industry is very fragmented. There are a few developers who also design and build on a large scale. For the most part, firms work through project alliances and outsource construction to subcontractors. Sales and leases are handled by yet another set of businesses, as is financing.

Summary

This chapter discusses three basic facets of the business within which the general manager must ensure that the most strategically appropriate levels of integration are employed. Managing the functional interfaces within a focused business, the relationships between and among independent strategic business units, and the prevailing opportunities for vertical integration are among the general manager's most complex tasks. In fact, these issues embody the essence of general management.

DISCUSSION QUESTIONS

1. What is meant by the term *integration*?
2. Which form of integration do you consider most important to a general manager?

3. Which factor is most important to "managing the functional interfaces," choosing the right functional managers or specifying the right rules for engagement?

4. Why are the concepts of free enterprise and competition important to the proper integration of the activities of subordinate business units?

5. What are the potential risks and rewards of deviating from industry norms in degrees of vertical integration?

21

EXECUTING

Execution is the process of converting strategies into detailed operational plans and then into action. The plans and associated actions are tactical, meaning that the management team focuses on how to perform the tasks (doing things right) as opposed to what actions to take (doing the right things), the latter representing the strategic view. Functional operating plans are devised to meet functional goals that align with the firm's strategies and are coordinated between the functions. These plans should consist of specific manageable actions and designate clearly who is to do what by when. They should include budgets and timetables, and if they extend over a period of time, milestones against which to measure progress.

At some point, the general manager and the organization should be ready to operate effectively with the right people properly organized in the right jobs. Likewise, a solid infrastructure of systems, equipment, and facilities should also be in place. Until these tasks are completed appropriately, operating difficulties may loom on the horizon. Ensuring their completion, though, may be part of executing the organization's plans.

The various parts of the organization should all be aware of the strategic objectives and the operating goals intended to be accomplished. Functional strategies should have been created that support the competitive strategy. This means knowing how the firm intends to create demand and then fulfill that demand profitably. There should be clarity of purpose in terms of who the firm's customers are, their needs and desires, which needs and desires the firm intends to meet, and the critical success factors required for doing so.

As with any trip undertaken, the firm must be steered in order to stay on course as the general manager and organization launch or continue the effort of executing strategy. The helmsman of a ship has a directional heading, but constantly has to make small adjustments to stay on that heading as winds and tides push the ship off course. Sometimes it is necessary to change the heading to get around a storm or other obstacle, and then return to course. Occasionally, though, a decision is made for some reason to change the destination, requiring the helmsman to steer in an entirely new direction. So it is with executing strategies. Plans and budgets provide benchmarks and guidance, but managers who consistently meet them precisely should be suspected of gaming the system. Similarly, strategic detours arise periodically that necessitate temporary adjustments to plans. Finally, at times a firm's management is compelled to change the firm's strategy outside the strategic planning cycle. While not a move to be sought out, such changes in strategy may be necessary to ensure long-term viability of the organization, and on occasion, immediate survival.

The Importance of Execution

Execution requires a clear understanding of the firm's strategies, set in place at the functional level to address the critical success factors. The critical success factors were identified when the customers and their needs were defined and were further refined when it was decided how the firm would compete. These functional strategies, in effect, become the firm's action plan, and management must remain focused on their effective execution. This commitment requires persistence and determination since many unexpected or unpreventable problems and/or opportunities will appear throughout the year (or other specified planning-cycle duration), especially when the organization is undertaking new and innovative endeavors. Frequently, there is no proven path to be followed and mistakes can be expected. Above all, management must be persistent.

Management also must be willing to "confront the brutal facts" of any situation. [1] The general manager should not rationalize, deny the existence of a problem, or fail to hold subordinate managers accountable. Management must be doggedly results oriented. If things are going well, management should aim to understand why, and learn to replicate the performance. If things are not going well, management should search out the root cause of the problem and learn to fix it. Innovation is essential because it is difficult to compete with organizations that are the most innovative in improving their products and processes.

The Nature of the Business and the Required Skills

Operating challenges vary with the size and type of business. Manufacturing has historically been the backbone of the U.S. economy. In recent years, however, as manufacturing jobs have moved around the world seeking lower costs, the service sector has become a powerful economic driver of the U.S. economy.

The service sector includes such widely diverse businesses as banks, insurance companies, the professions, health care, hospitality, transportation, and personal services. The manufacturing sector is also varied, consisting of products that are first classified as consumer goods or industrial equipment. Another major segmentation differentiates between durable goods (those with longer lives, such as refrigerators or automobiles) and nondurable goods (consumables like soap and toothpaste). Manufacturing companies also may be classified into businesses that manufacture for inventory (goods are produced for later sale) and those that manufacture on demand (goods are sold prior to or at production). Additional business types include natural resources companies, construction, and utilities.

Each of these various business types will have very different functional strategies, with different critical success factors. It is therefore difficult to generalize about execution. The general manager of every business, though, must identify its critical success factors and develop functional strategies to enhance the likelihood of success. The general manager must then set performance standards against which to measure results, and react decisively to deviations from plans.

As discussed earlier, the firm's functional strategies must support its strategy and approaches to gaining a competitive advantage. If the firm's strategy is to be the cost leader, it must take a product to market at a cost no competitor can meet. If the firm's strategy is to provide a differentiated good or service, its management must understand exactly what is intended and be focused on creating products and services that are, in fact, differentiated. Finally, if the firm is intent on dominating a specific market niche, everyone in the organization must understand the product characteristics and marketing approach that will achieve dominance of the targeted market niche. It is useful to reiterate that the three generic strategies—overall cost leadership or low-cost producer, differentiation, and focus or market niche—are not mutually exclusive. That is, a firm could simultaneously be the low-cost producer and still deliver a superbly differentiated product. Achieving more than one successful generic strategy, while challenging, would likely lead to a very profitable business.

The skills required to execute a strategy are discussed below in general terms.

Leadership

Leadership is critical to execution. There are clearly roles in a business for general managers who are visionaries and deal makers. It is also critical that there be leadership with an operating mentality. The general manager may possess the necessary operating skills, or if he or she does not, there should be someone on the management team who does.

A manager with an operating mentality is able to think in terms of systems and recognize how the various parts of the organization interact. At the same time, this manager knows how to manage details and bring about desired actions and results. The effective operating leader must know the business in detail, and ideally, he or she has the skills and values to demonstrate simultaneously the paradoxical traits of toughness (in holding people accountable) and compassion (in truly caring about them). Effective operating leaders must know how to get the right people in the right jobs, and organize and lead their efforts. These managers must not only make sound business decisions, but also personally demonstrate the behavior and values that they desire for the organization.

Focus, Discipline, and Dedication

Execution requires focus on the immediate tasks at hand with the discipline to follow plans and employ the best practices consistently, along with the dedication to see them through to meet the operating goals. This kind of rigorous determination should be tempered by a mental flexibility to steer—to make required adjustments on the fly to maintain the course and achieve the objectives in the face of changed or evolving conditions.

Performance and Progress Reports

Likewise, general managers must stay apprised of organizational happenings in a timely fashion. This important topic is discussed in Chapter 22, "Controlling and Reporting."

Coordinating and Communicating through Meetings

The preparation of detailed strategic plans is essential; planning for and coordinating tactical operations are equally critical. These plans are somewhat informal in some organizations, but are standardized and updated on a regular schedule in others. Operational plans usually require some meeting of the essential parties to coordinate commitments and schedules. It is important that these meetings be focused, efficient, and productive. Very often, they are too long and painful. A management team may, in fact, have too many meetings. The prevalent problem in many organizations is that the meetings are chronically ineffective. Patrick Lencioni, in *Death by Meeting,* points out that meetings fail when they lack a contextual structure.[2] He says there should be different meetings for different purposes and describes four types of operating meetings, each distinct. Lencioni's types of meeting include:

- Daily check-in meetings
- Weekly tactical meetings
- Monthly strategic meetings
- Quarterly off-site reviews

These meetings relate solely to the successful execution of strategic plans, and offer one logical approach to using meetings for strategic planning and strategy execution.

The *after-action review* is another type of meeting that some companies employ to advantage. After every major project or activity, those involved get together to review what went well and should be sustained, what needs improvement, and what lessons were learned.

Implicit in this discussion of meetings is that the right people are in attendance. If people who are not needed attend, their time is wasted. One major firm had a rule that only one person from any organizational unit could attend any meeting; the reasoning was that a second person from any organization would be redundant. Conversely, if the people who are needed are absent, the effectiveness of the meeting is diminished.

An experienced general manager also knows how to use one-on-one meetings to assess status, communicate instructions, and generally coordinate activities. A level of candor will often arise in such private meetings that may not be experienced in larger gatherings.

Creating Demand

Because all profits begin with a sale, executing the marketing strategy is a logical first order of business in most organizations. Two major components make up a marketing strategy: how to sell the product; and how to price the product.

Selling

Selling may be brand-driven, which means that it depends on advertising and reputation to create a pull for the goods or service. Alternatively, selling may be created by direct sales efforts, which create a push and usually depend on building a relationship with the customer.

If selling depends on advertising to establish a brand, the management must determine the target market, select the most appropriate media to reach it, and create an effective message. The critical skills for advertising include a deep understanding of the customers in the target market, the ability to select and utilize the media, and the skill to create compelling messages. Some businesses are very adept at this process and establish and maintain powerful brands. Others struggle with brand identification. For consumer products, marketing channel selection and packaging are also key variables.

If the marketing strategy is primarily one of direct sales, the firm must have well-trained, competent salespeople who systematically cover the target market. The best salespeople are those who can build relationships with their customers and prospects. The strongest direct sales effort is the consultative sell, in which the salesperson is recognized as an expert by the customer and provides advice on the product that will best meet the needs of customers and/or solve their problems.

The sales effort may, of course, utilize a combination of advertising and direct sales. Advertising provides an up-front means to create brand awareness, an image, and an interest in the product or service, after which the salesperson closes the sale.

Employees of every organization should strive to be customer-friendly, individually and collectively. Thus, any jobs that bring employees in contact with customers should be staffed with people who relate well to customers. This requirement applies to jobs at all levels of the organization. Businesses often spend a great deal of money to attract customers, and then create problems through unfriendly or incompetent employees who simply do not understand how to act in customer-friendly ways. These employees are either in the wrong positions or are the wrong people for the organization. Organizations should pay attention to customer feedback and carefully consider the cost of lost sales when making related staffing decisions. Of course, it is not always an easy task to find competent, customer-friendly workers, especially for low-wage service jobs. Organizations must carefully assess the value of such employees to the organization and find ways to hire and retain them.

Pricing

Pricing is among the most important tactical decisions that a manager makes on a day-to-day basis. The general manager effectively makes pricing decisions, either directly after consultation, or by the ratification of prices recommended by the manager of marketing and sales. Pricing plans are typically generated for the business plan, and play a primary role in the business model, as discussed in Chapter 10.

For the manager to set effective prices, he or she must know the competitive price levels in the market, the price elasticity of the market, and the product's cost structure. Vignette 21-1 describes the pricing dilemma faced by a very successful general manager.

In some businesses, pricing is a matter of negotiating, which has its own set of critical skills.

VIGNETTE 21-1

The general manager of a very profitable division of a major diversified, decentralized company found himself with a severe competitive problem. His division was a full-service operation competing with three different companies, each of which specialized in one of his three major product lines. In time, he found himself with lowered returns on investment resulting from large levels of inventories and receivables. An analysis of his product mix showed that the division was losing money on large numbers of products or SKUs (stock-keeping units) in all three product lines. He was determined to drive away this unprofitable business by raising prices. When the orders continued to arrive, he raised prices again, and yet again. This formerly unprofitable business became quite profitable after these actions. He later learned that his competitors had used high prices to send him unwanted business that involved small orders, high inventory levels, and hard-to-manufacture items. This problem had been brought on by his failure to monitor the prevailing prices in his markets.

Credit

If a business sells on credit, effective credit management (approval and collection policies) is an important skill. Retail businesses now benefit from their ability to accept credit cards, which solves this problem for some, but if the business extends credit on its own account, it must establish reasonable credit policies and be skilled at screening prospects for their creditworthiness.

Customer Service

The quality of customer service is a critical success factor in many businesses, as described in some detail in Chapter 20, "Integrating." The quality of customer service may be defined by the degree to which the transaction is convenient, on time, pleasant, and effective. Outstanding customer service may be a major component of a competitive advantage gained from differentiation.

A comparison of the service levels of companies operating in the same business will generally demonstrate a wide range of apparent effectiveness in this critical area. Those with high levels of service effectiveness usually spend a lot of time and energy perfecting these skills. They will have been innovative, hired carefully, and trained well. These efforts normally pay off handsomely in customer loyalty. Achieving high levels of customer service is very rewarding but difficult to accomplish, especially on a large scale, which is why many companies do not succeed in this crucial competitive arena.

In many businesses, the after-sale service is a major part of the sales experience. After-sale problems should be seen as an opportunity to gain customer goodwill if managed well. If the product or service is technical, the availability of expert assistance can be important. In durable product businesses, superior maintenance services may be a critical attribute, and a reputation for superior maintenance services may even lead to the sale itself.

Producing the Product or Providing the Service

Product production (which we will use to also designate service delivery) is at the core of execution because the related actions taken in the production/operations function reflect the basic intent of the business and its owners. Every business must have the capability to produce its products efficiently, to meet intended (acceptable) quality standards, and to meet delivery commitments. These activities require appropriate facilities; equipment and materials; trained personnel; adequate capacity and inventory; and well-defined performance, delivery, and quality standards.

The operating environment in which products are produced and services delivered varies across industries and businesses. What production personnel should share, though, is clarity of purpose, commitment to getting the job done, and the discipline and competence required to perform their tasks in a superior way on all important dimensions.

A positive, can-do attitude and pride in the work accomplished are also characteristics of strong operations personnel. An appreciation for innovation is also notable in this arena. Innovators characteristically love to tinker and are rarely content with the status quo. Management must recognize and accept that such creative thinking and subsequent actions constitute experimentation (with the best of intentions) in which mistakes inevitably will be made and failures will be experienced. As described in Chapter 3, the general manager must have the resolve to live with honest mistakes. Knowledge and skills required for success are often learned from the processes of failure and repeated efforts. This adventurous attitude is at the core of continuous improvement.

As we discuss in Part V, it is critical that organizations have controls in place to measure performance, react to deviations from standards, and learn from their experiences. Furthermore, the more decentralized a company is, the more important it is that management information systems are available to keep employees at all levels apprised of the status of the organization.

Managing Change through Execution

A general manager must be effective at managing change in executing strategies. When the operations involve doing things differently—changing or improving processes that involve learning new skills, or creating new products and services—a new dimension is introduced into the task of execution. The more dramatic the change, the greater the challenge presented.

Initiating and completing changes through execution often encompasses perfecting the intended new process or product on a small scale, perhaps by means of test models in laboratories or at beta sites. After management understands the nuances of the proposed changes, the organization must make a transition to a larger, more realistic scale. For a new process, this move requires putting the necessary equipment in place and training employees in its operation. After the new process is performing effectively, an appropriate transition from the old process to the new must be carefully planned and executed, in order to continue meeting targets for costs, quality, and deliveries. The time required for such changeovers typically varies with the complexity of the move.

Employing Projects

One-time projects are frequently used to bring about change. The complexity and significance of such projects may vary widely, ranging from simple to more complex. Simple projects may take a few hours or days and involve very few people. They are usually fairly straightforward to manage. More complex projects may take years and involve large numbers of people, often from many groups both inside and outside the organization. (For example, a complex project to bring about change might be the design, construction, and start-up of a new, more environmentally friendly plant; and a simple project might be an on-site Kaizen, or continuous improvement event.) Critical path scheduling was developed to assist in the management of one-time, very complex military projects. This project management methodology has been adapted for use in numerous nonmilitary industries, including the construction industry, filmmaking, and disaster relief. Many specialized books and software programs are available to assist the general manager in understanding the details of project management and critical path scheduling.

One-time projects typically require the following:

- A clear charge or purpose, which should have measurable outcomes regarding schedules, budgets, quality, and performance standards.
- A designated project manager who is responsible for the project and may be held accountable for results.
- An understanding by all involved of who holds veto authority over the project (usually the person to whom the responsible manager reports). This authority may approve, change, or reject the recommendations of the project manager.
- The right people for the project, including those parties who can contribute to the project and those whose support is needed for its implementation.
- A well-defined action plan.

Managing Acquisitions and Divestitures

A general manager must have, or have access to, a number of key skills in order to complete deals for acquisitions and divestitures. We mention in Chapter 3 that some general managers have these skills and others never gain proficiency at closing deals. Thus, some general managers are able to close numerous deals while others never seem to hone the required skills. Chapter 20 also briefly reviews the process of integrating acquisitions.

In general, successful acquisitions have the following characteristics:

- A strategic fit with the acquirer.
- A reasonable or advantageous price paid. Paying too much for an acquisition turns an otherwise good deal into a poor deal, regardless of the fit.
- Effective negotiating/bargaining skills on the acquirer's part. For most acquisitions, a wide range of terms must be negotiated.
- Effective due diligence. The acquirer must have sound estimates of (at least) the acquired company's customer base, earning power, personnel, assets, and liabilities.
- Effective and efficient integration.

General managers should also be willing to engage in divestitures when they would create value. Earlier, in discussing strategy and strategic goals, we noted that the general manager should sell businesses when they no longer fit the firm's strategy, when they are worth more to someone else than to the current owner, and when the corporate management is not adding value. It is possible that a divested business, when emerging from under the umbrella of a larger corporate structure, becomes profitable for its new owners when it is free from the burden of corporate overhead, and when management understands clearly that what happens going forward is to their personal benefit or at their cost. Divested businesses may also provide substantial returns on investment when new owners use a sizable portion of debt to fund the acquisition. In these cases, the new owners' equity investment is relatively small related to the total capital invested and, as a result, the return on their investment may be rather large.

Summary

All of the attention given to strategy formulation and implementation in a business is wasted unless there is strong, focused execution. Many observers of business, including academics, financial analysts, and the media, realize that execution is far more than half of the task of the general management. As we described earlier, effective strategies may be derailed by poor execution and marginal strategies may sometimes succeed through superior execution. It is reasonable to assert that few great strategies succeed without strong execution. These perceived facts have led many companies, their boards of directors, and their chief executive officers (CEOs) to designate a very strong chief operating officer (COO) whose total focus is on executing the strategic plans. The COO is often provided with a companion title of president.

In Chapter 22, we move on to the related tasks of controlling and reporting, which play a role in assessing the effectiveness of the execution efforts of management.

DISCUSSION QUESTIONS

1. What is the relative importance of strategy formulation versus execution?
2. What are the roles of the functional strategies in execution?
3. What role do meetings play in successful execution?
4. Why is the execution of one-time projects closely identified with managing change?

PART

V

IN SUMMATION

We reach Part V of this book having covered the basics of general management, beginning in the three chapters of Part I with the economic and organizational contexts within which the general manager functions and a delineation of the general manager's roles and tasks. The six chapters in Part II describe the strategic management process, beginning with the factors that impel a general manager to engage in strategic management and ending with the three key planning documents—the strategic plan, the multiyear business plan, and the annual plan or budget. The seven chapters in Part III present a set of analytical concepts that should be useful to the general manager, both personally and to enhance his or her ability to deal with functional specialists. Part IV covers the important aspects of general managers taking action, including organizing and aligning, staffing, integrating, and executing. The four chapters in Part V remind us of the material covered earlier with an emphasis on controlling, learning, and innovation (continuous improvement), public relations and advocacy (the means to get the word out about the firm), and some final reflections on general management.

Chapter 22, "Controlling and Reporting," covers the activities defined as "knowing what is happening and being able to take effective action." The general manager needs status information to be collected and reported in a timely fashion and in appropriate detail. This effort begins with obtaining information as close to the events in time and place as possible; with the ultimate reporting systems operating in "real time," providing for the maximum control of events and enabling management to intervene as necessary. Most organizations do a reasonable job of measuring the historical financial results, but they do not do as well in reporting nonfinancial strategic and operating results. It is important to recognize that indicators of strategic performance are effective leading indicators of financial performance. Strong financial performance results from harvesting the positive results of prior strategic actions, while strong strategic performance may not yet have shown up in financial results.

Chapter 23, "Learning and Innovation," discusses the development of knowledge and experience that can lead to innovation through new and better ideas. The ability of an organization to learn and innovate may be its only sustainable competitive advantage. The organizations that will excel in the future will be those that create a commitment and capacity to learn at all levels of the organization and encourage innovative thinking and actions. Learning is the foundation of continuous improvement. Organizations that embrace learning, and the implementation of what they have learned, eventually set themselves apart from those that simply carry on as before.

Chapter 24, "Public Relations and Advocacy," discusses how the general manager must be an advocate for the interests of the organization, both within and outside the business. There is a wide range of constituencies whose support is essential to the organization's success. Public relations and advocacy are important aspects of the general manager's responsibilities, although they are generally given little emphasis in the curricula of most business schools. They deal with developing and maintaining effective relationships with key stakeholders and the external community. While public relations is primarily about building and maintaining a company's image, advocacy is about protecting and advancing the interests of the business with the rule makers and rule enforcers in governments and other relevant institutions.

Chapter 25, "Reflections on General Management," reviews some of the authors' final thoughts—some that have been mentioned before and some that are introduced here. They are the personal observations and conclusions of the authors and will hopefully provide a useful overview of the roles and tasks of the general manager.

22

CONTROLLING AND REPORTING

Controlling may be defined as guiding or managing an organization in response to understanding what is happening within the organization and in its environment. In smaller businesses, the general manager generally participates in or directly observes the activities of the organization. As businesses grow, however, general managers are led by circumstances to delegate, first to one subordinate management level, and eventually to personnel in a number of organizational levels.

Delegation brings its own set of managerial challenges. The general manager is often quite removed in time and space from delegated activities, so there is little opportunity for him or her to personally experience what has transpired. Delegation without control may become abdication of the general manager's responsibilities. As a result, when the general manager is removed from events, information about what actually happened must be collected and reported in a timely fashion and in appropriate detail.

The implementation of an effective system for controlling and reporting requires the development of a sound management model. Attributes of this model should address the following:

- The prerequisites for effective control
  - Knowledge of the business
  - Clarity of purpose
  - Getting the right people

- Aligning the interest of the people with the goals of the organization
- The prerequisites for effective reporting
  - Mutually-agreed-upon goals and standards
  - Knowledge of what is happening
  - Evaluating performance
  - Taking appropriate action

The Prerequisites for Effective Control

Effective control takes place in a broad context within a business and requires that certain conditions must be present. If management knows what it wants accomplished and the right people are in the right jobs, the required results should be forthcoming. If, on the other hand, management is not clear about what it wants done, or does not have the right people in place, the preferred results are not likely to be achieved.

Many organizations overcontrol. They place too much emphasis on the 'brakes" by which actions and programs are reined in. Effective organizations, though, learn to empower the right people, allowing them to direct parts of the organization and their rates of progress.

Knowledge of the Business

Knowledge of the business, including the markets, customers, competitors, technology, and the organization's strengths and weaknesses, enables a general manager to make effective decisions. Over time, knowledge of the business evolves into the development of the "intuitive feel" that is so important in making entrepreneurial judgments about what is possible.

The relationships that provide access to information about other people's experiences, what is going on in the industry, and elements shaping the future are important ingredients of industry expertise. For instance, the general manager who has a strong relationship with a customer can readily learn that customer's major problems or thoughts about the future. Industry suppliers who are creating the materials and equipment that the business purchases are also major sources of information. If a general manager has close relationships with suppliers, much can be learned about their current situations and their plans for the future. Interestingly, suppliers are often great sources of information about competitors, particularly a supplier's salesperson. An effective general manager uses such opportunities to learn as much as possible about his or her competitors and emerging trends.

These relationships are complemented by a number of activities that usually provide a great deal of additional information to those in the industry. The general manager should read all of the appropriate trade journals for his or her industry, and attend industry workshops and conventions. These activities should not be limited to the industry in which the firm competes, though, but should include the industries of the firm's important business customers and those of the firm's major suppliers.

The accumulation of experience may provide the best means to build knowledge of the business and industry. The general manager should learn, over time, which actions are effective and which are not, as well as whom he or she may or may not trust. The general manager should also understand the economics of the business and the firm's business model. Effective general managers will experiment, learning more about initiatives that might succeed from initiatives that failed.

In the end, management must have a deep knowledge of the competitive marketplace, and of the firm's customers and their needs and desires, as well as the skills and resources that are critical for success in fulfilling those needs and desires. The general manager must also understand the realities of the firm's strengths and weaknesses and how they relate to those critical skills and resources, as well as the firm's competitive position. This knowledge should contribute to sound judgments about what the firm is capable of undertaking successfully.

The resulting knowledge of the business will have been gained through personal relationships, constant studying and learning, and years of experience.

Have Clarity of Purpose

As noted, the management team should understand clearly the customer base the firm intends to serve, the needs and desires of the customers, and the ways in which the firm intends to fulfill those needs and desires. This information should form the foundation of the firm's mission statement. Companies that do not have clarity of purpose often struggle with a lack of understanding of their core customers and their needs.

Furthermore, the general manager should be clear about the direction in which he or she wants to take the business, which relates to the vision of the organization, or the broadest objective. Clarity about the firm's mission and vision not only focuses management on what the firm needs to do, but also sets the boundaries that assist in identifying what it should not do.

Get the Right People

As emphasized previously, general managers must create the ability within the organization to select the right people, put them into the right jobs, and then emphasize training and development. General managers should also be rigorous about removing the wrong people from the organization. Control issues are much simpler when competent and well-trained people are in place.

Aligning the Interests of the People with the Goals of the Organization

The right people are motivated to do the right things. This is partly a reflection of their character; they understand and are committed to fulfilling their responsibilities and duties. Being human, though, they also are strongly influenced by their personal self-interests.

The tangible alignment of employees' self-interests with those of owners appears in performance-based compensation and profit-sharing arrangements. This alignment should explicitly extend to address the organization's values, strategic initiatives, goals, and objectives. Culture also may contribute to focus on alignment; the general manager should recognize the value of a culture of pride in achievement and competence.

The Prerequisites for Effective Reporting

Mutually-Agreed-Upon Goals and Standards

An initial step in establishing firm control of any organization is articulating what it is that the firm is trying to accomplish—that is, what would characterize success. This effort encompasses identifying the ultimate goals of the organization as well as the critical success factors that influence their attainment. Performance indicators of the critical success factors must be identified and requisite metrics determined for each indicator. Goals or standards may then be established related to these metrics, and used as a basis for evaluating actual performance. Identifying the critical success factors and their performance indicators and metrics requires a deep knowledge of the way the business should operate, as illustrated in Vignette 22-1.

The importance of mutually-agreed-upon goals cannot be overstated. When goals are handed down from the top management, some resistance is almost a certainty among the people who are required to achieve them. Equally important, if the achievement of the goals is not supported by some plan, they are of little use. Two unproductive related dynamics may occur, with senior managers identifying goals that strongly challenge the lower-level managers, and the lower-level managers, if asked for their perception of realistic goals, suggesting easily attainable targets. In short, performance goals can be set unrealistically high or low, depending on who sets them. The most effective goals involve some element of "stretch," but definitely are perceived by all to be "achievable." Often, management will establish two sets of goals, segregating and labeling stretch goals. A key element of the goals is that they be mutually agreed to, so that those who must attain them see them as their own goals and are committed to their achievement.

VIGNETTE 22-1

Wal-Mart has executed its low-price strategy extremely well. One of the company's key success factors has been the use of technology to control its investment in inventory. A key performance indicator for any retailer is inventory turns, a metric typically representing the value of inventory units on hand divided into the value of units sold annually. The goal is to have a very high inventory turn rate.

Other performance indicators include the number and estimated volume of stock outs that result in lost sales. A useful metric might be the number of stock outs in a month, by region or store.

Communication and collaboration within management are necessary to establish a requirement for improvement, focus on the challenges to attaining improvement, and lead to plans to overcome the challenges.

Organizations frequently employ the following four types of goals:

- Financial goals
- Operating goals
- Strategic goals
- Change goals

FINANCIAL GOALS Managers have the most experience with financial goals, in part because of the imperative for a business to earn a profit. Financial goals are normally quantitative, straightforward to set, and rooted in the financial statements—the income statement, the balance sheet, and the statement of cash flow. They usually reflect the desire for improvement or positive change, including such goals as those to increase revenues, reduce expenses, and reduce investments in assets (for example, accounts receivable or inventories). The most important financial goal is often recognized as the profit goal. Other important goals may relate to achieving targeted levels of cash flow and growth in revenues.

Another way of approaching financial goals is through ratios—the relationship between two elements of the statements. For the income statement, a common approach is margin analysis, which computes expenses and profit as a percent of sales. On the balance sheet, the ratios relate to the efficiency in utilization of assets, or asset turnover ratios such as sales/net assets. The balance sheet also is the source of ratios that describe the capital structure (the relationship of debt to equity or total capital) and liquidity.

It is very important that the financial statements be disaggregated into the subsets that drive profitability, as described earlier within the annual plan. For instance, management will want to disaggregate the business into its strategic business units (divisions or profit centers). They will want to understand volume and profitability by key marketing segments—customers (or customer groups), products, geography, and so forth. Effectively breaking the business down into its basic elements is a key to understanding the prevailing economic models of the business units and setting realistic and effective financial goals.

OPERATING GOALS Operating goals relate to operational activities and include measuring the effectiveness of sales activities, the degree of competitiveness, the level of customer service, operating efficiency, product or service quality, delivery reliability, employee satisfaction, safety, and more.

Operating goals should be both quantitative and qualitative. Those that lend themselves to quantitative indicators are generally fairly straightforward. The specification of qualitative goals, on the other hand, provides a challenge for management. How does management deal with something that is known to be important, but is not readily measurable? Effective measures may usually be found (eventually). This process requires some ingenuity, and a deep understanding of the activity.

Customer satisfaction, for instance, is an important qualitative issue. This can be measured by well-designed interviews and surveys. Repeating patterns of regular business statistics provide additional indicators. In one business, the customer service representatives who were closest to the account were asked monthly to assign their customers into one of four categories: very satisfied, satisfied, having concerns, and dissatisfied. The results were accumulated by customer service representatives and totaled. For those customers thought to be having concerns or who were assumed to be dissatisfied, actions were developed to correct the perceived problems. The accuracy of the measurement system was validated in part by reviewing the ratings for all customers who did not renew their contracts. The salesperson on the account followed up after every contact and produced an estimated rating, not knowing the rating prepared by the customer service representative. These ratings were compared and any disagreements were explored further.

STRATEGIC GOALS These are higher-order goals that drive operating decisions. For instance, a goal to increase market share could result in increased market coverage by adding salespeople or increasing advertising expenditures. Such a goal might also require expanded plant locations or capacity, or trigger an acquisition.

CHANGE GOALS Many goals imply some sort of change in behavior by various people. Change goals deal more specifically with the projects that are being undertaken to enhance the likelihood of the change occurring within the organization. Change goals are frequently expressed in terms of time and budget, although they may have some qualitative measures, as well. For instance, a desired change might be that a building attains increased aesthetic attributes. This stated (not well-defined) qualitative goal may be simply expressed as being brought about within a specified time period at an expenditure of no more than a specified amount of money.

Change goals may emanate from a general question regarding the changes needed to successfully achieve the strategic goals. For instance: What kinds of employee knowledge and skills, and what kind of systems does management need, to operate the firm's internal business processes to produce the results the customers would like, and to achieve the financial outcomes the owners would like?

Such questioning should have been addressed through the strategic planning process. Either within or outside the strategic planning process, a starting point may encompass development of several broad themes of change that are needed to drive the firm's strategy. An example of a theme might be the desire to gain market share. A theme may then lead management to adopt a number of approaches. Each approach requires one or more initiatives, each of which has one or more indicators of success. Measurement metrics need to be developed for each indicator, and then targets or standards.

An example from a manufacturing business is as follows:

> The Theme: Increase productivity
> Approaches:
> a.   Increase output per worker hour
> b.   Reduce waste

The table in Exhibit 22-1 demonstrates a systematic methodology for the approach of increasing output per worker hour. The intended likely effects on perspectives (financial results, customers, internal business processes, and learning/growth) are arrayed along with initiatives, the indicators of success, and the measurement metrics.

The process of specifying the initiatives required to execute a strategy or carry out an approach to change substantially improves management's knowledge of the business and the actions that need to be taken. Being

EXHIBIT 22-1 Approaches to Increase Output per Worker Hour

	Perspective			
	Financial	*Customer*	*Operational*	*Workforce*
Initiative	Reduce cost	Improve reliability	Improve machine maintenance	Train employees
Indicator	Variable costs	Delivery commitments met	Machine availability	Output rate and quality
Metric	Cost per unit	Percent of on-time deliveries; Overdue orders in days' production time	Percent of time machinery is operational	Percent of quality rejects; Output per worker hour

clear about the indicators and their related metrics permits management to set targets, and to measure the success of the initiatives. One key to success in goal setting is to concentrate at any one time on only a few themes, and a few strategies within the themes. The management may then learn to identify those indicators that are really important to the success of the strategy, and determine how to measure them.

Knowledge of What Is Happening

Every employee, from executive to entry-level hourly worker, must understand his or her responsibilities, along with the goals and standards that apply to the corresponding work. Employees must also know what performance level is being attained, and compare it to the goal or standard. When unacceptable or substantial deviation is found, employees should identify the underlying or assignable cause, if possible, and attempt to fix it. This approach is the essence of all efforts aimed at continuous improvement. If the advantageous deviations can be sustained, the goal or standard will eventually be raised.

DATA COLLECTION Knowing what is happening within the organization begins with data collection. The basic building blocks in a management information system are the transactions that are occurring constantly, everywhere the business is operating. The information about these transactions—for example, a retail sale, the speed of a machine, or a sales inquiry—should be made available immediately to those who are responsible for the transaction so that they may evaluate it and take appropriate action. The summarized results should be available to higher levels of management in an organized process. The process of collecting and acting upon data is illustrated in Vignette 22-2.

Data collection emanates from both formal and informal systems. Identifying the information that should be collected, the people for whom it is to be collected, and when it is needed are the key aspects of designing a management information system.

The formal systems capture relevant information about each business transaction and then transmit it to the people who need it, in the form in which they need it, in a timely way. One of the benefits of designing effective data collection and management information systems is that the design process forces management to understand how the business functions and the installed system will tend to enforce conformity to the practices they desire. Another approach to formal reporting is for the senior managers to meet with their subordinates, who explain what has been happening and what is likely to happen. Such meetings often are settings for the discussion of performance (results) versus goals.

Informal systems are often as important as formal systems. Informal systems reflect the style of the manager. The phrase, "management by walking around," is used to describe efforts by a manager to directly observe what is going on. The manager spends a substantial amount of time

---

VIGNETTE 22-2

Many major retailers have installed very sophisticated data collection systems at their cash registers. The data collected are transmitted through equally sophisticated communications systems to a centralized computer system that manages inventory purchases and restocking, and provides data that support pricing decisions. This data collection process is at the core of creating higher profits and lower costs by increasing inventory turns.

Federal Express and UPS, for instance, utilize package-tracking systems that record pickups and deliveries in real time as reported by the drivers. This enables these companies to know where a package is at any time, as well as lets them know what loads are developing for the day's work. These data collection systems are at the center of the business strategies of these firms.

talking to employees at all levels, customers, suppliers, and competitors, and simply observing what is happening. Information obtained from a variety of sources allows the manager to judge whether the sources are presenting a consistent picture. By interacting with personnel at all levels of the organization, the leader bypasses the chain of command that might otherwise filter the information he or she receives.

Generally speaking, the closer the receipt of information is to the time of an event, the more value it has to the recipient. Recent advances have created the ability for management to have effective, real-time reporting of information. This information may come through formal reporting channels, such as reports generated by automated systems, or informal channels, such as e-mail and Web postings.

Within the organization, the information system accumulates and summarizes data and sends it along up the chain of command, permitting senior managers to hold subordinates accountable for results. Maintaining the data over time also permits the identification of trends, which typically are important in making decisions about the future.

Evaluating Performance

After the data have been received by the appropriate managers, the actual performance must be compared to the plans, goals, and/or standards. This exercise reveals both desirable and undesirable deviations from management expectations. It is important for managers to recognize that the actual performance is not an accident, instead that it is driven by some underlying cause. Digging to find that cause is an important element of management control because a problem usually may not be addressed fully until it is understood. These control efforts should result, over time, in continuous learning and improvement throughout the organization.

Taking Appropriate Action

After due consideration, the manager must decide what action, if any, needs to be taken. In well-run, successful companies, most problems or opportunities require nothing more than a quick fix or a modest adjustment in how things are done. The general manager should determine, first, if the responsible manager recognizes and understands the problem, and is willing to address it. Managers who are having performance problems will occasionally become very defensive or rationalize the situation to avoid blame. They may, in fact, be in some sort of denial—if the problem is not understood, it is highly unlikely that it can be corrected.

If the problem is recognized and understood, the general manager should then determine if the manager who is accountable has a plan for dealing with it. If there is a plan, it can be evaluated; if there is no plan, one obviously must be developed. If the manager puts forth a plan, the general manager must make a judgment as to whether the manager who is accountable is capable of executing the plan successfully. If the answer to any of these questions is negative, there must be a strong intervention. If the manager is otherwise effective, the general manager can provide for some form of assistance—either an inside or outside consultant. It may be necessary, though, to deal more aggressively with the situation, using methods that may include advice, training, a direct order, demotion, transfer, or termination.

Unfortunately, many companies wait too long to confront performance issues. In these cases, a problem might fester and cause an operation or even the company to go into a downward spiral. One of the major characteristics of successful general managers is that they know when and how to deal with their nonperformers.

In an environment in which managers are asked to be innovative and to take risks by trying new ideas, an overly harsh reaction to failures may work against the very innovation and risk taking that the company needs and wants. In the world of research and development (R&D), experimentation is essential and failures are expected. They are seen in those environments as learning events that may (but not always) lead to a successful answer. Businesses need to think about innovation in a similar way.

As described above, the options of the general manager to intervene are limited by the resources and skills he or she can bring to bear on the situation. It is both difficult and easy to remove a subordinate, but the general manager must think ahead to the next step and assess whether he or she can, in fact, improve the situation with a replacement.

Many chief executive officers (CEOs) find it necessary to have strong corporate staffs so as to have the ability to know what is going on and when to intervene. The problem is that the stronger the parent company's staff, the more centralized decision making becomes, and, hence, the more bureaucratic the organization becomes. Students of management recognize the dangers of strong central staffs, even though such personnel may provide the CEO with a seductive sense of control and security.

Summary

Delegation without effective control systems results in abdication. A reporting system that informs management in a timely way about what is going on as compared to goals and standards is an essential element of an effective management control system. The information that is generated from a control system is an important ingredient in the strategic management process laid out in Chapter 5, as well as the learning process, described in Chapter 23.

DISCUSSION QUESTIONS

1. Why are controls and reporting so important?
2. What are the four types of goals?
3. What are the prerequisites for an effective control system?
4. What are the prerequisites for an effective reporting system?
5. How might the general manager know when to intervene?

23

LEARNING AND INNOVATION

Learning is one of the most important skills of a general manager and his or her collective organization. The pace of change through the first half of the twentieth century was quite slow when compared to today. For generations, craftsmen could learn their trades at a young age and pursue them for a lifetime. Improvements were primarily in tools and machines that did not obsolete the craft skills. An example was the Linotype machine used to set type for printing, which was a mechanical marvel when it was invented in 1885. With minor, evolutionary improvements, the machine was used as the primary device for setting type until the 1950s.

In the past, businesses could similarly develop a product or a process, perfect it, and expect it to have a relatively long competitive life. With stable products and processes, managers could train their workers to do the same things repetitively, which established and maintained high levels of productivity. There was little need for additional learning after a worker was trained or a process perfected. The goal was to make all work repetitive in order to gain maximum efficiency.

The technology revolution that had its origins in discoveries of the 1930s to the 1950s has changed the situation. Product and process lives are now much shorter, and workers now must commit to lifelong learning to remain productive. Businesses similarly have to deal with the continuous introduction of new processes or process improvements and learn how to become proficient in their utilization.

The importance of continuous learning in a changing world cannot be overstated. All living beings and organizations have to learn to adapt to changing environments or perish. An organization may be viewed in a similar light. When the pace of change outside an organization is greater than within, problems are in the offing. The situation demands continuous learning. The continuous learning process experienced by a business school professor is described in Vignette 23-1. It is not dissimilar from those of most managers and most organizations.

VIGNETTE 23-1

A professor joined the faculty of a graduate business school after completing a doctorate in quantitative analysis (QA, or operations research/management science). At the time of joining the business school faculty, he had accumulated seven years of experience as an analyst and manager in a high-technology firm and seven years of teaching experience on a part-time basis at three universities. Within a year of joining the faculty, he was asked to teach the required course in production and operations management to fill a need of the school. He was comfortable in this assignment since much of his practical business experience had been focused on the application of quantitative techniques to inventory and scheduling problems in large-scale manufacturing facilities.

As he settled into the teaching routine, he was also being engaged regularly as a consultant to work on operational problems and systems for manufacturing managers in a variety of industries. The style of the academic was built on the premise that his assignment was to change behavior, not to give advice. He therefore developed strong working relationships with the functional managers, built on mutual trust. As this work made a contribution to the success of the clients, many of the manufacturing managers were promoted to general manager or chief executive officer (CEO) positions within their companies. Because they were comfortable with the working style of the academic, they invited him to assist them in developing solutions to the problems and opportunities they faced in their new responsibilities as general managers.

The academic was subsequently invited by a number of companies to join their boards of directors. Some were consulting clients and some were companies in which he was an investor. He held fifteen directorships over his career. He thus has had a continuous, uplifting learning experience as he moved from a focus as a functional specialist to consider broader issues from the perspective of a general manager (responsibility for profit and loss and the management of the interfaces among the functional departments—marketing, manufacturing, engineering,

(continued)

VIGNETTE 23-1 (*continued*)

and finance). Finally, he learned about the perspective of a board member and chairman (representing the owners of the business).

His career thus paralleled that of many of his graduated students, who began their careers as analysts, progressed to become first-line supervisors, moved on to manage one or perhaps two functional departments, managed a profit center (division), became CEOs, and often became directors or chairs of their boards of directors.

Engaged individuals never reach the end of their learning odysseys.

Learning begins with the critical and creative thinking that produces and/or internalizes new ideas. The ability of an organization to learn and innovate may be the foundation for its only sustainable competitive advantage. The organizations that will excel in the future are those that discover how to tap the commitment and capacity of employees at all levels to learn and encourage innovative thinking and actions.

Management literature has recognized the importance of learning to the success of an organization, and has adopted the phrase *the learning organization*. David Garvin of the Harvard Business School has described the learning organization as one "skilled at creating, acquiring and transferring knowledge, and at modifying its behavior to reflect new knowledge and insights."[1] The challenge for the general manager is to understand the importance of learning, and then to make it a priority in the organization. This, like many tasks, is easier said than done; an organization must "learn how to learn."

How Individuals and Organizations Learn

There are essentially two ways in which individuals learn—via formal education and via experience. Formal education may be defined as learning from others through course work, reading, and research. This is essentially transferring current knowledge to a new recipient. One of the reasons that some organizations advance so much farther and faster than others is that they build upon the experience of the organization. Each succeeding generation does not have to rediscover what the previous ones have learned. In fact, the experience base enhances the learning of the next team or generation.

In 1990, Cohen and Levinthal coined the term *absorptive capacity* (mentioned briefly in Chapter 17).[2] This term represents the capability of individuals or firms to recognize the value of new ideas or information from external sources and then to assimilate the new ideas into their own thinking and situation. Management's skill at accomplishing these results determines the firm's absorptive capacity. The concept is that individuals and organizations with high absorptive capacity are more effective than others at creating positive change.

An organization should also want to create new knowledge. It commonly does this through experiential learning (learning and developing from experience), which uses existing knowledge as a foundation. New ideas are developed from experiential learning and related innovative thinking. Continuous improvement and breakthroughs are mechanisms that spur the creation of new knowledge within the organization.

The General Manager as Learning Advocate

The people who tend to learn the most are those who have a thirst for knowledge fueled by intellectual curiosity. They want to learn from others in formal and informal settings. Beyond being conventionally studious, however, they experiment in a systematic way to observe the effectiveness of various actions. With this mind-set, failures become learning experiences that lead to enhanced understanding.

Consider the important issue of what general managers should know personally, given that no individual can know everything required to execute broad responsibilities for a large organization. General managers must rely on the knowledge and skills of specialists in numerous specific areas and therefore should know how to evaluate the specialists' expert advice. The general manager should also develop expertise in the following seven broad areas:

- *Self-knowledge or personal mastery:* His or her values and strengths and weaknesses.
- *Management principles and tools:* The broad range of principles and tools taught in business schools.
- *Administrative principles and tools:* How to analyze situations and

make decisions, taught in many business schools through the use of case studies.

- *Laws and regulations:* What he or she *must* do and the limits on what can and cannot be done.
- *Industry expertise:* How the relevant principles and tools are applied in his or her specific industry, along with an understanding of how the industry functions and the relationships that are critical for success. These insights are gained through study and experience in the industry.
- *Technology:* All general managers should understand information technology and its application to their businesses. They also should understand the technology imbedded in their processes and products or services.
- *Interpersonal skills:* This is a broad topic that encompasses the ability to create and maintain relationships, communicate effectively, and influence others (individually and in groups, and internally as well as externally). It extends to being a good judge of people.

The relative importance of these areas will vary with the nature of the business and its competitive environment. Where the general manager is weak, he or she should have advisors or subordinates with complementary strengths.

The creation of an innovative learning organization requires leadership. Employees in all organizations are interested in what their leader promotes and the behavior the leader demonstrates. The leader should build a culture supportive of learning and innovation at every level of the organization, which usually requires the creation of a particular mind-set within an organization. The traditional management mind-set has been focused on efficiency, cost control, and minimizing risks, a rather focused approach of staying close to what the organization knows how to do. Its goals have encompassed meeting current customer needs by means of an emphasis on developing plans, setting goals, and holding people accountable for meeting them. Process and structure have been very important.

The managers of learning organizations do not abandon these disciplines, but extend them. As they consider their current operations, they seek more creative ways to operate by exploring what they do not know, which obviously requires taking risks. They attempt to anticipate future customer needs and the likely impact of the driving forces of change. They closely observe emerging trends, and remain flexible because they expect and embrace change. They encourage people to think creatively and to take risks with less emphasis on process and more on unstructured interactions.

Learning Is Difficult

Learning is a challenge for general managers when the material is complicated and experience with it or an aptitude for it is lacking. Organizational learning involves discovering something new and implementing the related changes. A natural resistance to change, though, is embedded in the persona of most people and organizations, based on comfort with the known, a perceived interest in maintaining the status quo, and/or a strong fear of uncertainty.

If a crisis must be confronted or a compelling vision embraced, there may be an effective impetus for many to learn and change, sometimes referred to as a "burning platform." It is more difficult to overcome the resistance, however, when the perceived need is less crucial. Effective learning and the implementation of the related changes should be built on a culture of continuous improvement that encourages innovation and risk taking. While the values of the organization should not change, management should always be willing to change processes for the better.

Experiential learning is essentially acquired by trial and error, and many organizations will not tolerate the inherent errors. The process of learning and change is straightforward when an experiment takes little time, has a clear outcome, and can be repeated at a known cost. Experimentation in a business environment may take a long time, have less-clear outcomes, be repeated only at great cost, and prove extremely difficult. The demands of meeting today's obligations leave little room for thinking and experimenting; management must consciously make the future a priority alongside if not over the present.

In every organization, the culture is the legacy of past practices. Nearly all successful organizations have spent years building competencies that have proven themselves over time. There is a tendency to stay with those things that have succeeded in the past. We are all familiar with the not-invented-here syndrome and have all heard the objection, "That's not the way we do it here," when considering something new and different. It is very difficult to change staff, organizational structures, systems, and cultures; yet learning and change often require such actions, which are costly in effort, time, and money, particularly given the need to align them all.

Learning and Planning

Learning in a business is closely related to planning. The process encompasses an assessment of the current situation compared to what management would ultimately like—the vision. As noted previously, the challenge for management is to determine what must be done to move from the present state to the preferred future. An important balance must be struck. Bold, competitive, and demanding leadership may encourage overly aggressive goals that encourage excessive risk taking. The firm, in effect, overreaches, with aspirations that exceed its competencies. On the other hand, reasonable, diligent, and conservative leadership may be too risk averse, rewarding steady-as-you-go behavior and penalizing the risk taking that provides informative learning experiences.

The Skills and Tools Required for Learning

Systematic Problem Solving

The skills required for learning emanate from the decision-making processes that embrace systematic problem solving. One goal of a learning organization is to build a detailed knowledge of the current business, including an internal perspective of how the firm functions and an external perspective of the dynamics of the market. While management confronts the realities of the present situation effectively, it must consider the future by attempting to identify the driving forces of change, understand trends, and project their likely future impact on the business.

A rational learning process begins with the collection of data. Facts and observations are accumulated and analyzed, their meanings are evaluated, and then estimates are made of what might happen in the future. A parallel intuitive process similarly collects softer data that provide an additional "feel" for the situation—data that cannot be proven as factual. These intuitive data contain many uncertainties and ambiguities. Most decisions made by the experienced general manager reflect a combination of outputs of these two processes—the rational and the uncertain/ambiguous.

Experimentation with New Approaches

One key to experiential learning is a predilection for asking the question, "How might we do this better?" The general manager of a business that is committed to learning will want to ask further, "How can this be done differently?" These questions refer to current practices. The important question is, "What can we do that has not yet been done?" The greatest breakthroughs in business require experimentation—learning what works and what does not work, and understanding why. The more innovative the thinking, the more unique the solutions are likely to be.

Effective learning organizations embody cultures of continuous learning and improvement within which people at every level are experimenting with new ideas. They learn to become more efficient, to improve quality, and to create more innovative product or service features. In addition to learning from their own experiences, they seek to learn from others by identifying and internalizing best practices wherever they may be found. After a breakthrough occurs, the essentials are taught to others in the organization. This activity may be as simple as one worker showing another an improved technique, or it may be the genesis of a new training workshop to which many are exposed.

The Learning Methodologies

Experiential learning is much more effective when it is supported by a systematic methodology. Consider the following three types of learning situations:

- Learning before doing (planning)
- Learning while doing (execution)
- Learning after doing (evaluation)

These learning situations were described by David A. Garvin of the Harvard Business School.[3]

Learning before Doing (Planning)

Learning before doing may be thought of as a series of planning stages, as in building a house or developing a software program. Building a house begins with a conceptual stage in which the kind of house desired is determined. Details require clarity about the size, the style, and the key characteristics of the house. These variables define the dilemma. As a start, the architect develops a feasible design, illustrated by floor plans showing the number of rooms and their relationships to each other. Views of the outside elevations are drawn that show the way the house will sit on the land. This process goes through numerous iterations until all parties are satisfied with the product. We do not deal with the details at this stage, but clearly describe the desired concept. The feasibility of the design should be tested, assessing, for example, whether it will fit on the site and whether its costs are within the budget.

After the concept has been settled upon and its feasibility determined, the process moves to the next stage—the schematic design. More precise specifications are developed in this stage. For example, the dimensions of the house, the materials to be used, and the mechanical, plumbing, and electrical systems are settled. Windows, doors, and electrical outlets are placed. Architectural details are developed for both inside and outside parameters. This step in the process adds broad specifications to the conceptual design. The last design stage is the preparation of working drawings. These are the detailed specifications from which the building can be built. They are usually sent out to builders to obtain bids, and are then used by the builders to create the building.

Developing a computer program moves through similar stages. The concept stage settles what the program is intended to do, and is followed by the development of a schematic design using flowcharts. The working drawings go into more detail about the amount and structure of the data to be input, processed, and output. The software program may then be written and installed for use.

The logic of building a structure or writing a program applies to projects in a business environment. If the project involves a new innovation or something the business has not done before, it is important to recognize the process as a learning opportunity. The learning should have as an early or initial step research into how others have dealt with similar situations. The process involves identifying alternatives, experimenting with their implementation, and evaluating the results. Successful, innovative actions will set the firm apart. The more unique the innovation, the more distinctive a successful solution will be; it may also entail the greatest risk because it is new and untried.

Learning while Doing (Execution)

Learning readily takes place when an individual is experimenting with better ways to do his or her job. Encouragement for this kind of behavior comes from individual training and a supportive culture. Every employee should be thinking continually about ways to do his or her job better. Because teams are the basic building blocks of organizations, they too must be monitoring performance and seeking ways to improve. This requires a perpetual dissatisfaction with the status quo.

Many problems cannot be solved by an individual, or even a work team, because they involve other parts of the organization. How these problems are best solved is an important fundamental question. One approach is to focus the efforts of a team of five to ten employees on a real business problem or opportunity. The team is generally cross-functional, has the requisite skills and experience, and represents all segments of the organization that are impacted by the problem or opportunity. This type of work has been called action-learning projects.

Top management sponsorship provides the support, resources, direction, and motivation to succeed in such endeavors. The people on the team thus know that what they are doing will not be stymied by bureaucratic red tape. The team organizes a process (work plan) that reflects the nature and complexity of the problem. Most process designs begin with defining the problem or opportunity. The team then assesses the current situation to understand any prevailing barriers to improvement or a solution. At this point, the team develops alternative solutions and examines the pros and cons of each. They select the solution to be recommended to members of management, who respond with a definitive yes or no answer, usually at the end of the presentation.

Learning after Doing (Evaluation)

After a task, a presentation, or a project has been completed, a post audit or autopsy should be conducted, not to place blame but to determine what can be learned. Management should understand what was done well in order to continue it in the future. It is also imperative to understand what was not done so well, in the interest of continuous improvement. The U.S. Army has developed a process called "After Action Reviews." The leaders involved in an exercise are required to debrief the participants immediately to determine what can be learned. The findings are recorded for later study and analysis to identify trends and to enable sharing with other organizations.

Many businesses have developed similar procedures, but perhaps with less discipline. In the press of daily priorities, just getting the job done ranks highest for employees, and pressure mounts to move to the next job. Finding the time to think about and record what went on previously can be a challenge, but learning organizations find ways to complete the autopsies in a timely manner. Autopsies are most effective when the actual participants in the project complete the review.

At this point, learning ties once again to planning. If the project team identified activities that were critical for success, indicators of performance designated for those activities, metrics identified for those indicators, and goals or standards related to the metrics, effective benchmarks should be in place. Management then should collect the performance data and compare the results to the goals or standards. Where the results fail to meet the goal or standard, there may be a problem with poor performance or an inaccurate standard. In either case, management may come to understand the deviation and deal with the problem. Likewise, if the goal or standard is being exceeded, management would want to know why. This kind of planning and data management enables continuous learning and improvement.

This methodology may be used to measure the effectiveness of strategy formulation and implementation as well as operational performance. Strategy may go awry because it is flawed or because it is good but poorly executed. Management may assess the effectiveness of the strategy by reviewing the assumptions on which the strategy was built. Were the assumptions accurate? Did unforeseen changes occur in the environment? For instance, did the needs of customers change, or did the competitive situation change? If the strategy still appears valid, then its execution should be examined. What did not go as planned can be identified—was there a volume problem (not enough demand was generated); a capacity problem (what was sold could not be produced); or were problems encountered with quality, efficiency, or costs? What were the underlying causes? With this information, management can begin to develop solutions and learn from the process.

Why Smart Executives Fail to Learn

Often, it is difficult to explain why very smart people who have been successful fail to learn. Sometimes the answer is that the manager has moved beyond his or her experience and intellectual capacity. A good general manager is constantly aware of his or her limits. When the business is moving into new areas where experience is lacking, management should recognize the need for and seek the requisite expertise. Managers in this situation might learn eventually, but perhaps not fast enough to handle the existing situation, or the subject may be too technical or specialized, and they choose to rely on others. This approach is often an efficient use of management time.

Arrogance or hubris may also be in play. Some successful people often believe that they already know much more than they really do. In these cases, there is a tendency for such a manager to blame others for problems, and to deny personal responsibility. The manager may have very deep-seated beliefs, and he or she may assume that a world not conforming to those beliefs is wrong.

One attribute of great general managers is a paradoxical combination of self-confidence and intellectual humility. These managers are willing to make tough decisions, and at the same time, they are very introspective. They are quite aware of what they do not know, and are constantly trying to learn more in order to improve their performance. This attitude opens the door to lifelong learning.

Summary

There is an increasing need for lifelong learning in business as the pace of change has quickened in recent years. All employees—especially managers and aspiring managers—must commit to a lifetime of continuous rejuvenation. Similarly, organizations must be open to self-examination and learning. There are certain fundamentals related to every business and its competitive environment that the general manager must master. Systems thinking should shape the general manager's approach to the challenges of the moment because the independent, ad hoc actions of individuals are steadily being replaced by effective systems that guarantee the repeatability of successful actions. These systems require effective planning, execution, and examination within the learning organization. Finally, companies must ensure that their most talented managers continue to learn; to relax in place will not suffice for the business environment of the future.

DISCUSSION QUESTIONS

1. Why is continuous learning so important to the general manager?
2. What attributes characterize a learning organization?
3. Why is systems thinking important?
4. Explain the meaning of the terms, learning before doing, learning while doing, and learning after doing. Is one more important than the others?
5. When you are a general manager, how will you ensure that your organization learns continuously?

24

PUBLIC RELATIONS AND ADVOCACY

Public relations and advocacy are important aspects of the general manager's responsibilities, although they are generally given little emphasis in the curricula of most business schools. They are similar functions in that they both deal with relationships with key stakeholders and the external community. While public relations is primarily about building and maintaining the corporate image, advocacy is about protecting and advancing the interests of the business with the rule makers and rule enforcers at all levels of government and in other relevant institutions. For certain CEOs whose organizations have operations in countries around the globe, advocacy may even encompass elements of diplomacy.

The chief executive officer (CEO) is the custodian of the corporate image. As such, he or she is the chief spokesperson, and often the public symbol of the company. These roles include, but go beyond, public relations to being the chief advocate and spokesperson along with his or her other duties. These roles may be more important in large, publicly held corporations that have high visibility in an industry, the economy, and politics. But they are also present in smaller public corporations and, to a lesser degree, in privately owned businesses.

Some businesses opt for a celebrity leader—a person with public name recognition and relationships with those whom the business wants to influence. Most businesses, however, select their CEOs based on general management competencies, not on the basis of celebrity status.

Credibility and Integrity

The CEO must have credibility to be effective in these public roles. The CEO gains credibility through the demonstration of two attributes in particular—competence and integrity. An advocate needs to be seen as knowledgeable about what he or she is talking about as well as honest and trustworthy. He or she must be able to communicate the intended message well. Competence is demonstrated by a record of achievement, which speaks for itself. There is a temptation for CEOs to use clever public relations efforts to cover weak records. This is where the integrity that builds trust is important. If CEOs tell the truth, they build trust over time. If they misrepresent the situation or their prospects, they rapidly destroy trust. Vignette 24-1 describes the importance of honesty and integrity.

The television sound bite, interviews, and speeches as well as more informal conversations and situations all come into play in creating the pub-

VIGNETTE 24-1

It is well understood that managing a business in a free-enterprise, competitive environment is fraught with risks. A general manager and his or her business have to contend with challenges from competitors, fluctuations in the value of currencies, conflicts with labor unions, unpredictable interest rates, and general economic conditions, among other perturbations. It is not surprising that a large percentage of new businesses do not survive their first two years. It is axiomatic that CEOs and their businesses can fail "honorably" or "dishonorably."

With wide understanding of the pitfalls attendant to running a business, there is a natural sympathy for the manager who, in spite of his or her best efforts, sees the business fail. The interested parties—suppliers, employees, customers, and investors—will be sympathetic as long as the general manager has failed "honorably," taking every precaution to protect the best interests of everyone involved. That general manager may gain a second chance to start or run another business, even from those adversely affected by the situation. The manager who fails "dishonorably," however, will have great difficulty ever securing a second chance. Not telling the truth to the various constituencies, attempts at fraud, dealing unfairly with employees, or visible troubles with legal or regulatory bodies will leave the tainted party with "no way back."

In short, failing "honorably" could happen to any of us. Failing "dishonorably" leaves a manager with little room for future maneuvering.

lic's impression of a general manager and his or her company. The public role of the leader of a business varies with the situation. In the normal course of business, an effective CEO helps maintain positive relationships with all of the company's constituents. The CEO's reputation can become critical when there are major events of public interest or in dealing with a crisis of some type.

Managing a public image is not an easy task, and it can raise many complex questions about which the leader must give careful thought. Think of the public perceptions of Microsoft and Wal-Mart, two of the most successful businesses of the past decade. Both have had issues with their public image, due in part to their success, but also resulting from substantive policies that they have followed. For instance, Wal-Mart has been criticized for its pay scales, offshore sourcing, and aggressive domestic purchasing practices. Its stores are also not welcome in many communities because of their impact on local merchants. Are these just public-image problems, or are they substantive issues with which the firm could and should have dealt more effectively? Microsoft has succeeded in a very competitive industry by creating product standards and effectiveness that in many cases have given it almost monopolistic power. Could it have been equally successful without being such a tough competitor?

In short, is the questioned image of these two companies the price they have had to pay for success? Many people resent winners (sometimes called the curse of the front-runner) and government regulators routinely equate size and market share to monopolistic control. Could they have done the same things but been more adept at managing their images? Or, should they have changed their strategies to achieve a more positive image, even if it meant more modest success? Is it possible there might have been even more long-term success with somewhat modified strategies?

These are the kinds of questions regarding public perceptions that, in the end, the CEO must resolve. There are no perfect answers, since almost every situation involves trade-offs. The CEO has the ultimate responsibility for the course the company chooses. In terms of crisis management, the standard of excellence is the way that Johnson & Johnson managed its Tylenol scare. A few bottles of the medicine were tampered with in a major city, causing several deaths, which received wide publicity because of the broad use of the medicine across the country. Johnson & Johnson immediately withdrew all of the product from store shelves at great expense, while it sought to understand the nature and extent of the problem. It actually used the problem to improve its public image—a short-term cost with great long-term benefits.

A complex public relations battle has been fought for years in the tobacco industry. The scientific evidence has been strong that smoking creates health problems. For many years, the courts held that since smokers knew this when they chose to smoke, based on the doctrine of contributory negligence, the cigarette companies were not held liable. But the opponents waged a persistent long-term public relations and legal battle that the tobacco companies ultimately lost. The low point of this battle may well have been the moment that the CEOs of tobacco companies sat before a congressional committee and jointly swore that they did not think smoking was a health hazard. What could the tobacco companies have done differently in a really difficult situation?

While these stories provide examples of public-image issues, they serve to make the point that this is an area in which the CEO must exert leadership, and that the stakes are often very high.

Fundamental Principles

There are two fundamental principles in public relations and advocacy. The first is that "it is in understanding that we are understood." The general manager must understand his or her audiences and adversaries if messages intended to influence their thinking and behavior are to be successfully crafted. This often runs contrary to our nature. It is somewhat natural to be so caught up in our own point of view that we present it with passion and, in the process, turn off the people we would like to influence.

The second principle is that there must be a well-thought-out proactive program. Such a program would aim to identify those the general manager wants to or needs to influence, to understand their views and interests, and then to build the communications and relationships that are most apt to win them over. It cannot be done with ad hoc, impulsive reactions to events, after the fact.

Public Relations Tools

Relationships

Whom we know matters. If a CEO wants to be able to influence others, he or she must have credibility, which encompasses having positive relationships with credible people. This does not mean that the relationships must be warm and personal, although that can help. Personal relationships might, in fact, backfire if there are appearances of cronyism or buying influence.

Strong professional relationships that are marked by respect and trust open the door to candor. Such relationships are especially important when natural conflicts of interest arise. Resolving them usually involves compromises that are hammered out in negotiations. This is not to suggest that a strong bargaining position is not important, because it is. When one sits down across the negotiating table from people with different interests, however, the presence or absence of trust and respect goes a long way to determining the tone of the discussions.

Another variable in establishing relationships and influence is the CEO's ego. Successful managers tend to have strong personalities. Success may often go to their head, and they may enjoy their power. They may be accustomed to having their way. They become acclimated to "the good life," often defined by a corporate jet and a life of luxury. When they are acclimated in this way, they can come across as autocratic and arrogant, and they may not have the kind of relationships that promote the best interests of the business.

The Media

We live in a world with many alternative media for reaching intended audiences. It is very important that the appropriate medium be chosen to deliver corporate communications and that the message is then delivered effectively. The CEO needs to know how this is done or hire advisors who know. The media can be characterized as direct, small-group, or mass communications. Direct communication can be subdivided into one-on-one communications in person, by telephone, or in writing (it used to be letters and is now often e-mail). Small group and mass communications can be in person, via conference call or electronic media, or in some form of print.

The medium that works best in a given situation depends on a number of variables. The nature of the message, the urgency, the economics, and the number of people to be reached all play a part. For the majority of general managers, the most efficacious way to deliver a message is in person— individually, in small group settings, or by making speeches. This clearly requires that the general manager be a strong communicator. Complex messages generally have to be delivered in some form of print. For many reasons, it is always effective to distill the message to its simplest possible form. Consistency of message and repetition are also important.

Choosing Advisors

The public relations and advocacy functions require specialized knowledge, experience, and skill sets. A general manager is usually well advised to work with public relations specialists to select appropriate media and prepare to deliver messages effectively. Selecting good advisors is very important. A primary consideration is to minimize conflicts of interest—the selected advisors should be independent and objective. Further, they should not have a bias in the direction of a specific medium. For instance, they should not be in a position to profit from the use of one medium more than from another. After the medium is selected, experts in that arena should be engaged, but that should be a second-order decision.

Evaluating the competence of specialists in these areas can be very subjective because communicating is, at its core, very much an art. The general manager can examine examples of past work, try to evaluate the specialists' understanding of the company's situation, and listen carefully to their recommendations. Too often, however, effective salespeople can sell more than they can deliver. As with everything else the CEO does, the results will be determined by his or her ability to choose the right people.

The Roles of the CEO in Public Relations and Advocacy

The CEO as the leader of the organization plays a number of essential roles in the public relations and advocacy functions. He or she may depend heavily on advisors or may be active in formulating and executing the business's communications strategies. In between the extremes are the usual general management roles of delegating to key persons, advising and consenting, overseeing, and holding subordinates or outside agencies accountable.

Public Spokesperson

The most visible role of the CEO is as the ultimate spokesperson for the company. Some choose to play this role very privately, staying as much behind the scenes as possible. Others choose to be very out front, often assuming celebrity status within their communities and industries, and even on a national and international level.

Either extreme has distinct risks. The behind-the-scenes role can be effective when things are going very well and there are no public pressures or controversies. When there are problems that must be dealt with publicly, however, the very private CEO may not have much credibility with the external world. The celebrity CEO, on the other hand, can appear to be promoting him- or herself instead of the interests of the company, and may not be attending to the company's business very well.

The middle road is generally more comfortable for most CEOs. The CEO has visibility and relationships with the important constituencies, but does not play a singular role in delivering the messages. When appropriate, he or she holds meetings and makes speeches. But the bulk of the public relations work is delegated to others, with close scrutiny.

Customer Relations

Among the most important constituencies in every company is the customer. It is crucial for customers to have a positive view of the business in general, and more particularly, its brands. Ultimate success depends on how well the delivered products or services perform. With outstanding product and service performance as the foundation, success is enhanced when the company's offerings are perceived as being cost-effective (good value) and supported by excellent advertising and sales programs. Success is further enhanced by keeping the company's brands in front of customers and by providing after-sales service and support that turns problems into opportunities.

One of the most effective ways of building brand awareness is to understand the customer experience at every contact point. It is amazing how many businesses spend small fortunes to create demand, and then fail to follow through to provide those attracted with a positive experience.

Some CEOs are very visible in ads and other sales promotions. For a few with a good public persona, this can be positive. Many, however, are just not cut out to make a positive impression, and should leave this work to others who are more competent. One mark of great CEOs is that they stay in touch with customers and thoroughly understand their needs and wants.

Employee Relations

In a similar vein, effective CEOs know and are known by their employees. They maintain open, two-way communications with employees at all levels of the organization, listening more than talking. They inform the employees about important aspects of the business. They are candid about the situation, holding themselves accountable to the employees for job security, working conditions, and compensation. They visualize their mutual relationship as a partnership created to serve the customer. Effective employee relations must penetrate deep into the organization. An incompetent or abusive frontline supervisor can undo all of the values espoused by the general manager. The performance of managers at all levels must therefore be monitored to ensure conformance with the company's values.

Supplier Relations

In situations where supplier bargaining power is limited, supplier relations may not be very important. When the business is dependent on its suppliers, however—for access to critical raw materials, equipment, or for technical support—maintaining strong relations with them can be crucial. Top managers frequently maintain relationships with their counterparts in the supplier organization. Many businesses find that striving to be a good customer over many years—dealing fairly and loyally—is a good business practice. This attitude may not be as prevalent today as it once was.

Investor Relations

Investor relations is an area in which the CEOs of publicly held companies spend a substantial portion of their time. Investor relations are critically important in determining the stock prices of public companies. The company story must be told honestly and skillfully, so that the investment community and other stakeholders can understand and believe it. The quality of stockholder communications is thus very important. There is an important middleman in stockholder relations—the financial analyst. The general manager wants as many investment firms (analysts) as possible to follow the stock and make "buy" recommendations to their clients. In recent years, the investment industry has changed so that there are fewer analysts than previously. The available analysts can choose from thousands of firms, and can effectively follow only a very small number. Thus, getting analysts to follow a company is a challenge—especially if it is a small-cap company with little trading volume.

These thoughts are summarized in Vignette 24-2.

The rules have also been tightened on what is allowable to say to analysts and stockholders, and when it is allowed to be said. The basic thrust of government regulators has been to reduce trading on insider information. The related goal is that any released information should be available at the same time to every investor or potential investor (in effect, the public). Thus, off-the-record, one-on-one conversations with analysts are virtually forbidden. The result is that much effort is made to present effectively the company's situation and prospects through all of the appropriate media—in-person meetings, print and Internet messages, and the stockholders' annual meeting and the related proxy statements and annual report.

Government Relations—Legislative

Many businesses, because of their nature, find it necessary to maintain close relationships with local, state, and federal legislative bodies, both

VIGNETTE 24-2

The analysts must like the company's story and trust the management.

in their home country and in other nations in which they conduct a substantial amount of business. For instance, a local real estate developer should have good relationships with the planning commission and the city council or county board of supervisors. It is in his or her best interests to influence community master plans and zoning ordinances. On an individual level, developers want to benefit from favorable action on their applications.

At the state and federal levels, general managers are concerned about laws and budgets that affect their industries. Typically, related efforts are largely managed through industry associations. In the case of very large companies, however, they may act on their own behalf as well. The efforts to maintain relationships begin with backing political candidates who are sympathetic to their interests. They may also employ salaried lobbyists who have long-term relationships with the elected officials and their staffs. At the worst, these efforts are seen as, and can be, payoffs for past or future favors. At the best, they provide the decision makers with pertinent information that helps them make effective laws.

Government Relations — Regulatory

All U.S. companies are regulated by agencies such as the Internal Revenue Service, the Department of Justice (antitrust), the Fair Trade Commission, the Department of Labor, the Equal Employment Opportunity Commission (EEOC), the Occupational Safety and Health Administration (OSHA), and their counterparts at the state level, to mention only a few. Publicly owned companies must also deal with the Securities and Exchange Commission (SEC), and similar state bodies.

In addition to these agencies, some industries have business practices that are closely regulated. Utilities and communications companies that are holders of public franchises must account to those whom they serve for the quality of their services and the prices charged (levels of profitability and returns on investment). Transportation companies were highly regulated for many years, but these regulations have been relaxed recently, leading to dramatic changes in industry structure — not all propitious. Other industries, such as banking and financial services, are under close scrutiny from regulators who attempt to protect depositors.

A fundamental first step in dealing with regulators is to understand the laws and the regulations as they apply to a given company. These can be very complicated, so many general managers engage counsel (lawyers) or other specialists to manage this function. This is the area where advocacy becomes paramount, beginning with having close, personal connections. The fact that defense contractors hire former military and government officials is no accident. Such advocacy efforts move to the use of lobbyists and efforts to be proactive on the political scene. These efforts can also extend to creating extensive public-awareness programs.

At a minimum, these advocacy activities are defensive in nature—simply attempting to thwart the efforts of groups that are attacking a company or its industry. They can also include offensive actions to change the status quo in favor of the company and its industry. The activities are characteristically pursued in markets, both domestic and international, in which a company has or aims to have a substantial amount of business.

Industry Leader

Virtually every industry has trade and professional organizations to represent the industry in legal affairs and to provide information and other services to its members. These services can range from education and training to the cooperative procurement of specialized products such as insurance or retirement plans. One of the choices the general manager has to make is whether he or she wants to be involved in these industry groups as an active member or leader. The costs are time and money. The benefits are getting to know competitors and learning from others who have similar challenges. Most political-advocacy efforts are channeled through industry associations or related political-action groups.

Community Leader

In a similar manner, a general manager has to decide the role that he or she wants to play in the communities in which the company has operations. The corporate presence can make a huge difference to local communities in terms of resources and expertise by helping local governments and nonprofit organizations do a better job of solving community problems and serving constituents, particularly the disadvantaged. The choices here range from total indifference to extensive involvement.

The benefits to the general manager and the firm are indirectly derived from operating in a more prosperous and healthy community, and from fulfilling perceived moral obligations of good citizenship. If general managers and their businesses are not heavily involved in their communities, they leave the decision making to other groups who may not be as interested in creating a favorable business climate.

Summary

The requirements for the CEO or general manager to reach out beyond the business are substantial. The general manager must assume many roles with regard to numerous constituencies in the arena of public relations and advocacy. Professional help may be engaged to assist with these important relationships, but the CEO or general manager is ultimately responsible in matters related to the company.

DISCUSSION QUESTIONS

1. What is the difference between public relations and advocacy?
2. Why are relationships so important?
3. What are the key relationships for a CEO?
4. Why is the Tylenol story so instructive?
5. What percentage of a general manager's time and energy should be devoted to public relations and advocacy?

25

REFLECTIONS ON GENERAL MANAGEMENT

In this closing chapter, we reflect on the general manager and general management from the perspectives provided within the earlier chapters. Our view is that the concept of general management must be well understood by all persons involved in governance and management because of its importance to an organization's success. An organization that does not have effective general management eventually will be incoherent, uncoordinated, and unsuccessful.

The success of the business is important to the people who are invested in it—those who invest their capital, the employees who invest their time and careers, the customers who depend on its products and services, and the numerous other stakeholders described in earlier chapters. Finally, in a capitalist, free-enterprise, competitive system, the success of a business is important to the broader economy, the prosperity of which depends, in large part, on the prosperity of its businesses.

General Management in Review

The term general manager is used to differentiate the role from that of a functional manager. A business achieves its goals through performance at the functional level, and a functional manager heads each function. There are normally three line functions: marketing (creating demand), engineering or research and development (creating product and process design), and production or operations (providing the product or service). There also are usually three support or staff functions: finance, human resources, and administration. Imbedded in all six functions is the task of managing information.

Functional managers have specialized knowledge, skills, and experience in their functional areas. The careers of most employees start with a job within a functional area, and these early positions create opportunities for aspirant managers to demonstrate leadership traits. Employees are promoted as they gain experience and build functional and management expertise. The ultimate position within a function is that of functional manager, which often is known by the title of director or vice president, for example, vice president of marketing. The role of the general manager, though, is largely differentiated from that of functional managers by two factors:

- The managers of functional departments are responsible for revenue or cost centers, while the general manager is responsible for both revenue and expenses, and hence profit and loss.
- The general manager is responsible for effectively managing the interfaces among the functional departments.

In many companies, an observer might gain the impression that one or perhaps another function is more important than the others. This might be the impression regarding research and development (R&D)/engineering at Intel, marketing at General Mills, finance at Goldman Sachs, or operations at Toyota. For most companies, however, every function is vital to success, and it is imperative that the general manager pay proper attention to the performance of each. As described earlier, the strategic, business, and annual plans for a firm should include specific performance goals, whose achievement by each of the functional departments will contribute to the success of the enterprise. The general manager should take care to emphasize the importance of all functional units to the success of the business in his or her dealings with the various parts of the organization.

An organization will not be successful over the long term if any one of its major functional areas is performing poorly. For example, a business's marketing function will be unable to sell profitably what the manufacturing function provides at an uncompetitive cost. Similarly, if no customers are interested in a particular product, the marketing function will be unable to sell it, regardless of how well it was produced by manufacturing. Furthermore, if the firm does not have the financial resources to fund the business adequately and an effective economic model for making a profit, the business will not survive.

General management must ensure that all of the business's major components are functioning well for it to run in a sustained, profitable mode. Ensuring this balance requires that the crucial decisions involving the interrelationships among the functions reflect an independent judgment on the part of the general manager. General managers will normally have demonstrated expertise in one or more functions, but that by itself is not what makes them effective. They must transcend performing as an expert to be effective as a generalist in the role of general manager. In a similar pattern, a division head within a decentralized organization who wishes to make the move to effective chief executive officer (CEO) must move away from being an integrator of functions toward being a leader of independent company presidents. The principal characteristics that tend to increase the effectiveness of general managers include the following:

- Having perspective; an ability to see the big picture and think strategically, taking the viewpoint of the total enterprise.
- Knowing how to identify multi- and cross-functional problems, determine their root causes, and make the changes necessary to solve them.
- Knowing how to convert strategies to action.
- Aggressively assuming profit and loss (P&L), "bottom-line" responsibility. As Harry Truman said, "The buck stops here." The notion of the bottom line comes from the profit line at the bottom of a firm's income statement. In the broader sense, it represents the responsibility for ensuring that the organization functions profitably and fulfills its purpose by achieving its strategic and operational goals.
- Having an appropriate attitude. Attitude determines how a general manager perceives the world. Successful general managers have a "can do" approach to solving problems and simultaneously seeking out opportunities. As a rule, they are industrious.

- Being a leader. Effective leadership is important to the success of any organization, and very few organizations progress beyond the capabilities and aspirations of their leadership. The leader who gets the right people into the right jobs and creates an environment within which they can be effective should be given credit for their success and be willing to take the blame for their failures.

In summary, general management is about getting results in the context of the total enterprise. It requires the ability to think strategically combined with the ability to execute strategies by taking action and managing change.

Becoming an Effective General Manager

Within the context of the modern corporation, there are essentially three ways for employees to earn a living. Employees may succeed as specialists who are compensated for "what they know," for instance, as tax experts or computer specialists. They may also succeed very nicely based on "what they can do," as welders, surgeons, management consultants, or highly skilled investment bankers, for example. Or, they may "manage the work of others," providing the insights and leadership that leverage efforts by and the collective accomplishments of those managed. The very best performers of each of these types of workers are handsomely rewarded in our free-enterprise economy. The question for each of us is how best to utilize our skills and abilities to our natural advantage. We focus in this book on the attributes most likely to enhance the careers of those who choose to manage. For managers, the ultimate prize in our economic system is the position of general manager.

Functional Experience

The work experience of most people in business begins within a functional unit of an organization. As one develops functional competencies, he or she should learn to work effectively as part of a team, which comes more easily to some than others. Those who are introverted, overly competitive, or very controlling often find collaboration and the sharing of responsibility and credit extremely difficult. Some jobs may be done effectively in isolation and may offer more comfortable placement for those who have difficulty working with others. For most jobs in business, however, teamwork is essential.

Team Leader or First-Line Supervisor

The first step up the management ladder usually involves promotion to the position of team leader or first-line supervisor. This position is known by a range of titles across different businesses and provides the new manager with a first taste of coordinating the activities of others and managing their performance. The task of building a high-performing team requires many of the characteristics of general management, but on a much smaller scale. The right people should be positioned in the right jobs and an organizational structure appropriate for the nature of the work should be created. People must be trained and developed, and proper concern for motivation and morale demonstrated. Strong performance should be recognized and rewarded and poor performance and unacceptable behavior must be dealt with. For the newly initiated manager, many of these tasks may be challenging and even seem beyond the authority of the position. They deserve attention, though, for they have the potential to greatly affect the probability of success. Beyond the management of subordinates, the manager should attend to the relationships of his or her team with other teams (the interfaces) in a way that ensures the effectiveness of their mutual efforts.

Manager of a Functional Department

The path from team leader to functional manager usually consists of promotions through a series of positions with progressively greater responsibilities, although in small companies, the number of layers through which to move may be rather limited. The pool from which a business draws its general managers includes those who are successful functional leaders. Not all functional leaders, though, will be qualified for or want to pursue the step into general management, and as a result, a natural selection process occurs. Many well-run organizations identify employees seen as having general management potential and provide them with a variety of assignments to broaden and deepen their experience and perspective. These assignments may be supplemented with training programs, either within the company or through short courses at industry or business schools. Such high-potential employees are a very valuable resource of the organization, and many companies dedicate tremendous effort to tracking their experiences and performance.

Strong functional expertise gathered through functional assignments and managerial roles is an important attribute of nearly all general managers. In fact, it is typically quite beneficial for an aspiring general manager to have demonstrated strong capabilities in managing two or more functional areas. Thus, a manager might begin in a sales or marketing capacity and eventually become vice president of sales and marketing. If the manager then gained experience as an operations manager, the likelihood of an assignment as a general manager would be greatly enhanced. Of course, this kind of rotational experience is more feasible in diversified, decentralized companies with a holding-company structure, as the availability of multiple profit centers or divisions increases the odds of such cross-training assignments.

General Manager

Most successful companies learn to develop their management talent primarily from within. Such an approach may more easily be done in larger businesses, but leaders of businesses of all sizes should be mindful of the need to create a talent pool to provide for orderly succession at all levels of management. To do so, managers may have to seek new talent that occasionally will need to be brought in from outside the company. While nearly all organizations have the option of hiring from outside, a very few do not. Vignette 25-1 discusses one such situation.

Becoming an effective general manager of a business is a career-long journey along four development paths. These paths encompass the following:

- Personal development
- Administrative competence
- Technical competence
- Interpersonal competence

Every situation requires some mix of these competencies, but their relative importance varies by situation. Successful general managers understand

VIGNETTE 25-1

The military model of development and promotion is instructive. The U.S. military promotes entirely from within. It brings in personnel as enlisted persons or as commissioned officers, depending on their qualifications, education, training, and experience. The enlisted personnel have career paths to the noncommissioned officer (NCO) ranks, and the outstanding ones have an opportunity to become commissioned officers. The NCOs are the backbone of the troop force, providing small-unit leadership and technical skills. The commissioned officers serve as managers. The junior officers are the frontline company managers, the majors and lieutenant colonels manage battalions (collections of companies), and the senior officers (colonels and generals) are the general managers. Personnel are promoted through the ranks based on merit, with the weaker ones being culled out at each step along the way. The process is essentially an "up-or-out" approach to promotion, especially after the first twenty years of service and at the higher ranks.

what is needed in a particular situation and whether those needs match their personal strengths.

PERSONAL DEVELOPMENT Based on the authors' observations, effective general managers have an intellectual curiosity that compels lifelong learning. They continuously work to develop their understanding of themselves, of others, of their businesses, and of the world around them. They possess well-defined values that are the foundation of their character, and a sound self-knowledge. Because of the diverse demands of their positions, personal development tends to occur across all of the dimensions of their lives, especially intellectually and emotionally. The natural outgrowth of these efforts is self-confidence that carries a general manager through tough decisions and challenging times.

Personal values naturally influence decisions and, consequently, managers promoted within an organization typically find alignment between their own values and those of the organization, both formal and informal. Effective general managers develop and employ a strong work ethic, setting a standard of performance for their subordinates. To direct their efforts, successful general managers discern when and how to take the initiative to make things happen, guided by goals and desired results. In response to an increasingly uncertain environment, though, they learn to remain flexible, adjusting quickly to changing circumstances.

Other observations of effective general managers include that they value results over their status, and are willing to hold people accountable at the risk of becoming unpopular. Also, they are open to and skilled at questioning the points of view of others. Evidence of their effectiveness comes in the trust and respect of subordinates, peers, and superiors.

ADMINISTRATIVE SKILLS A general manager's administrative skills result from his or her abilities to efficiently analyze, make decisions, and organize others. Because time is a scarce resource for most general managers, time management is a central facet of administrative skills. In learning to allocate time to tasks, the general manager must learn to distinguish between what is important and must be done personally, what should be delegated to others, and what would be of little value or a waste of time.

As a further distinction, managers will find that even among their important tasks, certain issues have an urgency to which they must respond immediately, and others may be of great importance but not urgent, and hence may be deferred to a later time. Urgent matters usually are related to current activities and involve deadlines. A general manager must develop strong discipline and organizational skills in order to become more proactive in what he or she chooses to do, and to deal with those important things that can, but should not, be deferred. An example of one executive's implementation of this approach is captured in Vignette 25-2.

TECHNICAL COMPETENCE It has been said that success results from who we are, whom we know, and what we know, this final factor

---

VIGNETTE 25-2

One experienced general manager split his day into three parts: administrative time, react time, and project time.

- *Administrative time:* During this deliberately dedicated period, the general manager performed many tasks, including managing his calendar, completing essential paperwork, writing letters, and returning calls and e-mails. He worked to keep an empty in-box. When the executive had a backlog of urgent administrative tasks, he relied on a capable personal assistant to aid him.

> • *React time:* During this second portion of the executive's day, he was available to direct reports, and "managed by walking around." It was also the time when he reviewed current operating reports and generally stayed in touch. This period of the day was basically unstructured.
> • *Project time:* The final portion of the day was dedicated to meetings and specific projects. The manager found that he was able to use this time efficiently by setting priorities for projects, reserving blocks of time for meetings, and ensuring that effective staff work preceded meetings.
>
> The amount of time spent on each activity varied depending on the existing circumstances and how much of the work at hand could be delegated to others.

including our technical competence. General managers paradoxically have to know a little about a variety of subjects, and yet understand and stay focused on what is really important. They should also recognize what it is they don't know, and learn how to obtain competent advice in those areas.

The technical competence of general managers should include a sound understanding of significant economic and management principles and concepts. For example, general managers need to understand concepts such as economies of scale, market share, and return on investment, and have a solid feel for how to adjust budgets for varying volumes and how to compensate people. General managers also must have a sufficient understanding of the functional activities to understand the reports, suggestions, and opinions they receive from functional managers; to supervise and evaluate the performance of their functional specialists; and to effectively integrate the plans and actions of the functional areas.

Industry expertise is also an important facet of a general manager's technical competence. Industry knowledge should include an understanding of the current and likely future states of the economics of the industry, its competitive structure, and its critical success factors. Industry expertise also includes establishing and cultivating long-standing relationships with customers, suppliers, competitors, and regulators, where applicable. Efficient access to information about what others know and what they are doing keeps a general manager well informed.

Some argue that a professional manager can be successful anywhere, and that industry expertise can quickly be acquired or hired. Occasionally, this transfer occurs, particularly in cases where the professional managers are truly exceptional. Often, these general managers' achievements are rooted in somewhat more specialized skills such as turnaround expertise or marketing savvy. Most managers, though, find industry expertise a valuable resource in performing their duties.

INTERPERSONAL SKILLS A general manager is dependent on the support and effectiveness of numerous individuals to achieve the goals of the organization. To be effective in managing, delegating to, and interacting with the necessary breadth of professionals and constituents, a general manager requires strong interpersonal skills that begin with being a good judge of people. A general manager must be able to assess the character and personality of others, along with their competencies, if he or she is going to get the "right people into the right jobs." An understanding of human nature is at the center of this facet of the general manager's job.

After the "right people" are in place, the general manager must be able to influence how they act. One element of this influence involves creating and maintaining positive relationships. Communication naturally has a role in these activities and is generally most effective in candid and trusting relationships. Numerous barriers to effective relationships exist, though, including personality conflicts, conflicts of interest, and a lack of trust. A good communicator recognizes these barriers when they exist and attempts to work through them, building on an understanding of the positions of the parties involved.

Of course, communication involves listening as well as speaking. Many managers make the mistake of viewing communication as a one-way street, with information flowing from manager to subordinates. Listening is a necessary component of the general manager's task to assess the environment and internal situation of the organization. Numerous means of communicating are available to the general manager, including through behavior, verbally, and via a variety of media, most commonly the written word. Vignette 25-3 illustrates one general manager's approach to communicating with his subordinates.

In summary, a general manager has to maintain a spectrum of relationships ranging from very personal, one-on-one relationships with key managers, to

VIGNETTE 25-3

One general manager met regularly with groups of twenty or so line employees. He began the meetings by saying that it was *their* meeting; he was there to listen to their ideas, suggestions, and concerns. He said that he had no secrets, that he was as accountable to them for their jobs and working conditions—the investment of their time—as he was to the stockholders for their investment of money. He listened, answered questions, and took actions that indicated he had heard them.

Some might think that this would be an invitation to a grievance session or a forum for the expression of unreasonable demands. On occasion, this did occur, but the general manager found that the employees truly cared about what was best for the company and were very fair-minded. He not only got many outstanding ideas and a good sense of morale from the meetings, but he also built trusting relationships with the employees.

a broader relationship with his or her management team, to a very broad relationship with the entire organization. The ability to build and sustain these relationships is essential to long-term success. Healthy and mutually beneficial relationships take time to establish; they may, however, be destroyed quickly by thoughtless or malevolent words or actions.

The General Manager Is Characterized by a Management Style

The management style of a general manager will normally reflect his or her personality and values. To be successful in the long term, the general manager's style must also be consistent with the nature of the work and the culture of the organization. A person's management style is shaped first by his or her motives, including personal ambitions for prestige, power, and wealth for some, and building a great organization and developing its people for others.

We should not forget, however, the "invisible hand of self-interest," proposed by eighteenth-century economist and philosopher Adam Smith. Many positive aspects of the world we know today can be traced to the efforts of people who were driven by their personal ambitions and self-interest. Most general managers act with some elements of both self-interest and servitude. Ideally, a compensation package would align the two through incentives.

The integrity of the general manager is closely associated with the means by which objectives will be sought. Integrity is not negotiable in great organizations, nor is it defined solely in moral terms. It also includes intellectual honesty, which is the ability to see things as they are, and deal with them without rationalizing, denying, or "spinning" them.

Perhaps the most prominent feature of a general manager's style is how decisions are made. The spectrum of styles ranges from autocratic, through which the leader pronounces decisions and issues edicts, to hands-off, where the leader delegates responsibility and authority for decisions to others. Most managers find a style somewhere between the two extremes, usually soliciting the advice of others before personally making significant decisions.

Another important element of a general manager's management style is his or her orientation toward performance. Strong general managers normally place a great deal of emphasis on continuous improvement and holding employees accountable for behavior and results. They are demanding yet fair.

Finally, managers have varying desires regarding the development of personal relationships with their subordinates. These proclivities relate to the personalities of the managers as well as their beliefs about how to best serve the interests of the organization. Some managers prefer an arm's-length relationship, noting that this approach keeps them objective when reviewing the performance of those they must evaluate. Others prefer to develop strong, personal bonds and trusting relationships, which they often see as enhancing the collective work of those involved.

Why General Managers Fail

General managers fail in their positions for numerous reasons, most of which are not mutually exclusive. As a result, organizations are often disadvantaged by the occurrence of more than one of the following causes of failure:

- Incompetence
- Inability to relate to others

- Ego and excessive ambition
- Greed
- Overreaching
- Conflicting values
- Inappropriate focus
- Inability to make difficult decisions

Incompetence

Management incompetence occurs when there is a misfit between the manager's skills and the requirements of the job. The lack of fit may be the result of inadequate training, intellect, natural ability, or experience. It may occur when a manager's job changes for some reason, and the skills and experience required by the change exceed the skills of a previously effective manager. Well-meaning incompetence is the source of far more lost value than dishonesty in most businesses.

The Inability to Relate to Others

Success as a general manager, though, depends on much more than just being competent. A general manager must be able to build relationships with members of the board of directors and senior managers so that their confidence is earned and effective communications ensue. Leaders cannot lead if the followers will not follow. Thus, the general manager also must establish a relationship with subordinates as well as the rank and file so that they will support his or her decisions. Problems frequently result from an abrasive personality or a dysfunctional management style.

Ego and Excessive Ambition

Many successful people are driven by considerable ambitions and huge egos. Everything is about *them*. Too little ambition may result in inadequate efforts to get a job done, but too much ambition may create political or unethical behaviors in attempts to get ahead that eventually prove self-defeating. In the same vein, success may feed an ego so that the general manager has no sense of humility. Ego can delude a person into a sense of infallibility. Organizations may attempt to curtail such problems with 360-degree evaluation mechanisms, in which all employees are evaluated by subordinates, colleagues, and supervisors, but boards and senior management must be willing to confront such behavior in order for this technique to be effective.

Greed

Greed is closely related to ego and ambition. For greedy individuals, the more they acquire, the more they tend to want, whether it is power, wealth, or adulation. Ego often fuels greed, convincing the greedy they deserve ever more of whatever it is they seek, and ambition drives them to find ways of obtaining it. Greed will offend reasonable associates and often leads to poor decisions that put the organization at risk.

Overreaching the Organization's Capabilities

The poor decisions likely to flow from ambition and greed include overreaching the organization's capabilities and resources, and committing it in some way to deliver products or results when it is unable. Such overcommitment may also stem from a deficiency in understanding the organization's limitations and the demands likely to be created by a decision to expand or change the business in some way.

Values Conflict

When values of key managers, owners, and/or board members conflict, differences of opinion are inevitable and often lead to an eventual parting of ways. It is almost impossible to maintain two sets of values under one roof. If an honest, performance-oriented general manager is working for a passive board of directors or senior executive, problems are likely, especially when definitive action is required. Conversely, a passive or dishonest general manager will run into problems in an organization that is performance-oriented and values integrity.

A Single Inappropriate Focus

Problems frequently occur when the general manager has primarily a single functional perspective and fails to understand or properly appreciate the value of the other functions. Such a bias may result from an excessive degree of loyalty to the function in which the general manager gained his or her early experience. Organizations should aim to rotate managers among the functions in preparation for a general management role. At the same time, general managers should be mindful of the necessity and contributions of each of the functions to the success of the business.

Inability to Make Difficult Decisions

A common cause of failure of general managers is the inability to make difficult decisions. This shortcoming keeps a general manager from committing to a course of action when alternatives encompass risky or unpleasant endeavors. Examples of such decisions include whether or not to move jobs offshore, close an underutilized and unprofitable plant, or reduce a bloated workforce. Even with strong supporting economic data, some managers are incapable of committing to taking action on such issues. Frequently, they evolve into a string of "wait-and-see" reviews, until the financial consequences take a toll or become too large to ignore. In essence, these managers choose the status quo over other options, often putting their organizations at risk. In many cases, the situation requires a new general manager with a different perspective and less emotional attachment to resolve the situation.

The Bottom Line on Getting into Trouble

One way for a general manager to avoid the kinds of mistakes identified here is to be introspective and honest about his or her performance. When a general manager constantly engages in self-assessment, takes personal responsibility for what happens, and is performance oriented and driven by the best interests of the organization and its shareholders, these problems are much less likely to occur.

Some Miscellaneous Observations on General Management

The Search for the Ultimate Weapon

There has been a continuous debate for decades over the relative importance of strategy formulation versus execution. In order to bring clarity to the issue, consider the analogy between strategy in the business context and the search for the ultimate weapon prevalent in military organizations throughout recorded history. Competitive advantages based on strategies are almost always short-lived, as most are readily copied. A well-thought-out business strategy may provide a temporary competitive advantage, but creating a sustainable competitive advantage requires effective, supporting functional strategies in marketing, operations, R&D or engineering, and finance. Such sustainable competitive advantages are often brought about by a firm that achieves a position as the low-cost producer in its market segments and reinvests a portion of its high margins into price reductions or other "investments" intended to gain volume and market share, placing steady pressure on competitors. The long-run application of effective functional strategies can lead to a position as the low-cost producer that, together with steady price reductions, eventually leads to dominance of a market segment.

Finally, we want to recognize the crucial importance of each of two aspects of corporate strategy. First, the strategic planning process begins with decisions regarding the firm's strategic goals and objectives, followed by the formulation of strategies for their attainment. Second, plans must be devised for implementing the strategies and managing the myriad of detailed actions that are required to execute the strategies effectively. In many ways, this strategic planning process in the business world is analogous to the longing for the "ultimate weapon" that has characterized military leaders throughout history. In seeking "sustainable competitive advantage," commanders have hoped to acquire access to a weapon so unique that it would tip the battle in their favor.

Unfortunately, this hope has, for the most part, been futile. Consider the small number of ultimate weapons we recall, and the relatively short time during which they afforded their initiators a competitive advantage. From the spear, bow and arrow, crossbow, longbow, gunpowder, and firearms, to machine guns, artillery, and nuclear weapons, the competitive advantage lasted only until opponents internalized the design and advantages of each weapon and copied them. Even with all of the science and technology involved with nuclear weapons, the competitive advantage was sustainable for only three years.

Consider, on the other hand, the success of the Greek phalanx, the Roman legion, Genghis Khan's cavalry, modern military logistics, and the ever-present use of alliances to rein in those who appear too powerful. It is apparent that, for the most part, history has belonged to the "organizers and implementers" and only for fleeting periods to those with some undefeatable ultimate weapon. So it is with business. Unique strategies are few and can seldom be perpetuated for very long. Even patents expire at the end of some specified time interval.

As a result, in our system of free enterprise and competition, with unprecedented capabilities for communication, ideas rarely remain proprietary for very long. Competitors become aware of the strategies of others from suppliers, customers, industry connections, former employees, and the CEOs' statements in the press and annual reports of public companies. Success in the business environment is surely dependent on the derivation of effective strategies, but it is at least equally dependent on superior ability to execute the strategies.

Those firms with superior strategies and the ability to execute them are the champions in our free enterprise system of capitalism and competition. This dual theme of strategy formulation and related superior execution has been reinforced throughout the chapters and vignettes of this book.

Managing Change

We have emphasized the dual needs to manage change effectively and to move decisively in implementation of decisions. In fact, the entire process of strategic planning and execution is dependent for success on the ability of the CEO to lead change and execute decisions swiftly and decisively. We learn from the master of understanding and explaining human nature, Niccolò Machiavelli, that certain traits are essential for the "prince" who wishes to defend and expand his realm (read business).

Machiavelli wrote, in 1513, that "there is nothing more difficult to execute, nor more dubious of success, nor more dangerous to administer than to introduce a new order of things,"[1] thus warning of the difficulties of implementing changes. He also wrote that, "in taking a state, its conqueror should weigh all the harmful things he must do and do them all at once so as not to have to repeat them every day, and in not repeating them to be able to make men feel secure and to win them over to the benefits he bestows upon them."[2] Our experience reinforces this notion that when a difficult decision must be implemented, it is far better to take the action swiftly and decisively, thus getting the period of unrest over as rapidly as possible and allowing the people affected to get on with their activities and establish a new routine.

Critical Thinking and Decision Making

It is important for the general manager to learn to ask the right questions and seek the best answers. An essential requirement for these activities is objectivity—the ability to see reality uninfluenced by self-interests and/or emotions. Within the organization, strong decision making is also supported by a norm of open and candid conversation. Employees and management team members must be able to express their opinions openly and honestly, and others must be willing to listen with an open mind. Respectful dissent should be encouraged in order to fully explore drawbacks and benefits of issues under discussion. The objective for the general manager is to provide a rule of reason and merit, not of power or politics, to encourage identification of viable alternatives as well as shortcomings of those already under scrutiny.

Managers must follow a disciplined decision-making process after the issues have been identified and analyzed and the thoughts and opinions of all who can contribute materially have been drawn in. Participants in this process should know who has the responsibility for making a decision and who has veto or approval authority. One of the frequent problems with the work of groups or teams is a tendency to desire and attempt to manage by total consensus. Building consensus is always an attractive goal, but sometimes it is not possible. When this is the case, a lack of consensus should not be permitted to paralyze the decision-making process. Too much emphasis on consensus can result in a "tyranny of a minority" that effectively maintains the status quo. There are times when a leader must assert his or her authority to ensure that a group arrives at a decision, recognizing that some involved will not find the outcome to their liking. To avoid this definitive act is a failure to lead.

Creative Thinking and Innovation

Strategic planning necessarily involves creative and innovative thinking. Because different results should not be expected if the status quo is perpetuated, general managers who want dramatic change to occur within their organizations must act and likely think in a different way. If they want to distinguish their organizations from competitors', they must search for solutions that are different from what others are doing, while maintaining a focus on customer needs and desires. These change leaders need to understand their customers' businesses and problems and focus strategies on providing innovative solutions. In summary, they must be entrepreneurial.

Additional Reflections

The effective general manager will be cognizant of the following fundamental aspects of any business:

- Public relations matter today. General managers must ensure that their organizations are recognized for strong performance and their constituents are well informed about potential shortfalls or crises.
- Governments set the rules of competition for business (or decide not to), but not in a vacuum. The general manager has the opportunity and responsibility to try to influence the formation of the rules in ethical and legal ways.
- Free cash flow is among the most important attributes of a business. Without cash, a business loses viability, regardless of the structure of its balance sheet. This issue is particularly relevant for smaller, growing businesses that need cash to get established but may not have ready access to additional financing.
- Excess cash is a dual-edged sword. It represents one of the most important strategic tools management can possess, but it also can weigh down returns.
- Systems are critical for the effective continuity of the business and necessary for sustained excellence. Systems include information management, planning, budgeting, compensation and evaluation, and reporting.
- Capital structure is the foundation for a successful business. Too much leverage, in particular, can lead to the demise of a business. Too little leverage leaves potential efficiencies unrealized.

Summary

The task of summarizing the multitude of aspects of general management is daunting. In writing this section, we simply would like to point out the importance of the role of general manager in the current global political economy and note that the position is the preeminent management role in today's dominant system of capitalism, free enterprise, and competition. The success of free-market systems, including that of the United States, relies on the performance of general managers in all sizes of organizations to marshal employees and inputs to serve customer needs and desires and to create value. The task is demanding and its requirements broad, but the outcomes contribute to the performance of economic systems that are perpetually raising standards of living on a broad scale. We salute this achievement and wish all managers and management students success in their personal quests to become effective general managers.

DISCUSSION QUESTIONS

1. What is general management?
2. How does one become an effective general manager?
3. What kind of general manager do you want to be?
4. Why do some general managers fail?
5. Why is the general management position the ultimate corporate job in our economic system?

NOTES

Chapter 1: General Management in Economic Context

1. Adam Smith, *An Inquiry into the Nature and Causes of the Wealth of Nations* (New York: Random House/Modern Library, 1994).

2. Jack Beatty (ed.), *Colossus: How the Corporation Changed America* (New York: Broadway Books, 2000), 6.

3. Paul Johnson, *A History of the American People* (New York: Harper Perennial, 1997), 560.

4. *Abstract of the Census of Manufactures* (Washington, D.C.: 1919), Table 195, 340.

5. Thomas L. Friedman, *The World Is Flat: A Brief History of the Twenty-first Century* (New York: Farrar, Straus, and Giroux, 2005).

6. William Pfaff, "A Pathological Mutation in Capitalism," *International Herald Tribune*, September 9, 2002, 8.

Chapter 3: The Roles and Tasks of the General Manager

1. *Warfighting,* U.S. Marine Corps, 1997.

Chapter 4: The Efficacy of Strategic Management

1. *Fortune*, April 17, 2006, F-27.

2. Louis V. Gerstner, Jr., *Who Says Elephants Can't Dance?* (New York: Harper Business, 2002), 68.

Chapter 5: The Strategic Management Process

1. James C. Collins and Jerry I. Porras, "Building Your Company's Vision," *Harvard Business Review,* September–October 1996.

Chapter 6: Fundamentals of Strategy Formulation

1. Michael E. Porter, *Competitive Strategy: Techniques for Analyzing Industries and Competitors* (New York: The Free Press, 1980), Chapter 1.
2. Ibid, 35.

Chapter 11: The Relationship between Cash Flow and Growth

1. All formulas in this chapter are derived in detail in the Darden Graduate School of Business Administration Technical Note, *Analytical Relationships among Growth, Profit, and Investment Goals*, UVA-OM-0881.
2. This growth rate (G) results from both real growth and inflation.
3. Fixed asset additions include the reinvestment of depreciation and FA(G).

Chapter 13: Relating Productivity and Firm Growth

1. F. W. Taylor, *The Principles of Scientific Management* (New York: Harper and Row, 1911).
2. T. P. Wright, "Factors Affecting the Cost of Airplanes," *Journal of the Aeronautical Sciences* 3 (February 1936): 122–28.
3. Jacqueline L. Doyle, "Economies of Growth: A Study of Corporate and Productivity Growth Rates in Two Service Industries" (dissertation submitted in partial fulfillment of the degree of Doctor of Philosophy in Business Administration, Darden Graduate School of Business Administration, The University of Virginia, Charlottesville, VA, 1995).

Chapter 14: Residual Income, EVA, and Corporate Capital Charges

1. *Fortune*, "The Real Key to Creating Wealth," September 30, 1993, 38.
2. *CFO*, "All about EVA," November 1996, 13.
3. *CFO*, "Metric Wars," October 1996, 14.
4. *The Stern Stewart Performance 1000: The Definitive Guide of MVA and EVA*.

Chapter 15: The Allocation (Redeployment) of Capital (Cash)

1. H. Mintzberg, *The Rise and Fall of Strategic Planning* (New York: The Free Press, 1994).
2. T. Lewis, "Surviving in the Software Economy," *Upside*, March 1996.
3. R. Shim, *Wal-Mart to Throw Its Weight Behind RFID*. CNET News.com, June 5, 2003.
4. R. A. Brealey and S. C. Myers, *Principles of Corporate Finance* (New York: McGraw-Hill/Irwin, 2003).

Chapter 16: Share Repurchases

1. All formulas in this chapter are derived in detail in the Darden Graduate School of Business Administration Technical Note, *Share Repurchases in the U.S.*, UVA-OM-1017, 2001.

2. E. Richard Brownlee, Kenneth R. Ferris, and Mark E. Haskins, *Corporate Financial Reporting* (New York: McGraw-Hill/Irwin, 2001), 4th edition, 146.

3. Marc Bertoneche, "Share Buy-Backs: The European and Japanese Experience," Harvard Business School Case No. 9-298-134, p. 3.

4. R. A. Brealey and S. C. Myers, *Principles of Corporate Finance* (New York: McGraw-Hill/Irwin, 2003), 442.

5. Ibid., 443.

6. Ibid., 442.

7. William W. Sihler, "Framework for Financial Decisions," *Harvard Business Review*, No. 71211, 1971, p. 133.

8. Brealey and Myers, 441–42.

9. Ibid., 442, 446.

10. Erik Lie and Heidi J. Lei, "The Role of Personal Taxes in Corporate Decisions: An Empirical Analysis of Share Repurchases and Dividends," *Journal of Finance and Quantitative Analysis* (December 1999), 542.

11. Brealey and Myers, 441.

12. Ibid., 446.

13. Ibid.

Chapter 17: Making Effective Decisions

1. Lawrence M. Miller, *Barbarians to Bureaucrats: Corporate Life Cycle Strategies* (New York: Random House, 1989).

2. This vignette is based on a case study by Michael J. Roberts, *The Johnsonville Sausage Company (A)* (Boston: Harvard Business School, 1986).

3. Funding Universe.com, Company Histories, Johnsonville Sausage, LLC.

Chapter 18: Organizing and Aligning

1. Alfred D. Chandler, Jr., *Strategy and Structure: Chapters in the History of the American Industrial Enterprise* (Cambridge, MA: M.I.T. Press, 1962).

Chapter 19: Staffing

1. Based on ideas from www.jimcollins.com.

2. Bill George, *Authentic Leadership* (San Francisco: Jossey-Bass, 2003), 72.

Chapter 20: Integrating

1. Vertical integration is the expansion of the value chain backward into suppliers or forward into distribution outlets. Horizontal integration is the development of new

markets for existing products, or new products for existing markets. Both types of integration are usually accomplished through acquisitions, although the new products may be developed internally.

Chapter 21: Executing

1. The notion of *confronting the brutal facts of our current reality* has been popularized by Jim Collins in his book, *Good to Great* (New York: HarperCollins, 2001). Collins attributes the concept to Admiral Jim Stockdale (pp. 83–87).

2. Patrick Lencioni, *Death by Meeting* (San Francisco: Jossey-Bass, 2004).

Chapter 23: Learning and Innovation

1. David A. Garvin, "Building a Learning Organization," *Harvard Business Review*, July–August 1993, p. 80.

2. W. Cohen and D. Levinthal, "Absorptive Capacity: A New Perspective on Learning and Innovation," *Administrative Science Quarterly* 35, no. 1 (1990): 128–52.

3. Garvin, "Building a Learning Organization."

Chapter 25: Reflections on General Management

1. Niccolò Machiavelli, *The Prince* (1532), from *The Portable Machiavelli*, edited and translated by Peter Bondanella and Mark Musa (Hammondsworth, Eng.: Penguin Books, 1979), 94.

2. Ibid., 106–107.

BIBLIOGRAPHY

"A Most Unusual Executive Bonus Plan." *Washington Post,* October 21, 1991, AI.

Abbott, Charles C. *Governance—A Guide for Trustees and Directors.* Boston, Mass: The Cheswick Center, 1979.

Abegglen, James C., and George Stalk. Kaisha: *The Japanese Corporation.* New York: Basic Books, 1985.

Abernathy, W. J., and K. Wayne. "Limits of the Learning Curve." *Harvard Business Review* 52 (September–October 1974): 109–19.

Ackoff, Russell. "The Future of Operational Research Is Past." *Journal of Operational Research Society* 30, no. 1 (Pergamon Press, 1979): 93–104.

Adler, Paul. "Shared Learning." *Management Science* 36, no. 8 (August 1990): 938–57.

Adler, Paul, and Kim B. Clark. "Behind the Learning Curve: A Sketch of the Learning Process." *Management Science* 37, no. 3 (March 1991): 267–81.

Allen, Julius W. "Increasing Productivity in the United States: Ways in Which the Private and Public Sectors Can Contribute to Productivity Improvement." In *Productivity: The Foundation of Growth: Studies/Prepared for the Use of the Special Study on Economic Change of the Joint Economic Committee, Congress of the United States.* Washington, D.C.: U.S. Government Printing Office, 1980, 67–100.

Andrews, Kenneth. *The Concept of Corporate Strategy.* New York: Irwin, 1971.

Argote, Linda, Sara L. Beckman, and Dennis Epple. "The Persistence and Transfer of Learning in Industrial Settings." *Management Science* 36, no. 2 (February 1990): 140–54.

Arthur, W. Brian. "Increasing Returns and the New World of Business." *Harvard Business Review* (July–August 1996): 100–109.

Baloff, Nicholas. "The Learning Curve—Some Controversial Issues." *Journal of Industrial Economics* 14, no. 3 (July 1966): 275–82.

Baloff, Nicholas, and John W. Kennelly. "Accounting Implications of Product and

Process Start Ups." *Journal of Accounting Research* 5, no. 2 (Autumn 1967): 131–43.

Baumol, William J., and Kenneth McLennan. "Toward an Effective Productivity Program." In *Productivity Growth and U.S. Competitiveness,* a supplementary paper of the Committee for Economic Development, eds. William J. Baumol and Kenneth McLennan, 185–224. New York: Oxford University Press, 1985.

———. "U.S. Productivity Performance and Its Implications." In *Productivity Growth and U.S. Competitiveness,* a supplementary paper of the Committee for Economic Development, eds. William J. Baumol and Kenneth McLennan, 3–28. New York: Oxford University Press, 1985.

Beatty, Jack, ed. *Colossus: How the Corporation Changed America*. New York: Broadway Books, 2000, 6.

Bertoneche, Marc. "Share Buy-Backs: The European and Japanese Experience." Harvard Business School Case No. 9-298-134, p. 3.

Bodde, David. "Riding the Experience Curve." *Technology Review* 78, no. 5 (March/April 1976): 53–59.

Bowen, D. E. "Managing Customers as Human Resources in Service Organizations." *Human Resource Management* 25, no. 3 (Fall 1986): 371–84.

Brealey, R. A., and S. C. Myers. *Principles of Corporate Finance*. New York: McGraw-Hill/Irwin, 2003.

Brodsky, Norm. "The Return of Customer Loyalty." *Inc.*, September 1997, 39–40.

Brownlee, E. Richard, Kenneth R. Ferris, and Mark E. Haskins. *Corporate Financial Reporting*. 4th ed. New York: McGraw-Hill/Irwin, 2001, 146.

Buckman, Rebecca. "These Days, Online Trading Can Become an Addiction." *Wall Street Journal*, February 1999, C1, C9.

Burck, Charles. "A Fresh Look at Productivity." *Fortune* 119, no. 4 (February 13, 1989): 28.

"Business Brief: Warren Buffett Gives General Dynamics a Proxy to Vote Berkshire's 15% Stake." *Wall Street Journal,* September 18, 1992.

Byczkowski, John. "Service Please: Industry Overtakes Manufacturing With 76% of Jobs." *Cincinnati Enquirer* 151, no. 223, November 18, 1991, Sec D, 1.

Carlson, John G. "Cubic Learning Curves: Precision Tool for Labor Estimating." *Manufacturing Engineering & Management,* 71, 5 (November 1973), 22–5.

———. "How Management Can Use the Improvement Phenomenon." *California Management Review* 3, no. 2 (Winter 1961): 83–94.

Carver, John. *Boards That Make a Difference*. San Francisco, Calif.: Jossey-Bass, 1990, 2–3, 6–7.

Chandler, Alfred D., Jr. *Strategy and Structure: Chapters in the History of the American Industrial Enterprise*. Cambridge, Mass.: M.I.T. Press, 1962.

———. *Strategy and Structure: Chapters in the History of the American Industrial Enterprise*. Boston: MIT Paperback Press Edition, 1969.

———. *The Visible Hand: The Managerial Revolution in American Business*. Cambridge, Mass.: Belknap Press, 1977.

Chase, Richard B., and Nicholas J. Aquilano. *Production and Operations Management: A Life Cycle Approach*. rev. ed. Homewood, Ill.: Richard D. Irwin, Inc., 1977.

Christainsen, Gregory B., and Robert H. Haveman. "The Determinants of the Decline in Measured Productivity Growth: An Evaluation." In *Productivity: The Foundation of Growth: Studies/Prepared for the Use of the Special Study on Economic Change of the Joint Economic Committee, Congress of the United States*. Washington, D.C.: U.S. Government Printing Office, 1980, 1–17.

Cohen, W., and D. Levinthal. "Absorptive Capacity: A New Perspective on Learning and Innovation." *Administrative Science Quarterly* 35, no. 1 (1990): 128–152.

Colley, John L., Jr. *Corporate & Divisional Planning: Text and Cases*. Reston Va.: Reston Publishing Company, 1984.

Colley, John L., Jr., Robert D. Landel, and Robert R. Fair. *Operations Planning and Control*. San Francisco, Calif.: Holden-Day, 1978.

Collins, James C., and Jerry I. Porras. "Built to Last." *Harper Business*, 1994.

Conley, Patrick. "Experience Curves as a Planning Tool." *IEEE Spectrum* 7, no. 6 (June 1970): 63–68.

Conway, R. W., and Andrew Schultz, Jr. "The Manufacturing Progress Function." *Journal of Industrial Engineering* 10, no. 1 (January–February 1959), 39–53.

"The Corporation's Cost of Capital and the Weighted-Average Cost of Capital." Charlottesville, Va.: Darden Graduate School of Business, Technical Note UVA-F-0910 (October 1990).

Courtney, Hugh, Jane Kirkland, and Patrick Viguerie. "Strategy Under Uncertainty." *Harvard Business Review*, November–December, 1997.

Covey, Stephen R. *The Seven Habits of Effective People*. New York: Simon and Schuster, 1989.

The Crystal Report on Executive Compensation, vol. 4, no. 8, October 1992.

Cushing, Woodrow W., and James E. McNulty. "The Behavior of Operating Costs at Large Commercial Banks." *The Mid-Atlantic Journal of Business* 29, no. 1 (March 1993): 27–40.

Day, George S., and David B. Montgomery. "Diagnosing the Experience Curve." *Journal of Marketing* 47 (Spring 1983): 44–58.

Dean, Joel. "Pricing Policies for New Products." *Harvard Business Review* (November 1950): 45–53.

DeBlasi, Michelle. "Stocking Up on Buybacks." *Bloomberg*, May 1999, 109.

Denison, Edward F. *The Sources of Economic Growth in the United States and the Alternatives Before Us*. Supplementary Paper No. 13, Committee for Economic Development, New York, 1962.

Dess, Gregory G., and G. T. Lumpkin. *Strategic Management: Creating Competitive Advantages*. New York: McGraw-Hill, 2003.

Dorroh, James R., Thomas R. Gulledge, Jr., and Norman Keith Womer. "A Generalization of the Learning Curve." *European Journal of Operational Research* (1986): 205–16.

Dowling, Grahame, and Mark Uncles. "Do Customer Loyalty Programs Really Work?" *Sloan Management Review* (Summer 1997): 71–82.

Doyle, Jacqueline L. "Economies of Growth: A Study of Corporate and Productivity Growth Rates in Two Service Industries." Dissertation submitted in partial fulfillment of the degree of Doctor of Philosophy in Business Administration, The Darden Graduate School of Business Administration, Charlottesville, Va.: The University of Virginia, 1995.

Doyle, Jacqueline L., and John L. Colley, Jr. "Pizza Hut, Inc." Charlottesville, Va.: Darden Graduate Business School, UVA-OM 0698, rev. 10/92.

Drucker, Peter. *The Practice of Management*. New York: Harper & Row, 1954.

Drucker, Peter F. *Innovation and Entrepreneurship*. New York: Harper & Row, 1985.

———. *Managing in Turbulent Times*. New York: Harper & Row, 1980.

Dutton, John M., and Annie Thomas. "Treating Progress Functions as a Managerial Opportunity." *Academy of Management Review* 9, no. 2 (April 1984): 235–47.

Eppes, Thomas E. "Keeping Customers Is Just as Important as Winning New Ones." *Business Marketing* (November 1997): 9.

Farris, Paul W., and Michael J. Moore, eds. *The Profit Impact of Marketing Strategy Project: Retrospect and Prospects*. Cambridge, UK: Cambridge University Press, 2004, 7.

Follett, Mary Parker. "Prophet of Management," ed. Pauline Graham. *Harvard Business Press*, 1995, released from 1920.

Franklin, Roger. *The Defender: The Story of General Dynamics*. New York: Harper and Row, 1986.

Freeman, R. Edward. *The Blackwell's Handbook of Strategic Management*. eds. M. Hitt and J. Harrison. Oxford: Basil Blackwell, 2001.

———. *Business Ethics: The State of the Art*. New York: Oxford University Press, 1991.

———. *Corporate Strategy and the Search for Ethics*. With Daniel Gilbert. Englewood Cliffs, N.J.: Prentice-Hall, 1988. (Translated into German as *Unternehmensstrategie, Ethick uan personliche Verantwortung*, Frankfurt: Campus Verlag.)

———. *Management*. 6th ed., with James Stoner and Daniel Gilbert, translated into Spanish, Portuguese, Dutch, Bahasa Indonesian, and Polish. Englewood Cliffs, N.J.: Prentice Hall, 1995.

———. *The Ruffin Series in Business Ethics*. New York: Oxford University Press, 1989–2001.

———. *Strategic Management: A Stakeholder Approach*. Boston: Pitman, 1984.

Friedman, Thomas L. *The World Is Flat: A Brief History of the Twenty-first Century*. New York: Farrar, Straus, and Giroux, 2005.

Garvin, David A. "Building a Learning Organization." *Harvard Business Review* (July–August 1993): 80.

———. "Quality on the Line," *Harvard Business Review* (September–October 1983): 64–75.

George, Bill. *Authentic Leadership*. San Francisco: Jossey-Bass, 2003, 72.

Gerstner, Louis V., Jr. *Who Says Elephants Can't Dance?* New York: Harper Business, 2002, 68.

Globerson, Shlomo, and Abraham Seidmann. "The Effects of Imposed Learning Curves on Performance Improvements." *IIE Transactions* 20, no. 3 (September 1988): 317–23.

Goldratt, Eliyahu M. *The Goal*. Croton-on-Hudson, New York: North River Press, 1992.

Goodwin, Jacob. *Brotherhood of Arms*. New York: Random House, 1985.

Graham, John R. "Eight Ways to Build Customer Loyalty." *Incentive* (October 1997): 124.

Graham, Pauline. "Mary Parker Follett: Prophet of Management," *Harvard Business Press*, 1995.

Grayson, Jackson, Jr. "The U.S. Economy and Productivity: Where Do We Go From Here?" In *Productivity: The Foundation of Growth: Studies/Prepared for the Use of the Special Study on Economic Change of the Joint Economic Committee, Congress of the United States*. Washington, D.C.: U.S. Government Printing Office, 1980, 18–45.

Griliches, Zvi. "Productivity, R&D, and the Data Constraint." *American Economic Review* 84, no. 1 (March 1994): 1–23.

Gupta, Vinod K. "Labor Productivity, Establishment Size, and Scale Economies." *Southern Economic Journal* 49 (January 1983): 853–59.

Hagstrom, Robert G., Jr. *The Warren Buffett Way*. New York: John Wiley and Sons, 1994.

Hambrick, Donald C., and Johnson, J. "Outside Directors with a Stake: The Linchpin in Improving Governance." *California Management Review* 42, no. 4 (Summer 2000).

Hamel, Gary. "Strategy as Revolution." *Harvard Business Review* (July–August 1996): 69–71.

Hart, Christopher W. L. "The Power of Unconditional Service Guarantees." *Harvard Business Review* (July–August 1988): 54–62.

Harvard Business School. "General Dynamics: Compensation and Strategy (B)." Boston: Harvard Business School, Case study no. 9-494-049, rev. December 3, 1997.

——. "Sustainable Growth and the Interdependence of Financial Goals and Policies." Boston: Harvard Business School, Case study no. 9-282-045, 1982.

Hayes, Robert H., and Kim B. Clark. "Exploring the Sources of Productivity Differences at the Factory Level." In Kim B. Clark, Robert H. Hayes, and Christopher Lorenz, *The Uneasy Alliance: Managing the Productivity-Technology Dilemma*, Boston: Harvard Business School Press, 1985.

Hayes, Robert H., and Steven C. Wheelwright. *Restoring Our Competitive Edge: Competing through Manufacturing*. New York: John Wiley and Sons, 1984.

Heineke, John M. "Notes on Estimating Experience Curves: Econometric Issues." *IEEE Transactions on Engineering Management* EM-33, no. 2 (May 1986): 113–19.

Hesselbein, Frances, Marshall Goldsmith, and Richard Beckhard, eds. *The Leader of the Future*. San Francisco: Jossey-Bass, The Drucker Foundation, 1996.

———. *The Organization of the Future*. San Francisco: Jossey-Bass, The Drucker Foundation, 1997.

Hirschmann, Winfred B. "Profit from the Learning Curve." *Harvard Business Review* 42 (January–February 1964): 125–39.

Humphrey, David B. "Why Do Estimates of Bank Scale Economies Differ?" *Economic Review* 76, Federal Reserve Bank of Richmond (September/October 1990): 38–50.

Johnson, Paul. *A History of the American People*. New York: Harper Perennial, 1997, 559–60.

Jorion, Philippe. *Value at Risk: The New Benchmark for Controlling Market Risk*. New York: McGraw-Hill, 1997.

Kaufmann, Patrick J. "Pizza Hut, Inc.: Home Delivery." Boston: HBS Case Services, Harvard Business School (unnumbered), 1987.

Kotter, John. *Leading Change*. Boston: Harvard Business School Press, 1996.

"Layoffs on the Line, Bonuses in the Executive Suite." *Business Week,* October 21, 1991, 34.

Lee, L. Douglas. "Productivity, Inflation, and Economic Growth." In *Productivity: The Foundation of Growth: Studies/Prepared for the Use of the Special Study on Economic Change of the Joint Economic Committee, Congress of the United States*. Washington, D.C.: U.S. Government Printing Office, 1980, 46–57.

Leftwich, Richard H. *The Price System and Resource Allocation*. rev. ed. New York: Holt Rinehart & Winston, 1961.

Lencioni, Patrick. *Death by Meeting*. San Francisco: Jossey-Bass, 2004.

Lenz, Ralph C., and Linda L. Bricker. "Relationships between Market Growth and Productivity." *Business Horizons,* May–June 1983, 36–41.

Levy, Ferdinand K. "Adaptation in the Production Process." *Management Science* 11, no. 6 (April 1965): B136–54.

Lie, Erik, and Heidi J. Lei. "The Role of Personal Taxes in Corporate Decisions: An Empirical Analysis of Share Repurchases and Dividends." *Journal of Finance and Quantitative Analysis* (December 1999): 542.

Lorsch, Jay W. *Pawns or Potentates: The Reality of America's Corporate Boards*. Boston: Harvard Business School Press, 1989, 7.

Machiavelli, Niccolò. *The Prince*. From *The Portable Machiavelli*, eds. and trans. Peter Bondanella and Mark Musa. Hammondsworth, Eng.: Penguin Books, 1979, 94, 106–107.

Magretta, Joan. "The Power of Virtual Integration: An Interview with Dell Computer's Michael Dell." *Harvard Business Review* (March–April 1998): 72–84.

Malkiel, Burton G. *A Random Walk Down Wall Street: Including a Life-Cycle Guide to Personal Investing*. New York: Norton, 1996.

March, James, and Herbert Simon. *Organizations*. New York: Wiley, 1958.

McDonald, John. "A New Model for Learning Curves, DARM." *Journal of Business & Economic Statistics* 5, no. 3 (July 1987): 329–35.

McGee, John S. *Industrial Organization*. Englewood Cliffs, N.J.: Prentice Hall, 1988.

Miller, Edward M. "Extent of Economies of Scale: The Effect of Firm Size on Labor Productivity and Wage Rates." *Southern Economic Journal* (January 1978): 470–87.

Mintzberg, H. *The Rise and Fall of Strategic Planning*. New York: The Free Press, 1994.

Morris, Barbara, and Robert Johnston. "Dealing with Inherent Variability: The Difference Between Manufacturing and Service." *International Journal of Operations and Production Management* 7, no. 4 (1987): 13–22.

The New Nonprofit Almanac and Desk Reference. New York: Jossey-Bass, Urban Institute, 2002, 4–5, 13, 33, 91.

Pattison, Diane D., and Charles J. Teplitz. "Are Learning Curves Still Relevant?" *Management Accounting* 70 (February 1989): 37–40.

Peles, Yoram C. "On Deviations from Learning Curves." *Journal of Accounting, Auditing & Finance* NS6 (Summer 1991): 349–63.

PepsiCo. Presentation to MS Global Consumer Conference, November 7, 2001.

Peter Senge. *The Fifth Discipline: The Art and Practice of the Learning Organization*. New York: Currency Doubleday, 1990.

Peters, Thomas J., and Robert H. Waterman, Jr. *In Search of Excellence: Lessons from America's Best-Run Companies*. New York: Harper & Row, 1982.

Pine, B. J. *Mass Customization*. Boston: Harvard Business School Press, 1993.

Porter, Michael. *The Competitive Advantage of Nations*. New York: The Free Press, 1980.

Porter, Michael E. *Competitive Advantage*. New York: The Free Press, Macmillan, 1985, 1–11.

Rader, Louis T. "Rader's Rules." Unpublished notes, Charlottesville, Va.: Darden Graduate School of Business Administration.

Reicheld, Frederick, and W. Earl Sasser, Jr. "Zero Defections: Quality Comes to Services." In *Keeping Customers,* eds. Benson P. Shapiro and John Svolka. Boston: Harvard Business School Press, 1992.

Roser, Sherman R., and Lawrence C. Sundby. "Learning Curves and Inflation." *Cost & Management* (July–August 1985): 30–34.

Samuelson, Paul A., and William D. Nordhaus. *Economics*. 14th ed. New York: McGraw-Hill, 1992.

Sasser, W. Earl, and William E. Fulmer. "Creating Personalized Service Delivery Systems." In *Service Management Effectiveness,* eds. David Bowen, Richard B. Chase, Thomas G. Cumming, and associates. San Francisco: Jossey-Bass, 1990.

Sasser, W. Earl, R. Paul Olsen, and D. Daryl Wyckoff. *Management of Service Operations: Text, Cases and Readings*. Boston: Allyn and Bacon, 1978.

Scherer, F. M. *Industrial Market Structure and Economic Performance*. 2nd ed. Chicago: Rand McNally College Publishing Company, 1980.

Schlender, Brent. "The Bill and Warren Show." *Fortune* (July 1998): 48.

Schonberger, Richard J. *Japanese Manufacturing Techniques*. New York: The Free Press, 1982.

Schroeder, Roger G. *Operations Management: Decision Making in the Operations Function.* 3rd ed. New York: McGraw-Hill, 1989.

Shapiro, Benson P., Adrian J. Slywotzky, and Stephen X. Doyle. "Strategic Sales Management: A Boardroom Issue." *Strategy and Business* (1997): 29–46.

Shi, David E. *The Simple Life.* New York: Oxford University Press, 1985, 8.

Shiller, Robert J. *Market Volatility.* Boston: MIT Press, 1989.

Siferd, Sue Perrott, W. C. Benton, and Larry P. Ritzman. "Strategies for Service Systems." *European Journal of Operational Research* 56 (1992): 291–303.

Sihler, William W. "Framework for Financial Decisions." *Harvard Business Review* 71211 (1971): 133.

Skinner, Wickham. "The Productivity Paradox," *Harvard Business Review* (July–August 1986): 55–59.

Sloan, Alfred. *My Years with General Motors.* Garden City, N.Y.: Doubleday, 1964.

Sloan, Allan. "Reality Bites." *Newsweek* (November 1997): 39–43.

Smith, Adam. *An Inquiry into the Nature and Causes of the Wealth of Nations.* New York: Random House/Modern Library, 1994.

Smith, David B., and Jan L. Larsson. "The Impact of Learning on Cost: The Case of Heart Transplantation." *Hospital & Health Services Administration* 34, no. 1 (Spring 1989): 85–97.

The Stern Stewart Performance 1000: The Definitive Guide of MVA and EVA.

Stewart, G. Bennett. "The Quest for Value." *Harper Business,* 1990.

Stobaugh, Robert B., and Phillip L. Townsend. "Price Forecasting and Strategic Planning: The Case of Petrochemicals." *Journal of Marketing Research* 12 (February 1975): 19–29.

Stoner, A. F., R. Edward Freeman, and Daniel R. Gilbert, Jr. *Management.* Englewood Cliffs, N.J.: Prentice Hall, 1995.

Thomas, Dan R. E. "Strategy Is Different in Service Business." *Harvard Business Review* 56, no. 4 (July–August 1978): 158–65.

Thompson, Arthur, and A. J. Strickland, III. *Crafting and Executing Strategy: Text and Readings.* 12th ed. Boston, Mass.: McGraw-Hill Irwin, 2001, 60.

Tichy, Noel M., and Sherman, Stratford. "Control Your Own Destiny or Someone Else Will." *Harper Business,* 1993.

Towill, Denis R. "Forecasting Learning Curves." *International Journal of Forecasting* 6 (1990): 25–38.

U.S. Bureau of the Census. *Statistical Abstract of the United States: 1992* (112th ed.). Washington, D.C., 1992.

———. *Statistical Abstract of the United States: 1993* (113th ed.). Washington, D.C., 1993.

U.S. Department of Labor, Bureau of Labor Statistics. *Employment Cost Indexes and Levels, 1975* 90 (Bulletin 2372), Washington, D.C., 1975.

———. *CPI Detailed Report: Data for December 1992,* Washington, D.C., 1993.

Vancil, Richard F., and Benjamin R. Makela, eds. *The CFO's Handbook.* Homewood, Ill.: Dow Jones-Irwin, 1986.

Ward's Business Directory of U.S. Private and Public Companies. Detroit, Mich.: Gale Research, Inc., 1991.

Warfighting. U.S. Marine Corps, 1997.

Winger, Richard, and David Edelman. "Segment of One Marketing." In *Perspective on Strategy.* Boston: Boston Consulting Group, John Wiley and Sons, 1998.

Womack, James P., and Daniel T. Jones. *Lean Thinking: Banish Waste and Create Wealth in Your Corporation.* New York: Simon and Schuster, 1996.

Yelle, Samuel. "The Learning Curve: Historical Review and Comprehensive Survey." *Decision Sciences* 10, no. 2 (April 1979): 302–28.

INDEX

Taylor, Frederick W., 225
TBR. *See* total business return
team leaders, 419
teams: employees in, 33; in execution,
    399; for strategic planning, 49
technical competence: of GM, 422–23
technology, 267; as driving force, 126;
    industry attractiveness of, *70*; knowl-
    edge of, 394; learning and, 390
termination, 340; of employees, 336
threats: in strategic planning, 132–35
3M Corporation, 264
tobacco industry, 406
tone: of organization, 302
total business return (TBR), 248
Toyota, 416
trading capital: in projected balance
    sheet, 172
training and development, 336–38; career
    management, 338; formal, 337; indoc-
    trination in, 336–37; on-the-job, 337;
    as staff function, 34; strategic plan
    and, 149; of talent, 44
transaction costs, 42
trial and error, 395
Tricon Global Restaurants, 272
Tropicana Food Products, 272
Truman, Harry S., 44, 417
trust, 319
TSSC. *See* The Smith's Snackfoods
    Company
turnover: of employees, 329–30
two-way performance mapping,
    237–38, *238*
Tylenol, 405–6
tyranny of minority, 432

Ubelhart, Mark, 248
ultimate weapon, 430
uncertainty: in decision making, 290–91;
    management of, 58
undercapitalization, 298
unit cost, 199
unit cost forecast, 161, *162*; quarterly,
    182, *184*
unit pricing forecast, 161, *161*; quarterly,
    182, *183*

unit sales: input data for, 160
unit sales forecast, *160*, 160–61; quarterly,
    182, *182*
UPS, 386
U.S. Army, 400
USA Today, 327

value chain, 41
values: conflict with, 428; definition of,
    116; demonstrated, *339*; of GM, 428; as
    performance measure, 166; shared,
    319; in strategic planning, 115–16, 143
variable budgets, 187–88
variable costs, 156; in profit structure,
    197
vendors. *See* suppliers
venture capital, 298
vertical integration, 37, 346; economic
    model and, 158; of SBUs, 355
vertical isolation, 347
vesting period: employment agreement
    and, 27; for equity-based compensa-
    tion, 26
vice presidents, 416; of divisions, 36;
    group, 3–4
Virginia Company of London, 8
vision: of business, 49; as catalyst for ac-
    tion, 98–99; definition of, 116; in logi-
    cal starting point, 104; in strategic
    planning, 115–16, 143
volume, 157, 158; in business model,
    51; value of, 199–200; variation
    in, 199
volume/capacity plan, 171

Wal-Mart, 265–66, 381, 405
Warfighting, 55
weekly tactical meetings, 365
workforce/staffing plan, 171
work plan, 399
worst case scenario, 152; sensitivity analy-
    ses and, 168

yes-men, 2

zero-based approach: in annual
    plan, 178

DATE DUE

OHIOLINK

Demco, Inc. 38-293